A Zone of Engagement

A Zone of Engagement

PERRY ANDERSON

VERSO

London · New York

First published by Verso 1992
© Perry Anderson 1992
All rights reserved

Verso
UK: 6 Meard Street, London W1V 3HR
USA: 29 West 35th Street, New York, NY 10001-2291

Verso is the imprint of New Left Books

ISBN 0-86091-377-5
ISBN 0-86091-595-6 (pbk)

British Library Cataloguing in Publication Data
A catalogue record for this book is available from the British Library

Library of Congress Cataloging-in-Publication Data
A catalogue record for this book is available from the Library of Congress

Typeset in Sabon by York House Typographic Ltd, London
Printed in Great Britain by Biddles Ltd

Contents

Acknowledgements

'Geoffrey de Ste. Croix and the Ancient World' first appeared in *History Workshop Journal* 16, spring 1983. 'Marshall Berman: Modernity and Revolution' was originally given as a lecture at a Conference on Marxism and the Interpretation of Culture at the University of Illinois at Urbana–Champaign in July 1983, and was first published in *New Left Review* 144, March–April 1984; the postscript was presented at a colloquium of the Fundación Pablo Iglesias in Madrid on post-modernism in May 1985. 'The Legacy of Isaac Deutscher' was written as an introduction to the posthumous collection *Marxism, Wars and Revolutions,* issued by Verso in spring 1985. 'Michael Mann's Sociology of Power' was published in *The Times Literary Supplement,* 12–18 December 1986. 'The Affinities of Norberto Bobbio' appeared in *New Left Review* 170, July–August 1988. 'Roberto Unger and the Politics of Empowerment' was published in a shorter version in *The Times Literary Supplement* of 13–19 January 1989, and fully in *New Left Review* 173, January–February 1989. 'W.G. Runciman: A New Evolutionism' appeared in *The London Review of Books,* 6 July 1989. 'On Emplotment: Andreas Hillgruber' was a contribution to a Conference on the Final Solution and the Limits of Representation at UCLA in April 1990. 'Max Weber and Ernest Gellner: Science, Politics, Enchantment' appears in John Hall and Ian Jarvie, eds., *Transition to Modernity,* a festschrift for Ernest Gellner, CUP 1992. 'Nocturnal Enquiry: Carlo Ginzburg', 'The Pluralism of Isaiah Berlin', and 'Fernand Braudel and National Identity' were all published in *The London Review of Books,* respectively in the issues of 8 November 1990, 20 December 1990 and 9 May 1991.

I would like to thank my two principal editors, Robin Blackburn and Mary-Kay Wilmers, for their special encouragement and stimulus; and my colleague Carlo Ginzburg, whose conversation inspired the final essay in this volume.

S

Foreword

The engagement to which the title of this book refers needs a few words of explanation. The texts below are critical essays on a variety of thinkers of the post-war period. In disciplinary range, these figures include historians of different fields, from antiquity to the recent past; sociologists who have taken the set of human societies as their subject; philosophers and critics of the political and cultural problems of modernity. In geographical setting, the writers involved have worked in what is still the principal region of intellectual production at large: the four leading countries of Western Europe – German, France, England, Italy – and the United States. If the contrasts in interest and outlook among the individual figures discussed are often wide, the ideas of all pass, in one way or another, by the crossroads between history and politics. This is the area that has taken up most of my intellectual life, and explains the cast of this volume.

The selection of authors considered here is partly a product of circumstance, as opportunity or solicitation arose. But it also corresponds to a temperamental choice. Out of the various possible motives for writing about the work of others, one combination has typically prompted me. The principal impulse behind these essays is one of admiration. Without this, none would have been written. In a general intellectual survey, I can be as hostile or dismissive – to the point of destruction – as anyone. The condition of a specific engagement, however, has always been respect. But I also need to feel a significant dissent. Without that, the precipitant of the form most natural to me seems to be lacking. So while this book is a record of different admirations, it is not an inventory of affinities or influences. The one exception is the piece on Isaac Deutscher, written as an introduction to a posthumous collection of his essays, rather than as a critical assessment of his major work, and so in a category apart. Generally speaking, I find it difficult to write about those to whom I feel, in one way or another, too intellectually close: which explains why, for example, this volume contains no appreciations of Eric

Hobsbawm, or Fredric Jameson, or Sebastiano Timpanaro, about all of whom I would like to have written. Some grain of resistance seems necessary to irritate a liking into a capacity for writing.

In recent years, intellectual history has become a battleground of rival procedures. The approach adopted below is at some distance from most of these. Roughly, three antagonistic programmes now dominate the field. The first and most long-standing takes single concepts or themes as its unit of enquiry, tracing their vicissitudes across time in the work of successive thinkers. This is the method practised by Isaiah Berlin, and discussed in the chapter here devoted to him. The second studies 'discourses' as the collective language of ideologies current at any given time, rejecting any extrapolation of particular notions from them, and subordinating the contribution of individual authors to historically limited moves within them. Quentin Skinner has been the leading advocate of this way of treating, in particular, political ideas. Thirdly, of course, there is the deconstruction of texts developed by Jacques Derrida, which refuses stability of meaning to anything that is written, seeking to show the systematic dependence of all that is enounced on what it denies, and the dissolution of the author into an infinite chain of unauthorized significations. The essays collected here are of different lengths and registers, but they imply a common norm of reading that is distinct from these modes. They are centred on individual authors – not concepts, discourses or texts – whose work they aim to reconstruct, so far as possible, as an intentional unity, situated within the intellectual and political currents of their time. They assume neither automatic coherence nor inherent dispersion in the writing of their subjects. Rather they try to locate specific contradictions of argument where these occur, generally treating them not as random lapses but as symptomatic points of tension, either within the body of thought itself, or with the evidence beyond it. Such contradictions can take the form of capsizals of meaning, but they need not do so. They may indicate a limitation of reasoning, or a complication of it; be signs perhaps of a critical infirmity, or a productively unresolved complexity, of argument. There is no general rule for reckoning their upshot: each case has to be judged on its own merits.

The first attempt I made at an intellectual history of this kind was an essay on Antonio Gramsci, written in 1976.[1] Gramsci, as it happens, was a writer whose notes in prison were rife with extreme contradic-

---

1. 'The Antinomies of Antonio Gramsci', *New Left Review*, 100, November 1976–January 1977, pp. 5–78; published as a book in Italy under the title *Ambiguità di Gramsci*, Rome 1978.

tions, of concepts and of arguments, that a circumspect secondary literature had looked away from. Reading them closely led me to something like an analytic tableau – formalizing the logic of the sliding bases of his key notions: hegemony, civil society, war of position, and others – and at the same time, to a detailed reconstruction of the historical debates – involving Delbrück, Kautsky, Luxemburg, Axelrod, Lenin, Trotsky, Lukács, Bordiga and others – that proved to be a condition of understanding his oscillations. The result was an approach allying elements of what could be thought of as the deconstructive and discursive programmes – in the service, however, of a rational decipherment of the originality of one, supremely deliberate, thinker. The historical method and findings of this essay seem to me to have lost none of their validity. But its aim was also political. Written in the wake of the Portuguese Revolution of the mid seventies, after the better part of a decade of radical ferment in Western Europe, this was an account of Gramsci that sought to draw a balance-sheet of the last great strategic debate of the international labour movement, for struggles still pending. That, at any rate, was my expressed intention. When it appeared, however, I received a letter from my friend Franco Moretti in Italy, the country still most buffeted by social turbulence, telling me that I had written a farewell in fitting style to the revolutionary Marxist tradition. In those days, this was not a verdict I was disposed to accept. But, not for the last time, his judgement proved better than mine.

In the next years, I found myself facing problems in the history of ideas in a second setting. If the heritage of European Marxism was one tradition in which I was formed, leading to reflections on Gramsci, the experience of the New Left in Britain was another background. Its leading thinkers were Raymond Williams and Edward Thompson. In 1978 I collaborated in the production of a volume of interviews with the former.[2] The result was a critical dialogue, across texts and contexts, reviewing all of Williams's writings to that date – a sustained exchange of a kind that is still perhaps unusual; certainly one essential to an understanding of the writer. Soon afterwards, a book about Edward Thompson sought to marry the form of the polemic, of which he is a master, with that of the profile, which calls for another kind of balance, in an attempt to capture his record as a Reasoner.[3] Theoretical and historical issues were mainly at stake. Politically, the conclu-

---

2. Raymond Williams, *Politics and Letters*, London 1979.
3. *Arguments within English Marxism*, London 1980.

sions of that work, though not unduly insisted on, remained close to those of the retrospect of Gramsci.

Such was roughly the starting-point of the essays in this volume. The first three of these, on Geoffrey de Ste. Croix, Isaac Deutscher and Marshall Berman, written in the early eighties, are substantially continuous, in concern and conviction, with texts of the seventies. The first two deal with eminent Marxist historians, the third with a cultural theorist of *soixante-huitard* sweep, whose work took its title from the *Manifesto*. These were, so to speak, intra-mural surveys within the intellectual world of the revolutionary Left, from a particular standpoint within it – one criticized by Marshall Berman, in his rejoinder to my account of him.[4] It was by now clear, politically, that the unrest of the recent period was over – that the end of fascism in Portugal had been a conclusion, not a harbinger; and intellectually, that Latin Marxism, at any rate, had expired. Registering these general changes at the time, my view was that the tradition of historical materialism could only benefit from losing pretensions, which had always been untenable, of absorbing the culture of socialism; but that it would retain its central position on the intellectual map of the Left so long as no alternative theory of historical development, genuinely comparable in scope, emerged to challenge it – something that not even the greatest classical sociology had produced.[5] Meanwhile, the international scene looked once again much as it had done before the disturbances of the sixties.

It was these conditions that changed abruptly in the second half of the eighties. The fourth and fifth essays below mark the turning-point in my own reactions. With the publication of the first volume of Michael Mann's historical sociology of power, it was immediately clear that there now existed a developed analytic theory of the pattern of human development, exceeding in explanatory ambition and empirical detail any Marxist account. Some of the criticisms that can be made of it are set down here; others developed elsewhere. But no work in a Marxist tradition could ignore the magnitude of the theoretical enterprise it represented. At the same time, against the background of perestroika, the political coordinates of the post-war world were starting to shift, as the societal ascendancy of the West became increasingly uncontested. The philosopher of the Left who, more than any other, came into his own in this new conjuncture was Norberto Bobbio. The distinctive synthesis of liberalism and socialism for which he stood had

---

4. See 'The Signs in the Streets: A Response to Perry Anderson', *New Left Review*, 144, March–April 1984, pp. 114–123.

5. See *In the Tracks of Historical Materialism*, London 1983, pp. 86–88.

no exact counterpart elsewhere. Defended since 1945, through the Liberation and the Cold War, it first acquired influence in Italy in the context of debates affected by the Portuguese Revolution – the same background against which my survey of Gramsci, whose conclusions Bobbio's arguments could have been directed against, had been written. A decade later his case appeared in a different light, and the insight of his work a benchmark of the difficulties facing the Left. Bobbio's origins and certainties, but also his hesitations, are the object of the reconstruction attempted here. Bobbio commented on this account in an exchange of correspondence subsequently published in Italy, which clarifies points of difference and of convergence between us.[6]

The change of focus in these texts gives the direction of the rest of the essays in this volume. For anyone working on broad comparative enquiries into the past – in my case, centred around the division of Europe, after the epoch of absolutism – the emergence of a formidable body of historical sociology was the most significant intellectual development of these years. The essays on W.G. Runciman and Ernest Gellner, with Weber as a common ancestor, pursue this interest. Further considerations on the trio of English sociologists discussed in these pages can be found in the companion volume to this one, which canvasses works not dealt with here.[7] Political concerns of these years are reflected in overlapping fashion, with two principal areas of emphasis. The liberalism Bobbio sought to wed to socialism takes less radical, yet still markedly original, forms in the writings of Isaiah Berlin and of Ernest Gellner. The most imaginative recent challenge to it has come from Roberto Unger, whose politics rest on a historical interpretation of the past equivalent to another macro-sociology. At the same time, modern liberalisms have typically involved a commitment to value-pluralism, whose most explosive problem is posed by the nature and record of nationalism. The relations between the two are a recurrent theme explored here in the work of Weber, of Gellner and of Berlin. Beyond them, the issue of national identity itself has become a crux of contemporary debate in Europe, not least in the final books of two leading historians of their countries, Fernand Braudel and Andreas Hillgruber.

Set against all themes of cultural difference, on the other hand, is the pursuit of human nature. The most striking historical investigation of this issue in many years is Carlo Ginzburg's account of the millennial

---

6. 'Un Carteggio tra Norberto Bobbio e Perry Anderson', *Teoria Politica*, V, nos 2–3, 1989, pp. 293–308.
7. See *English Questions*, London 1992, pp. 205–238.

persistence of shamanistic motifs in popular imagination. The essay devoted to his work takes the liberties of friendship, to which he has warmly responded.[8] What it does not say, though it is a general lesson from a range of writers considered here, is that a significant research programme is never spent as soon as its critics suppose. This has proved true of the tradition of structuralism, adapted by Ginzburg; of evolutionism, renewed by Runciman; of functionalism, animated by Gellner; of existentialism, socialized by Unger. All these doctrines were regarded as back numbers in the recent past. Today, in cases like these, it is their vigour which impresses. The future of Marxism is unlikely to be different. Its most powerful intellectual challengers, the various historical sociologies now arrayed against it, share a blind side whose importance is constantly increasing. They have little, if anything, to say about the dynamics of the capitalist economy that now rules without rival over the fate of the earth. Here the normative theory which has accompanied its triumph is equally – indeed avowedly – bereft: the Hayekian synthesis, for all its other strengths, disclaiming systematic explanation of the paths of long-term growth or of structural crisis. The come-back of historical materialism will probably be on this terrain, where already the signs of trouble are accumulating.

The last chapter in this book, unlike the others in considering a number of authors, brings some of its strands together in a survey of the different ways in which the end of history has been imagined since Hegel. The contemporary version of greatest force is that of Francis Fukuyama, in which a liberalism of the Right seeks to make sense of the times as the final victory of capitalist democracy. In this enterprise another intellectual tradition, dismissed for much longer, has displayed unexpected strength – German idealism. The end of history has been conceived in rival doctrines as well, and the essay tries to situate these, and their relationship to the Hegelian variant, in the context of the long-term development of liberal capitalism. From the mid nineteenth century onwards, this was a discourse that always also alluded to the destiny of socialism, sometimes with remarkable insight, in its sounding of the future. The book concludes with some reflections on where the socialist tradition stands today.

---

8. See his reply in the *London Review of Books* 13, 1, 10 January 1991; *Micromega*, 3, 1991, pp. 225–229. There is an attractive further glimpse of Ginzburg's theme in his forthcoming essay, 'Gli Europei scoprono (o riscoprono) gli sciamani'.

For, and against, Franco Moretti

Geoffrey de Ste. Croix
and the Ancient World

The appearance of Geoffrey de Ste. Croix's *The Class Struggle in the Ancient Greek World* alters, significantly and unexpectedly, the image of materialist history in Britain. Part of this change lies simply in the surprise of the author itself. It would have been reasonable to think that the remarkable company of Marxist historians formed in the years immediately before or during the Second World War had long since become a finite pleiad, its names familiar to every reader of *History Workshop Journal*. But it is now clear how mistaken such an assumption would have been. Alongside Hill or Hobsbawm, Hilton or Thompson, Ste. Croix must be entered as a comparable magnitude. The paradox is that he is older than any of these.[1] The great work before us – avowedly designed for 'students of Marx' and the 'general reader' as well as for specialist scholars – was written during his seventh decade.

The second change that Ste. Croix's book brings is to widen once again – one hopes once and for all – the horizons of historical materialism to embrace the classical world as a central field of intellectual enquiry. Raphael Samuel has pointed out how important the 'class struggle in Antiquity' was for the terms of intellectual and political debate among Marxists around 1900 – yet how 'almost entirely forgotten' it became afterwards.[2] The reasons for this shift will have been complex. But among them, ironically, may have been the very rise of 'people's history', in its modern sense. The term lends itself, perhaps inescapably, to national horizons and definitions more easily than to universal ones: for obvious reasons, it is difficult to stretch the notion

---

1. Ste. Croix was born in 1910; Hill in 1912; Hilton in 1916; Hobsbawm in 1917; Thompson in 1924.
2. 'British Marxist Historians, 1880–1980: I', *New Left Review* 120, March–April 1980, p. 29.

from, say, the English 'people' back to the Roman *populus*. The peculiar pattern of evidence that has survived from the classical past, too, is drastically taciturn on the lives of the exploited and oppressed – providing little immediate purchase for the kind of detailed and imaginative investigations of them associated with the best of 'history from below'. But whatever its causes, the result of this shift of sensibility and interest has commonly been to separate Classical from 'European' – let alone British – history, in the mental repertoires of many Marxists. Such intellectual separation, of course, itself reproduces the institutional division between Ancient and Modern History (every other type) entrenched in academic departments. The effect of Ste. Croix's work is to overturn this situation. It restores the classical world to a natural and central position within the explanatory universe of Marxism.

It does so, however, in an especially pointed and challenging way. For its proposed reintegration of Antiquity involves more than simply a 'temporal' expansion of materialist historiography: it also invites a reconstruction of its concepts. *The Class Struggle in the Ancient Greek World* is one of the most strenuously theoretical works of history ever to have been produced in this country. Direct exposition and sustained critical discussion of Marxist concepts, at a very high level of analytic rigour, occupy a position in the overall design of Ste. Croix's book without equivalent in the practice of his peers. For that reason alone its repercussions will make themselves felt wherever social classes and the conflicts between them remain an organizing theme in the writing of history. It seems only appropriate that one of the incidental hallmarks (and pleasures) of Ste. Croix's writing should be the liberty and pungency of his topical asides – on the Conservative Party or the Welfare State, the Cold War or the Christian religion.

Two inter-related facts appear to have set Ste. Croix apart from his generation, among Marxist historians. He started his career much later, studying as an undergraduate in his thirties at University College, London (1946–1949), under A.H.M. Jones; and he came to classical studies after a decade of professional life as a solicitor before the War (1931–1939).[3] His first book – his only one till *The Class Struggle in the Ancient Greek World* – was a survey of *The Origins of the Peloponnesian War*, published in 1972. This brilliant study, already revealing many of his gifts and idiosyncrasies, advanced a radical reinterpretation of the springs of the conflict between Athens and

---

3. See the entry in *Who's Who*, 1982.

Sparta in the fifth century BC, whose upshot was to shift primary responsibility for the outbreak of the war from the former to the latter, while emphasizing the unappeasable nature of the long-term antagonism between the democratic and oligarchic polities of these two slave-owning societies. Methodologically, the distinctive feature of the book is the extraordinary delicacy and precision of the textual analysis it deploys, in scrutinizing and revising the evidence for the origins of the Peloponnesian conflict. The two *tours de force* – one technical, the other philosophical – of Ste. Croix's approach here were his demolition of the traditional view of the Megarian decrees (generally seen as vindictive economic reprisals by Athens against a neighbouring city that provoked hostilities in Greece, which he argued were in all probability religious sanctions of rather limited significance, exploited for propaganda purposes by Sparta), and his reconstruction of Thucydides' vision of history at large. His sombre account of the Thucydidean thought-world, especially its conviction of the essential amorality of the relations between states, is of unforgettable power.[4] It alone gives *The Origins of the Peloponnesian War* enduring importance for the general reader.

In these passages, as throughout the book, the marks of the highest kind of legal training are unmistakable: a capacity to analyse, with the utmost ingenuity and vigilance, the finest nuance and most elusive context, by means of comparison or precedent, in a contradictory set of written documents, in order to arrive at the most plausible final rendition of meaning or event. At the same time, a lawyer's presentation is not always, as everyone knows, the easiest for a layperson. *The Origins of the Peloponnesian War* shuns the attractions of any narrative. Its chapters are severely organized by problematics, virtually discontinuous from each other, with a minimum of linkage. Discussion of *res gestae* is constantly interwoven with criticism of accounts of them, in a manner more usual for a specialist article than for a book: other authorities are cited and cross-examined in detail, over many pages, within the body of the text itself. The title bears a somewhat wilful relation to the contents of the book, which include reflections on the end of the Peloponnesian War, and even the fall of Sparta or Athens a century later. Moreover, in what must be some sort of record for a recent historian, indifference to conventional expectations of story-telling, or even argument-setting, generates no fewer than forty-seven appendices, covering well over a hundred pages, after the conclusion of

---

4. *The Origins of the Peloponnesian War*, London 1972, pp. 22–25.

the main narrative itself – a formidable cliff for any reader, perhaps even the contemporary classicist, to scale. A more substantive criticism of the book, finally, might be that an element of involuntary advocacy creeps into Ste. Croix's allocation of responsibilities for the Peloponnesian War: Spartan policy, at all events, earns a series of judgements and epithets – 'selfish', 'cynical', 'expansionist', 'aggressive', 'repressive'[5] – from which Athenian is generally exempt, even at times directly exculpated. Here the sympathies of the historian are at variance with the axioms of politics he draws from Thucydides, whose central lesson was that the logic of contention between all states in the ancient world was so implacable that their external policies could by nature never be other than ruthless and rapacious. With more reason to distribute political blame, for a catastrophe from which he suffered himself, Thucydides yielded less to it.

The Class Struggle in the Ancient Greek World is a very different kind of work. Constructed on a monumental scale, it surveys 1400 years of history – from 'Archaic Greece to the Arab conquests' – across 700 pages; and what pages. In a prose of exhilarating sharpness and clarity, Ste. Croix attacks the huge task of unravelling the successive class structures that spanned the evolution of the Ancient World. To this end the book summons up a fabulous range of sources. Classical historians have in some ways always needed to be more polymathic than most of their colleagues, for the stock of evidence that has survived from the Ancient World can be regarded in most respects – effectively all save its archaeological residue – as a closed inventory. Just because that quantity is for many purposes so limited, it tends to impose exceptional qualitative dexterity on those who investigate it: that is, an ability to move – and arbitrate – between different sorts of evidence that in later periods of history would rarely be brought together within the compass of any one programme of research. In The Class Struggle in the Ancient Greek World, these peculiar skills are practised in virtuoso style. Ste. Croix mobilizes his evidence from lyric poems, municipal inscriptions, legal corpuses, imperial constitutions, patristic polemics, narrative annals, philosophical discourses, medical anecdotes, biblical texts, senatorial correspondence, popular tomb-stones, administrative papyri, numismatic slogans – not indiscrimina-tely, but in each case incisively and critically. Some of the idiosyncrasies of his earlier writing persist. The title of the book is again misleading – more so, indeed, since Ste. Croix in no way confines himself to the

---

5. Ibid., pp. 158–166.

'Greek' world: his treatment of Roman history is actually considerably longer and fuller. Its architecture is less abrupt than that of its predecessor, proceeding from general theoretical and sociological sections (Part I) to sequential historical accounts (Part II). But space is very unevenly distributed within the latter, which themselves contain interpolations of extraneous material, where the author has effectively incorporated the substance of previously written articles into the text. This waywardness often produces some of the most enjoyable passages in the book – such as the splendid excursus on Jesus' relation to the world of the Graeco–Roman *polis*[6] or on Jewish and Christian attitudes towards women;[7] but it also introduces a certain arbitrary element into the composition of the work as a whole, curiously inseparable from its grandeur.

If these aspects of *The Class Struggle in the Ancient Greek World* recall *The Origins of the Peloponnesian War*, the decisive difference lies in the theoretical scope and ambition of the new work. Here too, it is difficult not to see the influence of Ste. Croix's legal formation. It is a commonplace that when historians come to write about historiography and its typically provisional procedures of enquiry, verification and judgement, they have frequently resorted to analogies from law – as opposed, that is, to science. Two of the most recent and famous examples are Edward Thompson's extended metaphor linking historical and legal courts in *The Poverty of Theory*, and Oscar Handlin's earlier and more comprehensive comparison of the two disciplines, which it in some ways echoes.[8] Yet despite this, in the present century at least, it has been rather rare for a major historian to have any real experience of the law: even most legal historians have not usually been practitioners. This may account for the fact that the conventional construal of wherein juridical virtues lie should have tended to be so partial. The traditional analogies essentially emphasize the empirical

---

6. *The Class Struggle in the Ancient Greek World*, London 1981, pp. 426–433. Henceforward CSAGW.

7. CSAGW, pp. 103–111.

8. Compare Edward Thompson, *The Poverty of Theory*. London 1978, p. 237; with Oscar Handlin, 'Principles of Historical Criticism,' in *The Harvard Guide to American History*, Cambridge, Mass. 1954, pp. 23–25 – whose reflections concluded: 'A judge and a jury, indeed, would go mad if they had to decide cases on evidence which will often seem more than satisfactory to the historian. But there is no escape; the historian, if he is to interpret at all, will try and convict on evidence which a court would throw out as circumstantial or hearsay. The victims of the historical process have to seek their compensation in the fact that history provides them with a far more flexible appellate procedure. The historian's sentences are in a continuous state of review; few of his verdicts are ever final.'

dimensions of legal or judicial practice: case-by-case examination of evidence, with attendant protocols of proof. But, of course, law also involves – even preeminently consists of – concepts. Real jurisprudence, in other words, demands the highest capacity for rigorously abstract analysis of formalized categories – their distinction, interrelation, modification. In this respect, it is much closer as a discipline to classical sociology than to most varieties of descriptive or narrative history, as they are usually practised. It is no accident, then, that Ste. Croix should show such an eloquent appreciation of the two-sided demands of any genuine historical materialism – the need, that is, for the Marxist historian 'to reconcile full and scrupulous attention to all forms of evidence for his chosen subject and a study of the modern literature relating to it with a grasp of general historical methodology and sociological theory sufficient to enable him to make the most of what he learns'.[9] Ste. Croix's mastery of evidence has already been noted. Its complement is his command of concepts, his declared and deliberate 'use of categories of social analysis which are not only *precise*, in the sense that I can define them, but also *general*, in the sense that they can be applied to the analysis of other societies'.[10] A large part of *The Class Struggle in the Ancient Greek World* is devoted to the work of systematic clarification and foundation of Marxist social categories, a work performed in no spirit of grudging preliminary penance but with the energy of a natural theoretical temperament.

The central purpose of Ste. Croix's work is to show the material structures of oppression and exploitation which laid the historical basis for successive forms of state and society in Antiquity. A full-colour reproduction of Van Gogh's *Potato Eaters*, for Ste. Croix 'the most profound and moving representation in art' of the primary producers on the land, serves as frontispiece to the book. 'These are the voiceless toilers, the great majority – let us not forget it – of the population of the Greek and Roman world, upon whom was built a great civilization which despised them and did all it could to forget them.'[11] To establish the exact and various identities of these toilers, Ste. Croix starts out with a general discussion of class, of far-reaching consequence for theory and history alike. Against the grain of most Marxist historical writing of the sixties and seventies, he insists that class should not be primarily defined as a subjective 'happening', whose essential criteria are therefore cultural consciousness or political autonomy – self-

---

9. CSAGW, p. 34.
10. CSAGW, p. 35.
11. CSAGW, pp. 209–210.

awareness or self-making. Ste. Croix respectfully but firmly rejects the different versions of this position that he finds in the work of fellow-Marxist historians. Classes, he contends, are primarily objective formations, defined by social relationships of exploitation that secure the extraction of surplus labour from the immediate producers. That exploitation may, or may not, generate a sense of collective unity and interest in the exploited – outcomes depending on the determinate possibilities for common action open to them. Consciousness of class identity, in other words, varies enormously among the dominated classes – the dominant classes, by contrast, will always possess a strong measure of it. What will not vary in the same way, however, is the fact of resistance to exploitation: for Ste. Croix, this is the other, equally objective, pole of the relationship constituting social class as such. That resistance, however, need be neither conscious nor collective, nor yet obviously visible in the recorded traces of the past which have survived the filters of prejudice and privilege. Class struggle is inherent in the class relationship itself, as the practices of exploitation, or resistance to them. It thus exists even where 'there may be no explicit common awareness of class on either side, no specifically political struggle at all, and perhaps even little consciousness of struggle of any kind.'[12] Ste. Croix is fully alive to the theoretical and political implications of this position. 'To adopt the very common conception of class struggle which refuses to regard it as such unless it includes class consciousness and active political conflict (as some Marxists do) is to water it down to the point where it virtually disappears in many situations. It is then possible to deny altogether the very existence of class struggle today in the United States of America or between employers and immigrant workers in northern Europe, and between masters and slaves in antiquity, merely because in each case the exploited class concerned does not or did not have any "class consciousness" or take any political action in common except on very rare occasions and to a very limited degree. But this, I would say, makes nonsense not merely of *The Communist Manifesto* but of the greater part of Marx's work.'[13]

Having defined class in general, Ste. Croix then proceeds to discuss the problem of slavery in the Ancient World, and its position within the Greek and Roman economies. It is well known how much controversy has surrounded this issue in recent years. Roughly speaking, opinion has divided into two camps: those who argue that slavery was constitu-

---

12. CSAGW, p. 57.
13. CSAGW, p. 57.

tive of the nature of Ancient civilization, and point to the structural scale of slave ownership at its peak periods, and those who deny that slavery was central to it, on the grounds that independent or dependent small producers were in general more numerous overall than slaves. Among the latter, some would restrict their claim to classical Greece, or even just Athens, as opposed to the Roman order that ultimately succeeded it.[14] Frequently, though not invariably, tenants of the second position have tended to reduce the slave condition to an essentially cultural or juridical phenomenon, athwart economic divisions – closer to a Weberian 'status' than a Marxist class. Ste. Croix resolves these arguments with a decisive clarification of their terms. The bulk of the labour performed in Antiquity, he maintains, may nearly always have been the work of non-slave producers – whether smallholders, artisans or dependent tenants. But the surplus labour that provided the income and wealth of the dominant classes was essentially extorted from slaves, until the advent of generalized serfdom in the later Roman Empire. Ste. Croix reminds us that it was the latter category which was expressly theorized by Marx as the basis for his periodization of modes of production in history, in *Capital* and elsewhere: 'What I think has often been overlooked is that what Marx is concentrating on as the really distinctive feature of each society is not the way in which the bulk of the labour of production is done, but how the extraction of the surplus from the immediate producer is secured.'[15]

---

14. See, for example, Ellen Meiksins Wood's 'Marxism and Ancient Greece', *History Workshop Journal* 11, Spring 1981. (Wood has since been an ingenious critic of Ste. Croix's view of Athenian slavery in her *Peasant-Citizen and Slave. The Foundations of Athenian Democracy*, London 1988, pp. 64–80, which argues that the dominant forms of exploitation in the Attic countryside must have been rental arrangements between wealthier landowners and tenants, rather than slavery. The difficulty with this alternative is that it leaves unexplained the very large numerical predominance of slaves over citizens – a ratio of 3:1 – in the classical period. Seeking to relegate slavery essentially to domestic service in urban households, Wood overlooks the obvious problem of the massive surplus necessary to maintain an unproductive labour force on this scale, demanding levels of rent extraction far beyond anything the scant evidence on leasing permits, and a degree of peasant depression quite incompatible with the general image of the sturdy Athenian smallholder it is the purpose of the book to uphold. For all its many merits – it contains a brilliant reconstruction of the possible path from the Mycenaean-style tribute kingdom to the early Greek *polis* – the work remains too much a negative polemic to afford a satisfactory account of the dynamics of Athenian society: the structural inter-relationships between peasant autonomy and widespread slavery are never really explored, leaving the promise of its title unfulfilled, as if the foundations of Athenian democracy were simply to be found in the first, not the second – rather than in the connexion between them. This is a mistake Ste. Croix never makes.)

15. CSAGW, p. 52.

Arraying the uneven but unquestionable evidence for the presence of slave-labour on agricultural estates, not only in the Roman Republic or Principate but in classical Attica as well, Ste. Croix points out that if this is to be regarded as insufficient, then there is far less evidence for any other form of agrarian exploitation by the wealthy in these epochs. 'How then,' he asks, 'if not by slave labour, was the agricultural work done for the propertied class? How otherwise did that class derive its surplus?'[16] Not merely is there no sign empirically that wage-labour or leasing, the only alternatives, were more widespread: logically too, he demonstrates, neither could have yielded rates of exploitation comparable to the use of slave-labour in the conditions of the time. The conclusion, then, is irresistible. Reinstating the classical Marxist vision of the role of slavery in Antiquity, but now on the basis of the most exhaustive modern scholarship, Ste. Croix sums up: 'Slavery increased the surplus in the hands of the propertied class to an extent which could not otherwise have been achieved and was therefore an essential precondition of the magnificent achievements of Classical civilization.'[17] This holds good, he makes clear, for Athenian democracy itself, which well-meaning writers have on occasion sought to absolve from the taint of slavery. Yielding to none in his admiration for that democracy, of which he gives a memorable account,[18] Ste. Croix nevertheless insists that it was a 'dictatorship by the minority of the population', albeit not a small minority; that 'just because it was a democracy and the poorer citizens were to some extent protected against the powerful, the very most had to be made out of the classes below the citizens'; and that therefore 'we need not be surprised if we find a more intense development of slavery at Athens than at most other places in the Greek world: if the humbler citizens could not be fully exploited, and it was inexpedient to try to put too much pressure on the metics, then it was necessary to rely to an exceptional degree on exploiting the labour of slaves.'[19] It was thus no accident that it was slaveowners – 'men liberated from toil' – who 'produced virtually all Greek art and literature and science and philosophy, and provided a good proportion of the armies which won remarkable victories by land over the Persian invaders at Marathon in 490 and at Plataea in 479 BC. In a very real sense most of them were parasitic upon other men, their slaves above all: most of them were not supporters of the democracy

---

16. CSAGW, p. 172.
17. CSAGW, p. 40.
18. CSAGW, pp. 283–84.
19. CSAGW, p. 141.

which ancient Greece invented and which was its great contribution to political progress, although they did supply almost all its leaders' – 'what we know as Greek civilization expressed itself in and through them above all.'[20]

While the centrality of slavery is copiously documented, it is one of the great strengths of *The Class Struggle in the Ancient Greek World* that Ste. Croix gives full and proper attention to the various other forms of exploitation characteristic of Antiquity, and to the different types of small producers who were so densely represented within it. Detailed discussions of independent smallholders, free artisans, rural *laoi*, later *coloni*, provide a wide panorama of these distinct subordinate classes. Two aspects of Ste. Croix's treatment of them perhaps stand out. The first is his contention that *laoi* or *coloni* – that is, dependent cultivators tied to the land – can be described without reservation as 'serfs', a term often withheld from them because of its mediaeval connotations. The second is his claim that women in Antiquity must be regarded as a separate class, because their special position in 'the earliest and most fundamental of all divisions of labour', monopolizing the reproductive function (in its broadest sense), made them an exploited group with inferior property and other legal rights, dependent on men.

However numerically and humanly important these other oppressed strata were – preponderant even, in census terms, at most times – for Ste. Croix they do not provide the guiding thread of ancient history. That lies within the exploitative structures of slave-labour itself. For it is part of the principal theme of *The Class Struggle in the Ancient Greek World* that slavery not only provided the surplus-labour on which the fortunes of the propertied classes were based in the peak periods of Greek and Roman civilization, but also furnishes the explanation for the long-run evolution of the ancient world. Contrasting Marxist theory, which dynamically relates social classes to each other in antagonistic conflicts that generate historical change, with Weberian theory, in which status groups are juxtaposed inertly in a hierarchy without internal tendency or momentum, Ste. Croix argues that one test of the former is precisely its ability to *explain*, rather than merely describe, the decline and fall of Roman imperial civilization. Much of the second half of his book is devoted to such an explanation. He starts by suggesting, as we have seen, that slavery was generally the most efficient form of extraction of surplus-labour in Antiquity – maximiz-

---

20. CSAGW, p. 115.

ing the rate of exploitation for the propertied classes, and therefore always preferred by them when circumstances permitted. He then notes, as many other scholars have done before him, perhaps especially Weber, that once the frontiers of the Roman Empire were stabilized after Trajan, the supply of slaves captured in war tailed off, with the result that slave-breeding became more widespread, as landowners strove to maintain the labour force on their estates. At this point, Ste. Croix introduces the crucial link – in his view, hitherto missing – in the causal chain that led to the subsequent colonate, and thereafter to the collapse of the imperial order itself.

To promote more regular reproduction, he argues, slaveowners must perforce have given more leeway to female slaves to bear and bring up children, rather than till the fields, and maintained more female slaves *tout court*, as well as allowing greater elements of stable cohabitation between the sexes. Such changes from the lop-sided *ergastulum* of Republican days could only have lowered the rate at which slave-labour as a whole was exploited. 'Breeding slaves inside the economy, then, instead of mainly bringing them in from outside, either cheap or even (as a consequence of the enslavement of war captives) virtually gratis, necessarily imposes a greater burden on the economy as a whole, especially in a society like ancient Greece (and Rome), with a high infant and maternal death-rate.'[21] The logical reaction of the propertied classes was then to try to compensate for the declining profitability of slave-labour by extending their mechanisms of extortion to hitherto free labour, and depressing it to a serf-like level: 'The inevitable consequence is that the propertied class cannot maintain the same rate of profit from slave labour, and, to prevent its standard of living from falling, is likely to be driven to increase the rate of exploitation of the humbler free population – as I believe the Roman ruling class now actually did, by degrees.'[22]

The result was the series of social and juridical changes that set in from the second century onwards, steadily degrading the position of the lower classes in the Empire – what came to be called the *humiliores* in the legal terminology that emerged during the Antonine Age, until eventually a uniform class of *coloni*, including former slaves and smallholders alike, emerged on the land by the fourth century: a population of tied serfs, paying rents to their landowners and taxes to the state. The average rate of exploitation in the new system must have

---

21. CSAGW, p. 231.
22. CSAGW, p. 231.

gone down: but its volume, as surplus labour was extracted on a far wider scale in the countryside, undoubtedly went up, as the escalating size of senatorial fortunes, not to speak of imperial indictions or clerical prebends, attests. The result was a social polarization of late Roman society so extreme, thrusting even the bulk of the curial class of provincial gentry downwards, as to fatally weaken its capacity to maintain either vigorous military forces of the Republican type (armies recruited from independent smallholders), or to generate any civilian loyalty and resistance in the face of external enemies. The barbarian invasions could then finish off a social order undone from within, by its own immanent logic.

*   *   *

Such are the overarching themes of *The Class Struggle in the Ancient Greek World*. Space precludes any adequate account of the richness of detail and digression with which they are developed. Nor can any lay reader hope to do more than suggest a few possible queries or qualifications, from within the complex edifice of Ste. Croix's argument itself, as it were. These do not touch on the central theoretical statement of the book. Ste. Croix's redefinition of class, and redrawing of the place of slavery in the class societies of Antiquity, have compelling force. It is difficult to imagine that discussion of either could ever be exactly the same again. Where grounds for further exploration start, is in some of the more strictly historical proposals within his conceptual framework. Three areas stand out here, relating respectively to the frontiers of class, the role of class struggle, and the dynamic of the mode of production in which such struggle may have occurred.

The first raises an issue that is in fact marginal to Ste. Croix's book as a whole, but an absorbing one for all that. Granted his definition of social class, can women in Antiquity have constituted one? Ste. Croix makes his case by two moves. Firstly, he assimilates 'reproduction' to 'production', as simply another form of the latter. Secondly, he emphasizes the inferior legal position of women, as reproducers, in Antiquity – especially their lesser property rights, token of their exploitation by men. 'Greek wives, I have argued, and therefore potentially all Greek women, should be regarded as a distinct economic class, in the technical Marxist sense, since their productive role – the very fact that they were the half of the human race which supported the main part of the burden of reproduction – led directly to their being subjected to men, politically, economically and socially.'[23] Ste. Croix remarks in this connection, plausibly enough, that individuals can in principle belong to a plurality of classes, if they combine a number of social roles in their person: but that one of these roles will normally preponderate, and so for most purposes define that person's class identity. The partners and daughters of slaves or smallholders, therefore, could be primarily slaves or smallholders, given the common destitution of both sexes in these groups, whereas the wives or female offspring of slaveowners would be primarily women by class position, given the great disparity of rights between them and their husbands or fathers. 'In Classical Athens I would see the class position of a citizen woman belonging to the highest class as largely determined by her sex, by the fact that she belonged to the class of women, for her father, brothers, husband and sons would all be property owners, while she would be virtually destitute of property rights, and her class position would therefore be greatly inferior to theirs. The humble peasant woman, however, would not in practice be in nearly such an inferior position to the men of her family, who would have very little property; and partly owing to the fact that she would to some extent participate in their agricultural activities and work alongside them (in so far as her child-bearing and child-rearing permitted), her membership of the class of poor peasants might be a far more important determinant of her class position than her sex.'[24]

It is possible to doubt the strength of these two arguments. For reproduction, however central a human function it may be in the generation of life, clearly is not production in the conventional sense of the term. It does not provide the necessities of life, still less yield a surplus over and above them; nor is it amenable to any yardstick of 'productivity', for Marx a central criterion for distinguishing any one type of historical economy from another. Moreover, there is obviously something paradoxical in arguing that the only women to form a truly separate exploited class were those from privileged backgrounds. For these were precisely the women who would dispose of domestic servants, generally slaves, not to speak of the other material comforts of wealthy households. What surplus labour was extracted from them, by Ste. Croix's own criteria? The social and cultural discrimination from which they suffered in Greece was, of course, real and grievous enough. But to speak of their 'economic exploitation' seems captious. It might be added that Roman women of the upper class – here,

---

23. CSAGW, p. 101.
24. CSAGW, pp. 100–101.

unusually, excluded from the discussion by Ste. Croix – in fact possessed very extensive legal and property rights, enjoying a measure of formal equality with their men that has struck many feminist observers from Simone de Beauvoir onwards. Ste. Croix's discussion of these questions is more tentative than that of his main themes, and he rightly looks forward to further research that may clarify them.

A second area where some readers might feel Ste. Croix's choices of coverage were a trifle disconcerting concern the 'class struggle in Antiquity' itself. For despite its salience in the title of the book, and its foregrounding in Part I, it could be argued that the actual manifestations of class struggle in Part II, which surveys the historical development of Greek and Roman civilization, are registered rather patchily, at times perhaps even underplayed. The most obvious lacuna here is any account of the great slave rebellions of the Roman Republic. Spartacus earns no more than three passing references; Eunus, leader of the Sicilian rising that preceded the era of Gracchan agitation, receives not one. It might be argued that these fall outside Ste. Croix's brief, as belonging to Roman history prior to its final incorporation of the Greek East. But in fact Ste. Croix devotes a fascinating chapter to class struggles within the citizen body of Republican Rome, from the conflict between 'patricians' and 'plebeians' to the popular tumults against the late oligarchy in the epoch of Cicero and Clodius. Given his own insistence on the centrality of slavery as a class relationship, the pattern of attention here seems inconsistent. For that matter, it might also be objected that the discussion of specifically Greek class struggle – promised by the title – is by comparison unduly terse. Certainly, two of its outstanding episodes are accorded scant space: the successful revolt of the Messenian helots against Sparta, in conjunction with Theban penetration of the Peloponnese, and the extraordinary attempt at social regeneration by a sweeping programme of reforms that included the emancipation of the Laconian helots, of the Spartan king Nabis in the second century BC – an enterprise that unleashed fierce class struggle within the Spartiate body itself. These absences must inspire a special regret, since no historian has displayed a more gripping mastery of Spartan society, in all its intricacy and obscurity, than Ste. Croix himself, in the very substantial sections devoted to it in *The Origins of the Peloponnesian War*.

In part, the apparent imbalances of topical concentration within the second part of *The Class Struggle in the Ancient Greek World* no doubt reflect the heterodox temper of the author himself, as impatient of conventional norms of composition as of received notions of any sort. But they also indicate an underlying issue in the treatment of the curve of ancient civilization that warrants further elucidation. Does the class struggle, as Ste. Croix formulates it, provide the direct key to the dynamic of successive classical societies? In Part I, he emphatically claims that it does. The irregularities of Part II, so far at any rate as direct accounts of the resistance of the exploited go, might be a symptom of the difficulties of that claim. The cruces here are obviously the 'destruction of Greek democracy' and the 'decline and fall of the Roman Empire' – the two most momentous changes in the political history of Antiquity. What is Ste. Croix's explanation of the first? Why was classical Greek society eclipsed by the end of the fourth century BC? His general answer seems to be that there was an inbuilt tendency for the economically stronger groups within the city-states to increase their political power at the expense of the poorer citizens, which in the long run had to lead to the contraction and subversion of democratic institutions: 'the basic economic situation asserted itself in the long run, as it always does: the Greek propertied classes, with the assistance first of their Macedonian overlords and later of their Roman masters, gradually undermined and in the end entirely destroyed Greek democracy.'[25] After the turn of the fourth century, he suggests, a 'slow regression' began in Greece: 'there was widespread and serious poverty among the mass of the people, at the same time as the few rich were perhaps growing richer' (p. 294) – this in a region that never possessed great natural resources anyway. The result was rising social tension and internecine conflicts in many of the city-states. These were then exploited by the Macedonian monarchy, which – given its own aristocratic character – found natural allies in the local propertied classes in its drive into Greece.

How persuasive is such a compressed account? A major drawback of it would seem to be its lack of any sufficiently specific temporal logic. Ste. Croix argues, in both his books, that Greek democracy should be seen essentially as a mechanism whereby the humbler citizens protected themselves against the economic threat to them by the propertied. If successful defence was possible in the fifth century, however, why not also in the fourth? In fact, Athenian democracy did indeed prove relatively stable after the Peloponnesian War. The major change in its operation was not so much any greater power accruing to the rich within the city, as the lesser power rich and poor alike now enjoyed outside the city, with the disappearance of the Athenian Empire. Ste. Croix cites the financial crisis provoked by the stoppage of imperial

---

25. CSAGW, p. 97.

tribute, and the ensuing difficulty for Athens in mobilizing adequate naval forces. But these factors are not integrated into his main explanation of the 'fall of Greece'. Yet an alternative account of the decline of Hellenic democracy might be constructed in terms, not so much of internal social polarization within the *polis*, as of the external limitations of the democratic state-form in Antiquity, which – just because of its radically direct character, exemplified above all at Athens – could never transcend municipal size without contradicting itself by issuing into an imperial domination over other cities. Only such domination, however, could provide it with sufficient territorial and material resources to compete militarily with centralized monarchies or oligarchic republics. In this sense, loss of empire may be said to have doomed Athens, and with Athens the smaller cities that maintained popular constitutions in its shadow.

The immediate agent of their downfall, however, was the Macedonian monarchy, treated by Ste. Croix as a more or less exogenous force in the whole process. But this understates the degree of symbiosis between urban Greece and its tribal periphery: the increasing strength and sophistication of the Macedonian polity and nobility under Philip II was itself the product of a cumulative acculturation within the orbit of classical civilization proper, in the peninsula. Classical Greece drew its own destroyer onto it, in this sense. The struggle that was directly at stake here, it might be said, was one between ruling groups: a mountain aristocracy and municipal citizenries. While Macedonian policy was indeed socially and politically conservative in Greece, ruling out radical innovations in the cities that fell under its control, it is significant that it showed no immediate hostility to Athenian democracy as such, once its suzerainty was established over it; as Ste. Croix concedes, neither Philip II nor Alexander interfered in any way with the Athenian constitution. It was not until the Lamian War, a generalized Greek revolt against Macedonian rule after Alexander's death, that Antipater temporarily imposed a more oligarchic regime on Athens – even then a fairly broad one, based on a hoplite census. But, of course, the vitality of any municipal polity could not in the long run survive the abolition of external autonomy, and the classical institutions of Greek democracy inevitably became ever more convulsed and weakened within the new Hellenistic universe of royal overlords, until finally Roman conquest effectively put an end to them.

If we now turn to the decline of the Roman imperial order itself, Ste. Croix's account does not this time take as its point of departure the class struggle as such. It is a systemic contradiction, rather than social struggle, that sets in motion the secular process of dissolution. A decline in the supply of slave-labour, consequent on low rates of internal reproduction, leads to offsetting attempts at slave-breeding which decrease the rate of exploitation, thus necessitating a complementary depression of free labour to sustain overall levels of surplus extraction. The major manifestations of class struggle between slaves and their owners – slave revolts – play no causal role here. This is surely why they figure so fleetingly in Ste. Croix's text: they bear little or no explanatory weight. Empirically, the soundness of Ste. Croix's judgement here brooks little doubt. Attempts to make of slave resistance – in a recent version, if not rebellion then mass desertion[26] – the lever of the diminution of slavery in the Ancient World are uniformly unconvincing. The real mechanisms, indicated by Ste. Croix, rather form an instance of that other fundamental theme of historical materialism: namely, that modes of production change when the forces and relations of production enter into decisive contradiction with each other. The maturing of such a contradiction need involve no conscious class agency on either side, by exploiters and exploited – no set battle for the future of economy and society; although its subsequent unfolding, on the other hand, is likely to unleash relentless social struggles between opposing forces. This is, in fact, just the sequence that Ste. Croix's interpretation of the final centuries of Antiquity tends to suggest. It is striking how closely the theoretical and historical issues here resemble those posed by the dissolution of feudalism a millennium later. There too, Marxist writers – the most illustrious was Maurice Dobb – have sometimes been inclined to read the crisis of the late mediaeval economy as the direct outcome of class struggle between lords and peasants, with ever mounting exactions of the former leading to a collapse of production by the latter. In fact, the demographic and ecological limits of the feudal mode of production in Western Europe cannot be ignored in an analysis of its contradictory logic: it was the objective deadlock they imposed on the societies of the fourteenth century, as forces of production struck against insuperable barriers within existing relations of production, that precipitated the economic disasters of the time, which then set off the most spectacular episodes of pitched conflict on the land.

The capital difference between the two processes, mediaeval and ancient, was of course that the one led to general emancipation of the direct producers in the countryside, the other to their general subjec-

---

26. See Pierre Dockès, *Mediaeval Slavery and Liberation*, London 1982, pp. 216–17, a work derivative from a once influential *maoisant* milieu in France.

tion – final exit as against initial entry into a serf-like condition, as it were (provided all the discontinuities and dissimilarities between villeins and *coloni* are remembered). To note this is to register some of the unsolved problems of the slow change of labour system in the later Roman Empire. The formidable cogency of Ste. Croix's reconstruction of the shift from slavery to colonate as predominant form of surplus extraction – superior to any alternative account available – rests more on logical deduction than on any empirical documentation. Given the absence of sources, this could not be otherwise. But it is in the nature of his argument to raise a number of further questions about the process it offers to explain. The first of these concerns the issue of slave reproduction. The central thrust of Ste. Croix's argument is that slave-breeding, increasingly necessary once the great windfalls of conquest ceased, was economically less profitable than slave capture – hence the pressure to complement it with depression of tenants or smallholders, if the income of the propertied classes was to be preserved. Could there have been a cultural spur to this change as well? Ste. Croix emphasizes, in his discussion of Greek slavery, the crucial advantages to slaveowners of a labour force that was ethnically not only alien but also heterogeneous, at once demarcated from the rest of the population and deprived of common springs of resistance.[27] It was the absence of these two qualities, he writes, which rendered the Messenian helots so much more dangerous than Attic slaves ever were. The vast bulk of Roman slaves, as the empire expanded, were of course constituted from non-Latin peoples. There too, when there occurred an unduly large concentration of captives from any one region, enslaved and imported into Italy, insurrection could break out in Republican days: the revolt led by Eunus, for example, massed recent prisoners from Syria and Asia Minor in common resistance in Sicily. But after the Augustan Age, the relative stabilization of the workforce must – in the absence of any colour bar – have led to widespread assimilation, in language and customs, between slaves and free poor over large areas of the Western Empire. An episode like the plebeian riots in protest against a mass execution of domestic slaves in Rome under Nero, cited by Ste. Croix, suggests such a cultural convergence. In these conditions, it may be wondered whether one of the further limitations of slave-breeding as a remedy to supply shortages was not its tendency to weaken ideological and coercive control over the slave population itself, which as time went on would become ever less immediately distinguishable as such –

---

27. CSAGW, p. 93.

perhaps facilitating flight, if not manumission (always higher in the Latin than in the Greek world anyway, possibly for reasons to do with Roman patterns of patronage, in Ste. Croix's view),[28] while at the same time rendering the poor free population ever less perceptibly separate from the slave. Here might lie one of the ancillary reasons for the social and juridical changes of the Antonine epoch.

However that may be, the consequence of these changes was vastly to extend the network of rural exploitation. The second question that Ste. Croix's account brings home very sharply is how this exploitation was organized. Two distinct problems are involved here. How was the surplus actually extracted from the immediate producers? How was it realized by the ultimate exploiters? The adjectives require emphasis here, because the obscurity of each process lies essentially in the intermediary agents and mechanisms ensuring them. Ste. Croix does not address the first problem directly. We know from the detailed descriptions in Columella how a slave villa was supposed to function in the first century AD: through an elaborate division of the workforce itself, involving a hierarchy of supervisory, skilled, unskilled and chained slaves, toiling in small labour teams each with their own drivers, coordinated by foremen and commanded by the bailiff or *villicus*. Differentiation of rank, cooperation of task, and invigilation of rhythm, backed by lash and fetter, made up the prescriptive model of slave agriculture, whose average units of exploitation were probably no more than 150–200 acres. This transparency, however, disappears once the focus shifts to the way in which slaveowners marketed the produce of their estates: as Ste. Croix comments, in an important passage, 'we have extraordinarily little evidence about this kind of activity'.[29] He goes on to agree that landowners will have typically sold their output (corn, oil, wine) on local markets. But this only compounds the mystery of the administration of very large fortunes on the land, since these frequently involved a wide scatter of estates – which, in the late Republic or early Principate, say, might be distributed up and down the length of Italy. How was the income from such disparate sources effectively gathered and centralized?

This issue, far from clear for the period of large-scale slave agricul-

---

28. See pp. 174–75. Ste. Croix does not discuss the persuasive arguments advanced by Keith Hopkins that Roman manumission may have had a twofold economic rationale for many masters: the prospect of emancipation ensuring good work performance by the slave, and then the purchase of it yielding a satisfactory sum at the end of that performance: *Conquerors and Slaves*, Cambridge 1978, pp. 125–29.

29. CSAGW, p. 129.

ture itself, becomes more acutely perplexing once a shift to the colonate has occurred. For on the one hand, direct supervision of the labour process by landowners necessarily declined, and with it the extraction of surplus at the point of production itself. But on the other hand, if the rate of exploitation decreased, the range of exploitation actually increased with the generalization of predial dependency in the Later Empire. Ste. Croix, in one of the most arresting statements in his book, writes: 'There is one phenomenon in particular which strongly suggests that in the Roman empire the peasantry was more thoroughly and effectively exploited than in most other societies which rely largely upon peasant populations for their food supply. It has often been noticed that peasants have usually been able to survive famines better than their town-dwelling fellow-countrymen, because they can hide away for themselves some of the food they produce and may still have something to eat when there is starvation in the towns. It was not so in the Roman empire' – there, again and again 'we find peasants crowding into the nearest city in time of famine, because only in the city is there any edible food to be had.'[30] What he does not perhaps sufficiently underline, however, is the fact that all the examples he gives date from the epoch subsequent to the decline of slavery, or fourth to sixth centuries AD.[31] The extraordinary 'efficiency' of the agrarian exploitation of the ruling class in this age finds confirmation, on the other side of the coin, in the gigantic size of senatorial fortunes in the Western Empire – by the fourth century some five times larger on average than those of the first century.

Yet how were these enormous sums levied from the immediate producers? What immensely ramified systems of rent collection, enforced by which forms of compulsion, operated by how many levels of intermediaries, secured the steady, lethal puncture of so many peasant livings in countless remote regions, without good transport or communications, to the profit of a magnate family in Rome? The geographical scale of the process, at its maximum reaches, was more like that of a modern multinational corporation than of any conceivable mediaeval holding. Melania, a noblewoman of the early fifth century, owned estates in Campania, Apulia, Sicily, Tunisia, Numidia, Mauretania, Spain and Britain: literally transcontinental domains. On these estates were still thousands of slaves; but many more will have been *coloni*. By what channels was their produce converted into her

---

30. CSAGW, p. 14.
31. CSAGW, pp. 219–220.

income of 1600 pounds of gold a year? Ste. Croix makes a point of calling *coloni* 'serfs', but their relationship to their landlords never approached the potent ideological compact of mediaeval serfdom, lacking either the feudal rights of the seigneur over the family of the villein (merchet, heriot, etc.) or the loyalties owed by the villein to the juridical authority of the lord. Yet, pressed less close to the ground, the Roman system yielded more.

Part of the reason why it could do so, of course, was the sheer weight of the late Imperial State itself. This figures less directly in Ste. Croix's concluding chapters than perhaps it is entitled to do. At any rate, there is no analysis as such of the deep and prolonged crisis of the Empire in the third century AD, between the death of Alexander Severus and the elevation of Diocletian, when endemic anarchy, invasion, plague and inflation seemed to threaten its existence for fifty years. The structural approach – by problematic, rather than period – preferred by Ste. Croix bypasses this watershed. It may in fact be the case that sources are so scant for these broken years – Jones compared them to a black tunnel[32] – that no useful hypotheses can be advanced about their overall meaning. But the coincidence between their timing and the transition in the countryside seems unlikely to have been fortuitous. Any history that sacrifices narrative too austerely will pay a certain price for its analytic clarity. In this case, the cost is any close reflection on the metamorphosis of the imperial state in the third century, which yet must be of central relevance to Ste. Croix's own explanatory purpose. It looks as if a kind of servo-mechanism may have been at work in this epoch. The great increase in the size of the imperial army and bureaucracy must have borne some relation to the enhanced capacity of the propertied classes to squeeze the peasantry ever more pervasively; the central apparatus of repression and coercion was

---

32. Their most recent historian repeats and enlarges the image: 'On the earlier edge of the least-known stretch of Roman history, one feels first the chilly shadow like a traveller approaching the Alps towards the close of an autumn day. No more than a setting sun shines on the Antonines; Severan times grow darker yet; and at their end, with the murder of the young Alexander in 235, blackness settles down. The historian thereafter pursues his way through what he feels to be a complex mass of many vast events almost hidden from him by the obscurity of his sources. He emerges into a gradually clearing light, but into a different country – as if he had entered the depths of Monte Bianco and discovered an exit from Mont Blanc': Ramsey Macmullen, *Roman Government's Response to Crisis, A.D. 235–337*, New Haven 1976, p. vii. Macmullen's main emphasis, which in keeping with his title is more concerned with the pattern of official response than with the nature of the socio-economic crisis itself, falls on the novelty and efficacy of the state's requisitioning capacities from Diocletian onwards: pp. 207–208.

enormously strengthened by the end of these decades. On the other hand, the growth of this apparatus in turn put remorseless further pressure on the same direct producers, in the shape of the much greater fiscal burden imposed for its upkeep – so depressing their economic position sharply in its own right, and thereby rendering them ever more liable to fall into the servitude of the colonate. The fourth and fifth century phenomenon of the *patrocinium* points very clearly to this dialectic: peasants 'voluntarily' putting themselves at the mercy of a landowner, to secure some relief from the attentions of the tax collector. It is necessary to keep the complex logic of this circuit in mind. If Finley – with whom Ste. Croix polemicizes unremittingly, and exaggeratedly – unduly hypostatizes what he calls 'the iron law of absolutist bureaucracy that it grows both in numbers and in cost',[33] as a virtually supernal process detached from the determinate functions of such bureaucracy, Ste. Croix for his part fails to allow sufficiently for the degree of autonomy that the imperial state henceforward acquired from the aristocratic class that it served, by its very overhaul.

For while the socio-economic privileges of the late imperial nobility were fortified and extended under the bureaucratic canopy of the Dominate, its political power was clipped where it had once most counted – in the military machinery of the state, which now acquired quite novel proportions (an army of over 600,000 to a civilian bureaucracy of about 30,000). The senatorial order was excluded from military commands by Diocletian, and never recovered them. The result in the West, where the aristocracy was wealthiest and most powerful, seems to have been widespread indifference by the rich to the defence needs of the state in the face of external pressures or emergencies – an indifference expressed in generalized tax evasion, withholding of conscripts and hostility to the professional officers (by now often of barbarian origin) trying to muster imperial forces in the region. Ste. Croix argues that it was the disappearance of an independent peasantry that undermined the vitality of the Roman armies during the fifth century. But in fact conscription, reintroduced under the Dominate, produced a large and relatively reliable military machine, whose soldiers enjoyed a series of material privileges that set them above the mass

---

33. M.I. Finley, *Ancient Slavery and Modern Ideology*, London 1980, p. 146; see also the similar formulation in *The Ancient Economy*, London 1973, p. 90. In general, 'iron laws' have an unhappy ancestry, from Lassalle's theory of wages which drew Marx's strictures, onwards. Much of Finley's general argument, however, is more concordant with Ste. Croix's than the latter's comments would suggest, even if the causal sequences it advances are less clear. For the issue of surplus labour, for example, see *Ancient Slavery and Modern Ideology*, pp. 81–82.

of the peasantry from which they came. After contending that 'the morale (and probably the physique) of the army deteriorated'[34] because of the debasement of the peasantry, Ste. Croix concedes a few pages later that the army of the late Empire 'developed a most remarkable discipline and *esprit de corps* of its own: the rank-and-file soldiers became entirely detached from their origins and were usually the obedient instruments, if not of their emperors, then of their actual officers'[35] – which seems closer to the mark. While popular apathy towards the barbarian invasions is manifest as a civilian phenomenon, it was patrician alienation that affected most directly the strictly military capabilities of the Roman order in the west. The armies gave a good account of themselves so long as they were kept up to strength. It was when they were neglected, in the final decades of the fourth century, under a series of emperors who were little more than aristocratic figureheads, that disaster struck.

Even so, the Empire did not fall simply from its own internal weaknesses. External assaults were the necessary agent of its execution. Here again Ste. Croix's picture of the process of decline needs to be complemented by some reference to the historical changes in the barbarian periphery of the Empire. The increasing pressure from the Germanic peoples in the north, from the third century onwards, cannot have been unconnected with the economic, political and cultural impact on them of the magnetic civilization to their south. Growing social differentiation and military sophistication were bound to be concomitants of any long-term proximity of primitive tribal societies to an advanced urban and commercial culture of the classical type. Here Ste. Croix's account needs to be complemented by the outstanding work that documents just this process, by his fellow-Marxist historian Edward Arthur Thompson – one of the most original contributions to classical studies since the war.[36] In fact, the evidence he himself marshals – in a valuable Appendix on barbarian settlers within the Empire prior to its fall, who he reckons numbered 'hundreds of thousands' – speaks directly of the creeping interpenetration of the two worlds. In this sense, an analogy could be ventured with the fall of Greece. Just as the latter developed at a distance its backward periphery in Macedonia, and thereby eventually drew its conqueror down upon

---

34. CSAGW, p. 261.
35. CSAGW, p. 265.
36. E.A. Thompson: *The Early Germans*, Oxford 1965; *The Visigoths in the Time of Ulfila*, Oxford 1966; *The Goths in Spain*, Oxford 1969; *Romans and Barbarians*, Madison 1982; as well as his classic, *A History of Attila and the Huns*, Oxford 1948.

itself, so the fall of Rome ultimately occurred when its rudimentary borderlands in Germany had evolved, under the force of its attraction, social and military forces capable of overwhelming it in its extremity. The difference, of course, was that Macedonia was politically a centralized monarchy and culturally a Hellenized society, sharing language and traditions with a classical Greece still intellectually and civically vigorous – the result being the great expansion of Hellenistic civilization; whereas the Germanic invaders were no Latinate country cousins, but still loose tribal confederations, while classical Roman society had long since been hollowed out from within – the result being the Dark Ages.

Recollection of these external aspects of the collapse of the Western Empire, however, does not alter the essential conclusion to which Ste. Croix conveys us at the end of his long work. 'As I see it,' he writes, 'the Roman political system facilitated a most intense and ultimately destructive exploitation of the great mass of the people, whether slave or free, and it made radical reform impossible. The result was that the propertied class, the men of real wealth, who had deliberately created this system for their own benefit, drained the life-blood from their world and thus destroyed Graeco–Roman civilization over a large part of the Empire – Britain, Gaul, Spain and north Africa in the fifth century; much of Italy and the Balkans in the sixth; and in the seventh, Egypt, Syria and Mesopotamia, and again north Africa, which had been reconquered by Justinian's generals in the sixth century. That, I believe, was the principal reason for the decline of Classical civilization.'[37] This summing-up, with its emphasis on the main lineaments of the process, can be accepted entirely. Characteristically, in an explicit contrast with the dictum of his gifted non-Marxist colleague Peter Brown, that 'the prosperity of the Mediterranean world seems to have drained to the top' by the fourth century, Ste. Croix concludes: 'If I were in search of a metaphor to describe the great and growing concentration of wealth in the hands of the upper classes, I would not incline towards anything so innocent and so automatic as drainage: I should want to think in terms of something much more purposive and deliberate – perhaps the vampire bat.'[38] That judgement is unlikely to be forgotten.

1982

---

37. CSAGW, pp. 502–503.
38. CSAGW, p. 503.

2

Marshall Berman:
Modernity and Revolution

Relations between the ideas of 'modernity' and of 'revolution' have been a focus of intellectual debate and political passion for the greater part of this century. The recent publication of Marshall Berman's *All That Is Solid Melts into Air* reopens that debate, with such renewed passion, and such undeniable power, that no contemporary reflection on these issues can avoid coming to terms with it. To pick out the main argument of the book is not to do justice to it as a whole, which will not be attempted here. Any compressed reconstruction of its general scheme must sacrifice the sheer imaginative sweep, the breadth of cultural sympathy, the force of intelligence, that give much of its splendour to *All That Is Solid Melts into Air* – qualities that over time will make it a classic in its field. Let us simply say at the outset that a stripped-down analysis of the principal case of the book is no adequate measure of the importance, and attraction, of the work to hand.

Berman's visionary argument starts as follows: 'There is a mode of vital experience – experience of space and time, of the self and others, of life's possibilities and perils – that is shared by men and women all over the world today. I will call this body of experience "modernity". To be modern is to find ourselves in an environment that promises us adventure, power, joy, growth, transformation of ourselves and the world – and, at the same time, that threatens to destroy everything we have, everything we know, everything we are. Modern environments and experiences cut across all boundaries of geography and ethnicity, of class and nationality, of religion and ideology: in this sense, modernity can be said to unite all mankind. But it is a paradoxical unity, a unity of disunity: it pours all into a maelstrom of perpetual disintegration and renewal, of struggle and contradiction, of ambiguity and anguish. To be modern is to be part of a universe in which, as Marx said, "All that is solid melts into air".'[1]

What generates this maelstrom? For Berman, it is a host of social processes – he lists scientific discoveries, industrial upheavals, demographic transformations, urban expansions, national states, mass movements – all propelled, in the last instance, by the 'ever-expanding, drastically fluctuating' capitalist world market. These processes he calls, for convenient shorthand, socio-economic *modernization*. Out of the experience born of modernization, in turn has emerged what he describes as the 'amazing variety of visions and ideas that aim to make men and women the subjects as well as the objects of modernization, to give them the power to change the world that is changing them, to make their way through the maelstrom and make it their own' – 'visions and values that have come to be loosely grouped together under the name of "modernism".' The ambition of his own book, then, is to reveal the 'dialectics of modern*ization* and modern*ism*'.[2]

Between these two lies, as we have seen, the key middle term of modern*ity* itself – neither economic process nor cultural vision but the historical experience mediating the one to the other. What constitutes the nature of the linkage between them? Essentially, for Berman, it is the idea of *development*. This is really the central concept of his book, and the source of most of its paradoxes – some of them lucidly and convincingly explored in its pages, others less seen by them. In *All That Is Solid Melts into Air*, development means two things simultaneously. On the one hand, it refers to the gigantic objective transformations of society unleashed by the advent of the capitalist world market: that is, essentially but not exclusively, *economic* development. On the other hand, it refers to the momentous subjective transformations of individual life and personality which occur under their impact: everything that is contained within the notion of *self*-development, as a heightening of human powers and widening of human experience. For Berman the combination of these two, under the compulsive beat of the world market, necessarily spells a dramatic tension within the individuals who undergo development in both senses. On the one hand, capitalism – in Marx's unforgettable phrase of the *Manifesto*, which forms the leitmotif of Berman's book – tears down every ancestral confinement and feudal restriction, social immobility and claustral tradition, in an immense clearing operation of cultural and customary debris across the

1. *All that Is Solid Melts into Air*, New York 1982, p. 15. Henceforward ASMA.
2. ASMA, p. 16.

globe. To that process corresponds a tremendous emancipation of the possibility and sensibility of the individual self, now increasingly released from the fixed social status and rigid role-hierarchy of the pre-capitalist past, with its narrow morality and cramped imaginative range. On the other hand, as Marx emphasized, the very same onrush of capitalist economic development also generates a brutally alienated and atomized society, marked by callous economic exploitation and cold social indifference, destructive of every cultural or political value whose potential it has itself brought into being. Likewise, on the psychological plane, self-development in these conditions could only mean a profound disorientation and insecurity, frustration and despair, concomitant with – indeed inseparable from – the sense of enlargement and exhilaration, the new capacities and feelings, liberated at the same time. 'This atmosphere,' Berman writes, 'of agitation and turbulence, psychic dizziness and drunkenness, expansion of experiential possibili-ties and destruction of moral boundaries and personal bonds, self-enlargement and self-derangement, phantoms in the street and in the soul – is the atmosphere in which modern sensibility is born.'[3]

That sensibility dates, in its initial manifestations, from the advent of the world market itself – 1500 or thereabouts. But in its first phase, which for Berman runs to about 1790, it still lacks any common vocabulary. A second phase then extends across the nineteenth century, and it is here that the experience of modernity is translated into the various classical visions of modernism, which he defines essentially by their firm ability to grasp both sides of the contradictions of capitalist development – at once celebrating and denouncing its unprecedented transformations of the material and spiritual world, without ever converting these attitudes into static or immutable antitheses. Goethe is prototypical of the new vision in his *Faust*, which Berman in a magnificent chapter analyses as a tragedy of the developer in this dual sense – unbinding the self in binding back the sea. Marx in the *Manifesto* and Baudelaire in his prose poems on Paris are shown as cousins in the same discovery of modernity – one prolonged, in the peculiar conditions of forced modernization from above in a backward society, in the long literary tradition of St Petersburg, from Pushkin and Gogol to Dostoevsky and Mandelstam. A condition of the sensibility so created – Berman argues – was a more or less unified public still possessing a memory of what it was like to live in a pre-modern world.

---

3. ASMA, p. 18.

In the twentieth century, that public simultaneously expanded and fragmented into incommensurable segments. Therewith the dialectical tension of the classical experience of modernity underwent a critical transformation. While modernist art registered more triumphs than ever before – the twentieth century, Berman says in an unguarded phrase, 'may well be the most brilliantly creative in the history of the world'[4] – this art has ceased to connect with or inform any common life: as he puts it, 'we don't know how to use our modernism'.[5] The result has been a drastic polarization in modern thought about the experience of modernity itself, flattening out its essentially ambiguous or dialectical character. On the one hand, from Weber through to Ortega, Eliot to Tate, Leavis to Marcuse, twentieth-century modernity has been relentlessly condemned as an iron cage of conformity and mediocrity, a spiritual wilderness of populations bleached of any organic community or vital autonomy. On the other hand, against these visions of cultural despair, in another tradition stretching from Marinetti to Le Corbusier, Buckminster Fuller to Marshall McLuhan, not to speak of outright apologists of capitalist 'modernization theory' itself, modernity has been fulsomely touted as the last word in sensory excitement and universal satisfaction, in which a machine-built civilization itself guarantees aesthetic thrills and social felicities. What each side has in common here is a simple identification of modernity with technology itself – radically excluding the people who produce and are produced by it. As Berman writes: 'Our nineteenth-century thinkers were simultaneously enthusiasts and enemies of modern life, wrestling inexhaustibly with its ambiguities and contradictions; their self-ironies and inner tensions were a primary source of their creative power. Their twentieth-century successors have lurched far more towards rigid polarities and flat totalizations. Modernity is either embraced with a blind and uncritical enthusiasm, or else condemned with a neo-Olympian remoteness and contempt; in either case it is conceived as a closed monolith, incapable of being shaped or changed by modern men. Open visions of life have been supplanted by closed ones, Both/And by Either/Or.'[6] The purpose of Berman's book is to help restore our sense of modernity, by reappropriating the classical visions of it. 'It may turn out, then, that going back can be a way to go forward: that remembering the modernisms of the nineteenth century can give us the vision and courage to create the modernisms of the twenty-first. This act of

---

4. ASMA, p. 24.
5. ASMA, p. 24.
6. ASMA, p. 24.

remembering can help us bring modernism back to its roots, so that it can nourish and renew itself, to confront the adventures and dangers that lie ahead.'[7]

Such is the general thrust of *All That Is Solid Melts into Air*. The book contains, however, a very important sub-text, which needs to be noted. Berman's title, and organizing theme, come from *The Communist Manifesto*, and his chapter on Marx is one of the most interesting in the book. It ends, however, by suggesting that Marx's own analysis of the dynamic of modernity ultimately undermines the very prospect of the communist future he thought it would lead to. For if the essence of liberation from bourgeois society would be for the first time a truly unlimited development of the individual – the limits of capital, with all its deformities, now being struck away – what could guarantee either the harmony of the individuals so emancipated, or the stability of any society composed of them? 'Even if,' Berman asks, 'the workers do build a successful communist movement, and even if that movement generates a successful revolution, how amid the flood tides of modern life, will they ever manage to build a solid communist society? What is to prevent the social forces that melt capitalism from melting communism as well? If all new relationships become obsolete before they can ossify, how can solidarity, fraternity and mutual aid be kept alive? A communist government might try to dam the flood by imposing radical restrictions, not merely on economic activity and enterprise (every socialist government has done this, along with every capitalist welfare state), but on personal, cultural and political expression. But insofar as such a policy succeeded, wouldn't it betray the Marxist aim of free development for each and all?'[8] On the other hand, 'if a triumphant communism should someday flow through the floodgates that free trade opens up, who knows what dreadful impulses might flow along with it, or in its wake, or impacted inside? It is easy to imagine how a society committed to the free development of each and all might develop its own distinctive varieties of nihilism. Indeed, a communist nihilism might turn out to be far more explosive and disintegrative than its bourgeois precursor – though also more daring and original – because while capitalism cuts the infinite possibilities of modern life with the limits of the bottom line, Marx's communism might launch the liberated self into immense unknown spaces with no limits at all.' Berman thus concludes: 'Ironically, then, we can see Marx's dialectic of

---

7. ASMA, p. 36.
8. ASMA, p. 104.

modernity re-enacting the fate of the society it describes, generating energies and ideas that melt it down into its own air.'[9]

Berman's argument is an original and arresting one, and it is presented with great skill and verve. It unites a generous political stance with a warm intellectual enthusiasm for its subject: the notions of both the modern and the revolutionary, it might be said, emerge morally redeemed in his pages. Indeed modernism is profoundly revolutionary, by definition, for Berman. As the jacket of the book proclaims: 'Contrary to conventional belief, the modernist revolution is not over.' A consideration of the logic behind this claim must start by looking at Berman's key terms 'modernization' and 'modernism', and then at the linkage between them through the two-headed notion of 'development'. If we do this, the first thing that must strike one is that while Berman has grasped with unequalled force of imagination one critical dimension of Marx's vision of history in *The Communist Manifesto*, he omits or overlooks another dimension that is no less critical for Marx, and complementary to it. Capital accumulation, for Marx, and the ceaseless expansion of the commodity form through the market, is indeed a universal dissolvent of the old social world, and can legitimately be presented as a process of 'constant revolutionizing of production, uninterrupted disturbance, everlasting uncertainty and agitation', in Marx's words. Note the three adjectives: constant, uninterrupted, everlasting. They denote a homogeneous historical time, in which each moment is perpetually different from every other by virtue of being next, but – by the same token – is also the same, as an interchangeable unit in a process of indefinite recurrence. Extrapolated from Marx's theory of capitalist development as a whole, this emphasis very quickly and easily yields the paradigm of modernization proper – an anti-Marxist theory, of course, politically. For our purposes, however, the relevant point is that the idea of modernization involves a conception of fundamentally planar development – a continuous-flow process in which there is no real differentiation of one conjuncture or epoch from another save in terms of the mere chronological succession of old and new, earlier and later, categories themselves subject to unceasing permutation of positions in one direction, as time goes by and the later becomes earlier, the newer older. Such is, of course, an accurate account of the temporality of the market and of the commodities that circulate across it.

But Marx's own conception of the historical time of capitalism as a

---

9. ASMA, p. 114.

mode of production was quite distinct from this: it was of a complex and differential temporality, in which episodes or eras were disconti-nuous from each other, and heterogeneous within themselves. The most obvious way in which this differential time enters into the very construction of Marx's model of capitalism is, of course, at the level of the social order generated by it. By and large, it can be said that classes as such scarcely figure in Berman's account at all. The one significant exception is a fine discussion of the extent to which the bourgeoisie has always failed to conform to the free-trade absolutism postulated by Marx in the *Manifesto*: but this has few repercussions in the architec-ture of his book as a whole, in which there is very little between economy on the one hand and psychology on the other, save for the culture of modernism that links the two. Society as such is effectively missing. But if we look at Marx's account of that society, what we find is something very different from any process of planar development. Rather, the trajectory of the bourgeois order as he conceived it was curvilinear. It traced, not a straight line ploughing endlessly forward, or a circle expanding infinitely outwards, but a marked parabola. Bour-geois society would experience an ascent, a stabilization and a descent. In the very passages of the *Grundrisse* which contain the most lyrical and unconditional affirmations of the unity of economic development and individual development that provides the pivot of Berman's argu-ment, when Marx writes of 'the point of flowering' of the basis of the capitalist mode of production, as 'the point at which it can be united with the highest development of productive forces, and thus also of the richest development of the individual' – he also stipulates expressly: 'It is nevertheless still this basis, this plant in flower, and therefore it fades after flowering and as a consequence of flowering.' 'As soon as this point has been reached,' he goes on, 'any further development takes the form of a decline.'[10] In contemporary terms, we could say that the history of capitalism must be periodized, and its particular paths reconstructed, if we are to have a sober understanding of what capita-list 'development' actually means. The concept of modernization, if uncritically employed, will occlude any possibility of that.

Let us now revert to Berman's complementary term 'modernism'. Although this post-dates modernization, in the sense that it signals the arrival of a coherent vocabulary for an experience of modernity that preceded it, once in place modernism too knows no internal principle of variation. It simply keeps on reproducing itself. It is significant that

---

10. *Grundrisse der Kritik der politischen Okonomie*, Berlin 1953, p. 439.

Berman is moved to claim that the art of modernism has flourished, is flourishing, as never before in the twentieth century – even while protesting at the trends of thought which prevent us from adequately incorporating this art into our lives. There are a number of obvious difficulties with such a position. The first is that modernism, as a specific set of aesthetic forms, is generally dated precisely from the twentieth century – indeed is typically construed by way of contrast with realist and other classical forms of the nineteenth, eighteenth or earlier centuries. Virtually all of the actual literary texts analysed so well by Berman – whether by Goethe or Baudelaire, Pushkin or Dostoevsky – precede modernism proper, in this usual sense of the word: the only exceptions are fictions by Bely and Mandelstam, from the early part of this century. In other words, by more conventional criteria, modernism too needs to be framed within some more differential conception of historical time. A second, and related, point is that once it is treated in this way, it is striking how uneven its distribution actually was, geographically. Even within the European or Western world generally, there are major areas that scarcely generated any modernist momentum at all. England, the pioneer of capitalist industrialization and master of the world market for a century, is of course a major case in point: beach-head for Eliot or Pound, offshore to Joyce, it produced virtually no significant native movement of a modernist type in the first decades of this century – unlike Germany or Italy, France or Russia, Holland or America. It is not surprising that it should be the great absentee from Berman's conspectus in *All That Is Solid Melts into Air* itself. The space of modernism too is thus heterogeneous.

A third objection to Berman's reading of modernism as a whole is that it establishes no distinctions either between very contrasted aesthetic tendencies, or within the range of aesthetic practices that comprise the arts themselves. But in fact it is the protean variety of relations to capitalist modernity that is most striking in the broad grouping of movements typically assembled under the common rubric of modernism. Symbolism, expressionism, cubism, futurism or constructivism, surrealism – there were perhaps five or six decisive currents of 'modernism' in the early decades of the century, from which nearly everything thereafter was a derivation or mutant. The antithetical nature of the doctrines and practices peculiar to these would suffice in itself, one would have thought, to preclude the possibility that there could have been any one characteristic *Stimmung* defining the classical modernist bearing towards modernity. Much of the art produced from within this range of positions already contained the makings of those very polarities decried by Berman in contemporary or subsequent theorizations of modern culture as a whole. German expressionism and Italian futurism, in their respectively contrasted tonalities, form a stark instance. A final difficulty with Berman's account is that it is unable, from within its own terms of reference, to provide any explanation of the divarication it deplores, between the art and thought, practice and theory, of modernity in the twentieth century. Here indeed time divides in his argument, in a significant way: something like a decline has occurred, intellectually, which his book seeks to reverse with a return to the classical spirit of modernism as a whole, informing art and thought alike. But that decline remains unintelligible within his schema, once modernization is itself conceived as a linear process of prolongation and expansion, which necessarily carries with it a constant renewal of the sources of modernist art.

An alternative way to understand the origins and adventures of modernism is to look more closely at the differential historical temporality in which it was inscribed. There is one famous way of doing this, within the Marxist tradition. That is the route taken by Lukács, who read off a direct equation between the change of political posture of European capital after the revolutions of 1848, and the fate of the cultural forms produced by or within the ambit of the bourgeoisie as a social class. After the mid nineteenth century, for Lukács, the bourgeoisie becomes purely reactionary – abandoning its conflict against the nobility, on a continental scale, for all-out struggle against the proletariat. Therewith it enters into a phase of ideological decadence, whose initial aesthetic expression is predominantly naturalist, but then eventually issues into early twentieth-century modernism. This schema is widely decried on the Left today. In fact, in Lukács's work, it often yielded rather acute local analyses in the field of philosophy proper: however marred by its postscript, *The Destruction of Reason* is not a negligible book. On the other hand, in the field of literature Lukács's application of it did indeed prove relatively sterile. There was never any Lukácsian exploration of a modernist work of art comparable in detail or depth to his treatment of the structure of ideas in Schelling or Schopenhauer, Kierkegaard or Nietzsche; by contrast Joyce and Kafka – to take two of his literary *bêtes noires* – are scarcely more than invoked: never studied in their own right. The basic error of Lukács's optic here was its evolutionism: time, that is, differs from one epoch to another, but within each epoch all sectors of social reality move in synchrony with each other, such that decline at one level must be reflected in descent at every other. The result is a plainly over-generalized notion of 'decadence' – one of course enormously affected, it can be said in extenuation, by the spectacle of the collapse of German society and most of its established culture, in which he had himself been formed, into Nazism.

But if neither Berman's perennialism nor Lukács's evolutionism provides satisfactory accounts of modernism, what is the alternative? The hypothesis I will briefly sketch here is that we should look rather for a *conjunctural* explanation of the set of aesthetic practices and doctrines subsequently grouped together as 'modernist'. Such an explanation would involve the intersection of different historical temporalities, to compose a typically overdetermined configuration. What were these various times? My suggestion will be that 'modernism' can best be understood as a cultural field of force *triangulated* by three principal coordinates. The first of these is something Berman perhaps hints at in one passage, but situates too far back in time, failing to capture it with sufficient precision. This was the codification of a highly formalized academicism in the visual and other arts, which itself was institutionalized within official regimes of state and society still massively pervaded, often dominated, by aristocratic or landowning classes: classes in one sense economically 'superseded', no doubt, but in others still setting the political and cultural tone in country after country of pre-First World War Europe. The connexions between these two phenomena are graphically brought home in Arno Mayer's recent and fundamental work *The Persistence of the Old Regime*, whose central theme is the extent to which European society down to 1914 was still dominated by agrarian or aristocratic ruling classes (the two were not necessarily identical, as the case of France makes clear), in economies in which modern heavy industry still constituted a surprisingly small sector of the labour force or pattern of output.[11] The second coordinate is then a logical complement of the first: that is, the still incipient, hence essentially novel, emergence within these societies of the key technologies or inventions of the second industrial revolution: telephone, radio, automobile, aircraft and so on. Mass consumption industries based on the new technologies had not yet been implanted anywhere in Europe, where clothing, food and furniture remained overwhelmingly the largest final-goods sectors in employment and turnover down to 1914.

The third coordinate of the modernist conjuncture, it can be argued, was the imaginative proximity of social revolution. The extent of hope or apprehension that the prospect of such revolution aroused varied widely: but over most of Europe, it was 'in the air' during the Belle

---

11. Arno Mayer, *The Persistence of the Old Regime*, New York 1981, pp. 189–273.

Epoque itself. The reason, again, is straightforward enough: forms of dynastic *ancien régime*, as Mayer calls them, did persist: imperial monarchies in Russia, Germany and Austria, a precarious royal order in Italy; even in Britain, the United Kingdom was threatened with regional disintegration and civil war in the years before the First World War. In no European state was bourgeois democracy completed as a form, or the labour movement integrated or coopted as a force. The possible revolutionary outcomes of a downfall of the old order were thus still profoundly ambiguous. Would a new order be more un-alloyedly and radically capitalist, or would it be socialist? The Russian Revolution of 1905–1907 – which focused the attention of all Europe – was emblematic of this ambiguity, an upheaval at once and inseparably bourgeois and proletarian.

What was the contribution of each of these coordinates to the emergence of the field of force defining modernism? Briefly, it may be suggested, the following: the persistence of the '*anciens régimes*', and the academicism concomitant with them, provided a critical range of cultural values *against which* insurgent forms of art could measure themselves, but also *in terms of which* they could partly articulate themselves. Without the common adversary of official academicism, the wide span of new aesthetic practices have little or no unity: their tension with the established or consecrated canons in front of them is constitutive of their definition as such. At the same time, however, the old order, precisely in its still partially aristocratic colouration, afforded a set of available codes and resources from which the ravages of the market as an organizational principle of culture and society – uniformly detested by every species of modernism – could also be resisted. The classical stocks of high culture still preserved – even if deformed and deadened – in late-nineteenth-century academicism, could be redeemed and released against it, as also against the commercial spirit of the age as many of these movements saw it. The relationship of imagists like Pound to Edwardian conventions or Roman lyric poetry alike, of the later Eliot to Dante or the metaphysicals, is typical of one side of this situation: the ironic proximity of Proust or Musil to the French or Austrian aristocracies of the other.

At the same time, for a different kind of 'modernist' sensibility, the energies and attractions of a new machine age were a powerful imaginative stimulus: one reflected, patently enough, in Parisian cubism, Italian futurism or Russian constructivism. The condition of this interest, however, was the abstraction of techniques and artefacts from the social relations of production that were generating them. In no case was capitalism as such ever exalted by any brand of 'modern-

ism'. But such extrapolation was precisely rendered possible by the
sheer incipience of the still unforeseeable socio-economic pattern that
was later to consolidate so inexorably around them. It was not obvious
where the new devices and inventions were going to lead. Hence the, so
to speak, ambidextrous celebration of them from Right to Left alike –
Marinetti or Mayakovsky. Finally, the haze of social revolution drift-
ing across the horizon of this epoch gave it much of its apocalyptic light
for those currents of modernism most unremittingly and violently
radical in their rejection of the social order as a whole, of which the
most significant was certainly German expressionism. European
modernism in the first years of this century thus flowered in the space
between a still usable classical past, a still indeterminate technical
present, and a still unpredictable political future. Or, put another way,
it arose at the intersection between a semi-aristocratic ruling order, a
semi-industrialized capitalist economy, and a semi-emergent, or
-insurgent, labour movement.

The First World War, when it came, altered all of these coordinates.
But it did not eliminate any of them. For another twenty years, they
lived on in a kind of hectic after-life. Politically, of course, the dynastic
states of Eastern and Central Europe disappeared. But the junker class
retained great power in post-war Germany; the agrarian-based Radical
Party continued to dominate the Third Republic in France, without
much break in tone; in Britain the more aristocratic of the two
traditional parties, the Conservatives, virtually wiped out their more
bourgeois rivals, the Liberals, and went on to dominate the whole inter-
war epoch. Socially, a distinctive upper-class mode of life persisted
right down to the end of the thirties, whose hallmark – setting it off
completely from the existence of the rich after the Second World War –
was the normalcy of servants. This was the last true leisure-class in
metropolitan history. England, where such continuity was strongest,
was to produce the greatest fictional representation of that world in
Anthony Powell's Dance to the Music of Time, a non-modernist
remembrance from the subsequent epoch. Economically, mass production industries based on the new technological inventions of the early
twentieth century achieved some foothold in two countries only –
Germany in the Weimar period, and England in the late thirties. But in
neither case was there any general or wholesale implantation of what
Gramsci was to call 'Fordism', on the lines of what had by then existed
for two decades in the USA. Europe was still over a generation behind
America in the structure of its civilian industry and pattern of consumption, on the eve of the Second World War. Finally, the prospect of
revolution was now more proximate and tangible than it had ever been

— a prospect that had triumphantly materialized in Russia, touched Hungary, Italy and Germany with its wing just after the First World War, and was to take on a new and dramatic immediacy in Spain at the end of this period. It was within this space, prolonging in its own way an earlier ground, that generically 'modernist' forms of art continued to show great vitality. Quite apart from the literary masterpieces published in these years but essentially nurtured in earlier ones, Brechtian theatre was one memorable product purely of the inter-war conjuncture, in Germany. Another was the first real emergence of architectural modernism as a movement, with the Bauhaus. A third was the appearance of what was in fact to prove the last of the great doctrines of the European avant-garde – surrealism, in France.

It was the Second World War – not the First – which destroyed all three of the historical coordinates under discussion, and therewith cut off the vitality of modernism. After 1945, the old semi-aristocratic or agrarian order and its appurtenances were finished, in every country. Bourgeois democracy was finally universalized. With that, certain critical links with a pre-capitalist past were snapped. At the same time, Fordism arrived in force. Mass production and consumption transformed the West European economies along North American lines. There could no longer be the smallest doubt as to what kind of society this technology would consolidate: an oppressively stable, monolithically industrial, capitalist civilization was now in place. In a wonderful passage of his book *Marxism and Form*, Fredric Jameson has admirably captured what this meant for the avant-garde traditions that had once treasured the novelties of the twenties or thirties for their oneiric, destabilizing potential: 'The Surrealist image', he remarks, was 'a convulsive effort to split open the commodity forms of the objective universe by striking them against each other with immense force.'[12] But the condition of its success was that 'these objects – the places of objective chance or of preternatural revelation – are immediately identifiable as the products of a not yet fully industrialized and systematized economy. This is to say, that the human origins of the products of this period – their relationship to the work from which they issued – have not yet been fully concealed; in their production they still show traces of an artisanal organization of labour while their distribution is still assured by a network of small shopkeepers . . . What prepares these products to receive the investment of psychic energy characteristic of their use by Surrealism is precisely the half-sketched,

---

12. *Marxism and Form*, Princeton 1971, p. 96.

uneffaced mark of human labour; they are still frozen gesture, not yet completely separated from subjectivity, and remain therefore potentially as mysterious and as expressive as the human body itself.'[13] Jameson then goes on: 'We need only exchange, for that environment of small workshops and store counters, for the *marché aux puces* and the stalls in the streets, the gasoline stations along American superhighways, the glossy photographs in the magazines, or the cellophane paradise of an American drugstore, in order to realize that the objects of Surrealism are gone without a trace. Henceforth, in what we may call post-industrial capitalism, the products with which we are furnished are utterly without depth: their plastic content is totally incapable of serving as a conductor of psychic energy. All libidinal investment in such objects is precluded from the outset, and we may well ask ourselves, if it is true that our object universe is henceforth unable to yield any "symbol apt at stirring human sensibility", whether we are not here in the presence of a cultural transformation of signal proportions, a historical break of an unexpectedly radical kind.'[14]

Finally, the image or hope of revolution faded away in the West. The onset of the Cold War, and the Sovietization of Eastern Europe, cancelled any realistic prospect of an overturn of advanced capitalism for a whole historical period. The ambiguity of aristocracy, the absurdity of academicism, the gaiety of the first cars or movies, the palpability of a socialist alternative, were all now gone. In their place, there now reigned a routinized, bureaucratized economy of universal commodity production, in which mass consumption and mass culture had become virtually interchangeable terms. The post-war avant-gardes were to be essentially defined against this quite new backdrop. It is not necessary to judge them from a Lukácsian tribunal to note the obvious: little of the literature, painting, music or architecture of this period can stand comparison with that of the antecedent epoch. Reflecting on what he calls 'the extraordinary concentration of literary masterpieces around the First World War', Franco Moretti in his recent book *Signs Taken for Wonders* writes: 'Extraordinary because of its quantity, as even the roughest list shows (Joyce and Valéry, Rilke and Kafka, Svevo and Proust, Hofmannsthal and Musil, Apollinaire, Mayakovsky), but even more than extraordinary because that abundance of works (as is by now clear, after more than half a century) constituted the last *literary season* of Western culture. Within a few years European

---

13. Ibid., pp. 103–104.
14. Ibid., p. 105.

literature gave its utmost and seemed on the verge of opening new and boundless horizons: instead it died. A few isolated icebergs, and many imitators; but nothing comparable to the past.'[15] There would be some exaggeration in generalizing this judgement to the other arts, but not – alas – all that much. Individual writers or painters, architects or musicians, of course produced significant work after the Second World War. But not only were the heights of the first two or three decades of the century rarely or never reached again. No new aesthetic movements of collective importance, operative across more than one art form, emerged either, after surrealism. In painting or sculpture alone, specialized schools and slogans succeeded each other ever more rapidly: but after the moment of abstract expressionism – the last genuine avant-garde of the West – these were now largely a function of a gallery-system necessitating regular output of new styles as materials for seasonal commercial display, along the lines of *haute couture*: an economic pattern corresponding to the *non*-reproducible character of 'original' works in these particular fields.

It was now, however, when all that had created the classical art of the early twentieth century was dead, that the ideology and cult of modernism was born. The conception itself is scarcely older than the 1950s, as a widespread currency. What it betokened was the pervasive collapse of the tension between the institutions and mechanisms of advanced capitalism, and the practices and programmes of advanced art, as the one annexed the other as its occasional decoration or diversion, or philanthropic *point d'honneur*. The few exceptions of the period suggest the power of the rule. The cinema of Jean-Luc Godard, in the sixties, is perhaps the most salient case in point. As the Fourth Republic belatedly passed into the Fifth, and rural and provincial France was suddenly transformed by a Gaullist industrialization appropriating the newest international technologies, something like a brief after-glow of the earlier conjuncture that had produced the classical innovatory art of the century flared into life again. Godard's cinema was marked in its own way by all three of the coordinates described earlier. Suffused with quotation and allusion to a high cultural past, Eliot-style; equivocal celebrant of the automobile and the airport, the camera and the carbine, Léger-style; expectant of revolutionary tempests from the East, Nizan-style. The upheaval of May–June 1968 in France was the validating historical terminus of this art form. Régis Debray was to describe the experience of that year

---

15. *Signs Taken for Wonders*, London 1983, p. 209.

sarcastically, after the event, as a voyage to China which – like that of Columbus – discovered only America: more especially, landing in California.[16] That is, a social and cultural turbulence which mistook itself for a French version of the Cultural Revolution, when in fact it signified no more than the arrival of a long-overdue permissive consumerism in France. But it was precisely this ambiguity – an openness of horizon, where the shapes of the future could alternatively assume the shifting forms of either a new type of capitalism, or the eruption of socialism – which was constitutive of so much of the original sensibility of what had come to be called modernism. Not surprisingly, it did not survive the Pompidou consolidation that succeeded, in Godard's cinema or anywhere else. What marks the typical situation of the contemporary artist in the West, it might be said, is, on the contrary, the closure of horizons: without an appropriable past, or imaginable future, in an interminably recurrent present.

This is not true, manifestly, of the Third World. It is significant that so many of Berman's examples of what he reckons to be the great modernist achievements of our time should be taken from Latin American literature. For in the Third World generally, a kind of shadow configuration of what once prevailed in the First World does exist today. Pre-capitalist oligarchies of various kinds, mostly of a landowning character, abound; capitalist development is typically far more rapid and dynamic, where it does occur, in these regions than in the metropolitan zones, but on the other hand is infinitely less stabilized or consolidated; social revolution haunts these societies as a permanent possibility, one indeed already realized in countries close to home – Cuba or Nicaragua, Angola or Vietnam. These are the conditions that have produced the genuine masterpieces of recent years that conform to Berman's categories: novels like Gabriel García Márquez's *One Hundred Years of Solitude*, or Salman Rushdie's *Midnight's Children*, from Colombia or India, or films like Yilmiz Güney's *Yol* from Turkey. Works such as these, however, are not timeless expressions of an ever-expanding process of modernization, but emerge in quite delimited constellations, in societies still at definite historical crossroads. The Third World furnishes no fountain of eternal youth to modernism.

So far, we have looked at two of Berman's organizing concepts – modernization and modernism. Let us now consider the mediating term that links them, modernity itself. That, it will be remembered, is

---

16. Régis Debray, 'A Modest Contribution to the Rites and Ceremonies of the Tenth Anniversary', *New Left Review* 115, May–June 1979, pp. 45–65.

defined as the *experience* undergone within modernization that gives
rise to modernism. What is this experience? For Berman, it is essentially
a subjective process of unlimited self-development, as traditional barriers of custom or role disintegrate – an experience necessarily lived at
once as emancipation and ordeal, elation and despair, frightening and
exhilarating. It is the momentum of this ceaselessly ongoing rush
towards the uncharted frontiers of the psyche that assures the world-
historical continuity of modernism: but it is also this momentum which
appears to undermine in advance any prospect of moral or institutional
stabilization under communism, indeed perhaps to disallow the cultural cohesion necessary for communism to exist at all, rendering it
something like a contradiction in terms. What should we make of this
argument?

To understand it, we need to ask ourselves: where does Berman's
vision of a completely unbounded dynamic of self-development come
from? His first book, *The Politics of Authenticity*, which contains two
studies – one of Montesquieu and the other of Rousseau – provides the
answer. Essentially, this idea derives from what the subtitle of the book
rightly designates the 'radical individualism' of Rousseau's concept of
humanity. Berman's analysis of the logical trajectory of Rousseau's
thought, as it sought to contend with the contradictory consequences
of this conception across successive works, is a *tour de force*. But for
our purposes the crucial point is the following. Berman demonstrates
the presence of the same paradox he ascribes to Marx within Rousseau:
if unlimited self-development is the goal of all, how will community
ever be possible? For Rousseau the answer is, in words that Berman
quotes, that: 'The love of man derives from love of oneself' – 'Extend
self-love to others and it is transformed into virtue.'[17] Berman comments: 'It was the road of self-expansion, not of self-repression, that led
to the palace of virtue . . . As each man learned to express and enlarge
himself, his capacity for identification with other men would expand,
his sympathy and empathy with them would deepen.'[18] The schema
here is clear enough: first the individual develops the self, then the self
can enter into relations of mutual satisfaction with others – relations
based on identification with the self. The difficulties this presumption
encounters once Rousseau tries to move – in his language – from the
'man' to the 'citizen', in the construction of a free community, are then
brilliantly explored by Berman. What is striking, however, is that

17. *The Politics of Authenticity*, New York 1970, p. 181.
18. Ibid., p. 181.

Berman nowhere himself disowns the starting-point of the dilemmas he demonstrates. On the contrary, he concludes by arguing: 'The pro- grammes of nineteenth-century socialism and anarchism, of the twen- tieth-century welfare state and the contemporary New Left, can all be seen as further developments of the structure of thought whose founda- tions Montesquieu and Rousseau laid down. What these very different movements share is a way of defining the crucial political task at hand: to make modern liberal society keep the promises it has made, to reform it – or revolutionize it – in order to realize the ideals of modern liberalism itself. The agenda for radical liberalism which Montesquieu and Rousseau brought up two centuries ago is still pending today.'[19] Likewise in *All That Is Solid Melts into Air*, he can refer to 'the depth of the individualism that underlies Marx's communism'[20] – a depth which, he then quite consistently goes on to note, must formally include the possibility of a radical nihilism.

If we look back, however, at Marx's actual texts, we find a very different conception of human reality at work. Here the self is not prior to, but is constituted by its relations with others, from the outset: women and men are social individuals, whose sociality is not subse- quent to but contemporaneous with their individuality. Marx wrote, after all, that 'only in community with others has each individual the means of cultivating his gifts in all directions: only in the community, therefore, is personal freedom possible.'[21] Berman cites the sentence, but without apparently seeing its consequences. If the development of the self is inherently imbricated in relations with others, its develop- ment could never be an *unlimited* dynamic in the monadological sense conjured up by Berman: for the coexistence of others would always *be such a limit*, without which *development itself could not occur*. Ber- man's postulate is thus, for Marx, a contradiction in terms.

Another way of saying this is that Berman has failed – with many others, of course – to see that Marx possesses a conception of human nature which rules out the kind of infinite ontological plasticity he assumes himself. That may seem a scandalous statement, given the reactionary cast of so many standard ideas of what human nature is. But it is the simple philological truth, as even a cursory inspection of Marx's work makes clear, and Norman Geras's recent book *Marx and*

---

19. Ibid., p. 317.
20. ASMA, p. 128.
21. *The German Ideology*, London 1970, p. 83; cited in ASMA, p. 97.

Human Nature – Refutation of a Legend makes irrefutable.[22] That nature, for Marx, includes a set of primary needs, powers and dispositions – what he calls in the *Grundrisse*, in the famous passages on human possibility under feudalism, capitalism and communism, *Bedürfnisse, Fähigkeiten, Kräfte, Anlagen* – all of them capable of enlargement and development, but not of erasure or replacement. The vision of an unhinged, nihilistic drive of the self towards a completely unbounded development is thus a chimera. Rather, the genuine 'free development of each' can only be realized if it proceeds in respect for the 'free development of all', given the common nature of what it is to be a human being. In the very pages of the *Grundrisse* on which Berman leans, Marx speaks without the slightest equivocation of 'the full development of human control over the forces of nature – including those of his own nature', of 'the absolute elaboration (*Herausarbeiten*) of his creative dispositions', in which 'the universality of the individual . . . is the universality of his real and ideal relationships'.[23] The cohesion and stability which Berman wonders whether communism could ever display lay, for Marx, in the very human nature that it would finally emancipate, one far from any mere cataract of formless desires. For all its exuberance, Berman's version of Marx, in its virtually exclusive emphasis on the release of the self, comes uncomfortably close – radical and decent though its accents are – to the assumptions of the culture of narcissism.

To conclude: where, then, does this leave revolution? Berman is quite consistent here. For him, as for so many others on the Left today, the notion of revolution is distended in duration. In effect, capitalism already brings us constant upheaval in our conditions of life, and in that sense is – as he puts it – a 'permanent revolution': one that obliges 'modern men and women' to 'learn to yearn for change: not merely to be open to changes in their personal and social lives, but positively to demand them, actively to seek them out and carry them through. They must learn not to long nostalgically for the "fixed, fast-frozen relationships" of the real or fantasized past, but to delight in mobility, to thrive on renewal, to look forward to future developments in their conditions of life and relations with their fellow men.'[24] The advent of socialism would not halt or check this process, but on the contrary immensely

---

22. Norman Geras, *Marx and Human Nature – Refutation of a Legend*, London 1983.

23. *Grundrisse*, pp. 387, 440.

24. ASMA, pp. 95–96.

accelerate and generalize it. The echoes of sixties radicalism are unmistakable here. Attraction to such notions has proved very widespread. But they are not, in fact, compatible either with the theory of historical materialism, strictly understood, or with the record of history itself, however theorized.

Revolution is a term with a precise meaning: the political overthrow from below of one state order, and its replacement by another. Nothing is to be gained by diluting it across time, or extending it over every department of social space. In the first case, it becomes indistinguishable from simple reform – political change, no matter now gradual or piecemeal, as such: as in the discourse of latter-day Eurocommunism, or cognate versions of Social Democracy; in the second case, it dwindles to a mere metaphor – one that can be reduced to no more than supposed psychological or moral conversions, as in the ideology of Maoism, with its proclamation of a 'Cultural Revolution'. Against these slack devaluations of the term, with all their political consequences, it is necessary to insist that revolution is a punctual and not a permanent process. That is: a revolution is an episode of convulsive political transformation, compressed in time and concentrated in target, that has a determinate beginning – when the old state apparatus is still intact – and a finite end, when that apparatus is decisively broken and a new one erected in its stead. What would be distinctive about a socialist revolution that created a genuine post-capitalist democracy is that the new state would be truly transitional towards the practicable limits of its own self-dissolution into the associated life of society as a whole.

In the advanced capitalist world today, it is the seeming absence of any such prospect as a proximate or even distant horizon – the lack, apparently, of any conjecturable alternative to the imperial status quo of a consumer capitalism – that blocks the likelihood of any profound cultural renovation comparable to the great Age of Aesthetic Discoveries in the first third of this century. Gramsci's words still hold good: 'The crisis consists,' he wrote, 'precisely in the fact that the old is dying and the new cannot be born; in this interregnum a great variety of morbid symptoms appears.'[25] It is legitimate to ask, however: could anything be said in advance as to what the new might be? One thing, perhaps, might be predicted. Modernism as a notion is the emptiest of all cultural categories. Unlike the terms Gothic, Renaissance, Baroque,

---

25. Antonio Gramsci, *Selections from the Prison Notebooks*, eds. Quintin Hoare and Geoffrey Nowell-Smith, London 1972, p. 276.

Mannerist, Romantic or Neo-Classical, it designates no describable object in its own right at all: it is entirely lacking in positive content. In fact, as we have seen, what is concealed beneath the label is a wide variety of very diverse – indeed incompatible – aesthetic practices: symbolism, constructivism, expressionism, surrealism. These, which do spell out specific programmes, were unified *post hoc* in a portmanteau concept whose only referent is the blank passage of time itself. Literally taken, there is no other aesthetic marker so vacant or vitiated. For what once was modern is soon obsolete. The futility of the term, and its attendant ideology, can be seen all too clearly from current attempts to cling to its wreckage and yet swim with the tide still further beyond it, in the coinage 'post-modernism': one void chasing another, in a serial regression of self-congratulatory chronology. If we ask ourselves, what would revolution (understood as a punctual break with the order of capital) have to do with modernism (understood as this flux of temporal vanities), the answer is: it would surely end it. For a genuine socialist culture would be one which did not insatiably seek the new, defined simply as what comes later, itself to be rapidly consigned to the detritus of the old, but rather one which multiplied the different, in a far greater variety of concurrent styles and practices than had ever existed before: a diversity founded on the far greater plurality and complexity of possible ways of living that any free community of equals, no longer divided by class, race or gender, would create. The axes of aesthetic life would, in other words, in this respect run horizontally, not vertically, as the calendar ceased to tyrannize, or organize, consciousness of art. The vocation of revolution, in that sense, would be neither to prolong nor to fulfil modernity, but to abolish it.

1983

Postscript

The two terms 'modernity' and 'revolution' appear to have a natural affinity. What is modern is newer than what it succeeds: what is revolutionary is more advanced than what it overthrows – 'tradition' in one case, 'reaction' in the other. The connexion between the two concepts lies in the common suggestion of a movement of progress, that each in its different way embodies. The most famous emblem of that relation is the proximity of the ideas of aesthetic and political 'vanguard'. Developed independently, in the Parisian art-world and the Russian revolutionary movement of the early twentieth century, these notions for a time even coalesced in the self-definition of surrealism, which sought to be in the forefront simultaneously of cultural and political change, in part precisely by abolishing the distinction between the two. The 'revolution of modernism' and 'modernizing revolutions' then became part of the standard vocabulary of the West after the Second World War, when surrealism itself had waned.

There is also, however, a disconnexion between the ideas of 'modernity' and 'revolution' that needs equal emphasis. The two did not enter history at the same moment. The term 'revolution' – whose original sense was the orbital movement of the stars, or the wheel of fortune – was first used in the late seventeenth century to denote the political overthrow of the fundamental structures of the state, and their replacement by a new order. The first, and formally unsuccessful breach in the Absolutist *ancien régime* in England – the Civil War that broke out in 1640 – was still called simply the 'Great Rebellion'. It was the successful sequel of 1688 that acquired the permanent title, for the English landowners and merchants who made it, of the 'Glorious Revolution'. By the eighteenth century, everyone – finally even Louis XVI himself – knew what the events of 1789 should be called: not a revolt, sire, but a revolution. 'Modernity' and 'modernization', on the other hand – as distinct from the simple usage of 'modern' in opposition to 'ancient', meaning no more than 'contemporary' or 'recent' – are coinages of the mid nineteenth century. They are products, not of the projects of bourgeois political emancipation – the ideals of Liberty, Equality and Fraternity – but of the impact of capitalist socio-economic transformation subsequent to them: the relentless onward march, above all, of Industry and Machinery.

The philology of these usages indicates a significant divergence between the later conceptions of 'modernity' and 'revolution', in the twentieth century. Each notion involves a different conception of temporality. The characteristic time of 'modernity' is continuous, and all-encompassing, like the process of industrialization itself: at its most extended, nothing less than the totality of the epoch itself. The time of a 'revolution', on the other hand, is discontinuous, and delimited: a finite rupture in the reproduction of the established order, by definition starting at one conjuncture and ending at another. The 'Glory', for the English bourgeoisie, of the 'Revolution' of 1688 lay above all in the speed and finality of the upheaval, and the closure of the settlement that concluded it. This distinction has its echo in linguistic convention as well. Because of it, in the twentieth century people could speak of modernism without strain – as the generic artistic expression of a perpetually ongoing experience of modernity; whereas the experience of revolution could not generate any semantic equivalent – the term 'revolutionism' precisely possessing a merely derisive meaning in the vocabulary of the great revolutionaries, denoting empty rhetoric and phrase-mongering. Each idea, 'modernity' and 'revolution', has thus always been endangered as a critical concept from opposite directions. The notion of modernity is extensive. Consequently it has always been threatened by the risk of dilution and banalization. If the modern is simply the new, and the passing of time assures its progress, everything in recent or current experience has acquired equal validity and meaning. A deep passivity and conformism then lies just around the corner, an inert adherence to what we might call the *motus quo*. By contrast, the notion of revolution is intensive. The danger it has always incurred is not a dissipation but an overloading of meaning. That is, the determinate act of overturning an established state apparatus, as the principal political barrier to social change, becomes surcharged with the apocalyptic significance of a total transvaluation of values, in which the telos of all history itself comes to be concentrated. In that conception, activism becomes voluntarism, and voluntarism messianism. The inflation of the two ideas of 'modernity' and 'revolution' thus leads in opposite directions. But it is significant that these could even be crossed, into a strange hybrid, in the work of the European thinker who more than any other tried to unite the motifs of the two – Walter Benjamin. His concept of *Jetztzeit* precisely combines the continuous flow of the new that is the hallmark of the modern, with the sudden transfiguring blast of the messianic into it, that is the sign of the revolution, in the over-pitched versions of either. Modernist alert and millennial expectation intertwine in the *Theses on the Philosophy of History*, without exhausting the richness of these, at the end of the thirties.

* * *

Today, the intellectual situation is very different from that of Benjamin's time. The notions of modernity and of revolution are under general assault. Not, however, equally so. The rejection of the idea of political or social revolution in the West predates the more recent questioning of modernity, and has been more absolute. But the two phenomena have been closely linked. Symptomatic in this regard has been the career of the leading contemporary prophet of 'post-modernity', the French theorist Jean-François Lyotard. Originally a militant of a Far Left group, *Socialisme ou Barbarie*, devoted to the goal of a libertarian socialist revolution, subsequently herald and enthusiast of the May Revolt in France, by the late seventies he was welcoming the conservative rule of Giscard d'Estaing as a barrier against the perils of communism, and is today a voice of the cultural establishment under the Mitterrand regime. The repudiation of revolution paved the way for the rescinding of a modernity all too contaminated – in Lyotard's eyes – with it. What essentially defines modernity for this theorist of post-modernity?

First and foremost, narrative structures that seek to render history intelligible as a developmental process: above all, naturally, Marxism. Such narratives, for Lyotard, bear with them the presumption of a universal subject and a predetermined goal – humanity and its eventual emancipation. Philosophically, their counterpart is the premise of an individual identity persistent or recoverable through even the most extreme psychic turbulence or fragmentation. The correlates of this identity in modernist aesthetics are the illusions of meaning and the residues of representation. Modern science, similarly, imagined that there was an overall logic of scientific enquiry involving general rules of research and common goals of ultimate agreement. All of these fading figurations of modernity are condemned by the verdict of the spectacular condition that has succeeded it – history without narrative; individuals without identity; discourse without meaning; art without representation; science without truth. In place of all these, Lyotard proposes the play of infinite language-games, the paralogism of incompatible conceptual planes, the insinuation of the unpresentable, the miniaturization of the past, and – above all – the cult of the unsayable intensities of the libidinal instant: in the end sole arbiter and value of post-modern existence. Politically, the consequences of this degraded ecstaticism are obvious enough. Everything else may disappear, volatilized in the mixer of post-modernism, but capitalism remains intact as the motor of its energetics. '*Le capital fait jouir*' – Lyotard's lesson[26] –

---

26. Jean-François Lyotard, *Economie Libidinale*, Paris 1974, pp. 117 ff.

is the slogan of Dionysus in Disneyland. Intellectually, this critique of modernity is trifling. No meta-narrative is so sweeping or speculative as that of the so-called 'post-modern condition' itself. The one identity that is certainly not in question is that of the author of it, ever ready to protest that his meaning has not been properly understood, and singularly available for representation in photograph or on television. The ultimate feebleness of these particular claims for the crisis of modernity, and the advent of post-modernity, can be seen in their attempt to garb themselves – notwithstanding – in the prestige of modernism, of which post-modernism is finally presented as either condition or completion, thereby signing its own certificate of redundancy.

* * *

Antithetical in spirit and substance to this parasitical construction of post-modernity is Marshall Berman's exploration of modernity in *All That Is Solid Melts into Air*. Berman's central theme is the connexion between capitalist socio-economic development – everything that from the nineteenth century onwards came to be designated 'modernization' – and that individual self-development which Marx in the *Grundrisse* argued was the measure of true modernity – 'that absolute working-out of creative potentialities which makes the development of all human powers as such the end in itself', such that man 'strives not to remain something he has become, but is in the absolute movement of becoming'. In the epoch of capitalist production, Marx wrote, 'this complete working-out of the human content appears as a complete emptying out, as a total alienation', against which 'the childish world of antiquity' could appear – and indeed really was – 'loftier in all matters where closed shapes, forms or given limits are sought for.' But this pre-modernity could only give 'satisfaction from a limited standpoint'. By contrast 'the modern gives no satisfaction; or where it appears satisfied with itself, it is mean.'[27] Berman's book is a sustained defence and illustration of the grandeur of that peculiarly modern dissatisfaction, as it has found expression in the successive forms of modernist art. Berman defines the essential characteristic of this modernity as the simultaneous experience of personal liberation and disorientation, exhilaration and anguish, brought on by the destruction of traditional and customary forms of life in the whirlpool of capitalist moderniza-tion – the sense of a self at once emancipated and jeopardized, without either the constraints or securities of the pre-capitalist social order.

---

27. *Grundrisse*, pp. 387–388.

Modernism is the aesthetic capture of this constitutive ambiguity of the experience of modernity – its artists from Baudelaire onwards both 'enemies and enthusiasts', as Berman puts it, of modern life, in which all that is solid – and so reassuring – evaporates into air.

It can be seen that Berman's account of modernism, whose emergence he traces from Goethe through Marx and Baudelaire to Dostoevsky and Mandelstam, and on to Robert Moses, ignores every prohibition of post-modernist ideology, which he expressly rejects in his conclusion. It generates a compelling historical narrative, itself built on a series of works of art that often remain classically representational, in order to trace not a metaphysical abolition of personal identity, but its profound social transformations in and through the massive impersonal forces wrenching it away from the fixity of its customary moorings. The power of Berman's vision comes from the imaginative depth at which it grasps the actual changes in the lives of millions of human beings as they were – and go on being – thrown into the vortex of capitalist industrialization, or now even de-industrialization. It is far from a mere intellectual construct, collated more or less superficially from an aesthetic trawl of the past. Politically too, it breathes an undaunted generosity and confidence in the possibilities of the future, without any trace of the complaisance towards the present of the characteristic discourse of post-modernity.

Yet there is an unresolved tension, it seems to me, in Berman's book. He argues that the experience of modernity which produced the classical works of modernism continues unceasingly today. Does it, then, also continue to reproduce a comparable contemporary modernism? Here, he appears to hesitate. On the one hand, he suggests that it does – that we are not short of works of the imagination fully equivalent to those of the nineteenth and early twentieth centuries. On the other hand, he insists on the importance of a *remembrance* of classical modernism, for the renewal of a wider cultural vitality – beyond isolated cases – today. Just as classical modernism never cut itself unilaterally off from prior traditions, so a contemporary modernism must not turn its back on its predecessor – as the discourse of post-modernism would have us do, in announcing a completely new sensibility and epoch, defined precisely by its indifference to that past. This emphasis of Berman's is not wholly easy to reconcile with the first. Is modernism a tradition to be recovered – hence in some sense temporarily mislaid, or forgotten – or is it a source that constantly renews itself, from the springs of ordinary contemporary life?

My own view is closer to the first of these positions, but with the difference that it is difficult to believe that classical modernism could ever be restored, since it seems so clearly to have been the product of a particular historical conjuncture that extends from the Belle Epoque to the Second World War, which has now passed in the metropolitan world – even if something like a version of it can be found in the underdeveloped world today. Nor, on the other hand, can it readily be maintained that the characteristic art which has succeeded classical modernism in the West is generally comparable to it in vitality or stature – let alone that some globally superior culture, embracing higher forms of history, philosophy, science and politics, has emerged beyond it. Quite the contrary: judged by the standards of 1900–1945, the last decades could well be regarded as an age of brass in the advanced capitalist countries – so long as one never forgets that such a judgement does not exclude peaks of eminence here and there. This relative stagnation – perhaps only pause – may in turn be related to the blockage of either hopes or fears of fundamental social change in the West.

Marshall Berman has replied eloquently and reproachfully to this critique.[28] The substance of his response is twofold. Why should the disappointment of revolutionary dreams condemn artists to silence? Did not, after all, the defeat of the French Revolution usher in the flowering of Romanticism? At the same time, does not any discounting of the mainstreams of contemporary culture, in the name of a better past, smack of a familiar elitism – more appropriate to the Right than to the Left? Since the basic social and existential experience of modernity, as described by Marx or Baudelaire, still manifestly continues, is not modernism as the creative response to it equally likely to persist? Berman remarks, very aptly, that it is an occupational hazard of intellectuals to lose touch with the stuff and flow of everyday life. But if we attend to that – as he does, in a series of vivid snapshots from the streets of New York – instead of looking vainly for lost masterpieces or missing revolutions, we will see that there is no reason to write any premature obituary for modernism. 'Life may be rough,' Berman writes, 'but people haven't given up: modernity is alive and well.'[29]

* * *

The force of this response is undeniable – like most of what Berman writes, in its own terms it is moving and persuasive. In particular, it resonates with one entirely understandable and salutary attitude to any

---

28. 'The Signs in the Street: a Response to Perry Anderson', *New Left Review* 144, March–April 1984, pp. 114–23.
29. Ibid., p. 121.

cultural recoil from the time, that must be felt especially strongly on the Left. We all have only one life to live, with one possible set of cultural experiences directly related to it. If we do not appreciate the one, must we not devalue the other? There appears to be something inherently disabling, self-destructive, in passing a limiting judgement on the collective self-expression of one's own epoch. Yet for all the force of this instinctive objection, socialists can and should make certain distinctions here. Berman is perfectly right to stress the constant sources of human creativity as such, regardless of historical conjuncture. If anything, he may have involuntarily tended to understate these in *All That Is Solid Melts into Air* itself, where any conception of natural humanity as such often appears to be dissolved. But this creative potential finds widely different realization in different societies and epochs. At the simplest and most everyday level, the ability to shape a life in immediate relationships of love and solidarity has not been equally distributed historically. The Third Reich did not permit as many chances of that as the Second, to cite only two forms of an oppressive class power – though, as the recent epic of the German cinema *Heimat* reminds us, even under Nazi rule, decent and dignified unpolitical lives were achieved. Reagan's America, for all its brutality and exploitation, allows far more space for that kind of realization – which is essentially, it seems to me, what Berman is talking about in his vignettes of New York. Contemporary Sweden would offer qualitatively more again.

The historical conditions of artistic creation are not identical with those of a modicum of popular fulfilment. The one is necessarily public, while the other can remain private. Above all, in class-divided societies the division of labour typically restricts the production of a wide range of art forms – those requiring the most specialized skills – to a relatively small and privileged catchment within the population. There is no necessary translation of popular experience into aesthetic creation, in this sense. When Berman argues that because 'people haven't given up', 'modernity is alive and well', it doesn't necessarily follow that modernism is consequently in equally good shape – as at times he seems about to concede himself. The social roots of cultural vitality are variable, and often enigmatic – though not, we must believe, ultimately undecipherable. But they have to be explored differentially in each case, conjuncture by conjuncture, country by country. That is why it seems sensible to discuss the origins of modernism in the twentieth century in greater detail. By tying down the kind of 'modernity' that generated it more specifically, we can perhaps also see why it has since declined. That judgement – of a decline – can scarcely be regarded as scandalous. An attachment to one's own epoch is humanly understandable, and politically indispensable for the will to change it. It is no accident that it was the greatest conservative politician of the post-war era, Charles de Gaulle, a man whose imagination was in many ways deeply held in the past, who nevertheless said: '*Il faut se marier à son temps*' – even if the conjugal metaphor, not necessarily wholly pleasurable, expressed his ambivalence. But culturally, more detachment is possible. No one doubts, or thinks it surprising, that English painting in the nineteenth century was generally sparse and mediocre compared with French, or that Spanish philosophy could not match German. Few would question that Roman letters in the first century AD were superior to those of the third century, or that Greek sculpture in the sixth century BC was less developed than that of the fourth. Contrasts of this sort – between countries, or across periods – are common currency in the history of art: not just natural, but unavoidable if it is to be written at all. There is no reason to withhold them from the twentieth century.

Finally, political insurgency is distinct again from either artistic expression or private life-experience, as a register of the realization of human potentiality. Revolutionary processes, in a world dominated by counter-revolution, do not bring any automatic fulfilment for those who participate in them, as the generation of 1789 or 1917 discovered. Nor, on the other hand, do they typically in themselves produce much great art – for which the circumstances of the Holy Alliance or Entente blockade were scarcely propitious. More usually, they have been preceded by major aesthetic schools or discoverers, which have then intermittently accompanied their ordeals – David or Boullée in France, Malevich or Lissitsky in Russia, perhaps Machado or Lorca in Spain. But fundamentally the times of the two are not the same. It was Antonio Gramsci who warned that 'changes in ways of thinking do not occur through rapid, simultaneous and generalized explosions', and that 'the explosion of political passions' in a revolutionary upheaval should 'not be confused with cultural transformations, which are slow and gradual.'[30] What connexion, then, exists between modernity and revolution in the twentieth century, if there is such a basic disjuncture between the rhythm and nature of the two?

Modernism, as a complex set of aesthetic practices that emerged primarily after 1900, although only baptized as such fifty years later, was the product of a historically unstable form of society and an undecided epoch, in which drastically variable futures were lived as immediately possible – among them, saliently but not exclusively, socialist revolution. That encompassing and vitalizing uncertainty was

---

30. *Selections from Cultural Writings*, London 1985, pp. 418–419.

constitutive for what came to be called modernism. Since the Second World War, the West has passed into an opposite constellation. Apart from the intense but brief social turbulence at the end of the sixties, all the basic institutional coordinates of the major industrial countries have remained fixed, as capitalism has anchored itself in the structures – however partial and imperfect – of liberal democracy and consumer prosperity, to become a self-reproducing order such as it very rarely was before 1945. Any widespread sense of possible alternative futures has receded: the only one generally felt today is nuclear war, which is precisely unlivable as a prospect. It is against this background that classical modernism has – as might have been predicted – dwindled away. This does not mean that societies just entering political and economic conditions long since routinized in the core zones of capital find themselves in the same situation. Manifestly, countries as diverse as Turkey or Brazil today – where constitutional democracy was itself only one possible future, among many worse alternatives, a brief historical moment ago, and Fordism remains uneven and precarious – are not. The relations between art and the social order are likely to look different there. Even in the central countries of advanced capitalism today, the lapsing of modernism does not mean that therefore all the sources of an oppositional culture have dried up. At least one very large sea-change has occurred in the most stabilized states of the West, with the gradual transformation still under way of the sexual division of labour within them. The movement of women's emancipation has – above all in the United States – thrown up a new range of art of its own, some of it indebted to modernist traditions, some of it not. Feminist writers have certainly staged their own kinds of aesthetic renewal.

But we still remain a long way from the clustered heights of early twentieth-century modernism. In the interim, the relations between capital and culture have been transformed in these societies. The critical distance of art from commerce and publicity has narrowed enormously; the capacity of the established order for absorption and corruption has increased vertiginously. In these conditions, any generalized aesthetic break-out of the kind that marked modernism is difficult to conceive, as piecemeal achievements and individual innovations are swiftly recycled back into official celebrations that live on them. A certain ideology of post-modernism makes a spurious virtue out of that necessity, exalting every corporate pastiche and opportune eclecticism as the liberating spirit of the age. Leopold Ranke was fond of saying that every epoch is equally close to God. That is precisely the view that a socialist must reject. For a consequent cultural relativism must be conservative. If all cultures are in principle equally valuable – as Lévi-

Strauss once claimed – why fight for a better one? The energies of modernity, once generated by capitalism, are now ever more trapped and compromised by it. That is another reason for remaining true to the hope of a passage beyond this world order, one soberly understood in its very limits as a radical political – and not a metaphysical – transformation.

1985

3

The Legacy of Isaac Deutscher

Isaac Deutscher, who died seventeen years ago, was one of the great socialist writers of this century. He was a Marxist and a historian, but the way in which these two vocations were connected in his work, and the place he occupies in the literature of each, are without close counterpart. Deutscher's fame rests, of course, on two masterpieces on the fate of the Russian Revolution, his biographies of Stalin and of Trotsky. In these, all Deutscher's powers were concentrated on the object of his life's study; and it is there that readers new to his work will continue to start. *Marxism, Wars and Revolutions* serves another purpose. The collection of essays and addresses it contains gives us an intellectual portrait of the biographer himself – of Deutscher as a mind. For the essayist, in the nature of the genre, spoke more directly and personally, and over a more various and unexpected range of topics, than the historian. Subjective experience and conviction find greater expression in these interventions than in the major objective reconstructions of the past themselves. From them, we can see Deutscher as a more complex and multi-dimensional figure than the terms by which he became best known in his lifetime would suggest: not simply a scholar, but a thinker of the Left; and beyond a commentator on events, a committed participant in them. This is a range of texts that gives a more comprehensive sense of Isaac Deutscher, as a fighter and a critic, an intellectual and militant, than any previously available.

What do they show? In the first instance, through their prism, the original context that nurtured Deutscher comes into view. The universal features of the mature writer tended to conceal these origins: but it was in fact a very particular regional experience that made possible the later cosmopolitanism. However, like that of another master of English prose, Joseph Conrad, his Polish past long lay partly hidden from sight, and can easily be misunderstood. Deutscher was born in the province of Krakow in 1907, and as a boy grew up in natural sympathy with

Polish traditions of literary experiment and political emancipation. But his family was not from the patriotic gentry, but from the Jewish middle class, where his father owned a printing business; and his youthful politics were early on socialist. A generation earlier, Rosa Luxemburg had come from a similar background in the neighbouring province of Lublin, where her father was in the timber trade.[1] Like her, Deutscher entered the Polish revolutionary movement while still in his teens, joining the Polish Communist Party in early 1927. Between the experiences of the two lay, of course, the change that had confounded one of Luxemburg's lifelong perspectives – the independence of Poland. But as Deutscher explains in *The Tragedy of the Polish Communist Party*, the predominant tradition in the political milieu in which he became a militant was still Luxemburgist. The way in which that tradition was weakened, compromised and finally snuffed out forms, in fact, the leitmotif of his moving evocation – at once analytically sharp and acutely felt – of the fate of pre-war communism in Poland. Deutscher's own formation, however, was in close continuity with Luxemburg's heritage. From it he took its moral independence, its spontaneous internationalism, its uncompromising revolutionary spirit – a Marxism that was as classical in its ease with the theory of historical materialism (Luxemburg had been the first Marxist to criticize the schemas of reproduction in *Capital*), as it was vigorous in its connection with the practical life of the workers' movement.

To these historical bequests there was added a specific geographical endowment as well. Poland lay between Germany and Russia, the two great powers that had decisively shaped – or misshaped – its destiny since the days of Napoleon. Luxemburg's career as a socialist had passed in the ambience of all three nations: organizing the clandestine labour movement in Poland from her student days, intervening in the debates of the Russian movement during the Revolution of 1905–1907, and leading the Left in the German movement in the final decade of her life. Nor was her case an isolated one. Her contemporary Karl Radek, from Brest, was equally at home from Bremen to Moscow. For a socialist of Deutscher's generation, Versailles Poland no longer afforded this kind of possibility. But the geopolitical position of the country still ensured that any Polish Marxist would be formed against the immediate horizons of events in Germany and Russia: in some ways more so than ever, as the October Revolution had now given birth to

---

1. The principal difference between the two was the language spoken at home: Polish in Luxemburg's case, Yiddish in Deutscher's.

the Soviet Union to the east, while the Comintern focused its greatest hopes on a second breakthrough in Weimar Germany to the west. It was thus quite logical that Deutscher's service in the Polish Communist Party should have come to an end, not over national issues as such – tortuously mishandled though these were by the Party under Soviet pressures, as his retrospect recalls – but over the growth of fascism in the neighbouring capitalist state. In 1932, he formed part of a minority opposition that attacked the sectarian passivity of the German Communist Party, imposed by the Stalinist leadership of the Comintern, towards the rise of Nazism – while also criticizing the results of the same 'third period' line, and the bureaucratic regime that accompanied it in the Polish party. These positions came to coincide with those of Trotsky in exile: and Deutscher was expelled from the Polish Communist Party as Trotsky's warnings of the terrible threat posed by Hitler's movement to European labour reached a crescendo.

If Germany was the immediate occasion for Deutscher's break with the official Communist movement, Russia was to be the lasting concern of his mature work as a Marxist. Already in 1931 he had travelled to the USSR for the Polish party, and witnessed at first hand the ravages of collectivization and famine, as well as the industrial feats of the first five-year plan. By this time, the policies of the Third International were entirely subordinated to the twists and turns of the Soviet party leadership, as Stalin remorselessly consolidated his power in Russia. With the victory of Nazism in Germany in 1933, the direction taken by the Russian Revolution would be decisive for the fate of the European labour movement as a whole. The text that opens the collection below, the pamphlet Deutscher wrote in October 1936 on the first of the great Moscow Trials, set the agenda for the rest of his life. Written with searing indignation, his hand – as Tamara Deutscher puts it – 'trembling with rage', Deutscher's protest nonetheless already displayed some of the distinctive qualities that were to mark his later work as a Marxist historian. Thus he was not content with dismantling the circumstantial absurdities of Stalinist 'evidence' at the Trials: even more conclusively, he dwelt on the psychological impossibility of an alleged 'terrorism' that abased itself before its accusers, an audacious 'conspiracy' collapsing into abject self-flagellation, and surmised the real mechanisms which extracted the confessions of Zinoviev, Kamenev and the rest – the GPU's secret promises of post-trial pardon in exchange for their moral suicide in the dock, that were promptly discharged by summary physical execution. The penetration of Deutscher's insight here – contrasting with the overblown speculations of so many of his contemporaries – has been confirmed by the evidence that has subsequently emerged about the Trials: a remarkable tribute to his gifts of historical reconstruction. He concluded the pamphlet with the ringing words: 'History still leaves socialism some time to save its burning edifice. Let us not lose faith in our ideals.'

Three years later, Deutscher left Warsaw for London. The small communist opposition in Poland was isolated and dispersed; he had rejected the formation of a new International by Trotsky, arguing that a 'period of intense reaction and depression' was 'wholly unfavourable' to the venture; a new European war was visibly imminent, as the ambitions of the Third Reich expanded. Deutscher settled down to master English and start a new journalistic career abroad.[2] War broke out a few months later, with the German invasion of Poland. Nazi victory in the west was followed by Soviet occupation of the east of the country, in accordance with the provisions of the Molotov–Ribbentrop Pact of 1939. With this partition, Deutscher's native land had once again disappeared from the map of Europe. Two years later, Hitler launched the Wehrmacht against the USSR itself, and within months was at the gates of Moscow. Deutscher, after a brief spell with Polish forces in Scotland, was now working as a journalist for *The Economist* in London. The second text in this collection is the record of his reaction to the titanic struggle under way in Russia. Written in February 1942, when the victory of Stalingrad still lay well ahead, Deutscher's article – addressed to Polish readers in exile – expresses, with impassioned eloquence, the other pole of his response to the drama of the Soviet Union under Stalin: after his scorn and disgust at the infamy of the Trials, his respect and admiration for the 'heroic resistance of the Russian workers and peasants' in which history had stripped off the mask of the bureaucracy and revealed 'the Revolution's true countenance: bleeding but dignified, suffering but fighting on'. Attacking both liberal myths of the 'solidarity of the two totalitarian-isms', and the Stalinist crimes that had given rise to them, he under-scored the real historical significance of the conflict between the USSR and Germany – a 'battle for the very existence of the workers' movement and the freedom of the European peoples – a freedom without which socialism cannot be achieved.' 'The destiny of the world now hangs in the balance across the vast spaces of the USSR', he wrote.

---

2. For this period of Deutscher's life, as for the whole of his youth, see Daniel Singer's invaluable biograpical essay 'Armed with a Pen,' in David Horowitz, ed., *Isaac Deutscher – The Man and His Work*, London 1971, an essential volume for understanding its subject.

'In the terse war communiqués we socialists read not only the reports about "normal" war operations: we are also reading in them the fate of the deadly struggle between revolution and counter-revolution.'

These early Polish-language texts, on the Purges and the Red Army at bay, were written with an incandescent intensity. *Reflections on the Russian Revolution*, published in *The Political Quarterly* in early 1944, as the Nazi armies were in full retreat before the advancing Soviet forces, and the end of the German invasion was near, is quite different in mode. Here Deutscher, setting aside any reference to current events, looked at the development of the Russian Revolution as a whole in a long historical perspective, comparing it with the English and the French Revolutions before. Stalin's dictatorship, he concluded, was closer to the Cromwellian Protectorate than the Napoleonic Empire in the paradoxical continuity of a repressive and hierarchical regime with the insurgent origins of October. But no stabilization was yet in sight. The 'Pandora's box of the Revolution is still open', he wrote, releasing 'its monsters and its fears' – but also 'the hope at the bottom of it', which alone had made it possible to 'sustain and keep together a nation which had drained the cup of defeat almost to the last bitter dregs', in the first months of the Nazi invasion. The future of the post-revolutionary bureaucracy formed under Stalin remained uncertain, once the struggle was over. 'Here the student of history can only put the question-mark without attempting to formulate any reply.' These concluding words announce the change in Deutscher's practice as a writer that was to occur in the years immediately following the peace. After 1945 Deutscher did not consider going back to Poland,[3] as Marx had never thought of resettling in Germany; renouncing immediate political engagements, he wrote *Stalin: A Political Biography* instead, which appeared in 1949. The fourth text devoted to the USSR below, *Two Revolutions*, is his introduction to the French edition. It extends his comparison of the Russian and French Revolutions, now with all the authority of that work, discussing in particular the analogy between their respective expansions beyond their borders, with the forcible creation of satellite states in Europe – hybrid products at once of emancipation and oppression. Revolt among his allies and satellites had contributed to the downfall of Napoleon, a precedent

---

3. Save once, after the Polish October, in 1956 – when informal overtures were made to him by the authorities to return to Poland. His reply was that he would do so if he could deliver a series of lectures on the history of Polish Communism, to be subsequently written up into a book: whereupon no more was heard of the offer.

that should give 'grave warning' to Stalin as he constructed a Soviet order in Eastern Europe – already against the rebellion of Tito. One of Napoleon's client states, he noted, had been the Duchy of Poland, where his legend had lived on long after his defeat, and was still alive to Deutscher as a schoolboy. The French system had not been saved by its redeeming features. But the verdict of history on its Stalinist counterpart was unlikely to be more severe than on the Napoleonic original.

By the time Deutscher's biography of Stalin appeared, the political conjuncture in the West had, of course, changed. From 1946 onwards, the Cold War had set in: a comprehensive anti-communism now dominated official culture and politics in the advanced capitalist countries. In a climate of conformity and fear, the Soviet experience became the object of a vast ideological campaign, orchestrated through government agencies, political parties, trade unions and intellectual institutions alike, depicting the Russian threat – of perpetual aggression and subversion – to the Free World. In other words, a period very like our own. Deutscher's response to it, which forms the theme of the second part of this collection, thus makes timely reading. *The Ex-Communist's Conscience* is a cool and devastating review of *The God That Failed*, a symposium of penitents with communist pasts. Deutscher compares their conversions – liberal or conservative – with those of disillusioned early admirers of the French Revolution such as Wordsworth or Coleridge, who rallied to the cause of Tory oligarchy and Holy Alliance in the struggle against Napoleon. This demeaning path he contrasted with the examples of three very different figures – Jefferson, Goethe and Shelley – who refused to choose between the two armed camps of their time, and whose judgement 'history has proved superior to the phobias and hatreds of their age'.

The next essay deals directly with the centrepiece of the phobic literature of the Cold War, George Orwell's *1984*. Deutscher, who knew Orwell quite well as a fellow-journalist, pens a remarkable portrait of him and the springs of his vision of Stalinism as the expression of a primordial sadism, wielding power and inflicting pain for their own sake – human evil detached from historical cause or social reason. Amidst so many suffuse tributes to Orwell's genius today, wanting any sense of the proportions of their object, the economy and severity of *1984 – The Mysticism of Cruelty* are a reminder of the function of real criticism. But if the celebrity of the book was created, in Deutscher's words, by the 'social demand' of the Cold War, what was the real character of the Cold War as an international conflict itself? The third piece in this section provides a broad historical retrospect, twenty years after Potsdam. Deutscher prepared this text for a speech at a National Teach-In in Washington during May 1965 on the war in Vietnam – a direct outcome of the original conflict unleashed by Western intervention (French, British and American) in Indochina in 1945. Accepting the inevitability of a world-wide clash between capitalist and anti-capitalist regimes and social forces, after their joint defeat of the Axis powers, Deutscher pointed out the drastic inequality of position and strength between the leading victor states, the USA and USSR – 'two colossi, one full-blooded, vigorous and erect, and the other prostrate and bled white'; and the absurdity of the claims that Russia was bent on a military assault on the West after its ordeal in the Second World War, or that Stalin sought – rather than feared – the spread of revolutions abroad. Nevertheless, despite the asymmetry of economic power and of political responsibility at the origins of the conflict, whose onus lay predominantly with the Anglo–American powers, 'effects outlive their causes', and 'the danger is only too obvious that this cold war may terminate in total nuclear war'. Moreover, Deutscher went on, in another decisive respect 'the cold war has already given us the foretaste of the fully-fledged nuclear war: its fall-out cannot be confined to enemy territory; it contaminates the moral texture, it destroys and warps the thinking processes of the popular masses in our countries, in all the countries engaged in waging the cold war.' To fight against the Cold War was not to abandon class struggle, but to release it from the morass of 'hysteria and insanity, myths and legends' in which it had become alienated and obscured, to allow it – adapting a phrase of Marx's about the Commune – to run through its different phases in the most rational and humane way,[4] so that 'the divisions may once again run within nations, rather than between them.'

Following the death of Stalin there opened a period in which there seemed for a time to be a real prospect of such a rationalization of East–West conflict. Deutscher was the first observer to predict the ferment of destalinization in the USSR after 1953. His book *Russia After Stalin* explored the different possible directions in which the

---

    4. 'The Commune does not do away with the class struggles through which the working classes strive to abolition of all classes and, therefore, all class rule, but it affords the rational medium in which that class struggle can run through its different phases in the most rational and humane way': Karl Marx, *The First International and After*, ed. David Fernbach, London 1974, p. 253.

Soviet state and society might move, as the first signs of the Thaw became visible. In these same years, which seemed to hold some promise of a revival within the international communist movement of pre-Stalinist traditions, he was preparing his monumental biography of Trotsky, the first volume of which – *The Prophet Armed* – appeared in 1954. The texts contained in the third part of this collection reflect these interlinked concerns, but also cast light on Deutscher's attitudes to Poland and the crisis of Stalinism in Eastern Europe, to Germany and the fate of socialism in Central Europe, and to Scandinavian Social Democracy in Western Europe. *The Tragedy of the Polish Communist Party*, as we have seen, recreates the world of pre-war Polish communism in which Deutscher was formed. But it was prompted by the Polish renewal of 1956, when the reforming current led by Gomulka defied Soviet intimidation with a significant liberalization of political and intellectual controls in Poland. Deutscher viewed these developments with a critical sympathy, hoping for a return of the better traditions of the past. His conclusion is striking testimony to the complete freedom of his spirit from all national cant. He insisted on the 'indestructible links between the Polish and Russian Revolutions' – links proved both 'negatively and positively', in 1918–1920, in 1939, in 1954 and again in 1956. Considering how often history had 'mocked and insulted Poland's national dignity and, in the first place, the dignity and independence of the Polish revolutionary movement', it was not surprising that the Polish people 'sought refuge in the jungle of our nationalist legends'. The Polish masses, he argued, would eventually understand that 'the bonds which unite their destiny with that of the Russian and other revolutions are indissoluble', but only 'after they have recovered from the blows and shocks inflicted on them in the past, and when they feel that nothing can ever again threaten their independence and national dignity.' Ten years later, Deutscher addressed a scathing *Open Letter* to Gomulka, denouncing the first trial of men who were to be the leaders of KOR in the eighties, and warning that with such persecutions Gomulka was 'compromising the future of socialism'. Deutscher's judgement on each occasion was vindicated. The final decline of the Gomulka regime into the squalid repressions of 1968 prepared the way for the moral discredit of communism in the country at large; yet the subsequent rise of Solidarity proved unable to transform Polish state and society, in the absence of any corresponding movement against the bureaucratic order in the Soviet Union. The 'negative bonds' between Polish and Russian experience still prevailed.

Deutscher's conversations and correspondence with Heinrich Brandler represent a very different kind of document, of great fascination of their own. For Brandler embodied a living mediation between the epoch of Luxemburg and Lenin, and that of Deutscher. Born in 1881, as a young Saxon building-worker he had joined the German Social Democratic Party, and become a friend and adherent of Rosa Luxemburg before the First World War. In 1918 he had participated in the founding of the German Communist Party, and found himself by 1921 at the head of it. In the following year there occurred the 'German October' – the ill-starred attempt at an insurrectionary rising in Central Germany by the KPD, on instructions from the Comintern in Moscow prompted by Zinoviev and Trotsky. Brandler, modest and cautious by temperament, neither believed in the prospects for a successful German Revolution in 1923, nor thought himself capable of leading one. But as a loyal Communist he obeyed instructions, and was then blamed for the failure of the enterprise. Expelled from the party for opposing the 'third period' line in 1929, he spent the Nazi years in exile in France and Cuba. Deutscher first met him on his return to Europe in 1948. Tamara Deutscher vividly evokes the friendship that ensued. During these initial encounters, Deutscher recorded his discussions with Brandler, in which the older man recollected the famous episodes of the twenties in which he had been a principal figure. Deutscher's ability to convey a personality – on this occasion obliquely – is once again notable. After his return to West Germany, Brandler organized a small Marxist formation, *Gruppe Arbeiterpolitik*, committed to revolutionary social- ism, and the two men continued to write to each other. Brandler had always been closer to Bukharin's Right Opposition in the twenties, while Deutscher's sympathies lay with Trotsky's Left Opposition, and this difference was reflected in the latter's more stringent overall hostility to Stalinism in the post-war years. When working-class riots erupted against the Ulbricht regime in East Germany in 1953, however, it was Brandler who viewed this upheaval with more unconditional approval, concentrating on its sociological character in the DDR itself, while Deutscher reminded him of the international context in which the rising was ideologically appropriated by the West, and of the setback to the cause of political reform in East Germany that it occasioned, paradoxically rescuing Ulbricht from the brink of political extinction as the Soviet leadership abandoned its intention of jettison- ing him. The debate between the two over the significance of this contemporary crisis was conducted on both sides in terms of its position within German historical development as a whole, since the epoch of Tilsit. The exchange printed here concludes with Brandler's reaction to Deutscher's treatment of the 'German October' thirty years earlier, in the second volume of his biography of Trotsky, *The Prophet*

Unarmed.[5] While admiring the character of the manuscript as a whole, he sought to clarify his own role in the disasters of that year, when many believed that the best single chance of a revolution in the West was missed. Deutscher's response to his objections is of especial interest, since here – in direct dialogue with an interlocutor of Lenin himself, both witness to the past and comrade-in-arms in the present – he sets out a memorable explanation of his practice as a Marxist historian, dealing with events in which his own revolutionary sympathies were fully engaged.

Deutscher's exchanges with the Norwegian Social Democrat Trygve Lie provide a caustic contrast. Lie had been Minister of Justice in the Labour government that had first – grudgingly – given asylum to Trotsky in 1935, then isolated and harassed, and finally expelled him, under combined bourgeois and bureaucratic pressures, in 1937. In the course of his research for the third volume of his biography of Trotsky, *The Prophet Outcast*, Deutscher interviewed Lie in 1956 about these events. The notes that he took of his findings give a revealing glimpse of a certain kind of West European Social Democracy, in all its meanness and hypocrisy, as it confronted the grandeur of the Bolshevik tradition in the person of Trotsky in Norway. Trygve Lie, of course, incarnated all that was worst in such Scandinavian traditions, irresistibly recalling Ibsen's most savage portraits to Deutscher. Above and beyond his role during Trotsky's exile, he was to be one of the most servile functionaries of US policy in the Cold War, when as the American appointee as Secretary-General of the United Nations, he introduced McCarthyism into the international civil service, demoralizing it for a decade to the disgust of even liberal colleagues. The moral and political gulf between a Brandler and a Lie brings home much of the human meaning of the original separation of the Third from the Second International on the morrow of the First World War.

The central focus of Deutscher's work was the fate of the Russian Revolution, the transformations of the Soviet state that emerged from it, and their impact on the European labour movement. Of all these, he had direct experience and first-hand knowledge, as a Marxist apprenticed in the Polish Communist Party, fluent in German and Russian,

---

5. For a fuller selection of the Deutscher–Brandler correspondence, see *New Left Review* 105, September–October 1977. The complete original series of letters had been edited by Hermann Weber, *Unabhängige Kommunisten – Der Briefwechsel zwischen Heinrich Brandler und Isaac Deutscher 1949 bis 1967*, Berlin 1981.

familiar with the Latin cultures, writer of a memorable English. This was the world of classical Marxism, native to Europe. The victory of the Chinese Revolution in 1949 transformed the boundaries of this universe, extending its problems to Asia in the setting of an ancient civilization with a longer continuous history than any in Europe, and a culture of traditional self-sufficiency. Deutscher immediately realized the world-historical significance of the overthrow of the Kuomintang. This was, indeed, the final emphasis of his essay *Two Revolutions* already mentioned, written within a few months of the entry of Mao's armies into Peking, where he argued that comparisons between the destiny of the French and Russian Revolutions found their natural stopping-place with the arrival of the Chinese Revolution. 'For this phenomenon we find no parallel in the epoch of the French revolution. To its very end the French revolution stood alone.' Deutscher watched with close interest the first years of Communist China, but it was not until the exhaustion of the reforming impetus in Khrushchevite Russia in the late fifties, and the Chinese challenge to Soviet direction of the international communist movement in the early sixties, that he turned his full attention to the specific historical character of Maoism. The result was one of his finest and most original essays, *Maoism – Its Origins and Outlook*, which surveyed the tensions and contradictions of the Chinese experience in the light of its Russian predecessor. The balance and complexity of his assessment, made without benefit of any specialized linguistic or area skills, have few equals in the subsequent literature. Maoism, he argued, could be seen as a kind of fulfilment of Marx's conjecture that late nineteenth-century Russia might develop directly from a primitive agrarian society to socialism, through a revolution based on the peasantry and its communal traditions, provided that the working class had come to power in the advanced industrial countries of Western Europe, and so could exert a gravitational pull on backward Russia. *Mutatis mutandis*, just such a sequence had occurred in China, but – ironically – with newly industrialized Russia playing the part Marx had assigned to Western Europe. Hence the paradoxes of Maoism. On the one hand, from its rural origins it rested more securely on the consent of the majority of the population than had Bolshevism, the movement of an urban minority: initially more confident relations with the peasantry were also assisted by coming to power after and not before a civil war, permitting the Maoist regime – unlike the Leninist – to proceed immediately to the constructive tasks of economic revival. On the other hand, the agrarian background of Maoism also meant a narrow cultural provincialism and uncontested political authoritarianism, in marked contrast to the broad internationalism and lively intellectual pluralism of the classical Bolshevik tradition. Socially, the Chinese regime was relatively more egalitarian than the Russian at a comparable stage of its post-revolutionary development; but its organizational monolithism, untouched by any more democratic past heritage, nevertheless gave it an unmistakable 'affinity with Stalinism'. Internationally, its preaching of the watchwords of irreconcilable class struggle and its campaign for radical resistance to imperialism, might be formally appealing. But Deutscher pointed to the incongruity of the cult of Stalin that accompanied them, and presciently asked how far 'Maoist professions of revolutionary internationalism' really reflected 'the frame of mind of the Chinese masses', and were 'not merely a response to Western provocation', with the continuing blockade of China by the USA? Thus already in 1964, at the height of apparent Maoist intransigence towards Western imperialism, Deutscher lucidly foresaw the prospect that if the 'Western powers were to try to play China against the Soviet Union' – 'might Peking not succumb to the temptation?' Less than a decade later, the answer was to be forthcoming.

Deutscher did not live to see the embrace with Washington of Mao's last years. But he did witness, and judge, the launching of the 'Cultural Revolution' in China that paved the way for it. Proclaimed in the name of the radical ideas of the Paris Commune, and a revolt against all hierarchy and bureaucracy, the Cultural Revolution was greeted with a wide range of indulgence and enthusiasm among the left intelligentsia of Europe and North America, forming a whole generation of *maoisant* sympathizers in the West. Credulity in the official propaganda of the Chinese regime, as purge succeeded purge in the ranks of party and state and the population at large, often persisted until the death of Mao himself. Deutscher was quite untouched by such fashionable illusions. From the outset, as can be seen from his trenchant piece *The Meaning of the 'Cultural Revolution'*, he indicted the crude intellectual nihilism, the mindless xenophobia, and the brutal persecutions unleashed by the 'Great Helmsman' in 1966. For all its apparently farcical aspects, he warned, 'the Maoist "cultural revolution" is a deadly serious affair. Its effect on China's spiritual and intellectual life is, in all probability, going to be just as devastating and lasting as were the consequences of the Stalinist witch-hunts. Its political meaning is also comparable. Like Russia in the last years of the Stalin era, so China has now plunged headlong into a self-centred isolationism and nationalism.' The result would be 'an irreparable loss to the nation: a gap in its cultural consciousness, a lowering of standards, and an impoverishment of spiritual life. Post-Stalinist Russia is still smarting under the loss, and so will Maoist and post-Maoist China.' Deutscher's clairvoyance did not halt here. He went on to predict, again with arresting accuracy, that the deliberately lowered economic horizons of the regime – its failure to advance Chinese industrialization with anything like Russian-style success under Stalin, its inability to resolve rural over-population and unemployment – were unlikely to provide a basis for political stabilization. 'Pressures for a more ambitious policy of economic progress will make themselves felt', and 'some reaction against the latest version of Maoism is all too likely to set in.' He concluded: 'Mao has been in one person China's Lenin and Stalin. But at the end of his road he shows more and more similarity to Stalin; and the latest orgy of his personality cult underlines the likeness. It is as if he had outlived himself and is already a relic of the past, an embodiment of China's backwardness and isolationism. When the reaction against these aspects of Maoism comes, his successor or successors, whoever they are, will have to act as its mouth-pieces and agents.' The profile of Deng Xiaoping and his associates is already delineated.

The final group of texts collected here is distinct in character from the rest. In these, which date from the sixties, Deutscher posed four of the most general and fundamental questions confronting any socialist in the second half of the twentieth century. How should the bureaucratic systems, that have emerged from every revolution in the backward countries so far, be viewed historically? What is the validity of the classical theory of Marxism for an analysis of capitalism in the advanced countries? Where does the role of violence lie in the transition to a society beyond capitalism? What would be the shaping forms of a socialist civilization? The first of these issues Deutscher explored in *The Roots of Bureaucracy*. It is often said that his conjunctural writing on Russian political development in the Khrushchevite epoch was overly optimistic about the prospects of democratization in the USSR and in the Soviet bloc generally; and it is true that he thought the failure of reforms in the early sixties was unlikely to be a durable one, given the wider changes in Soviet social structure as a whole. The protracted stabilization of Brezhnevism was a process he did not live to dissect. But in his most considered theoretical reflections on the historical phenomenon of bureaucracy as a whole, he left little ground for confidence in any short-term supersession of it in a society like the USSR, let alone China. For there, in his long-range interpretation, he located the social origins of bureaucracy in the division between mental and manual labour which lay 'buried on the border between the primitive communistic tribe and civilized society', with the first embryonic emergence of class society itself. After sketching the metamorphoses of bureaucratic administration, and its relations to successive modes of production from the Pharaohs and the Bourbons, Deutscher then argued that under capitalism 'the political power of the bureaucracy has always been in inverse proportion to the maturity, the vigour, the capacity for self-government of the strata constituting a given bourgeois society. On the other hand, when in highly-developed bourgeois societies class struggles have reached something like a deadlock, when contending classes have lain as if prostrate after a series of exhausting social and political struggles, then political leadership has almost automatically passed into the hands of a bureaucracy.' This was why Victorian England or Jacksonian America, with their self-assured bourgeoisies, were the least bureaucratic of the major capitalist powers in the nineteenth century, while the 'mutual exhaustion' of bourgeoisie and proletariat after 1848 gave rise to the Second Empire in France, and the 'many-sided deadlock' between junkers, industrialists and workers in Germany yielded the domination of Bismarck's officialdom.

It was this logic, transposed to societies where the capitalist class itself had been destroyed, yet the working class was still fragmented and weak, that explained the enormous growth in the power and longevity of post-revolutionary bureaucracies, against the background of the relentless hostility of the surrounding capitalism. These post-capitalist bureaucracies, however, for all their despotic arrogance and privilege, did not constitute new classes. To this day, Deutscher observed, 'the Soviet bureaucracy has not managed to acquire that social, economic and psychological identity of its own which would allow us to describe it as a new class. It is something like an amoeba covering post-revolutionary society with itself. It is an amoeba because it lacks a social backbone of its own, it is not a formed entity, not a historic force that comes on the scene in the way in which, for example, the old bourgeoisie came forth after the French Revolution.' Mined by its own contradictions, it would not last forever. In a society character-ized by widespread automation, shorter working-hours, civilized leis-ure and cultural independence, 'the antagonism between brain-work and manual labour really will wither away, and so will the division between the organizers and the organized.' Then, he predicted, but only then, 'it will be seen that if bureaucracy was a faint prelude to class society, bureaucracy will mark the fierce, ferocious epilogue to class society – no more than an epilogue.'

The three remaining texts in this group are all products of Deutscher's practical political interventions within the Left, once a mass movement of semi-revolutionary temper arose among a younger generation in the West towards the end of his life, with the emergence of widespread opposition to the American war in Vietnam and the beginnings of revolt on the campuses. These addresses show him grappling with the problems of socialism in the richest capitalist nations of the time, and indicate how wrong it is to think of Deutscher as only a historian, albeit of the major revolutionary experience of this century: for without ever ceasing to think historically, he also defended original political and ethical positions as well. *Marxism in Our Time* looks at the general situation of historical materialism as a theory of social emancipation, a century after *Capital*: one which he then judged to display 'simultaneous ascendancy and decline'. To the question – is Marxism obsolete? – Deutscher replied: 'There is one, only one essential element in the Marxist critique of capitalism. It is very simple and very plain, but in it are focused all the many-faceted analyses of the capitalist order. It is this: there is a striking contradiction between the increasingly social character of the process of production and the anti-social character of capitalist property. Our mode of existence, the whole manner of production, is becoming more and more social in the sense that the old free-lance producers can no longer go on producing in independence from each other, from generation to generation, as they did in the pre-capitalist system. Every element, every fraction, every tiny little organ of our society is dependent on all the rest. The whole process of production becomes one social process of production – and not only one national process of production but one international process of production. At the same time you have an anti-social kind of property, private property. This contradiction between the anti-social character of property and the social character of our production is the source of all anarchy and irrationality in capitalism.' The contradiction could not be reconciled in the long-run – a 'collision must come'. The nature of that collision could not be predicted in detail: but its general shape was not in doubt. On the one hand, Deutscher – at the height of the Kennedy–Johnson boom – expressed his disbelief in any 'further smooth, evolutionary development of Western capitalism': after twenty years of prosperity, slump would come again – as it did. On the other hand, the class struggle in the West had to be seen as a 'war against capitalism that has lasted many generations', and which had seen 'the mobilization of counter-revolution all over the world, in all its various forms, from fascism to the most refined social-democratic reformism, all mobilized in the defence of the existing social order.' Then, in a striking passage, Deutscher went on: 'Never yet, except in extraordinary moments like the Commune of Paris, has the working class mobilized itself even to a fraction of that intensity and strength at which the possessing and ruling classes have maintained their mobilization on an almost permanent footing. Even during the Commune the insurgents never really mobilized for a life-and-death struggle – we have all the descriptions showing their light-mindedness, their good-humoured and good-tempered optimism.'

It was the strengths, yet also the weaknesses, of such optimism that Deutscher reviewed in *The Dialectics of Violence and Non-Violence*, one of his sharpest and most unsettling pieces. In it, he started by stressing the traditional tension within the classical outlook of Marxism between the necessity of political violence as a means for overthrowing bourgeois class rule, and the aim of a classless society that for the first time in history would be truly free from violence. That essential and defensible dialectic was, however, overborne in the tragic vicissitudes of the Russian Revolution, when 'under overwhelming and inhuman pressures' terror was let loose and 'what was to have been but a glassful of violence became buckets and buckets full, and then rivers of violence', so that 'in the end the non-violent meaning of Marxism was suppressed under the massive, crushing weight of Stalinism.' But the two could not be cleanly separated. For, Deutscher argued, 'it would show a lack of moral courage in Marxism to draw the formal line of dissociation and say that we are not responsible for Stalinism, that that wasn't what we aimed at' – 'we cannot delete Stalinism from our records although we are not responsible for Stalinist crimes'. Why was this so? In a rare personal avowal, Deutscher went on: 'To some extent we (and when I say we I mean that generation of Marxists with which I as an individual identify morally, I mean Lenin, Trotsky, Bukharin, Zinoviev, the early Communist leaders in Europe) participated in this glorification of violence as a self-defence mechanism. Rosa Luxemburg understood this when she criticized the first faint signs of this attitude.' Yet this was self-criticism, not repudiation. Revolutionary violence, regretted and unglorified, might remain necessary against an enemy who had never shrunk from any extremity of it, as the murderous war in Vietnam that formed the context of his intervention demonstrated. But in advanced industrial societies like America itself, the potential balance of class forces was immensely more favourable to an undistorted outcome of revolutionary struggle than in backward and isolated Russia. There such violence could be 'rational and infinitesimal', if the vast majority of the exploited were ready to employ it to break the power of their exploiters, without making a virtue of it.

In the last text of the volume, *On Socialist Man*, Deutscher looked towards the future to ask what could be said, without relapse into utopian speculation, of human potential and limitation in a classless society once finally achieved. (The term 'man' should not deceive, as Deutscher's reference to the 'dependence of woman and child on the father' makes clear: it is gender-neutral, in the sense of the Russian *chelovek* or German *Mensch*.) Two features of his reply stand out. The first is the sobriety of his projection: socialism would not 'solve all predicaments of the human race' – indeed of Trotsky's trinity of 'hunger, sex and death', it could offer relief only for the first. Beyond class, human beings would still – *pace* Shelley – suffer guilt and pain, and feel the discomfort of civilizational restraints over instinctual drives. But these drives – and this is the second significant theme of his address – could in themselves be given neither the historical immobility nor the societal importance that Freud's theory attached to them. While respecting the warrant of psychoanalysis within its proper and restricted domain, Deutscher had no difficulty in dispatching its inflated claims for the interpretation of history, let alone intrusions of it into politics. As he drily pointed out, in discussing Freud's theory of aggression, 'throughout history men organized into armies have slaughtered each other over property or claims to property; but they have not so far, except in mythology, fought wars over "prerogative in the field of sexual relationships".' Whereas Marxism had tried to 'tackle from the right end the tasks confronting our society', and had moved mountains – both in victory and defeat – in so doing, the practical social effects of psychoanalysis were by comparison nugatory. In a period like the present, when an uncritical reception of psychoanalysis, even in ostentatiously idealist forms, coexists with a retreat from any form of historical materialism, Deutscher's calm reminder of the relations of truth and force between the two is a salutary one. Socialism, in his vision, would neither bring an impossible liberation from all human servitudes, nor stop at an imaginary immutability of all human instincts.

Isaac Deutscher died in August 1967. He was just sixty. It is difficult to compute the loss his disappearance has meant to Marxist culture since. The historical conditions that produced this singular revolutionary socialist have passed away. Neither the living connection with the world of Lenin or Luxemburg, nor the cosmopolitanism of an older East-Central Europe, was available to subsequent generations. Yet Deutscher's work continues to represent an indispensable source for the culture and politics of socialism, because of its peculiar combination of qualities.

Among these was the serene political fortitude with which Deutscher met the contingencies of his own period – his unshakable fidelity to the political ideals of his youth, amidst so many conflagrations in which one edifice of the Left after another burnt down, or had to be reconstructed. That fortitude was the product of his absolute independence of thought – the entire freedom of his person and outlook from those fashions and phobias which have swayed the intelligentsias of the Left in one direction after another – successively Stalinist or Maoist, structuralist or post-structuralist, advocates of the new working class or the new social movements, Eurocommunism or Eurosocialism. But this spiritual independence was the very opposite of sectarian or pharisaical isolation. Deutscher had an ability to communicate with a greater audience than any other socialist writer of his generation in English. His books were translated, his articles read, across the world. Such universality was given by literary power. But this was not simply an aesthetic gift: it reflected an intellectual command of a classical Marxism so close to its sources in the full range of European culture and enlightenment behind it that it had no need of a specialized vocabulary – required not the slightest technical strain – to find its words. The adoption of biography as his mode of writing history had a related meaning – a genre that has always possessed the widest appeal among the different kinds of literature about the past. In Deutscher's case, the biographical form had an additional, deeper meaning. In the life of an individual, he could join the discourses of morality and necessity that Marxism has often found it so hard to hold together. His Stalin and Trotsky are preeminently products of history, subject to the determinations of wider social forces that they expressed or rejected: but they are also moral agents, accountable for their actions and the consequences of them. Ethics traditionally refers to persons; causal dynamics to groups. Deutscher's exceptional psychological grasp was the medium in which the two – causality and responsibility – achieved synthesis in his writing. A socialist politics today needs to be informed by a sense of each in equal measure. Another way of putting this is to recall the actual contrasts between the trio Deutscher selected for their resistance to conformity in the Napoleonic age. Goethe, Shelley, Jefferson – serene olympian, visionary iconoclast, shrewd politician. He had an element of each in his own make-up. The culture of the Left needs them all.

1984

Postscript

The historian was survived for over two decades by his wife Tamara Deutscher. In his lifetime, she had been his intellectual companion and assistant. After his death, she became his editor and moral place-holder. The depth of her love for him gave her the courage to play this role, in which she was timid at first. But her background – she came from a family of radical intellectuals in the east of Poland – and her temperament, of generous intransigence, also equipped her for it. For more than twenty years, she personified the culture to which he had given expression, with a light warmth and beauty of her own. Deutscher's last published commentary on Soviet affairs saw the Brezhnev–Kosygin regime, still recently installed, as the dreary epi-logue to the failure of destalinization under Khrushchev, one that might be as short-lived as it would be sterile. Events proved otherwise, and it fell to her to follow the repressions that multiplied after the invasion of Czechoslovakia, and the growth of dissidence in Russia under the carapace of an obdurate tyranny. Watching for every sign of intellectual or political awakening in the USSR, she responded with alertness and hope, in the way he would have done, to the different kinds of opposition within the country which in one way or another moved downstream, however critically, from October; and when *perestroika* finally arrived, welcomed it, albeit with the scepticism she kept for all bureaucratic initiatives. The moral revival brought by the progress of democratization in the Soviet Union was for her the best source of confidence in the future. The gathering break with the whole legacy of Bolshevism disappointed, but it did not disillusion her. She viewed the trend of events under Gorbachev with a mixture of gaiety and sadness. Refusing to go to the USSR so long as Deutscher's work was still unpublished there, in the last months of her life she took part in a meeting in Barcelona between leading Soviet exiles and figures of the new wave at home, that gave voice to the emerging consensus in Russia. The unassertive dignity and independence of her person, as she expressed another kind of dissidence, made all the more impression. A few days before she died, she looked on television at the veiled face of Natalya in an archival film on Trotsky's life in Mexico, and said simply: 'Niobe'.

A year later, the Soviet experience came to its end. More than any other historian, grasping them within his own political memory, Deutscher had taken imaginative measure of its original grandeur and of its subsequent gangrene, together. He never lost his hope that the revolutionary impetus of 1917 would recover from the fate that had overtaken it, and finish in freedom. He hoped his work would one day contribute to that emancipation, believing his widest readership would eventually be Russian. Shortly before August 1991, the first book under his signature appeared in Moscow – a pirate edition of truncated parts of the second and third volumes of his biography of Trotsky, glossed by a local detractor of its subject. A connoisseur of the ironies of history, his sense of the future also allowed for this one too. He is mostly thought of, with justice, as a guarded optimist for the revolution. But it was distinctive of his vision that he also contemplated, directly and calmly, the historical prospect of restoration. The peoples of the Soviet Union, he thought, might yet have to go through the modern experience of a capitalism they had missed. 'Much of the record of these fifty years is utterly discredited in the eyes of the people', he wrote in 1967, such that 'at times the Soviet Union appears to be fraught with the moral–psychological potentiality of restoration that cannot become a political actuality.'[6] If the possibility became reality, it might – like other restorations – have its redeeming place in the complicated longer-run progress towards a common human liberty, in whose resumption he never doubted.

1991

---

6. *The Unfinished Revolution*, Oxford 1967, p. 105.

4

Michael Mann's
Sociology of Power

Who could fail to be intellectually stirred by the breadth of Michael Mann's horizon in this three-volume study? Its aim, in his own words, is nothing less than 'to provide a history and theory of power relations in human societies', an enterprise he thinks 'likely to be virtually synonymous with a history and theory of human society itself'.[1] Any initial misgivings that such a large promise must be idle or inflated are soon dispelled. The ambition of the conception is, against all conventional expectations, matched by the clarity and grandeur of the execution.

Mann's history of power begins with a survey of prehistoric evolution, and the reasons why it did not generally debouch into stable forms of social stratification. It then proceeds to an account of the emergence of civilization and the State in Mesopotamia, with some side-glances at other Near Eastern, Asian or American *Hochkulturen*. Sargon's Akkadian conquests are studied as the inauguration of a new configuration of power – 'empires of domination', of which the Assyrian and Persian subsequently receive separate treatment. Classical Greece arises as the heir jointly of Near Eastern riverine civilization, Iron Age plough agriculture coming from the North, and Mediterranean coastal trade pioneered by the Phoenicians: hoplite infantry, however, are the key to the construction of the class-divided polis, an ordering of power without regional or other precedent. The Roman world that succeeded it is defined by Mann as the first true 'territorial empire', capable of enforcing its rule uniformly across a vast geographical space rather than relying on indirect control through heterogeneous clients, as did the 'empires of domination'. The contradictory effects of the Roman

---

1. *The Sources of Social Power*, Vol. I, *A History of Power from the Beginning to A.D. 1760*, Cambridge 1986, p. 1. Henceforward SSP.

unification of the Mediterranean generate the spread of Christianity as a religion of salvation, which then provides the crucial moral carapace for decentralized economic growth in Europe during the Dark and Middle Ages, based on wet-soil agriculture and littoral commerce. In this environment the transition towards capitalism came to be inextricable from the growth of a multiplicity of 'organic' national states, with far greater effective power over their terrain – if lesser formal reach – than any ancient empire, each at once constructed and checked by warfare between them.

Such a simplified summary conveys little more than the chronological scope of Mann's survey – bold enough in itself. But it is the quality of his analytical narrative that is most impressive. Contemporary sociologists, however well-intentioned in their approach to the past, often tend to be gauche in their handling of it. Nothing could be less true in this case. Mann displays a formidably close command of the literature on his multifarious topics, and an intuitive realism of evidence that would do credit to any historian. To sustain these gifts evenly, without any appearance of strain, across a span that extends from Beaker bands to Hanoverian oligarchs is an astonishing achievement.

But it is not one super-added, as it were, to the sociological enquiry as a whole: rather it derives from it. For Mann's theory of power is what takes him so closely into his history. At one level, this theory is general and conventional enough. There are four sources of the social power invoked in the title: economic, ideological, political and military. Mann's justification of this quartet is somewhat cursory – no doubt he intends to return to a more extended foundation of it in his third volume. At all events, within his own scheme 'political' power (perhaps better transcribed as 'administrative', at any rate for the period of this volume) does not seem to possess the same categorical autonomy as the others: for any exercise of it manifestly depends on the possession of either ideological or military power, and normally a combination of both force and belief – while the converse does not hold, as the monks or marauders who cross his pages show. Political power in a 'pure' state cannot exist in the same sense.

With this reduction, however, the preliminary classification is unexceptionable, if not very novel. The originality of Mann's theory lies elsewhere, at a lower level of specificity: in his comprehensive concern with what he calls the 'exact infrastructures' of each kind of power[2] –

---

2. SSP, p. 30.

that is, the detail of their organizational techniques. The logistics of military mobility; the extent and quality of literacy; the technology of farming and transport capacities of trade; the incidence and range of judicial control; the pattern of fiscal revenue and expenditure are typical of the areas where Mann transforms our understanding of what the historical possibilities and realities of power have been, and how they have changed, over millennia.

Again and again, these investigations are bravura performances. Mann strenuously repudiates the 'false opposition' between idealism and materialism as modes of social explanation – a 'sterile dualism' he hopes to break down.[3] But in some ways his distinctive approach is best characterized in a phrase of his colleague John Hall's, whose essay *Powers and Liberties* can be taken as an elfin counterpoint to Mann's encyclopaedic study, as an 'organizational materialism'.[4] It is this common focus on the organization of contrasting types of power that confers such versatility on his sociology of it. Most practitioners, whatever their theoretical liberality in constructing or distinguishing different kinds of power, are usually at home with only one or two of them. Sociologists, like historians or the rest of us, tend to have temperamental affinities of a fairly selective sort. Weber was the great exception; and Mann is another. The validity of his claim to elude the ordinary connotations of idealism or materialism lies not in any – all too familiar presumption of a – philosophical supersession of them, but in the even-handed authority and fluency with which he moves from religious doctrine to tax structure, from military strategy to agrarian ecology, from class relations to state diplomacy. All of these are unified in a single analytic of power. That might seem forbidding. An obsession with power normally suggests sinister overtones. But although Mann's optic does involve a limitation of his field of vision, there is no trace of an authoritarian fascination with his object. On the contrary, his writing is singularly humane and democratic in temper. The monumentality of the enterprise is offset by an agreeable informality of style, a prose of short, vigorous, vivid sentences, without undue jargon or rhetoric, which engages the reader in direct argument – in that regard, a far cry from Weber.

Mann describes his view of social development, in a term of Ernest Gellner's, as 'neo-episodic' rather than evolutionary. Human power – and so human society – changes in staccato bursts, rather than through

---

3. SSP, p. 369.
4. *Powers and Liberties*, Harmondsworth 1985, p. 75.

any continuous growth, and its cumulative enhancement has been, he insists towards the end of the book, accidental. Much therefore depends on the choice of the episodes he singles out for attention, and the plausibility of his accounts of them.

What can be said of these? The first real crux in the book concerns his explanation of the rise of civilization and the State. Having argued that general social evolution did not lead in this direction, because tendencies to social hierarchy and inequality cyclically went into reverse as those who risked subordination in prehistoric groups moved on or away from them, Mann contends that the essential precondition for the emergence of civilization and acceptance of its discontents was a 'closing of escape routes' or ecological 'caging'.[5] This is a logical deduction, rather than a geographical or historical conclusion. His actual survey of the rise of civilization focuses overwhelmingly on Mesopotamia, where he subsequently has to note that there was not much ecological closure at all, but rather a topographical space marked by a 'lack of clear-cut external boundaries', yielding a 'civilization fuzzy at the edges', the product of 'various interaction networks' created as much as anything by 'ecological diversity'.[6] Tacitly redefining his starting-point in terms of the model he constructs of Mesopotamia, Mann then seeks to apply it to Egypt, which he finds a 'deviation' because it lacked 'overlapping regional networks', was, so to speak, too sequestered along the Nile.[7] These contradictions are left in the air as he moves to China or the Indus Valley – the two other regions of major alluvial agriculture – and to Crete or pre-Columbian America, which were not. Discussion of all these is desultory, even when they undermine the premises of the analysis most clearly ('the Maya were not particularly caged').[8]

The origins of civilization pose one of the most long-standing conundra of the social sciences, and Mann cannot be blamed for having failed to solve it. But here his method has let him down. Only a comparative analysis could offer a hope of coherent explanation. Such an account would, among other things, have to pay closer attention than Mann gives to the place of organized religion in the birth of the State – a point emphasized by a Marxist, Maurice Godelier[9] – and it would have to look more systematically at the range of economic

5. SSP, p. 75.
6. SSP, pp. 92, 102.
7. SSP, p. 108.
8. SSP, p. 119.
9. Maurice Godelier, *The Ideal and the Material*, London 1986, pp. 156–163.

surplus available for either. But above all, it could not privilege one region and treat all others as perfunctory adjuncts. Mann's opening Mesopotamian option is not, however, arbitrary – it has definite significance for what follows.

The second major theme of the book is the nature and import of 'empires of domination'. Sargon, Assurbanipal and Cyrus are the leading figures here: all establishing imperial states across the breadth of the Tigris and Euphrates. Mann's dissection of the mechanisms of rule that allowed these sprawling structures to be built in a world of desperately limited transport and communication, of ethnic and cultural localism, is excellent. The theoretical acuity – also empirical liveliness – of these pages make them far the best analysis of the early Near Eastern Empires that we possess. Mann himself puts great weight on their enforcement of what, after Herbert Spencer, he calls 'compulsory cooperation', or the extraction of a greater economic surplus via an increase in military coercion. His account of the potential benefits for production and circulation (if not for producers) from imperial repression and exploitation brings a formal precision and detail to the process it has not had before. But he is wrong in claiming that his view of such empires of domination is in this respect particularly heterodox. If anything, it has always been the standard judgement of most authorities – satirized indeed by E.P. Thompson in his poem on the First Emperor of Ch'in: 'However many the emperor slew / the scientific historian / (while taking note of contradiction) / affirms that productive forces grew.'[10]

Mann's third principal topic is the Classical World, or more especially the character and fate of the Roman Empire. His treatment of Greece is full of admiring insight, and shows the skill with which he can deploy class analysis (hitherto kept well in the background) when he judges it relevant; the distinctions he proposes, here and elsewhere, between the different kinds of class struggle observable in history are eminently sensible and useful, once freed from a procrustean reference to the 'institution' of Greek class struggle as a 'power jump'.[11] But there is relatively little articulation between the Greek and Roman episodes of his story, the former becoming something of a parenthesis in the narrative as a whole. The brunt of his interest falls on the Roman conquest and control of the Mediterranean, viewed as a higher stage of imperialism – the advent of the first true 'territorial empire'. Mann

---

10. 'Powers and Names', *London Review of Books*, 23 January 1986.
11. SSP, p. 195.

argues that the two axes of Roman power were the legionary army, an infantry force superior to any other in its day, and a ruling-class culture of unprecedented literacy capable of assimilating any conquered elite in its path. Following Keith Hopkins, he stresses the economic multiplier effects of the first, which generated the great prosperity of the first two centuries of the Principate; and the ideological divider effects of the second, once the material conditions of cultural universalism – in literacy, language and trade – spread beyond the ruling strata, and so subverted official cults to generate the triumph of Christianity under the Dominate.

Neither of these processes tells us much about the fall of the Empire. Mann does briefly broach relationships between the State and the landed classes, but in an uncharacteristically nebulous fashion that compares somewhat lamely with Chris Wickham's recent treatment of the same subject;[12] there is little sense of the increasing social polarization that gripped the Western Empire. Deprived of an internal dynamic, Mann therefore has to fall back on the familiar ground of increased external pressures to account for the end of the Roman order. But barbarian invasions notoriously cannot explain Byzantine survival; hence he is driven to ignore the subsequent life of the Eastern Empire altogether, his narrative consigning Byzantium to an oblivion into which even Gibbon did not venture to thrust it. The rise of Rome is far more memorable here than its decline.

One of the reasons for this is that Mann's interest is much more centrally engaged by another question: why and how did Christianity triumph in the Roman world? His discussion of this is in many ways a *tour de force*, one of the most original and compelling parts of the book, above all as it explores the social pathways by which the new faith asserted itself. But there is a suggestive bias to it. All religions have a dual existence: as systems of individual consolation within the cosmos, and as bonds of social cohesion within the community. Weber concentrated on the first, Durkheim on the second – respectively the sacred in human relationships with nature, and with society. Mann's interpretation of Christianity is single-mindedly Durkheimian. 'Christianity was not a response to material crisis, nor was it a spiritual alternative to the material world. The crisis was one of social identity: what society do I belong to?'[13] This blunt affirmation, whose lack of nuance contrasts with the general way complex evidence is handled in

12. Chris Wickham, 'The Other Transition: from the Ancient World to Feudalism', *Past and Present* 103, 1984.
13. SSP, p. 309.

his study, derives from Mann's overall angle of vision. In a work devoted to social power, religion must be thematically subsumed as a form of it. That can tell us part – an important part – of the truth about the rise of Christianity; but far from all of it. For the 'history of power' is not 'virtually synonymous' with human history *tout court*, contrary to his initial claim. In making it he veers close to the characteristic modern confusion that simply equates power and culture, whose foremost exponent has been Michel Foucault – otherwise far removed from his concerns. What Mann's account of Christianity casts radically aside is its intellectual setting within the classical thought-world: the extent to which it could exploit the moral and philosophical gap between a rationalized culture, capable of producing an Epicurus or Lucretius, and residualized cults, ever more degraded to the imperial ends of a Domitian or Elagabulus, in a new explanation of the universe. The role of the supernatural is all but banished from Mann's account of Christianity: the word 'miracle' never occurs in it. Yet it is upon these that contemporary polemics with paganism above all turned: not on alternative versions of the social order, but on divine intervention in the natural order. Mann's insensitivity to this dimension of Christianity is quite consistent, and leads him later on to the startlingly unhistorical judgement that the Church 'committed a terrible blunder' by rejecting scientific rationality from the seventeenth century onwards, since the physical world was a 'trivial area' for its concerns, which were 'overwhelmingly social, not natural'[14] – as if Galileo and Darwin could properly have been welcomed by the Holy See, if only occasional incumbents had been spryer.

Mann ends his book with an exploration of European development from 800 to 1760, which seeks to trace out the determining forces of its unique dynamism in a world-historical perspective. His explanation rests on the cumulation of what can reasonably be simplified again to three 'sources' of power. His account of the transformations of economic production and exchange between the Dark Ages and the Enlightenment is generally lucid and proficient, although it contains, as he himself notes, little that is novel as a contribution to an understanding of the transition from feudalism to capitalism. The fire-bursts of Eric Jones would in any case be a hard display to follow over environmental, demographic or technological terrain.[15] More significant, perhaps, is the sparseness of coverage devoted to property relations –

---

14. SSP, p. 464.
15. E.L. Jones, *The European Miracle*, Cambridge 1981, pp. 3–103.

here, as elsewhere throughout the book, Mann's polymathic range curiously omits the law for the most part.

On the other hand, his pathbreaking morphology of the politico-military structures of the state, from Offa to Frederick II, is magnificent: shaped around careful analysis of royal and public finances in the paradigmatic case of England, this reconstruction of the slow emergence of the European state system is the most decisive single demonstration in the book. Its gist is that the primary crucible of state-formation and transformation was always external military competition rather than the needs of internal political administration. No one has ever worked through the ensuing historical logic with such intellectual command. Yet this empirical centrepiece of the final part of the book is not its theoretical fulcrum. No more than 'decentralized' feudal agriculture is the multiple-state system of mediaeval or early modern times an explanatory innovation in the literature on the rise of the West. As Mann himself acknowledges, geo-strategic analysis of the latter was a leitmotif of the German tradition that culminated in Hintze.

What is new in Mann's explanation is the role he ascribes to his third source of power – ideology. The surprise hero of the tale is the Catholic Church. His argument, reduced to essentials, is that it was only the restraining and softening influence of Christian ethical teaching that 'pacified' violence between or within states in some measure and 'regulated' exchange of goods over any distance. The Church's preaching of 'consideration, decency and charity towards all Christians' imparted a 'common humanity' and 'social identity' to Europeans that acted as a 'substitute for coercive pacification normally required in previous extensive societies'.[16] In short, without sermons no peace and no trade. Religious faith here becomes the precondition of economic development and political civilization. As Mann points out, this is not a Weberian view insofar as it does not appeal to any particular relation between doctrine and labour or nature: it simply – far more drastically – entrusts to theology the virtues of sociality as such. Having laid out this claim in his discussion of the mediaeval Church, Mann drives the argument home without equivocation in his conclusion. After rehearsing the contribution of his 'four main power networks' (*sc.* three – the chapter is actually entitled 'Capitalism, Christendom, and States') to the dynamism of Europe, he declares: 'I have singled out one, Christendom, as *necessary* for all that followed. The others also made a

---

16. SSP, p. 381.

significant contribution to the resultant dynamic, but whether they were "necessary" is another matter.'[17] Christianity is *primus inter pares* as a cause of Occidental triumph. The last wisdom of social science rediscovers the first conviction of the conquistadors themselves.

There are, however, two obvious objections to Mann's view, which only the particular architecture of his book could have led him to overlook. The first is simply that 'Christendom', to use the term he persistently employs, was never confined to Western Europe. The massive reality of the Eastern Church is blotted out from Mann's account, once Byzantine history is dispatched down the oubliette. Where were the fructifying effects of Orthodox Christianity on economic and political life – why did it release no comparable development in Anatolia or the Balkans? Mann provides no principles of differentiation within the history of Christian doctrine or organization that could explain the divergence. Whatever else it may have lacked, Byzantium certainly did not want for normative regulation by religion. But the same is true, of course, of the Islamic world, let alone of early imperial China. By recasting a Weberian claim for the catalytic role of religion in generic Durkheimian form, Mann deprives himself of any reasonable basis for claiming special privileges for Christianity. 'Normative pacification' is a hold-all in the baggage of every major faith. There was a good deal more effective enforcement of it in Abbasid or T'ang lands than in the world of Charles the Bald. How can Mann screen out such evident reflections? The answer lies in an underlying *parti pris* of his work. The nature of his enterprise, he explains, is 'historical, not comparative, sociology'.[18] There are occasional sidelights – a very able one on Hindu caste, for example – but, fundamentally, Mann constructs just one, continuous pedigree of power. A gigantic narrative binds Sumer to the City of London in a single unfolding story, from Mesopotamia to Modern Europe. He theorizes such continuity as the 'macropattern' of a 'long-term drift', far antedating mediaeval experience, of the 'leading edge of civilization' towards the West and North-West because of 'political blockage' in the Orient – where this vanguard had to fight 'a defensive, and sometimes losing, battle against aggressive eastern neighbours', while finding favourable ecological opportunities westwards.[19] It is this meta-historical peregrination of progress towards the Occident that explains most of the weaknesses and blind spots of Mann's history noted above: Egypt treated as an

---

17. SSP, p. 507.
18. SSP, p. 503.
19. SSP, pp. 508–509.

anomaly in the emergence of civilization, and ignored as an empire of domination; China relegated to footnote condition as a territorial empire; Byzantium excluded from the ambit of Christendom; Islam disregarded as a force of normative pacification.

The book's most striking failure is not to give any proportionate weight or attention to Chinese experience. That alone disqualifies the subtitle of Mann's work, which is a touch of unnecessary hubris. Was Shang civilization ever environmentally 'caged'? Did the unification of Ch'in not long precede that of Rome? Has the family-responsibility system no place in the inventory of 'infrastructures of power'? Were literacy rates in the time of Han Wu-Ti less than under Hadrian? Can Confucianism be appropriately described as a 'salvation religion'? Was the countryside of the Southern Sung really a mere laggard beside the panorama of a twelfth-century Europe that was 'already the most agriculturally inventive civilization since the Iron Age'?[20] Joseph Needham might have written in vain for all the impact of his work on this series of assumptions. There was a period when a rudimentary immobility was all too often attributed to the early mediaeval economy. But the necessary correction has become, in Mann's vision, a giddy over-reaction which sees Europe 'leaping ahead by AD 1000' – Anglo-Saxons and Franks already germinating 'the major achievements of our scientific, industrial capitalist era'![21] Admonishing the reader that 'European self-denigration is misplaced', Mann neglects the worse danger of self-intoxication.

The springs of this error are not cultural, or any familiar kind of Eurocentrism. They lie in a theoretical fallacy: the idea that there cannot be a sociology at once historical and comparative. Mann gives no valid reason for counterposing the two. His remarks on the subject are fleeting and specious – comparative sociology is 'too difficult' (at any rate after Muhammad), or 'does not have enough cases' for its purpose.[22] By shutting out real comparisons from his history, however, he has denied himself indispensable empirical controls for too many of his hypotheses. It is difficult not to feel that the motive for this restriction may have been less the intellectual impossibility of creating a wider framework than the compositional gain of the narrower one. For Mann's history of power, precisely because it does tunnel into a multi-millennial exordium of the Industrial Revolution alone, acquires a headlong narrative drive quite unlike anything in the masterpieces of

20. SSP, p. 500.
21. SSP, p. 378.
22. SSP, pp. 371, 503.

classical sociology. Not lesser than *Economy and Society* itself in analytic stature, it is superior as literature.

It is these qualities which are likely to remain with the reader, long after any particular reservations about its method or conclusions have faded. All criticisms of *The Sources of Social Power* are bound to have something of the cat looking at the king. For this is, after all, only the first of three volumes, the next of which will trace the fate of nations and classes up to the present. No sociological enterprise of this magnitude has ever been undertaken that was not animated by some – tacit or explicit – political passion. One waits absorbed to see what that will prove to be. There can be little doubt that a great work is in the making.

1986

The Affinities of Norberto Bobbio

In early 1848, within a few weeks of each other, two antithetical texts were published in London, on the eve of European revolution. One was *The Communist Manifesto*, by Karl Marx and Friedrich Engels. The other was *Principles of Political Economy*, by John Stuart Mill. The former famously declared that the spectre of communism was haunting Europe, and would soon take possession of it. The latter, using the same imagery with scarcely less confidence, but in the opposite sense, dismissed socialist experiments as little more than chimeras that could never take on real shape as viable substitutes for private property.[1] The antithesis occasions little surprise for us now. Liberalism and Socialism have long been conventionally understood as antagonistic intellectual and political traditions; and with good reason, by virtue of both the apparent incompatibility of their theoretical starting-points – individual and societal, respectively – and of the actual record of conflict, often deadly, between the parties and movements inspired by each. However, at the very outset of this historical contention, it was strangely short-circuited in the trajectory of Mill himself. The risings of the urban poor across the principal capitals of Europe and the bloody battles that followed them stirred a warm solidarity in Harriet Taylor, the object of his affections. He set himself to study with a newly opened mind doctrines of common ownership; and soon – indeed in the very same work, *Principles of Political Economy*, in its revised edition of 1849 – pronounced the vision of socialists collectively to be 'one of the

---

1. *Principles of Political Economy*, London 1848, Vol. I, p. 255. Mill's judgement specifically referred to Saint-Simonian schemes, which – as he explained – he regarded as the most serious form of socialism. In his autobiography he used the same phrase for his initial view of any socialism, which could only be 'reckoned chimerical': *Autobiography*, London 1873, p. 231.

most valuable elements of human improvement now existing'.[2] Rarely has a fundamental political judgement been so rapidly and radically reversed. Thereafter, Mill always regarded himself as a liberal and a socialist; as he put it in his *Autobiography*, 'The social problem of the future we now considered to be how to unite the greatest individual liberty of action with a common ownership in the raw materials of the globe, and an equal participation of all in the benefits of combined labour.'[3] He defended the Paris Commune, and died working on a book on Socialism which he hoped would be more important than his study of Representative Government.

Mill's evolution, however striking, might be thought idiosyncratic or isolated. But it was not. There was to be a distinguished succession to it. England's most famous philosopher after Mill replicated the same movement. In 1895, Bertrand Russell wrote the first English-language study of German Social Democracy, the leading party of the Second International, after a study trip to Berlin. While decidedly sympathetic to the more moderate aims of the SPD, 'the point of view from which I wrote the book' – he noted seventy years later – 'was that of an orthodox liberal'.[4] At that time Russell deprecated what he called the 'boundless democracy' of the party's Erfurt Programme, and feared what he thought would be the 'foolish and disastrous experiments' that might ensue if it were not modified to respect 'natural inequalities'.[5] Within another two decades, he too had changed his mind thoroughly and permanently. It was the First World War which transformed his outlook, as 1848 had Mill's. The work he had planned to write jointly with D.H. Lawrence, *Principles of Social Reconstruction*, which appeared in 1916, if it contained caustic attacks on the state, private property and war, was still deemed insufficiently intransigent by Law-

---

2. *Principles of Political Economy*, London 1849, Vol. I, p. 266. Of the several versions of socialism, Mill now decided that Fourierism was the most skilful and formidable variant, an opinion he held to the end of his life. Of the difference between the first and second editions of his work, Mill later wrote: 'In the first edition the difficulties of socialism were stated so strongly, that the tone was on the whole that of opposition to it. In the year or two which followed, much time was given to the study of the best Socialistic writers of the Continent, and to meditation and discussion on the whole range of topics involved in the controversy: and the result was that most of what had been written on the subject in the first edition was cancelled, and replaced by arguments and reflections of a more advanced character': *Autobiography*, pp. 234–35.

3. *Autobiography*, p. 232.

4. *German Social-Democracy*, London 1965 (re-edition), p. v.

5. Ibid., pp. 141–43, 170.

rence, then urging a 'revolution' that would effect 'the nationalizing of all industries and means of communication, and of the land – in one fell blow'.[6] But Russell's next book, *Proposed Roads to Freedom*, written during his imprisonment for agitation against the war, was a full-scale discussion of Marxism, Anarchism and Syndicalism, which came out unequivocally for Guild Socialism as 'the best practicable system' – the form of common property he believed most conducive to individual liberty, as against the dangers of any too-powerful state.[7]

Another eminent contemporary who made the same transition was the economist J.A. Hobson. Best known at large for his work on *Imperialism*, because of Lenin's use and critique of it in his own later work on the subject, Hobson was a convinced English liberal when he published it in 1902. In his case too, it was the First World War which altered his course. By 1917, he was actually attacking West European Social Democracy from the left, writing that: 'The patriotic stampede of socialism in every country in the summer of 1914 is as convincing a testimony to its inadequacy to the task of overthrowing capitalism as could possibly be given.'[8] After the war, Hobson devoted his best energies to developing a theory of the socialist economy that would combine the structural exigencies of standardized production for basic needs, with sectoral conditions for personal liberty and technical innovation. The economist of over-saving whose influence Keynes acknowledged in *The General Theory* was himself meanwhile writing a work entitled *From Capitalism to Socialism*.[9]

The United States provides a final example. There too, the country's major philosophical mind, John Dewey, a staunch and outspoken liberal throughout his long career, traced the same curve. In his case it was not the First World War[10] but the Great Depression which led him to trenchant conclusions. In his book *Liberalism and Social Action*,

---

6. Ronald Clark, *The Life of Bertrand Russell*, London 1975, p. 263.

7. *Proposed Roads to Freedom*, London 1919, pp. xi–xii, 211–12: 'The communal ownership of land and capital, which constitutes the characteristic doctrine of Socialism and Anarchistic Communism, is a necessary step toward the removal of the evils from which the world suffers at present and the creation of such a society as any humane man must wish to see realized.'

8. *The Fight for Democracy*, Manchester 1917, p. 9.

9. Hobson's discussion both of the reasons for, and the limits of, socialization of the means of production, has a strikingly modern ring: see *From Capitalism to Socialism*, London 1932, pp. 32–48.

10. Dewey, after initially opposing US entry into the War, rallied to Wilson in 1917 – against the bitter protest of such devoted pupils as Randolph Bourne. The cast of his

published in 1935, Dewey – noting the historical absence in America of the Benthamite, as opposed to Lockean, moment of what he took to be the historic liberal legacy – forthrightly denounced laissez-faire ortho-doxies as 'apologetics for the existing economic regime' that masked its 'brutalities and inequities'. He went on, writing at the height of the New Deal: 'The control of the means of production by the few in legal possession operates as a standing agency of coercion of the many' – such coercion, backed by physical violence, being 'especially recurrent' in the US where in times of potential social change, 'our verbal and sentimental worship of the Constitution, with its guarantee of civil liberties of expression, publication and assemblage, readily goes over-board'. Dewey saw only one historical resolution for the tradition he continued to champion: 'The cause of liberalism will be lost,' he declared, 'if it is not prepared to socialize the forces of production now at hand', even – if necessary – resorting to 'intelligent force' to 'subdue and disarm the recalcitrant minority'. The aims of classical liberalism now required the achievement of socialism. For 'the socialized econ-omy is the means of free individual development.'[11]

It is timely to recall these illustrious examples today, because after a major interval we are seeing a significant new range of attempts to synthesize liberal and socialist traditions. The later work of C.B. Macpherson, in particular *The Life and Times of Liberal Democracy*, comes immediately to mind. The studied ambiguity of John Rawls's *Theory of Justice* can be – by some, has been – read as laying philosophical foundations for a similar project. More express in inten-tion is Robert Dahl, recently advocate not only of political pluralism but also of economic democracy. A younger generation of Anglo–American writers has produced a series of works, differing in temper and purpose, but comparable in political inspiration: David Held's *Models of Democracy* and John Dunn's *Politics of Socialism in Eng-land*, Joshua Cohen and Joel Rogers's *On Democracy* and Samuel

---

German Philosophy and Politics (1915) in many ways recalls that of Thomas Mann's antithetical *Reflections of an Unpolitical Man* (1918) on the other side. In it Dewey, drawing on Heine's famous forebodings, sought to link German Idealism to German militarism – as against an American Experimentalism proper to US democracy. This *Kulturpatriotismus* was in some degree qualified by Dewey's concluding repudiation of the whole 'philosophy of isolated national sovereignty' and call for the creation of an international legislature beyond it. In the twenties, Dewey's extensive travels outside America contributed substantially to the broadening of his political sympathies.

11. *Liberalism and Social Action*, in John Dewey, *The Later Works, 1925–1953*, Vol. XI, Carbondale–Edwardsville, Illinois 1987, pp. 22, 46; 61–62, 63.

Bowles and Herbert Gintis's *Capitalism and Democracy* in the USA. In France, Pierre Rosanvallon, among others, seeking to recover liberal traditions for the Second Left, has called for a reconsideration of the modern relevance, not just of de Tocqueville, but of Guizot too.[12]

I   Bobbio: Background, Career

In this current landscape there is one figure of outstanding moral and political significance, the Italian philosopher Norberto Bobbio. Although perhaps the most influential political theorist of his own country, with a wide audience in Spain and Latin America as well, Bobbio has hitherto been relatively little known in the Anglo-Saxon world. It is to be hoped that the recent translation into English of two of his principal works – *Which Socialism?* and *The Future of Democracy* – will alter this situation.[13] Any reflection on the relations between liberalism and socialism must take central stock of Bobbio's *oeuvre*. To understand this, however, something needs to be said of the life-experience behind it.

Norberto Bobbio was born in 1909 in Piedmont, and grew up in what he has described as a 'bourgeois-patriotic milieu', between 'those who had resisted fascism and those who had yielded to it'. He fell

---

12. Note the clustering of dates: John Rawls, *A Theory of Justice*, Cambridge, Mass. 1971; C.B. Macpherson, *The Life and Times of Liberal Democracy*, Oxford 1977 – then: Joshua Cohen and Joel Rogers, *On Democracy*, New York 1983; John Dunn, *The Politics of Socialism*, Cambridge 1984; Robet Dahl, *A Preface to Economic Democracy*, Berkeley 1985; Pierre Rosanvallon, *Le Moment Guizot*, Paris 1985; Samuel Bowles and Herbert Gintis, *Democracy and Capitalism*, New York 1986; David Held, *Models of Democracy*, Cambridge 1987.

13. Polity Press, London 1987; each with a fine introduction by Richard Bellamy. Publisher and editor are to be congratulated on the books' appearance. Bellamy discusses Bobbio further in his *Modern Italian Social Theory*, London 1987, pp. 141–156. The original Italian editions were *Quale Socialismo?*, Turin 1976, and *Il Future della Demorazia*, Turin 1983. The English translation of the former includes further essays not collected in the Italian original. References below to the English editions are abbreviated to WS and FD; the translations have sometimes been modified. Bobbio's full *oeuvre* is enormous. Carlo Violi, *Norberto Bobbio: A Critical Bibliography*, Milan 1984, published in honour of his 75th birthday, contains over 650 items – themselves amounting to no more than some sixty per cent of his production. Much of his work has been in the theory of law, which will scarcely be mentioned below.

I would like to thank Fernando Quesada and his colleagues at the Instituto de Filosofía in Madrid, whose seminar on modern theorists of democracy in 1986 originally prompted reflection on Bobbio.

initially under the influence of Gentile, philosopher of the regime, and did not reject Mussolini's order at the outset.[14] His early training was in political philosophy and jurisprudence at the University of Turin between 1928 and 1931. At that time, he recalls, the names of Marx or Marxism were unknown in the lecture-room – less officially banned than regarded as intellectually dead and buried – and Bobbio's own outlook was largely formed by Croce's historicism, like that of many of his generation. At the same time, his teacher in the philosophy of law, Gioele Solari, sought to develop a 'social idealism' also inspired by Hegel, but one more progressive than Crocean doctrine in political sympathy. In due course, after doctoral work on German phenomenology, Bobbio came by the mid thirties to form part of a Turinese intellectual milieu that was strongly liberal in conviction – descending directly from the memory of Piero Gobetti. This ambience provided the Piedmontese nucleus of *Giustizia e Libertà*, the anti-fascist organization founded by the Rosselli brothers in France. When its network fell to a police sweep in 1935, Bobbio was briefly arrested as a sympathizer. After his release, he taught at the universities of Camerino and then Siena before the Second World War. There, he joined the Liberal-Socialist movement formed in 1937 by Guido Calogero and Aldo Capitini, two philosophers at the Scuola Normale in Pisa. In 1940, he moved to the University of Padua, which was to become the heart of the Resistance in the Veneto. In the autumn of 1942, he helped found the *Partito d'Azione*, the political wing of the Resistance into which *Giustizia e Libertà* and the Liberal-Socialist movement converged. Now a member of the Committee of National Liberation in the Veneto, Bobbio was arrested a second time by Mussolini's regime in December 1943; he was released three months later.[15]

The following year, while fighting still raged in Northern Italy, Bobbio published a short polemical work entitled *The Philosophy of Decadentism – A Study of Existentialism*.[16] This text, a vehement denunciation of the aristocratism and individualism of Heidegger and Jaspers in the name of a democratic and social humanism, makes clear the impact on him of the labour movement that was the leading force in the Northern Resistance. Bobbio was later to explain: 'We abandoned

---

14. 'Cultura vecchia e politica nuova', in *Politica e Cultura*, Turin 1955, p. 198.

15. See *Italia Civile. Ritratti e Testimonianze*, Florence 1986 (re-edition), pp. 70–71, 95–96, 170, 276–77; *Italia Fedele. Il Mondo de Gobetti*, Florence 1986, pp. 157–58; *Maestri e Compagni*, Florence 1984, p. 191. These three volumes of 'portraits and testimonies' contain much of Bobbio's most personal writing.

16. An English translation was published by Oxford University Press in 1948.

decadentism, which was the ideological expression of a class in decline, because we were participating in the labour and in the hopes of a new class.' 'I am convinced,' he went on, 'that if we had not learnt from Marxism to see history from the point of view of the oppressed, gaining a new and immense perspective on the human world, there would have been no salvation for us.'[17] In speaking thus, Bobbio was describing a widespread reaction among the pleiad of younger intellectuals who had rallied to the *Partito d'Azione*. He himself was 'one of those who believed in the henceforward irresistible strength of the Communist Party'[18] and looked forward to common action between workers and intellectuals for a radical reform of the structures of the Italian state.

The avowed goal of such militants in the *Partito d'Azione* was precisely to realize a synthesis of liberalism and socialism. Since these had long been joint objects of fascist imprecations, it seemed logical to many of its thinkers to vindicate them together. In their eyes this would be the specific vocation of the *Partito d'Azione*, distinguishing it from the traditional parties of the working class. After the Liberation, however, in spite of its distinguished military role during the Resistance and its rich intellectual endowment, the party failed to win a durable position on the Italian political scene. After three years, it disappeared. No one has described the reasons for its eventual dissolution better than Bobbio himself, who – a decade later – wrote: 'We had clear and firm moral positions, but our political positions were subtle and dialectical – and therefore mobile and unstable, continually in search of an insertion in Italian political life. But we remained rootless in the Italian society of those years. Towards whom should we turn? Moralists above all, we advocated a complete renovation of Italian political life, beginning with its customs. But we thought that for such a renovation there was no need of a revolution. We were consequently rejected by the bourgeoisie, which wanted no renovation, and by the larger part of the proletariat, which did not want to renounce revolution. We were thus left *tête-à-tête* with the petty bourgeoisie, which was the class least inclined to follow us – and we were not followed. In truth it was a rather painful spectacle to see us – the *enfants terribles* of Italian culture – thrown together with the most fearful and feeble layers of Italian society, minds in perpetual motion trying to make contact with the most slothful and withered mentalities, provokers of scandal winking complicitly at the most timorous and conformist of citizens,

---

17. 'Libertà e potere', in *Politica e Cultura*, p. 281.
18. *Politicà e Cultura*, p. 199.

these super-intransigent moralists preaching to specialists in compromises. During the whole period in which the *Partito d'Azione* – leaders without an army – was active as a political movement, the Italian petty bourgeoisie – an army without leaders – was indifferentist. You can imagine whether a marriage between the two was feasible.'[19]

This judgement – hard and caustic – on the experience of the *Partito d'Azione* no doubt reflects the state of mind in which Bobbio withdrew from direct political involvement after the party had dissolved itself in 1947, and he took up a chair in the philosophy of law at the University of Turin. But although devoting himself mainly to work in his academic field, he did not do so exclusively. For, in the following years, he wrote a series of eloquent articles criticizing the polarization of Italian political and intellectual life during the High Cold War. In them he courteously yet pointedly took issue with the ideologies of both official communism and anti-communism, the Congress for Cultural Freedom (from its inception), and the Partisans of Peace. His principal interlocutor, however, was the PCI. Bobbio's aim was to dissuade it from unconditional allegiance to a Soviet state that he numbered – 'without being scandalized by the fact, since I hold that it reflects a hard historical necessity' – among totalitarian regimes;[20] and to persuade it of the permanent importance of liberal political institutions such as existed in the West. It is difficult to think of many other writers in Europe who achieved a tone of comparable civility and equanimity at that time.[21] The effect of these interventions was marginal until after the death of Stalin, when the changes in Russia started to loosen the ideological corsets of the Italian Communist movement a little. It was then that Bobbio published, in 1954, an article entitled 'Democracy and Dictatorship', which had a more significant outcome. Its theme was a serene but severe critique of the traditional Marxist conceptions of these two terms, insisting on the historic underestimation by Marxism of the value of the liberal legacies of the separation and limitation of powers, yet predicting that the PCI would evolve towards a greater

---

19. 'Inchiesta sul Partito d'Azione', *Il Ponte*, VII, No. 8, August 1951, p. 906. Paradoxically Togliatti's retrospective judgement of the party, in response to the same questionnaire, was less severe – for he could write: 'In essence there were only two great currents of resistance and effective, durable struggle against fascist tyranny: one was led by us Communists, the other by the Action movement, and it is not even certain that ours was always and everywhere the stronger.' *Il Ponte*, VII, No. 7, July 1951, p. 770.

20. *Politica e Cultura*, p. 48 – a volume which includes the principal interventions of this period: 'Invito al colloquio', 'Politica culturale e politica della cultura', 'Difesa della libertà', 'Pace e propaganda di pace', 'Libertà dell'arte e politica culturale', 'Intellettuali e vita politica in Italia', 'Spirito critico e impotenza politica'.

21. Both Russell and Dewey lost their heads at the onset of the Cold War.

understanding and acceptance of these, 'essential for its cohabitation with the Western world', in the years to come.[22]

This summons provoked an extended response from the leading Communist philosopher of the time, Galvano Della Volpe, who reproached Bobbio with regressing to the positions of the moderate liberalism of Benjamin Constant in the early nineteenth century, and maintained that Marxism was by contrast the heir of the more radical democratic tradition of Jean-Jacques Rousseau, theorist of a *libertas maior* as against Constant's *libertas minor*. Bobbio in turn replied to Della Volpe with a much longer essay than his original article, 'On Modern Liberty Compared with That of Posterity', in which he developed his argument and urged, in a friendly but firm tone, the Communists to beware of a 'too ardent progressivism' that risked sacrificing the conquests of an existing liberal democracy to the installation of a future proletarian dictatorship in the name of a perfected ulterior democracy. The weight of this second intervention was such that Palmiro Togliatti himself felt it necessary to respond to its arguments, under a pseudonym in *Rinascita*.[23] In his rejoinder to Togliatti's counter-arguments, Bobbio concluded with an autobiographical evocation and credo. Without a profound engagement with Marxism after the Liberation, he wrote, 'we would either have sought a haven in the refuge of interior life, or would have put ourselves at the service of the bosses. But, among those who were saved from these two fates, there were only a few of us who preserved a small bag in which, before throwing ourselves into the sea, we deposited for safekeeping the most salutary fruits of the European intellectual tradition, the value of enquiry, the ferment of doubt, a willingness to dialogue, a spirit of criticism, moderation of judgement, philological scruple, a sense of the complexity of things. Many, too many, deprived themselves of this baggage: they either abandoned it, considering it a useless weight; or they never possessed it, throwing themselves into the waters before having the time to acquire it. I do not reproach them; but I prefer the company of the others. Indeed, I suspect that this company is destined to grow, as the years bring wisdom and events shed new light on things.'[24]

The quiet confidence of the final sentence was going to prove

---

22. *Politica e Cultura*, p. 149.

23. Ibid., p. 194; the title of Bobbio's reply was, of course, a deliberately ironic reprise of Constant's famous essay of 1818, 'De la Liberté des Anciens Comparée à celle des Modernes'.

24. *Politica e Cultura*, pp. 281–82.

justified, if only in the long run – as no doubt Bobbio intended it. In the short run, the episode of his debate with Della Volpe and Togliatti had little major repercussion in Italian political culture, remaining relatively neglected for the next twenty years. It was not a prelude to any immediate wider audience for Bobbio, who continued to work essentially within the university. In 1964, the ruling Christian Democratic Party embarked on a coalition with the Italian Socialist Party for the first time, once the latter had broken its links with the Communist Party. For six years, Italy was governed by the formula of the so-called Centre–Left. Much later, Bobbio would describe this experience as, for better or worse, 'the happiest moment of Italian political development' in the post-war period.[25] One may wonder whether Bobbio really felt much enthusiasm at the time for the lacklustre governments of those years. But one thing is certain. In 1968, Bobbio for the first time entered the recently merged Unitary Socialist Party – a reunification of Nenni's PSI and Saragat's Social-Democratic PSDI. What ensued? A massive popular upheaval broke out in the universities and factories of the country – the famous Italian 1968–69. The vote of the newly unified PSU – instead of increasing – fell precipitously. The Italian middle classes, taking fright at the new student and worker militancy, shifted rightwards and the Centre–Left rapidly expired. All Bobbio's subsequent references to 1968–69 are tinged with reserve or bitterness. At the national level, his political calculation had been brusquely swept aside. At the same time, he had to confront the turbulence and disorder of the student rebellion in his own arena of professional activity.[26] He did not enjoy the experience, any more than the majority of his colleagues. The student assemblies of the time, in particular, seem to have shocked him a great deal, leaving disagreeable memories which can be read between the lines of the polemic which was going, in a subsequent phase of Italian politics, to make him a central figure of national debates for the first time.

This happened – could only happen – after the ebbing of the great social movements of the late sixties and early seventies. In late 1973, the Italian Communist Party proclaimed the goal of a strategic connubium with Christian Democracy – the so-called Historic Compromise – and the following year announced its general theoretical conversion to the principles of Eurocommunism. Twenty years after his debate with

---

25. 'La Crise Permanente', *Pouvoirs*, No. 18, 1981, p. 6.
26. One of his own sons was moreover a leader of *Lotta Continua*, of which he later became the historian. See Luigi Bobbio, *Lotta Continua – Storia di una Organizzazione Rivoluzionaria*, Rome 1979, a dignified and thoughtful retrospect.

Togliatti, Bobbio's predictions were now fully vindicated. A political terrain finally favourable for his theses on democracy and dictatorship, liberalism and Marxism, had opened up. Taking advantage of the opportunity, Bobbio wrote in 1975 two key essays in *Mondoperaio*, the theoretical journal of the Socialist Party – the first on the lack of any political theory in Marxism, the second on the absence of any alternative to representative democracy as the political form of a free society, with a clear warning against what he saw as the dangers of delusions to the contrary in the revolutionary process then under way in Portugal.[27] This time, Bobbio's interventions aroused an enormous interest in the Italian public, and a large number of politicians and intellectuals replied to them, from both the PCI and the PSI. At the end of an extended debate, Bobbio could – a year later – congratulate himself on the consensus which he thought he could now discern around his basic emphases. By 1976, the PCI had formally renounced the Leninism he had once criticized, and was about to make striking electoral gains that he could welcome. The PSI, too, was adapting its traditions. With some satisfaction, Bobbio noted that Pietro Nenni himself was using his arguments officially from the tribune of the Fortieth Congress of the Socialist Party.[28] In 1978, fortified by this unfamiliar prestige, he collaborated in the drafting of the new programme of the PSI, defending it against those who taxed it with being very little Marxist. In the wake of this influence, Bobbio became a major columnist on national politics for *La Stampa* – his first regular journalistic practice since the Liberation.

These were also the years which witnessed the rise of Bettino Craxi to the apex of the Socialist Party – initially in the name of a moral and political renovation of Italian Socialism, which would put it at the head of struggles for a better civic and secular democracy in Italy. Bobbio, who like many in his party was suspicious of the corporatist logic of the Historic Compromise, seems to have shared the hopes of a libertarian remoulding of the PSI, and its potential role in a national renewal. Disappointment was not long in coming. The governments of 'National Solidarity' yielded not a harvest of reforms, but the tares of terrorism. Parliamentary instability and corruption did not diminish: by 1981, Bobbio was writing that for the purposes of understanding the realities of national politics 'the yellowed map of the Italian Constitu-

---

27. 'Esiste una dottrina marxista dello stato?' and 'Quali alternative alla democrazia rappresentativa?' reprinted in *Quale Socialismo?*, Turin 1976, pp. 21–65, and now in WS, pp. 47–84.
28. *Quale Socialismo?*, pp. 66–68; WS, pp. 86–87.

tion' could be thrown away.[29] The PSI under Craxi was becoming an increasingly cynical and authoritarian machine, subordinated to a cult of the Leader decked out with a 'decisionist' rhetoric borrowed at one remove from Carl Schmitt. The *pentapartito* regimes of the eighties, jumbling DC, PSC, PSDI, Republicans and Liberals together in 'an unwonted and hitherto unthinkable combination of the Centre–Right and the Centre–Left', he has regarded as designed to exclude any more progressive alternative, under US veto.[30] Today, Bobbio's position has once again become that of a more or less independent *franc-tireur*, today a Life Senator nominated by the President, a kind of honorific Italian peer, the moral conscience of the Italian political order.

II Complexion, Location

Such has been, approximately, the *cursus vitae* of Norberto Bobbio – a life he once called 'a continual, slow, difficult apprenticeship: so difficult it has nearly always left me exhausted and unsatisfied, so slow that it is still not completed'.[31] What is its particular historical significance? Within the line of thinkers who have sought to reconcile liberalism and socialism, Bobbio differs from his principal predecessors in a number of important respects. One of these is simply the field of his special interests. Bobbio is a philosopher with a wide formation, who measured himself against the phenomenology of Husserl and Scheler before the war, the existentialism of Heidegger and Jaspers during the war, and the positivism of Carnap and Ayer after the war. His own epistemological preferences have always been empirical and scientific – going clean against the grain of what he dubs the 'Italian Ideology', congenitally speculative and idealist in bias.[32] In that respect he recalls

---

29. 'La Crise Permanente', p. 12. Given the importance Bobbio has always attached to constitutional norms, the judgement could scarcely be more drastic. Twenty years earlier he had co-authored a textbook of civic education expounding the Constitution for use in Italian high schools: Norberto Bobbio and Franco Pierandrei, *Introduzione alla Costituzione*, Bari 1960.

30. 'a situation over which it is useless to drape a pious veil': 'Introduzione', *Il Sistema Politico Italiano tra Crisi e Innovazione*, Milan 1984, p. 21.

31. *Italia Civile*, p. 10.

32. *Profilo Ideologico del Novecento Italiano*, Turin 1986, pp. 3–4. This work is Bobbio's major exercise in intellectual history: a brilliant, if often revealingly selective, survey.

Mill, Russell or Dewey. Unlike them, however, Bobbio is not an original philosopher of major stature; still less an economist, as were Mill and Hobson. But if he has made no comparable contribution to logic or epistemology, ethics or economics, his grasp of the principal traditions of Western political thought – from Plato to Aristotle to Aquinas or Althusius, Pufendorf and Grotius to Spinoza and Locke, Rousseau or Madison to Burke and Hegel, Constant and de Tocqueville to Weber or Kelsen – is greater, not just in point of time but in scope and depth. Bobbio's command of political philosophy is backed by a training in constitutional law and familiarity with political science. One element of this professional engagement is of especial consequence for the character of Bobbio's work. He is much more at home with the history of Marxism than any of his immediate forerunners. His philological ease with the various traditions of historical materialism is not uniform. Marx as a classic he knows well; but if he is familiar with texts of Kautsky and Lenin, it is in a more superficial way, and when he speaks – for example – of Gramsci he can commit surprising errors. Paradoxically, however, this limitation can be deemed virtually an advantage in the context of the dominant culture of the Italian Left up to the seventies – a culture all but suffocated by its too exclusive and internal reference to Marxism, leading to just those abuses of the 'principle of authority' that Bobbio was to single out for criticism.[33] His knapsack of non- or pre-Marxism, of which he spoke to Togliatti, kept him far from that, as did his transparently tolerant, sceptical and democratic temperament.

Another difference is that Bobbio's political coordinates are in some ways more complex than those of his principal predecessors. In effect, he stands at the crossroads of three major contending traditions. By primordial formation and conviction he is a liberal. But Italian liberal-ism has always been a phenomenon apart, within the European set. In England, its nineteenth-century homeland, liberalism achieved a pure consummation in the minimal state and free trade of the Gladstonian epoch; thereafter – its historical vocation as it were fulfilled – it had little more to do than to pass over into its brief social epilogue under Asquith and Lloyd George, and expire as a political force. In France, on the other hand, liberalism as a doctrine was an expression of the Restoration, theorizing the virtues of a censitary monarchy; hegemonic under the Orleanist regime, mimicked under the Second Empire, it was

---

33. *Quale Socialismo?*, p. 25; WS, p. 51.

thereby too compromised to survive the advent of a Third Republic based on untampered manhood suffrage. In Germany, notoriously, National Liberalism capitulated to Prussian conservatism under Bismarck, abandoning parliamentary principles for adhesion to military success against Austria; and after political abdication, it fell into economic disarray when free trade was subsequently discarded by the Second Reich. In Italy, however, by contrast with Germany, national unification was achieved not over the body but under the very banner of Liberalism. Moreover the liberalism that emerged victorious from the Risorgimento had a double legitimation: it was both the constitutional ideology of the Piedmontese Moderates, codifying the structure of their dominance under the monarchy, and the secular definition of an Italian state created against the will of the Roman Church.

This singular success acted as if to render superfluous for a long time the fulfilment of a normal liberal agenda in Italy. The name of liberalism was so thoroughly identified with the construction of the nation and the cause of the lay state that its leading statesmen and thinkers felt little pressure to improve electoral honesty or to further political liberty. This was the country where the oligarchic and manipulative regime of Giovanni Giolitti, with its large dose of repressive violence and cooptive corruption, defined itself as Liberal down to the Great War; where the major theoretical mind of economic liberalism, Vilfredo Pareto, called for a white terror to crush the workers' movement and sweep away parliamentary democracy; where the greatest Italian philosopher, Benedetto Croce, paladin of his own ethical liberalism, exalted the massacres of the First World War, and approved Mussolini's investiture in power. Yet it was, amongst other things, deformations like these which ironically helped to preserve the vigour and future of Italian liberalism well into the twentieth century. In no country was the fate of liberalism so polymorphous and paradoxical. For precisely because its classical ideals were at once so extolled and burlesqued in Italy, they retained a radical normative power they had lost elsewhere, and would prove capable of entering into the most unexpected and combustible patterns in opposition to the established order. Bobbio is himself a testament to the ambiguity of this legacy. He treats the figures of Giolitti and Pareto with respect and admiration; that of Croce at times with near veneration.[34] The imprint of Crocean

---

34. 'One of the most complex and inspired and meditated visions of history of this century': *Italia Civile*, p. 92.

historicism, in particular, is very strong on one side of his thinking. Yet he also stresses the indifference of Croce's philosophical teleology to every institutional value of the political liberalism he holds dear, its all but complete irrelevance to the practical agenda of a modern democracy – which in his view has required an atemporal natural-rights foundation that was anathema to Croce.[35] For Bobbio's own liberalism is essentially a doctrine of constitutional guarantees for individual freedom and civic rights in the empirical tradition of Mill, which he associates especially with England; and his greater heroes in Italy have been those thinkers who could be regarded as close to it – the less representative figures of Carlo Cattaneo, who defended Milan against the Austrians in 1848, and Luigi Einaudi and Gaetano Salvemini, who did not truckle to fascism in 1924.

Now in itself, of course, such an outlook – however eloquently expressed, as it is by Bobbio – has little that is original in the twentieth century. The whole interest of Bobbio's thought, however, derives from the confrontation of this classic political liberalism, mediated through the distinctive Italian experience, with two other theoretical traditions. The first of these is socialism; and here too the Italian context was formative. Bobbio, when he came to the Left at the end of the thirties, entered an intellectual and political field that was already uniquely – so to speak – cross-pollinated. For in the kaleidoscopic conditions of Italian society after the First World War, in which so many social and ideological elements were shaken into unfamiliar patterns, liberalism did not fade but took on some new and startling colours. Italy produced in these years what is still the only full-scale scholarly study of European liberalism over the previous century, Guido de Ruggiero's *Storia del Liberalismo Europeo* – a work not only of comparative historical synthesis but also of embattled political engagement, completed as fascism consolidated itself in power. De Ruggiero, a historicist with a marked respect for the German contribution of Kant and Hegel to the European idea of a *Rechtsstaat*, was himself from the political centre. Yet he could write that 'if we remember the mean and inhuman harshness displayed by early nineteenth-century Liberals towards the urgent social problems of their times, we cannot deny that socialism, for all the defects of its ideology, has been an immense advance on the earlier individualism, and, from the point of view of history, has been

---

35. See 'Benedetto Croce e il liberalismo', in *Politica e Cultura*, pp. 253–268.

justified in attempting to submerge it beneath its own social flood.'[36] Among a younger generation, further to the Left, the gravitational force of an insurgent working class – and sometimes of the Russian Revolution beyond it – produced an astonishing array of different attempts to weld proletarian and liberal values into a new political force. The first and most famous of these was the programme for a 'Liberal Revolution' of Piero Gobetti, who published Mill in Italian and upheld free trade, yet admired Lenin and collaborated with Gramsci in *L'Ordine Nuovo*, before launching his own *Rivoluzione Liberale* in 1922. Gobetti's liberalism was one that called on workers to conquer power from below and become the new rulers of society, as the only class capable of transforming it. Seeing itself as revolutionary in the full sense of the word, it shunned Italian socialism as too reformist, and expressed every sympathy for Russian communism.

Gobetti died in France in 1926. Two years earlier, his journal had published an essay by a young socialist critical of the traditions of the PSI, Carlo Rosselli. In confinement under Mussolini, in 1928 Rosselli wrote a book entitled *Socialismo Liberale* – before escaping to France, where he founded the movement of *Giustizia e Libertà* the next year. Rosselli's project for a synthesis came from the opposite direction to that of Gobetti. Admiring what he thought he knew of British labourism, he sought to purge socialism of its Marxist heritage and Soviet incarnation, and to recover for it the traditions of liberal democracy he believed were fundamental conquests of modern civilization. Rosselli and his brother were assassinated by fascist thugs in 1937. In that year, Guido Calogero and Aldo Capitini created a distinct current they called *Liberal-socialismo* in Pisa. The slight nuance of its name indicated a position intermediate between that of Rosselli and Gobetti. Capitini, in particular, at once more religious in outlook and more sympathetic to the Soviet experience, aimed at a future social order that would be both

---

36. *The History of European Liberalism*, Oxford 1927, p. 391; in a section entitled 'The Liberalism of Practical Socialism'. Bobbio's own feelings about de Ruggiero's work have been mixed. Confessing that it was once dear to him, he reproached it after the War with overestimating the value of German liberalism in general, and uncritically exalting the contribution of Hegel in particular – while, together with Croce, underestimating the achievements of English liberalism: 'What [the Italian idealists] could not perceive in the homeland of Milton and Mill, they imagined they had found in the country of Fichte and Bismarck': *Politica e Cultura*, pp. 253–56. Notwithstanding these objections, a number of Bobbio's own themes were anticipated by de Ruggiero, who during the Resistance was himself active in the formation and leadership of the *Partito d'Azione*.

'post-Christian' and 'post-communist', combining maximum legal and cultural liberty with maximum economic socialization. Calogero was closer to Rosselli, in a more philosophical idiom, rejecting Russia as a 'totalitarian' state and arguing against any general socialization of the means of production. When the two movements flowed into the *Partito d'Azione* in 1942, his advocacy of a mixed economy as the appropriate medium of a reconciliation of freedom and justice prevailed, and became part of the formal programme of the party. But it was contested within it by another current that described its goal – such were the possibilities of the time, and the country – as Liberal Communism. Its principal theorists, Augusto Monti and Silvio Trentin, were Gobetti's most direct descendants. From within *Giustizia e Libertà* in the thirties, Trentin had rejected the idea of a two-sector economy, and insisted on the need for a revolutionary socialization of property relations, while at the same time calling for a decentralized federative state – along Proudhonian lines – to safeguard liberty against the dangers of political despotism once capitalism was overthrown. For these thinkers, a communist revolution was anyway probable in post-war Italy, and the task was to think through the forms of the democratic revolution to come afterwards, that would historically 'right' it.[37]

Liberal Revolution, Socialist Liberalism, Liberal Socialism, Liberal Communism: has any other nation thrown up a range of such hybrids? They were possible in Italy because there had been no time for either bourgeois democracy or social democracy to set after the First World War, and establish a stable framework of demarcations for politics under capitalism. A decade of fascism meant that liberalism was still a peculiarly unconsummated force, while socialism became a relatively undivided one; and that together they confronted an enemy against whom resistance could in the last resort only be insurrectionary. In these conditions, the Italian Resistance could display every kind of generous syncretism. Bobbio is an heir of this exceptional moment, which was – he has often explained – the central political experience that shaped him.

Personally and morally closer to Capitini, his practical preferences were those of Calogero, although in his case they were combined with a lucid sense of the likely strength of the PCI after Liberation that would

---

37. For this intricate history, see Bobbio's several accounts in *Italia Fedele*, pp. 9–31; *Italia Civile*, pp. 45–48, 249–266; *Maestri e Compagni*, pp. 239–299; *Profilo Ideologico*, pp. 151–163.

lead him – more or less inescapably – to a much deeper engagement with Marxist culture. Once a liberal, Bobbio in these years became a socialist. But like his Anglo-Saxon predecessors, he was not only a liberal before being a socialist, but preeminently remained one after being so. That liberalism derived from a profound commitment to the constitutional state, rather than from any particular attachment to the free market. It was political, not economic – a difference formulable more sharply in Italian than other languages, in the distinction (made most famously by Croce) between *liberalismo* and *liberismo*.[38] Hence it could permit an egalitarian passage to socialism. Explaining his own conception of the relation between the two, Bobbio wrote much later: 'I personally hold the socialist ideal higher than the liberal.' For, he argued, the former comprises the latter, but not vice versa. 'While equality cannot be defined in terms of liberty, there is at least one case in which liberty can be defined in terms of equality' – namely 'that condition in which all members of a society consider themselves free because they are equal in power'.[39] Socialism is therefore the more inclusive term.

The logic of these convictions recalls Mill or Russell, Hobson or Dewey. What differentiates Bobbio's version of them is the historical experience out of which they spring. Unlike these earlier exemplars, Bobbio's bridge from liberalism to socialism was not a relatively isolated intellectual episode – it belonged to a collective movement that played a major political role in a time of civil and national war. The struggles, the passions, the memories behind it are far thicker. But just because these were so much more practically embodied, they were also more subject to the verdict of results. For Bobbio there was only one real, new ideology of the Italian Resistance – that of the *Partito*

---

38. Croce's essay *Liberalismo e Liberismo*, written in 1928 and directed against Einaudi, argued that liberty was a moral ideal compatible with a number of economic regimes – hence not to be identified with mere competition and free trade; a decade later he used the same arguments against Calogero to reject the notion of any possible synthesis between liberalism and socialism – 'liberty suffers no adjectives'. In 1941 he refused to join the *Partito d'Azione* because it advocated distribution of land to the peasants in the South. See Giovanni Di Luna, *Storia del Partito d'Azione*, Milan 1982, p. 25.

39. *La Ideologie e il Potere in Crisi*, Florence 1981, pp. 29–30. This volume is essentially a collection of Bobbio's articles in *La Stampa* between 1976 and 1980, texts in which he says – justly – that he 'nearly always tried to link problems of the day to general themes of political philosophy or political science.' They form a remarkable example of a kind of public prose that has all but disappeared in the European newspaper world.

d'Azione, which he terms 'the party of liberal socialists'.[40] His nostalgia for the time of hope it represented recurs again and again in his texts. But it is always accompanied by the irony we have already seen. Liberal socialism was an 'elite formula', whose 'doctrinaire philosophical positions' were 'doomed to defeat by great, real political forces that were moved by very concrete interests and powerful drives rather than by perfect syllogisms'.[41]

The two principal such forces were, of course, Christian Democracy and Communism. Bobbio has never had much to say about the DC. It was the PCI that dominated his post-war horizon, in dialogue or polemic. The unusual political tenor of his exchanges with it, for the years of the Cold War, has been noted. These debates mark a historic divide that separates, in a fundamental way, his conjugation of liberalism and socialism from that of his predecessors. They were typically formed within a comfortably established liberalism and then reacted against its outrages or its failures – vindictive repression, imperialist war, mass unemployment – by seeking a socialism beyond it. Bobbio, by contrast, became a liberal and a socialist in something like a single impulse in the struggle against fascism, and then reacted against the crimes of established socialism – the system of Stalin's tyranny. To register this difference is not to minimize the seriousness of the engagement of his two closest forerunners, in their time, with the revolutionary experiences of the twentieth century. Russell wrote the most penetrating – often uncannily prophetic – study of the Bolshevik regime of the Civil War period by any foreign observer, after his visit to the USSR in 1920.[42] Dewey arrived to work in China a few days before the May 4th Movement, where he upheld the cause of the Canton

---

40. *Italia Fedele*, p. 248. There is a historical ellipsis in the description which suggests how important that synthesis was to him, to the point of a certain optical illusion. For the *Partito d'Azione* also contained a significant force that had little to do with socialism – drawn from banking and business circles and led by Ugo La Malfa, the post-war architect of a Republican Party that was to be politically close to enlightened industrial capital. Bobbio's memory of the *Partito d'Azione* regularly passes it over. In fact it was La Malfa's group, centred on the Banca Commerciale, which actually took the initiative in creating the *Partito d'Azione* – accepting the programmatic ideals of the Liberal Socialists only reluctantly and tactically; and which also survived the eventual break-up of the party most effectively. See the excellent recent history by Giovanni De Luna, *Storia del Partito d'Azione*, pp. 35–42, 347–365.

41. *Italia Fedele*, p. 248.

42. *The Practice and Theory of Bolshevism* (London 1920) is an astonishing text in the number and sharpness of its premonitions. Russell foresaw the likelihood of a

government, attacking the role of British and Japanese imperialism in the country. He subsequently travelled to Turkey at the invitation of Kemal; to Mexico in the time of Calles, where he saw the realities of US imperialism – at work too in the Nicaragua of Sandino; and to Russia before the onset of collectivization. He wrote with sympathy about all of these.[43] In the late thirties, he famously and courageously helped to expose the Moscow Trials.

Nevertheless, such engagements were still in some sense honourable episodes rather than central preoccupations of men for whom, by background and native context, modern revolutionary movements inevitably remained somewhat remote. Bobbio, fresh from a Resistance movement whose leading force was the PCI, only a border away from the Yugoslav Revolution and little more from the newly created People's Democracies, in a country whose internal politics were a direct stake of the conflict between West and East, was in quite another historical situation. His engagement with socialism was necessarily of another order: at once far tenser and more intimate.

But there is also another element in the characteristic vision of Bobbio which separates him from his predecessors. One of the most striking common traits of the outlook of Mill, Russell and Dewey was their faith in the social power of education. The prospects of socialism hinged, for Mill, on a gradual cultural elevation of the working classes which only long-term processes of education could accomplish – till then it would always be premature. Dewey's major influence in America derived, of course, from the Laboratory School he founded in Chicago, developing a rational–instrumental (as distinct from romantic–expressive) variant of progressive education; his best-seller in the US always remained *Democracy and Education*. Russell combined a joint pedagogic enterprise at Beacon Hill with extensive advocacy of its

---

nationalist and bureaucratic involution of the Bolshevik state, the future scale of its industrialization, and the probable limits to Third International strategies based on Russian experience in Western Europe; he even glimpsed something like a far-off balance of nuclear terror. His verdict on the Soviet experience is never quite coherent, and he had no really credible alternative for the labour movement in the West. But these failings weigh little against the achievement of the whole.

43. Dewey described his time in China, on returning, as the most intellectually profitable of his life; it can be seen as one kind of watershed in his development. For his responses to the upheavals of the twenties, see his *Impressions of Soviet Russia and the Revolutionary World: Mexico–China–Turkey*, New York 1929, especially the chapter 'Imperialism Is Easy', pp. 181ff. Russell crossed paths with Dewey in Hunan and Peking in 1921: see his own work *The Problem of China*, London 1922, p. 224.

principles in *Education and the Social Order* and other writings.[44] In all three cases, the sovereign importance ascribed to education was linked to a particular conception of the intellectual as potentially exemplary educator.

Bobbio, on the other hand, has expressly rejected any such role for intellectuals – deeming it, indeed, the characteristic mirage of pre-war Italian thinkers, uniting such diverse figures as Croce, Salvemini, Gentile, Gobetti, Prezzolini and Gramsci himself in a common delusion that their task was to 'educate the nation'.[45] His sceptical reserve towards programmes of 'intellectual and moral reform', or overly ingenuous hopes in *Bildung*, is conversely accompanied by a marked respect for that tradition of 'political realism' which has been especially concerned with the role of power and violence in history. Its influence on Bobbio has been deep. This tradition, he observes, has nearly always been a conservative one.[46] In Europe, its supreme philosophical exponents were Hobbes, theorist *par excellence* of absolutism, for whom the law without a sword was but paper; and Hegel, for whom sovereignty was tested not so much in the enforcement of internal peace as in the prosecution of external war – the perpetual medium of the life of nations. In Italy this realism took the form not of a speculative rationalization but of a terrestrial exploration of the mechanics of domination, from Machiavelli to Mosca and Pareto. Bobbio has been a close and appreciative commentator of his country's elite theorists, to whom he owes certain significant elements of his sociological outlook.[47] But there is a sense in which his appropriation of the realist legacy has taken its distance from, or rather inflected, the specifically Italian tradition. For the latter has characteristically tended to issue into an obsessive culture of pure politics – that is to say, of politics conceived as a sheer subjective contest for power per se, as Machiavelli himself essentially saw it. What that tradition has lacked, by contrast, is

---

44. Russell's book appeared in 1932; Dewey published a text with the very same title in 1936.

45. 'Le Colpe dei Padri', *Il Ponte*, XXX, No. 6, June 1974, pp. 664–67; *Profilo Ideologico del Novenceto Italiano*, pp. 3–4. Bobbio traces the specifically Italian version of this idea back to Gioberti's legacy to the Risorgimento.

46. Bobbio develops this theme in many texts. See, among others, *Saggi sulla Scienza Politica in Italia*, Bari 1969, pp. 9, 197, 217; *Profilo Ideologico del Novecento Italiano*, p. 17.

47. See in particular his assessments of Pareto and Mosca in *Saggi sulla Scienza Politica*, published at the height of the student risings, against whose illusions Bobbio intimated they could serve as a salutary antidote: p. 252.

a real sense of the state – as an impersonal and objective complex of institutions. The reasons for this deficit are fairly evident – the long absence, and later persistent weakness, of an Italian national state. The originality of Bobbio's own reception of the Italian realist tradition has lain in his firm reorientation of it away from politics as such – the intricate mechanisms for gaining or losing power which so fascinated Machiavelli or Mosca, or even Gramsci (and in degraded daily detail the country's parliament and press to this day) – and towards the questions of the state which preoccupied far more Madison, Hegel or de Tocqueville.

There are two fixed points of the reflections on the state that follow. The first is Bobbio's unwavering insistence that all states rest in the last resort on force.[48] For him this is the great, pessimistic lesson of conservative realism. It was shared, he notes, by Marx and Lenin. But they combined a pessimistic view of the state with an optimistic view of human nature, that allowed the prospect of an eventual elimination of the one by an emancipation of the other – whereas for the mainstream realist tradition the incorrigibility of the passions required the permanent duress of organized power to restrain them.[49] Bobbio, without pronouncing directly on this question, remarks that in general 'political studies owe more to the sometimes ruthless insights of conservatives than to the rigorous but brittle constructions of reformers'.[50] His second emphasis does in fact uphold a conservative against a Marxist tradition. It falls on the irreducibly violent potential of inter-state relations, beyond all internal regulation, as constitutive of the nature of political sovereignty as such. Precisely insofar as the logic of war is thus independent of domestic class relations, it has been neglected by Marxism to its peril. The history and theory of military conflict are for Bobbio – as much as for Hegel or Treitschke – necessarily integral to any realistic reflection on the state. Paradoxically, it is just this sense of the centrality of war for the destiny of politics that has also made Bobbio – quite exceptionally in his country – a steadfast opponent of the nuclear arms race, who yet advocates a Hobbesian formula for international peace.[51] Contrasting his outlook with traditions that

---

48. *La Ideologie e il Potere in Crisi*, p. 165.

49. *Stato, Governo, Società*, Turin 1985, pp. 119–125; *Quale Socialismo?*, pp. 39–40; WS, pp. 62–63, 187– 190.

50. *Saggi sulla Scienza Politica*, p. 217.

51. That is, the investment of a monopoly of armed force in a single super-state with global jurisdiction. Bobbio contrasts this 'juridical' solution with what he terms the

descend from either Spencer or Marx, Bobbio expressly disavows any belief in the necessity of progress – here less than anywhere. On the whole, history reveals not so much the ruse of reason – unintended good coming out of intended evil – as the malignity of unreason – unintended evil let loose by intended good.[52] Acknowledging in their place the claims of even a thinker like de Maistre, Bobbio's thought is a liberalism simultaneously open to socialist and conservative, revolutionary and counter-revolutionary, discourses.

III Actually Existing Democracy: Two Critiques

What, then, has been the pattern of Bobbio's theoretical interventions over the last thirty years? The guiding thread of his writing in this period has been a defence and illustration of democracy as such. That democracy he defines procedurally rather than substantively. What are the criteria of Bobbio's democracy? Essentially, there are four. Firstly, equal and universal adult suffrage; secondly, civic rights which assure the free expression of opinions and the free organization of currents of opinion; thirdly, decisions taken by a numerical majority; and fourthly, guarantees of the rights of minorities against any abuses on the part of majorities. Defined in this way, Bobbio insists tirelessly, democracy is a method, the form of a political community, not its substance. But it is no less transcendent a historical value for that. Marxism, he argues, has always committed the fundamental error of underestimating it, insofar as historical materialism has been concerned with another question altogether: that of who rules in a given society, not of how they rule. For Marx and Lenin, this second problematic – what Bobbio calls the problem of the subjects, rather than the institutions, of power – obscured the first completely, to the point of generating a fatal confusion between dictatorship understood as any domination by one part or class of a society over another, and dictatorship understood as the

---

'social' solution classically envisaged by Marxism, in which international peace is assured by the disappearance of the state. He does not maintain that it would amount to a general pacification of social relations, since the state remains an 'institutionalization of violence'; only that it would provide the conditions for the elimination of nuclear weapons, which call for an unconditional conscientious objection today, together with a rejection of the theory of deterrence that justifies them. See *Il Problema della Guerra e le Vie della Pace*, Bologna 1979, esp. pp. 8–10, 21–50, 79–82, 114–16, 202–206.

52. *Quale Socialismo?*, pp. 102; WS, pp. 115, 209–212.

exercise of political force exempt from any law – in Lenin's famous definition; that is to say, between two wholly different meanings of the term – as a social order in a generic sense, and as a political regime in a narrower sense.[53] Bobbio observes that there was a pre-Marxist tradition which accepted the necessity of a revolutionary dictatorship to change society – one that extends from Babeuf to Buonarrotti through to Blanqui. What was new in Marxism was its transformation of this classical notion of dictatorship – as a government at once exceptional and ephemeral, as the Romans conceived it – into the universal and unalterable substance of all governments prior to the advent of communism, that is of a classless society.

Against this theoretical conflation, Bobbio underlines the irreplaceable importance of the emergence of liberal institutions – parliaments and civic liberties – within what is indeed a class society, dominated by a capitalist stratum, but one that exercises its dominion within a regulative framework guaranteeing certain basic freedoms to all individuals, whatever their class. This political democracy represents, historically and juridically, an indispensable bulwark against abuses of power. Liberal in its origins in the previous century, it continues to be liberal in its institutional format in this century. 'When I use the term liberal democracy,' he writes, 'it is not in a limitative sense' – since there could be no such thing as a non-liberal democracy – but to denote 'the only possible form of an effective democracy'.[54] The essential function of such a democracy is to assure the negative freedom of citizens from the prepotence – actual or possible – of the state: their ability to do what they like without external legal impediment. The mechanisms of this guarantee are dual – and structurally indissociable: on the one hand civic rights at the level of the individual, on the other a representative assembly at the level of the nation. The nexus between the two constitutes what Bobbio calls the irreducible nucleus of the Constitutional State, whatever the exact suffrage obtaining in the different epochs of its existence. As such it forms a legacy that can be utilized by any social class. Its historical origin, Bobbio argues, is as irrelevant to its contemporary usage as is that of any technological instrument, be it the railway or the telephone. There are no grounds why the working class cannot appropriate this complex in its own construction of socialism, and it has the most compelling reason for doing so. For in Bobbio's view, as he puts it in a deliberately pointed echo of tenets of

53. *Politica e Cultura*, pp. 150–52.
54. Ibid., p. 178.

historical materialism, 'liberal institutions belong to that material culture whose techniques it is essential to transmit from one civilization to another'.[55]

In his exchanges with Della Volpe and Togliatti, Bobbio naturally had no difficulty demonstrating the contrast between this liberal institutional nexus and the state of affairs in the Soviet Union, where a dictatorship of the proletariat was proclaimed – for him a dictatorship *tout court*, complete with 'the phenomenology of despotism of all times', the contrary of any kind of democracy.[56] But this initial contrast has encompassed only half of his polemical intent. For liberal democracy had in the course of time also to be distinguished and defended against another enemy, or at any rate another model. What was that? Liberal democracy, Bobbio has always insisted, is necessarily representative or indirect. The only alternative formally conceivable to it, therefore, would be a delegated or more direct democracy. By the seventies, there were few defenders of dictatorship – supposedly proletarian or otherwise – in Italy. But those who believed that a more direct form of democracy than the prevailing parliamentary order was possible and desirable were not so few. They looked forward to a conciliar democracy that would be as structurally proper to an advanced socialism as representative democracy was to advanced capitalism. The real target of Bobbio's theoretical interventions between 1975 and 1978 were these. His central attack was directed against what he called the 'fetish' of direct democracy. He did not deny the long pedigree of this idea from Antiquity through to Rousseau, before it was integrated into the tradition of historical materialism. But he rejected its validity or applicability to the industrial societies of today.

What are his arguments against it? They are twofold – structural and institutional. On general historical grounds, Bobbio reiterates the familiar case that the sheer scale and complexity of modern states preclude *ab initio* direct popular participation in national decision-making, as a technical possibility. This does not mean, he goes on, that he therefore regards the existing representative state as the *ne plus ultra* of democratic evolution. Representative democracy and direct democracy are not antitheses, but compose a continuum of forms. In this continuum, 'there is no form which is good or bad in an absolute sense,

55. Ibid., pp. 153–54, 142.
56. Ibid., p. 157.

but each is good or bad according to the time, the place, the issues, the agents.'[57] Such contextualization would seem to qualify the starkness of the initial contrast Bobbio makes between representative and direct democracy. But in practice, he criticizes or rejects every specific institutional form of direct democracy that he discusses. Firstly, referenda – the principal element of such democracy in the post-war Italian Constitution, which distinguishes it from more conservative counterparts elsewhere in Western Europe – may be tolerable for infrequent consultations of public opinion when the latter is divided into two more or less equal parts over some large and simple problem. But they are completely unsuitable for the bulk of legislative work, which far exceeds the capacity of the ordinary citizen to sustain an interest in public affairs – for voters cannot decide on a new law every day, as must the Italian Chamber of Deputies. Moreover, in referenda – Bobbio avers – the electorate is atomized, deprived of its normal guides or mediators in the shape of political parties. He has therefore deplored their multiplication in recent years.[58]

Nor are popular assemblies – as Rousseau once conceived them – viable either, as mechanisms of a direct democracy in modern societies. Practicable at best in small city-states of Antiquity, such bodies are physically impossible in contemporary nation-states with their millions of members. Moreover, even where they have briefly functioned at local level, in small settings, they have all too often proved easily distortable by demagogy or charisma, as the sad experience of the student movement demonstrated. Revocable mandates, for their part – a pivotal element in the conception of a more direct democracy for Marx or Lenin – are actively nefarious, for they are historically typical, Bobbio maintains, of autocracies in which the tyrant can dismiss his functionaries at any moment. Their positive complement, the imperative mandate, on the other hand exists de facto in modern European parliamentarism, in the form of the iron discipline of parties over their deputies, and as such is a weak point, to be lamented, of the democracy that already exists, rather than a strong point of any future democracy. The very notion of a binding mandate, for Bobbio, is incompatible with the principle that deputies represent general rather than sectoral interests which he holds to be essential to parliamentary democracy.[59] Thus his allowance that elements of direct democracy could be inte-

---

57. *Quale Socialismo?*, p. 98; WS, p. 112.
58. *Quale Socialismo?*, p. 59; WS, p. 79; 'La Crise Permanente', pp. 10–11, where Bobbio describes the 'burst' of referenda in the seventies as culpable of 'lese-democracy'.
59. *Quale Socialismo?*, pp. 59–62; WS, pp. 80–82.

grated as complements into representative institutions is largely nominal. The only actual example he mentions with approval is a faculty meeting. The spirit of his position is expressed in dismissals of the very idea of direct democracy by Bernstein and Kautsky that he cites as inspirations for his own vision of the problem.[60]

Defence of representative democracy; critique of direct democracy; rejection of revolutionary dictatorship. In its general lines, Bobbio's themes could so far be compared to the doctrine of any lucid liberal, or read as a more or less unconditional adhesion to the Western status quo. Where does his non-conformism begin, not to speak of his socialism? It is to be found in his critique of the representative democracy which we have – and which he otherwise lauds. Here is where the really neuralgic point of Bobbio's thought lies, where the intellectual tensions which permeate and confer on it all its political and theoretical interest can be most clearly seen. For on the one hand Bobbio enumerates a series of objective processes which, according to him, tend to diminish and undermine representative democracy as he himself prizes it: that is, the classical schema of a liberal-constitutional state based on universal adult suffrage, the pattern which became generalized throughout the advanced capitalist zone after the Second World War. What are these growing obstacles to the operation of representative democracy? They can be summarized approximately as follows.

In the first place, the autonomy of the individual citizen has been completely eclipsed by the predominance of large-scale organization. The size and complexity of modern industrial societies necessarily renders impracticable the kind of composition of individual wills into a collective will postulated by classic liberal-democratic thought. In its stead there emerges a conflict of consolidated and oligarchic groupings whose interplay – whether at the party-political, or the socio-economic level – typically takes the form of a corporative bargaining that undermines the very principle of free representation as it was understood by Burke or Mill. The entry of the masses into the political system, with the advent of universal suffrage, has not counteracted these tendencies. Rather it has itself fatally generated a hypertrophied

60. *Il Futuro della Democrazia*, pp. 34–41; FD, pp. 47–52; *Quale Socialismo?*, pp. 94–95; WS, pp. 109–110.

bureaucracy in the state – the outcome of justified popular pressures for the creation of welfare and social security administrations, which then paradoxically become ever more cumbersome and impermeable to any democratic control. Meanwhile, the technological advances of the Western economies make their governmental coordination and direction constantly more complex and specialized a function. The result is to open up an unbridgeable gulf between the competence – or rather incompetence – of the overwhelming majority of citizens in this area, and the qualifications of those few who alone know something of the matter: hence the constitution of a technocracy is inevitable. For their part, moreover, the citizens of the Western democracies tend to sink ever deeper into civic ignorance and apathy; one carefully maintained by the dominant media of commercial distraction and political manipulation. The consequence is that the actual electors evolve towards exactly the opposite of the well-educated and politically active subjects which should have been the human base of an operative democracy, in the eyes of the classical theorists of liberalism. Finally – here Bobbio rejoins a general refrain of the seventies – the combination of multiple corporative pressures, intractable weight of bureaucracy, isolation of technocrats, massification of citizenry, is an 'overload' of criss-crossing demands on the political system that sabotages its capacity to take effective decisions, leading to its growing paralysis and discredit.[61]

Such is the first line of criticisms Bobbio levels at our political order today. He sums up the gravamen of his charges by speaking of the 'unfulfilled promises' of representative democracy – expectations of liberty it has been unable to honour. But at the same time he insists that these promises could never have been redeemed. For the historical obstacles against which they were dashed have not been contingent. To Bobbio all the processes he enumerates so unsparingly, which have thwarted the hopes of the classical theorists of liberal democracy, are implacable – so many objective transformations of our conditions of social coexistence from which none can escape. They are, so to speak, necessary deficiencies of established representative democracy.

But at the same time, on occasion in the same texts, Bobbio advances a series of criticisms of this democracy whose effect is diametrically opposite. Here his objection to contemporary parliamentary demo-

---

61. See *Il Futuro della Democrazia*, pp. 10–24; FD, pp. 28–39: Bobbio's discussion is in some ways less well articulated than usual here – there is not, in fact, analytically much distinction between his 'unfulfilled promises' and his 'unforeseen obstacles'.

cracy is not promises it has failed to keep, but ones it has never given. For what Bobbio notes in this register is the general absence of any democracy in Western societies outside the precinct of legislative institutions themselves. Parliaments are held on either side in a rigid structural halter. On the one hand, the state itself comprises administrative apparatuses of a profoundly authoritarian character which, as he puts it, typically pre-existed the arrival of representative democracy and continue in large measure to be recalcitrant to it. 'What we call for the sake of brevity the "representative state" has always had to reckon with the existence of an administrative state which obeys a completely different logic of power, that descends from above rather than ascends from below, that is secret rather than public, based on hierarchy rather than autonomy' – and 'the first has never been able to make the second wholly submit to it.'[62] Army, bureaucracy and secret services constitute the occult underside of parliamentary democracy. 'Even the best Constitution shows only the facade of the huge, complicated edifice of the contemporary state. It reveals little or nothing of what is behind or within it – not to speak of the cellars below.'[63]

Outside the state, moreover, the characteristic institutions of civil society exhibit a virtually uniform lack of democracy. Representative principles occupy a relatively small space in social life as a whole. In factories, schools, churches or families, autocracy of one kind or another continues to be the rule. Bobbio does not treat the absence of democracy in these as of interchangeable significance. His emphases are those of classical Marxism. Remarking that 'the institutions the citizen succeeds in controlling are increasingly fictitious as centres of power', he writes that 'the various centres of power of a modern state, such as big business, or the major instruments of real power, like the army and bureaucracy, are subject to no democratic control';[64] 'the process of democratization has not even begun to scratch the surface of the two great blocks of descending and hierarchical power in every complex society, large corporations and public administration.'[65] His overall verdict on the balance of powers within the Western order is unequivocal: 'Even in a democratic society, autocratic power is far more widespread than democratic power.'[66]

---

62. *Quale Socialismo?*, p. 63; WS, pp. 82–83.
63. *La Ideologie e il Potere in Crisi*, p. 170.
64. *Quale Socialismo?*, p. 17; WS, p. 43.
65. *Il Futuro della Democrazia*, p. 47; FD, p. 57.
66. *Quale Socialismo?*, p. 100; WS, p. 113.

To remedy these autocratic patterns, Bobbio advocates a democratization of social life at large. By this he means primarily the spread of principles of a representative rather than a direct democracy: that is to say, the extension of rights of free organization and decision now confined to the political ballot to the basic cells of the daily existence – work, education, leisure, home – of the citizenry, wherever this extension is practicable. 'The present problem of democracy,' he writes, 'no longer concerns "who" votes, but "where" we vote.'[67] To pose this second question is not utopian today, for Bobbio argues that social development itself tends towards its resolution. Thus he writes that 'we are witnessing the extension of the process of democratization' – one in which 'quite traditional forms of democracy, such as representative democracy, are infiltrating new spaces, occupied till now by hierarchical or bureaucratic organizations.' In these circumstances, he remarks, 'I believe it is justified to talk of a genuine turning-point in the evolution of democratic institutions.'[68]

Now the contradiction – the fundamental incompatibility – of this register of Bobbio's thought with the previous one is patent. Here he insists on unnecessary deficiencies or limits of representative democracy. That is, he dwells on deficiencies which he presents as potentially superable by means of an extension of democratic principles themselves, beyond their existing boundaries – deeper into the state and across into civil society. There can be no doubt of the sincerity of his proposals here. But how can such a critique be relevant to a political order which cannot even realize its own principles within their current limits – and not for any want of subjective will, but under the weight of irresistible objective pressures? Either representative democracy is fatally destined to a contraction of its substance; or it is potentially amenable to an amplification of that substance. Both cannot be true at the same time. On occasion Bobbio seems to sense this and tries to soften the difficulty with formulas like: 'we seek ever more democracy in conditions that are ever worse for obtaining it.'[69] But such awareness is fleeting. On the whole Bobbio does not seem really conscious of how radical and central the contradiction is for his discourse as a whole. The basic antinomy of his theory of democracy never becomes the direct object of a reflexion on its meaning.

How are we to explain this? The answer seems to be that the

---

67. *Quale Socialismo?*, p. 100; WS, p. 114.
68. *Il Futuro della Democrazia*, pp. 43–45; FD, pp. 54–56.
69. *Quale Socialismo?*, p. 46; WS, p. 69.

contradiction is precisely the involuntary result of Bobbio's peculiar position at the confluence of the three diverse currents of thought discussed above. In effect, what happens is that he subjects his preferred ideal – liberal democracy – to two opposite and antagonistic kinds of criticism. The first of these is conservative: in the name of a sociological realism indebted to Pareto and Weber, it points out all those factors which pitilessly tend to evacuate the representative state of its vitality and worth, rendering it ever more a disappointing shadow of itself. The second is socialist: in the name of a conception of human (and not just political) emancipation derived from Marx, it points out all the areas of autocratic power in capitalist societies which the representative state leaves completely untouched, thereby depriving itself of the only social bases that would convert it into a true popular sovereignty. Bobbio cumulates the two conceptions, without being able to synthesize them. In reality, they are irreconcilable.

If that is so, we might suppose that Bobbio himself would not be able to maintain an equilibrium between the two – the temptation of a conservative realism and the solicitation of a socialist radicalism. To see the upshot of his thought here, it is necessary to put to him the question that provides the title of one of his major essays. Which socialism, finally, does Norberto Bobbio stand for? At first sight, the answer seems obvious enough – a moderate social democracy. Bobbio himself virtually proposes such a definition. A recurrent theme of his writing has been a contrast between the benefits Northern Europe has enjoyed from effective reforming government by social democracy, in contrast to the woes Italy has incurred from the divisions of a labour movement unable to challenge the arrogance and corruption of Christian Democratic hegemony. In the fifties Bobbio invoked the positive experience of the Attlee administration in Britain indirectly against the PCI.[70] In the sixties he depicted the formative period of Italian politics after the First World War as a time of tragic extremism in which the opposed but related forces of the subversive Right and the subversive Left overwhelmed the better impulses of moderate conservatism and moderate reformism, with disastrous consequences for Italian democracy.[71] In the seventies he criticized the PCI's formal advocacy of a 'Third Way' between Stalinism and social democracy as strategically empty rhetoric, that served only to conceal the need for a clear-cut

---

70. *Politica e Cultura*, p. 150.
71. *Profilo Ideologico*, pp. 114–15.

choice between dictatorial and democratic methods of social change – which between them exhausted the range of possible options. Declarations of Italian particularity as the basis for a superior Third Road were intellectual presumption, as if this backward country – whose relevant peculiarities were only the mafia, official corruption, tax evasion, bureaucratic ineptitude and clientelism, black economy and terrorism – could give lessons to the more modern societies of Europe.[72] In reality, Bobbio commented, ceremonial discourses apart, 'how can the practice to date of the two major parties of the Italian left be described other than as, in the most benevolent of hypotheses, social democratic?' – 'I say benevolent because to tell the truth, compared with the practice of the more advanced social-democratic parties, the Centre–Left already experienced and the Historic Compromise merely proposed can only be described the one as a makeshift and the other as a retreat.' He concluded his verdict on the Third Way of the Berlinguer years with these words: 'Once Leninism is excluded as inapplicable in advanced societies, which are anyway so different from Russia or China as to be incomparable, I frankly do not see how the Italian labour movement can avoid flowing into the great river of Social Democracy, abandoning the fascinating but inscrutable project of digging out a bed of its own – where the current would in all probability be weak in impetus and short in course.'[73]

Bobbio's endorsement of social democracy, apparently unambiguous in this judgement, nevertheless expressly concerns methods rather than aims. It does not underwrite the kind of society over which social democracy has so far presided in the West, and does not exclude the possibility of a third – for that matter, he notes, a fourth or fifth – model of society, alternative and preferable to the two antagonistic models now existing, as distinct from a third route towards one. The essential point is that any advance towards socialism in countries with liberal institutions must preserve them and proceed through them. Bobbio's historical realism prevents him from denying that there have been other roads to the overcoming of capitalism in other periods or other zones. Democracy is not a supra-historical value. 'The democratic method is a precious possession, but it is not appropriate for all times and all places.' In particular there may be situations of emergency or revolutionary upheaval, 'violent transitions from one order to

---

72. *La Ideologie e il Potere*, pp. 124–25.
73. Ibid., pp. 126–27.

another', where it is inapplicable.[74] Bobbio is under no illusions that the liberal order itself came into existence liberally. It was forged in 'a harsh struggle' against the *anciens régimes* by a 'minority of intellectuals and revolutionaries' – its founding episode the 'bloody outcome' of the 'pullulation of religious sects and political movements' in the English Civil War.[75] Likewise the basis of the democratic order that eventually succeeded it, the majority rule first glimpsed by the Levellers, 'did not generally itself have its genesis in the decision of a majority.'[76] Bobbio's capacity to register the insurgent origins of the *Rechtsstaat*, or the coercive matrix of a consensual democracy, is not just a token of his freedom from *bien-pensant* pieties of a conventional kind. It reflects that strain of his realism which derives from the tradition of the Italian elite theorists. Although this tradition started in the saturnine guise of the conservatism of Mosca and Pareto, it moved in the next generation into the hands of moderate democrats – men like Burzio and Salvemini, from whom Bobbio assimilated it without qualms. 'What regime is not the fruit of conscious and organized vanguards?' he once asked a Communist interlocutor.[77] 'Qualitative changes in history, or revolutionary processes, are the work of minorities.'[78]

But once a democratic political order is established, Bobbio excludes – taxatively – its transformation by any similar scenario. The past of liberal democracy is viewed with a cool historicism; its present with a categorical absolutism. The influence of Croce – famous for the *sang-froid* of his history of liberty, served even by crimes against it – informs the first attitude; a resort to natural rights theory, abhorred by Croce, underlies the second. In tacitly playing on both registers, German–Italian idealism and Anglo–French empiricism, Bobbio is undoubtedly inconsistent. But he is not in breach of a common liberalism, which virtually requires some amalgam of this kind.[79] The difficulty for him

---

74. *Quale Socialismo?*, p. 74; WS, p. 91.

75. *Politica e Cultura*, p. 55; *Liberalismo e Democrazia*, Milan 1985, p. 35. The latter text contains Bobbio's most extended discussion of the historical variants and vicissitudes of nineteenth-century liberalism, including a shrewd assessment of Mill.

76. *Liberalismo e Democrazia*, p. 36; 'Democrazia e maggioranza', *Revue Européenne des Sciences Sociales*, XIX, 1981, Nos. 54–55, p. 378.

77. *Politica e Cultura*, p. 55.

78. 'La regola di maggioranza e i suoi limiti', in V. Dini, ed., *Soggetti e Potere*, Naples 1983, p. 20.

79. Bobbio's philosophy of law reveals the same tension. On the one hand, he has been a more resolute exponent of legal positivism than Kelsen himself, pointing out the historically contingent character of the latter's 'fundamental norm' – one that can only be

arises at the next step. For all the countries where liberal democracy prevails are capitalist. How, within this framework, is socialism then to be reached? Bobbio's honesty and lucidity do not permit him to evade or obscure the problem. He gives no clear-cut answer to it – the hesitations of his thought are very evident here. But at the end of the day, the conclusion towards which he inclines is unmistakable. For he does look at the only two coherent strategies for a meaningful socialism available to him. These he describes as structural reforms from above, and widening of democratic participation from below. What is his verdict on them? He expresses a lethal scepticism about both. Writing of structural reforms, he asks: 'Let us assume that a total transformation can result from a series of partial reforms: up to what point is the system prepared to accept them? Who can exclude the possibility that the tolerance of the system has a limit, beyond which it will shatter rather than bend? If those whose interests are threatened react with violence, what is there to do except respond with violence?'[80] In other words, the central mechanisms of capitalist accumulation and reproduction may be inherently resistant to constitutional change, imposing a basic choice that forces the very notion of structural reform apart: either respect the structures, or transgress the reforms. Bobbio has himself never shown much interest in the strategy of structural reforms, whose history stretches back to Belgian and French debates in the thirties. But he has often dwelt on the prospect of a progressive democratization of civil society, as we have seen. He might be expected, therefore, to be more sanguine about the potential of this strategy. But

---

viewed as an expression of 'liberal ideology'. On the other hand, he shares the values of the *Rechtsstaat* as they were essentially conceived by Kelsen, and so is driven towards a natural-rights position of the kind that was the object of the original positivist critique – if one now transposed onto what Bobbio terms a 'meta-juridical plane'. For a delicate disentangling of the ensuing contradictions, see Sergio Cotta, 'Bobbio: un Positivista Inquieto', in Uberto Scarpelli, ed., *La Teoria Generale del Diritto – Problemi e Tendenze Attuale*, Milan 1983, pp. 41–55. The same conflict between an intellectual rejection and a political commitment to natural law foundations can be seen in Bobbio's treatment of human rights. These, he vigorously insists, form an ill-defined, shifting, often mutually incompatible congeries of claims – none of which can be deemed 'basic', since what seems fundamental is always particular to a given epoch or civilization. On the other hand, now that all governments acknowledge their codification in the UN Charter, the problems of their theoretical foundation have been resolved by the advent of their 'factual universality' – there is therefore no need to justify them philosophically, only to protect them politically. For this cutting of the Gordian knot, see 'Sul fondamento dei diritti dell'uomo' and 'Presente e avvenire dei diritti dell'uomo', in *Il Problema della Guerra e le Vie della Pace* (first edition), Bologna 1970, pp. 119–157.

80. *Quale Socialismo?*, p. 85; WS, pp. 100–101.

in fact his conclusion is equally bleak. 'There are good reasons to suspect that a progressive extension of the democratic basis of our society will encounter an insuperable barrier – I say insuperable within the system – at the factory-gates.'[81] The space for radical reform is closed by the very properties of the economic order that call out for it. Such doubts, concurrent in their logic, effectively tend to cut the ground from the parliamentary-democratic road to socialism to which Bobbio is formally committed.

Moreover, they are doubled by even more radical doubts as to what might be the fate of democracy under socialism, once a classless society were achieved. It has been seen that Bobbio's liberalism is not of the economic kind: he has never shown special attachment to the market. But for the same reason he has not shown much interest in economic alternatives to the market either. Capitalism as a system of production, as distinct from a set of injustices in distribution, is in some ways little more than a mildly reprehensible referential background for Bobbio – on the whole rejected, but never analysed. Consequently, when he thinks of socialism, its change in the ownership of the means of production conveys no positive value in itself for him. On the contrary socialization, beyond the limits of the mixed economy, tends only to conjure up the spectre of an all-powerful state, now master of economic as well as political life – an old liberal fear, of course. The result is that Bobbio ends up by predicting that not only will the same obstacles to democracy exist under socialism as under capitalism, but that the dangers to it will actually be greater: 'I am convinced that in a socialist society democracy will be even more difficult.'[82] A paradoxical conclusion for a democratic socialist, to say the least.

But these two reflexions – the probable unviability of a democratic road to socialism, the greater risks to democracy from socialism – throw into involuntary relief Bobbio's ultimate historical choice. Between liberalism and socialism, he in practice opts for the former. At times he justifies his preference with the claim that it is in reality the more radical. In a certain sense, he writes, democracy is 'a much more subversive idea than socialism itself.'[83] That claim is today by no

---

81. *Quale Socialismo?*, p. 85; WS, p. 101. Indeed recently the scope of Bobbio's scepticism has broadened from factory to civil society as a whole. 'The extension of democratic instances to civil society now seems to me more an illusion than a solution': '*Introduzione*', *Il Sistema Politico Italiano tra Crisi e Innovazione*, p. 20. Compare this dictum with the claim cited at note 68 above.

82. *Quale Socialismo?*, p. 83; WS, p. 99.

83. *Quale Socialismo?*, p. 53; WS, p. 74.

means confined to Bobbio. His way of redeeming it, too, is widespread – to redefine socialism as a sectoral specification of democracy, or local instantiation of a higher-order concept. Thus he declares his leaning to a conception of socialism which 'emphasizes control of economic power by an extension of the rules of the democratic game to the factory, or the firm in general, rather than the transition from one mode of production to another' that would involve an 'overall collectivization of the means of production'.[84] The significance of this move – one that has become virtually a *topos* of recent discussion – is in the substitution it makes. The reconceptualization of socialism as essentially economic democracy answers to a dual purpose. It serves at once to appropriate the central legitimation of the existing political order for the cause of social change, and to avoid the central ideological obstacle to the implementation of such change: namely, the institution of private property. Its logic is that of a circumvention – the word it would not speak is expropriation. As such, it has a long tradition behind it. In fact it was Mill himself who was probably the first explicit theorist of such a conception – envisaging socialism as the gradual growth of an industrial democracy that could afford to leave capitalist ownership of the means of production formally intact, if it elevated workers to managerial powers over them 'without violence or spoliation'.[85] The same intellectual move, made for the same motives, can be found in Russell, for whom 'self-government in industry' was 'the road by which Britain can best approach Communism'.[86] Dewey had his own version

---

84. 'La filosofia politica', – Intervista, *Mondoperaio*, January 1986, p. 115.

85. Mill's hope was that cooperative societies would prove so successful that workers would be increasingly unwilling to work only for wages any longer. In these circumstances 'both private capitalists and associations will gradually find it necessary to make the entire body of labourers participants in profits.' Through this process, he thought, there could eventually occur 'a change in society' which 'without violence or spoliation, or even any sudden disturbance of existing habits and expectations, would realize, at least in the industrial department, the best aspirations of the democratic spirit' – ultimately prompting capitalists to lend their capital to workers 'at a diminishing rate of interest, and at last perhaps, even to exchange their capital for terminable annuities.' Mill developed these notions in the 1852 and 1865 editions of his *Principles of Political Economy*: see *Collected Works*, Vol. III, Toronto 1963, p. 793. Of modern writers, Dahl is perhaps closest in inspiration to Mill here. See his arguments for cooperative ownership and his conception of experimental advances towards it in *A Preface to Economic Democracy*, pp. 148–160.

86. 'Capitalists value two things, their power and their money; many individuals among them value only the money. It is wiser to concentrate first on the power, as is done by seeking self-government in industry, without confiscation of capitalist incomes. By

of it, seeking to overcome 'autocratic methods of management' in enterprises that were 'harmful to democracy' because they militated against 'effective give-and-take communication' or 'free conversation'.[87] The reappearance of this substitution in Bobbio testifies to its persistence as a leitmotif of successive attempts to wed liberalism and socialism. If its practical fruit to date has been relatively small, the reason is in part that major social institutions do not generally allow themselves to be painlessly bypassed. The prerogatives of private property form an immensely strong bastion of the ruling ideology under capitalism, whose positive power is further fortified by the negative message inculcated by the division of labour – that organizational hierarchy is the condition of industrial efficiency. Together, these two have hitherto been more than a match for appeals to economic democracy they all too readily render *ultra vires*. Is it fortuitous that, contrary to the extensions of the suffrage on which they were optimistically modelled, the rights of co-determination in industry have so rarely, if ever, proved cumulative – have been so easily diluted or reversed?

Bobbio is too realistic to be unaware of these difficulties. His invocation of democracy as more subversive than socialism is more tactical than systematic. His real thought can be found elsewhere. Its actual conviction is the very opposite. 'The acceptance of a democratic regime presupposes the acceptance of a moderate ideology', he declares.[88] For 'majority decisions in a political order based on universal suffrage permit changes in the system, but they do not allow a change of the system.'[89] The permanence of capitalism as a social order

---

this means the capitalists are gradually turned into obvious drones, their active functions in industry become nil, and they can ultimately be dispossessed without dislocation and without the possibility of any successful struggle on their parts': *The Practice and Theory of Bolshevism*, London 1920, p. 183. It should be said that elsewhere Russell gave little reason for thinking that capitalists would set such small store by their power, as distinct from their income – the theme of *Power: a Social Analysis* was to be quite the reverse; or for assuming that an outcome obvious to their prospective dispossessors would not be so to them as well.

87. *German Philosophy and Politics*, New York 1942 (re-edition), p. 46. Here as elsewhere Dewey anticipated leading themes in the writing of Habermas. Arguing that America needed a philosophy that would 'articulate the methods and aims of the democratic way of life', he asserted that 'the philosophy which formulates that method will be one which acknowledges the primacy of communication' – given that 'prejudices of economic status, of race, of religion imperil democracy because they set up barriers to communication, or deflect and distort its operation': pp. 46–47.

88. 'La filosofia politica', p. 114.

89. 'La regola della maggioranza e i suoi limiti', p. 20.

becomes, in other words, a premise of any effective participation within the representative state. Paradoxically, as Bobbio himself candidly notes, this does not mean that if capitalism is untouchable, democracy is thereby inviolable. History has shown otherwise – 'one cannot change in a qualitative leap by democracy, but one can die by democracy'.[90] If a parliamentary road to socialism has yet to be seen, Italian and German experience between the wars is a reminder that there is a parliamentary road to fascism. This uncomfortable reality has to be faced. For Bobbio it does not qualify the value of liberal democracy, but enhances the need for constitutional safeguards to protect it.

These remain, in the end, his most abiding concern. Of the two problems – 'who rules? and how do they rule?' – Bobbio declared without ado in 1975 that 'there can be no doubt that the second has always been more important than the first'.[91] Always: in other words, what matters is not which class dominates, but the way it dominates. Here Bobbio's option, at the deepest level, for the liberal pole of his thought becomes manifest. For the same reason, of the two critiques of representative democracy in his writings, it is the conservative and not the socialist that has final weight. In his most recent writings, that critique even tends – in a familiar figure – to become a perverse apology. Thus, making of necessity a virtue, Bobbio can write: 'Political apathy is in no way a symptom of crisis in a democratic system, but usually a sign of good health.'[92] It signifies a 'benevolent indifference' to politics as such, that is founded on good sense. For in democratic societies major social change is generally not the result of political action at all, but of the progress of technological capacities and the evolution of cultural attitudes – involuntary molecular processes, rather than deliberate legislative intervention. Such 'continuous transformation' through the stream of inventions and the adjustment of mores greatly reduces the significance of even 'traditional reformism', whose importance social democracy – for all its moderation – has typically overestimated.[93] In these conditions, it is better to accept the political agenda of limited competition among elites rather than risk the stability of the constitutional framework by putting too ambitious demands on it. Bobbio expresses this with his habitual vivacity in the

---

90. Ibid., p. 21.
91. *Quale Socialismo?*, p. 38; WS, p. 61.
92. *Il Futuro della Democrazia*, p. 61; FD, p. 67.
93. 'Riformismo, socialismo, eguaglianza', *Mondoperaio*, May 1985, pp. 67–68.

phrase: 'Nothing risks killing democracy so much as an excess of it.'[94]
A fine elitist formula.

IV Conclusions, Questions

How are such concluding cadences to be judged? Their meaning may
be sought at two levels. At one of these, they without question reflect a
certain biographical experience that has shaped Bobbio profoundly,
and of which he is completely self-aware – that is, a specifically Italian
disappointment. In no country of Western Europe, one might say, were
political hopes on the left legitimately higher as the war came to an end
than in Italy – which had produced the largest popular Resistance, the
most vital intellectual ferment, the broadest radical labour movement;
a moment whose memory is perhaps still not wholly extinct even today,
something of it living on in the international aura of the PCI. But in
none, too, were such hopes so radically confounded over the subsequent decades. Bobbio's texts form a crystalline prism of this history. In
1945, he declared that 'the expedient of universal suffrage closes the
democratic experiment in the form of indirect democracy', and in the
name of the federal ideals of Cattaneo ardently advocated an advance
towards 'direct democracy' through a 'multiplication of the institutions
of self-government'.[95] Twenty-five years later, republishing this essay
together with others, he introduced it with the words: 'I do not hide
from myself that the balance-sheet of our generation has been disastrous. We pursued the "Alcinesque seductions" of Justice and Liberty;
we have achieved very little justice and are perhaps losing liberty.'[96]
These lines were written in the bitter year – for Bobbio – of 1970. His
fears that the freedom won by the Liberation would prove 'futile',
squandered by the established order and then destroyed by terrorist
subversion against it, reached their peak in the following period. By the

---

94. *Il Futuro della Democrazia*, p. 13; FD, p. 31. The thought is as old as the Roman
oligarchy. Cf. Cicero – 'Too much freedom will itself reduce a free people to servitude':
Republic, I, 68.

95. 'Stati Uniti d'Italia', republished in *Una Filosofia Militante. Studi su Carlo
Cattaneo*, Turin 1971, p. 55. In 1946, Bobbio recounts, when the *Partito d'Azione* was in
the throes of its internal crisis, 'I thundered against the idea of giving birth to a middle-
class party that would merely restore the old parliamentary democracy that had been
killed by fascism.' See his recent contribution to the special number of *Il Ponte* on liberal
socialism: XLII, No.1, January–February 1986, p. 145 (a text which also contains some
sharp comments on the destiny of the PSI).

96. *Una Filosofia Miltante*, p. xi.

mid eighties, he judged the worst dangers over and could observe with relief the relative stabilization of Italian democracy. The terms in which he did so, however, were scarcely a tribute to the civic spirit of the nation: 'One can be free by conviction or by mere habituation. I do not know how many Italians are really true lovers of liberty. Perhaps there are few. But there are many who, having breathed freedom for many years, could not do without it, even if they do not know it. To use a famous saying of Rousseau, in another context, Italians live in a society in which – for reasons of which most of them are ignorant and indifferent – they are "obliged to be free" by forces larger than themselves.'[97]

But this conclusion, withdrawing Bobbio's more apocalyptic predictions of the preceding decade, has not substantially softened his historical balance-sheet of the Republic he fought to create. Vindicating the values of the Resistance, a battle in which 'we were not mistaken', he has recently recalled once again the gap between the 'ideals of yesterday' and the 'reality of today', writing: 'We have learnt to face democratic society without illusions. We have not become more satisfied. We have become less demanding. The difference between our concerns then and our preoccupations now is all in that. The whole quality of our common life has not improved, indeed in certain respects it has worsened. It is we who have changed, becoming more realistic and less ingenuous.'[98] This frank avowal explains a good deal of Bobbio's apparent adjustment to the discoloured minimalism of the representative order in Italy, his willingness to find reasons – or consolations – for the mortification of popular interest in politics, under elites whose regimen has for much of the time meant little more than bread and scandals. He has explained his own outlook on that scene with a characteristically self-critical straightforwardness. After developing the casuistics of conformity cited above – the benevolent character of political indifference, the necessary constraints on political alternatives – he remarked: 'I do not know whether the reflections I have been formulating here can be deemed generally reasonable and realistic. But I do know that they will be considered disillusioning and discouraging by those who, faced with the degradation of public life in Italy, the shameful spectacle of corruption, sheer ignorance, careerism and cynicism with which the majority of our professional politicians present us every day, think that the channels allowed by the system are

---

97. *Profilo Ideologico del Novecento Italiano*, p. 183.
98. *Italia Civile*, p. 6.

inadequate to bring about reforms, let alone radically transform it.' Addressing these, Bobbio went on: 'The present writer belongs to a generation of people who lost their hopes more than thirty years ago, shortly after the end of the war, and have never recovered them except for occasional moments, as rare as they were fleeting, and which came to nothing. They came at the rate of one per decade: the revocation of the *Legge Truffa* (1953), the formation of the Centre–Left (1964), the great revival of the PCI (1975).' 'As someone who has been through many years of frustrated hopes, I have learned to be resigned to my own impotence . . . But I fully accept that these arguments carry no weight with the young in Italy, who have not known Fascism and know only this democracy of ours, which is less than mediocre, and so are not equally disposed to accept the argument of the lesser evil.'[99]

Such sentiments, and the experience behind them, divide Bobbio from his great predecessors. There is no reason to doubt their sincerity. But in one respect they fail to do him justice. There is a difference between ideal and influence. Disappointment is not necessarily impotence. Bobbio's early hopes were not realized, but it is notable how often his later admonitions were heeded. If one compares his record with that of Mill or Russell or Dewey, it is clear that he has never been an original thinker in the same way. He is the first to underline the derivative character of his own principal ideas, for him a common trait of post-war Italian culture as distinct from that of the first years of the century.[100] But his political impact in his own time has certainly been greater than theirs. Bobbio in effect urged Eurocommunism on the PCI, and foresaw its adoption, twenty years before the event. He played a significant role in the abandonment by the PSI of its Marxist past. He helped to discountenance the challenge of the Far Left in the same period. He anticipated the repudiation of the notion of a Third Road by both major parties of the Italian labour movement. It is difficult to think of another intellectual who has had such a real and visible effect on the political climate of their country since the war.[101] In successive debates Bobbio has earned his influence not only by an unusual combination of gifts of expression and of erudition, but by a singular

---

99. *Il Futuro della Democrazia*, pp. 64–65; FD, pp. 70–71.
100. 'Everything that was done then betrays haste, improvisation and has no originality. We were, at best, popularizers.' *Maestri e Compagni*, p. 26.
101. The one main exception to this record does him only honour – his opposition to nuclear weapons. See his bitter comments on the complete indifference of official Italian politics and culture to the issue in the second edition of *Il Problema della Guerra e le Vie della Pace*, Milan 1984, pp. 5–7: 'those who sound the alarm are like dogs howling at the moon.'

personal transparency and probity. Even when defending increasingly neo-moderate positions against more than justified criticisms from radical opponents, his moral and intellectual superiority over them has generally shown through.

Yet that moderatism has ended, as we have seen, by casting the whole project of marrying liberalism and socialism into doubt. Mill described socialist schemes as 'chimerical', before the change of mind that started the history of theoretical attempts to unite them with liberal principles. Bobbio, after participating in the practical movement of the *Partito d'Azione* to achieve such a liberal socialism, has since pronounced it 'chimerical' – 'no more than a lofty velleity'.[102] Beyond the historical reasons for this irony, inscribed in Bobbio's own political experience, there was an intellectual one too. From the outset, his theoretical formation included not only a socialist and a liberal but also a conservative strand. Bobbio has always remained sincerely, admirably progressive in his personal sympathies and intentions: by any standards an enlightenment thinker of nobility. But what his writings seem to show is a pattern of elective affinities at work, in spite of these intentions. For in Bobbio's texts, liberal socialism reveals itself to be an unstable compound: the two elements of liberalism and socialism, after seeming to attract each another, end by separating out, and in the same chemical process the liberalism moves towards conservatism.

How representative is that recombination? Beyond all Italian circumstances, how far are these elective affinities operative more widely – independently of the volition of individual thinkers – in modern political thought? As a term, liberalism first appeared in the world as a pennant of the 18th Brumaire of the Year VIII, when Napoleon brought the French Republic to an end, declaring that he took power to 'protect men of liberal ideas'.[103] Through all its subsequent vicissitudes, that originating motive has perhaps never quite disappeared. But it also is true that the First Empire generated elsewhere a more radical reception of the idea – the same term inspiring in Spain the first European revolution against the Restoration. When the Old Order was challenged on a continental scale in 1848, the recurrent attempt to extend liberalism beyond itself to meet new social classes and values

---

102. *Una Filosofia Militante*, p. 201; *Liberalismo e Democrazia*, p. 62: 'Whereas the conjugation of liberalism and socialism has so far remained a lofty velleity, the growing identification of liberalism with market forces is an incontestable reality.'

103. Otto Brunner, Werner Conze, Reinhart Koselleck, eds., *Geschichtliche Grundbegriffe*, vol. III, Stuttgart 1982, pp. 749–751.

began. To date, what is striking is the disproportion between the intellectual credentials and the political results of the successive projects that followed. For all the good will and talent expended on it, the synthesis of liberalism and socialism has so far failed to take. That is not to argue that it must. The renewed energies the conception now attracts – since who would wish for an illiberal socialism? – might point in the other direction. It is too soon to say. But a sense of the history of the undertaking is likely to be a condition of resuming it to good effect.

1988

Roberto Unger and the Politics of Empowerment

The largest industrial power of the Southern hemisphere has recently completed one of the most protracted and divisive processes of constitution-making in modern history. The fruits of nineteen months of labour by the Constituent Assembly of Brazil have already aroused violent reactions. 'Clauses on employment worthy of Cuba, on foreign enterprise reminiscent of Romania, on freedom of property fit for Guinea–Bissau. Not the faintest odour of civilization' – so said Roberto Campos from the Right, Minister of Planning and Ambassador in London for the generals, today Senator of the cattle-barons of Mato Grosso, on the practical shape of the new charter. By coincidence, the same months have seen the publication in the Northern hemisphere of a uniquely ambitious exercise in constitutional theory by a Brazilian–American, which seeks to lay out the design not only of a polity but of a concomitant economy and society. Its author, Roberto Mangabeira Unger, comes from one of the most famous political families of Bahia. His grandfather Otavio was Foreign Minister under the Old Republic, an oligarch of legendary eloquence who oscillated between fascism and liberalism in opposition to Vargas, while his grand-uncle João founded and led the small Brazilian Socialist Party. Roberto, a by-product of his grandfather's exile in the USA under the Estado Novo, had a mixed upbringing in the two countries. For the past decade he has taught critical legal theory at Harvard Law School, with recurrent forays into his native land – where he has been an acute critic of the new constitution from the left, for multiplying fictive welfare rights while legalizing further military fiats: Unger to his US audience, Mangabeira to his Brazilian. Like Edward Said or Salman Rushdie, he forms part of that constellation of Third World intellectuals, active and eminent in the First World without being assimilated by it, whose number and influence are destined to grow.

The originality of Unger's enterprise lies in its combination of aims:

'*Politics* presents an explanatory theory of society and a programme of social reconstruction. The theory works towards a radical alternative to Marxism. The programme advances a radical alternative to social democracy.'[1] It is the surprise of this two-edged challenge that gives the work its peculiar force. The vehicle chosen for it, however, does not always serve this purpose best. Crisply defined at the outset, Unger's project subsequently waylays and disperses itself through sheer multiplication of topics and repetition of themes. The huge spread-eagled text of *Politics* stretches over (so far) a thousand pages. The nominal organization of its three books by no means corresponds to its real architecture, whose foundation actually lies in a preceding work, *Passion – An Essay on Personality*, and whose lantern – as it were – will presumably be the ethics promised as 'Part II' of the whole in *False Necessity*. Intellectual ambition has won an expensive victory over political communication in such giganticism. In virtually any work of practical advocacy, there is some trade-off between length and effect. Here the impact of often striking programmatic proposals is inescapably reduced by the extravagant mass of unbound ideation surrounding them.

Unger's prose, unusual in the intensity of its rhetorical pressure, does not really relieve this difficulty. It displays an unremitting stylistic energy in the quest for a vocabulary free from every theoretical jargon or political cliché, with many memorable and felicitous results. But it can also resort to a less fortunate, quasi-revivalist register: 'Try to understand, reader, by an act of imaginative empathy, the bitterness a person might feel when he discovered that doctrines invented to emancipate and enlighten had now become instruments of confusion and surrender . . . It was an instance of illusion passing into prejudice. You wanted to write a book to set things right' – 'When the larger argument falls into confusion and obscurity, when I stagger and I stumble, help me. Refer to the purpose described in this book and revise what I say in the light of what I want.'[2] Disdaining any conventional apparatus of references, Unger appends instead an omnibus reading-list to *False Necessity*, whose concluding recommendation for the study of

---

1. *Politics, a Work in Constructive Theory* is the general title of Unger's opus, of which three volumes have appeared so far: *Social Theory: its Situation and Task*, or 'A Critical Introduction'; *False Necessity,* or 'Part I: Anti-Necessitarian Social Theory in the Service of Radical Democracy'; and Plasticity into Power, or 'Variations on Themes – Comparative–Historical Studies on the Institutional Conditions of Economic and Military Success'. All were published by Cambridge University Press in late 1987. Henceforward ST; FN; PP.

2. ST, pp. 78–79; 9.

cultural revolution (after Hegel or Kierkegaard) is: 'See *TV Guide*' – an unwise flourish, liable to bring recent preachers of the screen too readily to mind. It would be wrong to make overmuch of this histrionic side of the work; but vibrato interpellations intended to heighten attention risk distracting it from the serious core of Unger's argument.

The central premise of *Politics* is that 'the present forms of decentralized economies and pluralistic democracies (markets based on absolute property rights, democracies predicated on the sceptical quiescence of the citizenry) are neither the necessary nor the best expressions of inherited ideals of liberty and equality. They frustrate the very goals for whose sake we uphold them.'[3] The aim of the work is to develop a persuasive alternative beyond the limits of social democracy to these congealed forms – 'a particular way of reorganizing governments and economies that promises to realize more effectively both aspects of the radical commitment: the subversion of social division and hierarchy and the assertion of will over custom and compulsion.' Such institutional reconstruction is for Unger inseparable from cultural transvaluation, or a 'radical politics of personal relations' that will 'allow us to connect leftism and modernism'.[4]

These contemporary political purposes are set within a much vaster theory of history, from which they receive their warrant. Unger constructs this vision from a double rejection: principally of Marxism, for adhering to a vision of the past composed of a limited number of modes of production, conceived as integrated orders capable of replication in different epochs or environments – if also all other variants of 'deep structure theory'; and secondarily of sociological or historiographic positivism, for tending to deny the existence of societal totalities or qualitative discontinuities at all. Against the latter Unger insists that distinct and decisive structures do indeed exist – what he calls 'formative contexts', as opposed to the 'formed routines' subject to them. Against the former he argues that each such structure is at once internally dissociable and historically unique – the elements that comprise it do not have to fit together, and the combination of them never recurs. Formative contexts, so understood, exercise a formidable constraint over all social practices, forcing them into a specific mould of predictable routines. But they also embody a fundamental contingency, since there is no intrinsic logic binding their constituent parts

---

3. ST, pp. 6–7.
4. Ibid.

together. The conventional opposition in modern politics between reform and revolution, or piecemeal versus overall change – the one potentially ineffectual, the other hypothetically lethal – is therefore misguided. Formative contexts can be disassembled by bits, in partial moves that by the same token effect basic alterations. The real contrast is between 'context-revising' and 'context-preserving' conflicts. But there is no unbridgeable gulf between these. Rather they form a continuum, in which disputes over routines can always suddenly escalate into battles over structures.

Why is such escalation perpetually possible? Unger's answer appeals to a transhistorical attribute of the species which he calls its 'negative capability'. The meaning he attaches to this term is virtually the opposite of that intended by Keats. What it denotes is active will and restless imagination pitted against all circumstance or convention, a constitutive human capacity to transcend every given context by negating it in thought or deed. As such, Unger argues, its exercise has gradually expanded since the dawn of civilization, giving history what cumulative (though not irreversible) direction it appears to have. Today the goal of politics must be to increase the space of that negative capability, by creating institutional contexts permanently open to their own revision – so diminishing the gap between structures and routines, and 'disentrenching' social life as a whole.

Such disentrenchment represents both a pragmatic and a moral value. In the past, the economic and military success of states always depended on the degree to which they achieved what Unger terms 'plasticity', or the ability to promote a 'pitiless recombination' of the factors of production, communication or destruction to meet changing conditions or opportunities. But this kind of institutional flexibility typically consorted with predatory or despotic power – the rule of nomadic conquerors, agrarian bureaucracies, or mercantile oligarchies. Once modern popular sovereignty starts to emerge, however, it acquires normative force as a principle of social emancipation as well as material prosperity. For now the fixity of all traditional hierarchies and dependencies may be seen as a false necessity that can be undone by the general will. The advent of the *Rechtsstaat*, universal suffrage and social security are only the hesitant beginnings of this process. Unger looks beyond them towards a more radically 'empowered democracy', capable of freely remaking every dimension of its common life. His own programme for empowerment includes proposals for the reorganization of government, property, work, and personal relations alike, in a spirit intended to dispel the 'received, superstitious contrast' between liberalism and socialism.

Within Unger's extended construction, there are three distinct theoretical planes. The first and founding one is a philosophical anthropology. It is set out not in *Politics* but in the preceding work on which much of this trilogy depends, *Passion – An Essay on Personality* (1984). There Unger postulated a twofold model of the self: as on the one hand endowed with an infinite mobility in always finite conditions, on the other possessed of a constitutive yet perilous longing for others. The external world and all character are perpetually subject to transcendence by the self; but the self is subject to an unlimited need for others that is also an unlimited danger – of 'craven dependence' or collective conformity. There is no constant human nature, only an inherent tension between attachment to and fear of others. Unger improbably presents this vision as a restatement of the 'Christian-romantic image of man', fortified by a touch of Nietzsche. In fact, what is striking is its similarity with Sartre's account of consciousness in *Being and Nothingness* – the quicksilver capacity of the for-itself to elude all given determinations and the tormented dialectic of its relations with others. But where the early Sartre remained essentially asocial, his conclusions negative, Unger seeks to give a positive resolution to the same existential premises by projecting a society based on them. 'It is necessary to enact the modernist ideal as a form of social life.'[5] The unifying principle of such a form would be empowerment. Unger uses this notion simultaneously for the conversion of the individual capacity for transcendence into a collective power of context-revision; and for the 'mastery' of each individual's exposure to others, which requires satisfaction simultaneously of the need for passionate engagement and the need to avoid menacing dependence in intersubjective relations. The strain of yoking together these two quite different senses of 'empowerment' – the second visibly a wilful graft on the first – is pervasive in Unger's work. The two underlying ideals remain in effect dissociated, their forcible union producing the characteristically dissonant appeals to the paired virtues of 'ardour and gentleness', 'greatness and sweetness' that are a feature of his writing.[6]

The dominance of the first concern, inscribed if not avowed in his existential starting-point, emerges much more unambiguously once Unger moves to the historical issues which form the second major plane of his work. For Sartre, when he shifted onto the terrain of history in *Critique of Dialectical Reason*, the 'negative motor' of human develop-

---

5. *Passion – an Essay on Personality*, New York 1984, p. 17.
6. *Passion*, p. 270; FN, p. 595.

ment was scarcity. For Unger, the motor is negative only in name, through whimsical annexation of a term from Keats whose meaning he inverts. The driving force of history is actually the perpetual positive disposition of human beings to transcend their inherited contexts – development as *dépassement*. Scarcity and the practico-inert do not disappear altogether. But they are downgraded to secondary obstructions or intermissions in the pathway of this revisionary will, in the guise respectively of a need for 'coercive surplus extraction' (long superseded) and a persistence of 'sequential effects' (tending to diminish). The formal outline of Unger's theory of history can thus be read as an optimistic transcoding of Sartre's.

But unlike Sartre, Unger goes on to propose substantive analyses of major episodes in the course of history. Here his key conceptual instrument is the notion of formative context. This is presented expressly as an alternative to the mode of production in the Marxist tradition, rejected as too rigid and replicable. A formative context is something looser and more singular – an accidental institutional and ideological cluster that regulates both normal expectations and routine conflicts over the distribution of key resources. The contemporary North Atlantic example thus includes, for Unger: constitutional division of governmental powers, partisan rivalry incongruously related to class, market economies based on absolute property rights, bureaucratic supervision of business activity, differential unionization, taylorized work organization, vocabularies of private community, civic equality and voluntary contract.[7] The price for the looseness of configuration prized by its author is, in other words, vagueness of boundaries and indiscriminacy of elements. For the 'tangible and intangible' resources on whose control the whole definition of a formative context depends are never demarcated. The result is that the concept lacks any hierarchy of determination, and its only law of motion is cyclical – since a true dynamic has been identified from the outset not with the working, but precisely with the breaking of contexts by negative capability.

Unger provides two principal examples of such historical cycles. The first, and much the most extended, is what he calls the 'reversion cycle' in agrarian bureaucratic empires – Han, Roman, Byzantine, Korean, Mughal. These states, he argues, essentially rested on a monetary economy rather than coerced labour or barter. For a commercial agriculture, generating cash taxes was the precondition of the political autonomy of a central government capable of withstanding the fissi-

7. ST, p. 152.

parous power of local magnates. The normal base of these aristocrats was the large, autarkic estate; production for the market, on the other hand, was typically undertaken by small independent cultivators. The contradiction of the imperial regime was to be socially solidary with the dominance of the nobility, but economically dependent on the vitality of the peasantry. To keep magnate pressures at bay, the state could resort to a limited repertoire of policies, found again and again in the most widely separate epochs and areas: recruitment of an upstart bureaucratic staff, creation of a service nobility, or implantation of military–agrarian colonies. But over time, aristocratic power in the countryside all but invariably prevailed. The consequence was then the fatal erosion or disappearance of smallholders, the contraction of output for the market, the decline of fiscal catchment by the state, leading eventually to a full 'reversion crisis' or relapse into a natural economy, and therewith the disintegration of the imperial order.[8] Only Mediaeval Europe and Tokugawa Japan escaped this cycle. There the peasantry could withstand landlord exactions since there was no united front of power and privilege arrayed against it – in the absence of a bureaucratic state in Europe, and of a resident aristocracy in Japan; though the Ottoman and Ch'ing Empires succeeded in mitigating the cycle by drawing on their nomadic backgrounds to strengthen central checks to magnate autonomy, and so stabilize small agrarian property.

This is an ingenious and elegant schema. But it suffers from a fundamental empirical flaw. In pre-modern societies, there was no general affinity between peasants and markets of the kind presumed by Unger – quite the contrary. The overwhelming priority of the immediate producers was normally subsistence production for their own households. Commercial agriculture, where it emerged – far more patchily and precariously than Unger suggests – tended rather to be associated with the marketable surplus of medium or large estates whose proprietors were not tied to the needs of their own reproduction in the same way, because of the latitude of their material base. The most spectacular example, of course, was farming in the late Roman Republic and the Principate, where the advance of monetization spelt not the rise but a savage depression of the smallholder, as oligarchs amassed huge concentrations of land and servile labour for market production, and cash relations acquired historically unprecedented intensity. Unger registers this sequence, but not the depth of its discrepancy with his thesis.

---

8. PP, pp. 13–25.

Morever, if the development of Classical Rome effectively inverted the relation he postulates between markets and magnates, the evolution of Mediaeval Europe upsets no less his scenario for peasants and states. For having argued that the eclipse of centralized state machinery in the Dark Ages permitted the emergence of a degree of village autonomy in the countryside that was the key to feudal dynamism, Unger has no ready explanation for the scale of the crisis that overtook the latter in the fourteenth century. In fact, to account for what he deems its avoidance of 'outright' reversion, he is driven to invoking just the opposite of his initial principle, namely the vigour of 'the *non*-commercial parts' of the rural economy centred on the peasant plot and village community.[9] At the same time, he notes that the resolution of the crisis saw a strengthening of centralized aristocratic power in the new monarchies, rather than a weakening of it. The original terms of the argument are thus switched or scrambled in the two best-known chapters of the world-story it sets out to tell.

The analytic of pre-modernity in *Plasticity into Power* has its sequel in a genealogy of modernity in *False Necessity*. There Unger's concern is to establish the origins and nature of the formative context of the present OECD zone. He does so by means of a critique of what he calls its 'mythical history', shared by conservatives, liberals and Marxists alike – that is, the view that there was a convergent, irresistible logic in the long-run process which led to the contemporary configuration of market economy, mass-production industry and parliamentary democracy. Unger argues that this package was adventitious. The major institutional clusters of the West emerged separately, without particular congruence. Politically, a liberal constitutionalism of eighteenth-century cast became improbably coupled to mass parties, for which it had never been designed, in the course of the nineteenth century. The corporation came to dominate the organization of private property only later, after hard-fought contests against it. Assembly-line industry, exemplified by Fordism, arose more recently still, and is already receding. Yet out of these disparate histories a pervasive status quo has crystallized. Marked by preventively deadlocked government, unconditionally held property entitlements, massively concentrated business units and rigidly hierarchical work processes, this conformation was dictated by no immanent technological or social necessity. There was a

9. PP, p. 32.

real historical alternative to it, represented by the forces of 'petty-bourgeois radicalism' in the nineteenth and twentieth centuries. Unger uses this term in a broad sense for all those who resisted elite politics, big capital, large factories, unregulated markets, whether in the name of populist or utopian socialist ideals. His crucial claim is that smaller forms of property and production, based on flexible forms of work organization, were just as progressive technically – and therefore viable economically – as giant trusts and mass-production industry, as the experience of modern farming or selected textiles was to show. Their stabilization in either individual or cooperative form, however, required support by the state, a characteristic goal of their radical spokesmen from Proudhon or Lassalle to Demarest Lloyd. It was the political defeat of programmes like theirs which sealed the fate of this potential and preferable path of development, not any sociological impossibility of its realization.

What then decided the political issue itself? Unger's answer is essentially that the petty-bourgeois alternative posed more of a threat to the interest of traditional elites than its (should we say – bourgeois?) rival, which prevailed because it encountered less resistance from entrenched agrarian or patrician interests. Hence a realistic popular radicalism was crushed or constricted by force. In the terms of Unger's general historical theory, this is an appeal to the weight of 'sequential effects' – the practico-inert force of one formative context in shaping the next. Figured against these, the petty bourgeoisie represents the front-line of 'negative capability' of the modern epoch, as the peasantry did in the pre-modern world in Unger's vision – the bearers of the most creative economic forces. The industrial proletariat, creature of mass production and regimented work organization, is *eo ipso* tacitly disqualified from any vanguard role in this conception. Classical claims for it are never, however, tested in a direct comparison. For here there is a very striking lacuna in Unger's counter-history of modernity. He initially defines the contemporary formative context of the West by four institutional clusters: the work organization complex, the private rights complex, the governmental organization complex, and the occupational structure complex. But when he moves to his genealogy of it, he omits the last altogether, 'for the sake of simplicity'.[10]

Such simplification exacts a high price. For what it means is that Unger provides no analysis at all of the emergent social structure of the

---

10. Compare FN, pp. 69–79 with pp. 174 et seq.

societies he is discussing. He rejects the use of the term capitalism for them, on the grounds that it is either too general or too particular to be helpful. The merits or otherwise of this scruple are of less moment than the ensuing absence of any overall class map of these social formations. The petty bourgeoisie itself, the hero of Unger's parable, is in this respect virtually plucked out of thin air. For there are no surrounding class relationships into which it is inserted, in structural antagonism or dependence, affinity or ambivalence. Nobility or bourgeoisie, middle classes or working classes, are little more than smudges on the horizon. Indeed even the small producers themselves are only gesturally sketched. They are most consistently identified under the rubric of 'petty commodity production' – a term ostensibly taken from the vocabulary of Marx that Unger otherwise shuns. But the concept loses its direction in his usage. When Marx spoke of *einfache Warenproduktion* – 'simple' commodity production – he defined it not by the scale of its output but the nature of its key input: it was that form in which the producer marketed goods without resort to wage-labour (or servile dependants). For Unger, on the other hand, petty commodity production includes every kind of market enterprise short of the centralized factory and multidivisional firm – from the manufacture of cutlery in Solingen to computers in Silicon Valley. The connexion of this gamut of economic forms with even the widest notion of petty bourgeoisie is tenuous indeed. On the other hand Unger virtually ignores white-collar employees – the archetypal petty bourgeois of the big cities from the later nineteenth century onwards, epitomized in the *calicot* public of T.J. Clark's unforgettable portrait of Parisian popular culture of the period.[11]

Some sustained recovery of the forgotten visions of emancipation of small producers, whether populist or socialist, is an attractive and overdue project. The passionate, unfashionable plea Unger enters for the bearers of petty-bourgeois radicalism is in this regard likely to have only good effect. He is right too, of course, in insisting on their crucial role in the European insurgencies of the 1840s or American of the 1890s. But the argument that they could have remade the world for the better, wholesale, demands much more than this. The structural heterogeneity and ambiguity of the petty bourgeoisie alone, emphasized in nearly all the classical studies of it, militated against anything like that. Unger, lacking any theory of different class capacities for

---

11. *The Painting of Modern Life*, London 1984, pp. 205–258.

collective action, which must depend on a general account of social structure, overlooks these traits and their implications. Astonishingly, *Politics* contains not a single substantive reflection on – scarcely even a mention of – fascism: the political movement of the twentieth century for which petty-bourgeois forces, above all, provided the shock troops. Unger, after criticizing a 'mythical history' of modernity, describes his own as 'schematic and polemical', even frankly 'speculative'.[12] But, even short of fuller empirical documentation, the structure of his argument requires comparative controls of a kind he does not venture. If it was the power of traditional elites which thwarted the success of petty-bourgeois radicalism in Victorian Europe, why did not their relative absence permit it in North America? If small property generated the virtues of flexible work organization and ideals of democratized government, how could it rally so rapidly to the New Rome and the Third Reich?

But beyond these questions, Unger's alternative history poses a more drastic difficulty for his own theory. For it culminates in a contemporary landscape of monotonous sameness – the familiar, featureless plains of the world of G–7. In that panorama all advanced capitalist societies are subject, Unger argues, to the futile recurrence of a 'reform cycle' impotent to alter them – regularly swinging between meliorist attempts to guide investment and redistribute income, generating inflationary wage struggles that provoke loss of business confidence, followed by reactive drives to restore market dominance and fiscal discipline. The predictable movements of this pendulum he describes as an 'insult to the primacy of the will'.[13] Their determinant is the formative context finally consolidated as a general rule of the North Atlantic and Pacific regions in the post-war epoch. The millennial growth in negative capability that Unger ascribes to the overall course of human development, instead of yielding an ever greater variety of social invention, thus paradoxically issues into an end-state of massive uniformity. The historical contingency he insists upon as the mark of true volition enigmatically generates not the play of creative diversity, but a necessitarian identity. Unger on occasion senses the problem, and offers *ad hoc* responses to it, lamely invoking the similarity of problems facing societies or the pressure of leading states on late-comers to imitate them. But within the logical structure of his thought the contradiction seems radical and insoluble.

---

12. FN, pp. 7, 176.
13. FN, p. 52.

Yet whatever the anomalies of the philosophy or history advanced by Unger, it is politics that must be decisive for judgement of his work – as its title suggests. Here, however, its reception has been ironical. For controversy has focused on everything but this. Two polar reactions to the overall merits of *Politics* are represented, on the one hand, by the capacious symposium of a dozen admiring contributors drawn from a wide range of disciplines, across 350 pages in the *Northwestern University Law Review*; on the other, by the furious commination – 'Harvard's Greatest Fraud' – of *The New Republic*.[14] The rancour of the latter, a zealot for the Contras, is perhaps not hard to explain. Curiously, however, in both cases the actual political programme of the book is largely ignored – as if it were too hot to handle in the depoliticized atmosphere of the United States at the hour of Dukakis and Bush. But this is unquestionably the most seminal and powerful part of the work. Unger starts by asking whether social democracy, which he takes to be 'the single most attractive emergent model of social organization in the world today – least oppressive, most respectful of felt human needs', is for all that 'the best that mankind can hope for, for an indefinite time to come'. His answer is a firm negative. For 'social democracy makes the liberal project of the Enlightenment – the cause of liberty, equality and fraternity – unnecessarily hostage to a transitory and replaceable institutional order.'[15] The pillars of this order are: a state that requires and produces a quiescent citizenry; markets ruled by property rights that are absolute in duration and scope; work processes that are needlessly stultifying and inflexible. Social democracy pursues its ordinary aims within the parameters they set. By contrast Unger's over-riding objective is to reduce such fixed distance between contexts and routines, by making the fundamental institutions of society available for regular (as opposed to exceptional, or revolutionary) revision.

The programmatic proposals which ensue are systematically addressed to the existing forms of power, property and labour. Unger criticizes what he sees as the modal type of Western liberal state for effectively paralysing significant change from above, and precluding it from below, by constitutional checks and balances originally and deliberately designed for the restrictive purposes of eighteenth-century notables. But he does not endorse any call for a more direct democracy,

---

14. 'Symposium: Roberto Mangabeira Unger's Politics', *Northwestern University Law Review*, Vol. 81, Summer 1987, No. 4: 'The Professor of Smashing', *The New Republic*, 19 October 1987.

15. FN, pp. 25, 27.

along conciliar or other lines, which he regards as little more than an imaginary inversion of the prevailing model. Instead he argues for 'dualist' constitutions conferring rival power and initiative on two centres of authority, president and parliament, favouring creative conflict between them, with rapid resolution of deadlocks by popular consultation. The principle of this conception is an 'overlapping' rather than separating of powers – extended to the creation of a special instance for ensuring the democratization of information inside and outside the state itself. So constructed, Unger's republic is designed to mobilize the democratic energies of its citizens rather than to neuter them.

Yet its charter can be realized only if the economy is transformed. For 'such a democracy cannot flourish if the everyday world of work and exchange is organized in ways that not only differ from the principles of democratic government but limit their scope, undermine their influence, and disrupt their workings.'[16] The target of Unger's critique here is the assimilation of markets as decentralized arenas of exchange, with property rights as absolute claims to divisible portions of social capital. The former are indispensable, for freedom and for efficiency; the latter are unacceptable mechanisms of inequality and privilege. Their fusion in the current economic order 'withdraws the basic terms of collective prosperity from effective democratic choice and control'.[17] Unger's remedy is to transfer control over major productive assets to a 'rotating capital fund' which would disaggregate property rights down through a tier of capital-givers and capital-takers – an ultimate social fund controlled by the government, leasing capital to autonomous investment funds operating in given sectors, which then auction or ration resources to competitive teams of producers, for stipulated periods. Breaking up consolidated property rights in this way would then encourage more flexible forms of work organization, characteristic of small or medium vanguard enterprises today. The workings of the market, in which final capital-takers act as 'unrestricted gamblers', would be buffered by welfare rights guaranteeing a minimum income to all citizens.

Unger completes his programme by arguing that a transformation of personal relations is the necessary counterpart of institutional change. He calls this prospect 'cultural revolution' – significantly, the only time the latter term acquires salience in his vocabulary. Its contours are

---

16. FN, p. 483.
17. FN, p. 482.

much more elusive, in part because detailed treatment of them is deferred to a further volume on the 'microstructure of social life'. But two elements are already sketched. Interpersonal relations can be rewrought in the spirit of modernism by deliberate role-jumbling and confusion of expressive conventions, while the idea of a community should move from the seamless sharing of customary values to a heightening of mutual vulnerability, which accepts conflict as itself a positive value. Although these notions occur only as a tentative coda to *False Necessity*, they are of central importance to Unger, who insists that 'the qualities of our direct practical and passionate dealings always represent the ultimate object of our conflicts over the organization of society'.[18]

For sheer imaginative attack, Unger's project for social reconstruction has no contemporary counterpart. It certainly honours its promise to advance beyond – far beyond – the ambitions of social democracy. Perhaps the best way of grasping just how radical Unger's vision is would be to compare it with that of a thinker whose intellectual energy matches his own, and whose political sympathies are not so distant. Habermas too constructs his analysis of current capitalist society in dualist fashion, and develops his critique of it in the name of a normative modernity. For him the two levels of the social order are its systems – the economy and state, the domain of strategic action steered by the objective media of money and power, operating behind the back of individual agents; and its life-world – the private and public spheres that are the abode of communicative action, where intersubjective meaning and value arise, in cultural transmission or socialization. The drive of capitalist rationalization is towards the relentless colonization of the life-world by the systems – the invasion of every refuge of unforced sociability or aesthetic play by administrative rules or cash relations. For Habermas this process is pathological, and must be resisted: this is the vocation of the new social movements – ecological, pacific, feminist. But the actions of these will be for the most part experimental or defensive in scope, 'border conflicts' to safeguard the spaces of the life-world. What they cannot undertake, under pain of a dangerous regression, is any counterattack to reconquer the systems themselves. For these are necessarily beyond the intentional control of agents, as products of the structural differentiation that is a condition of modern industrial society.[19] The reappropriation of an alienated

---

18. FN, p. 556.
19. *Theory of Communicative Action*, Vol. II, London 1988, pp. 338–343, 393–96.

economic and political order by its producers and citizens as it was once envisaged by Marx, in other words, is tabooed by Habermas. It is just this demarcation, between what can and what cannot be reclaimed for conscious collective control, that Unger rejects. The whole force of his duality is exactly the opposite. Contexts are contrasted with routines in order to show how the frontiers between them are mutable and crossable. The aim of a democratic politics is to make a routine of the revision of contexts. Intellectually more remote than Habermas from the Marxist tradition, Unger is in this respect politically much closer to it.

At the same time the confidence and scope of his institutional programme separate him from nearly all conventional socialist discussion today. A general inhibition in this area has been a long-standing reflex of the lines of thought that descend from Marx. The all but complete silence of Habermas himself is a striking case in point. No such aversion to reconstructive detail marked the alternative utopian traditions that started with Saint-Simon, and Unger is right to claim their heritage. The boldness of his recovery of it can only be admired. But his particular proposals raise a number of difficulties. Unger's juridical background can be seen in a certain overestimate of the independent significance of constitutional arrangements as such. For all their real importance, the effect of these is always subject to the objective structure of the state and the actual balance of social forces. The Constitution of the Fifth Republic answers fairly closely to Unger's ideal of a governmental power divided between two potentially rival authorities, in the Presidency and Assembly, with rapid resolution of conflicts between them by popular consultation. The cohabitation of Mitterrand and Chirac, and the successive elections of 1988 which wound it up, fit this description very well. But far from mobilizing the democratic energies of the French, the experience lowered them to a post-war nadir – a third to a half of the electorate abstaining. The example of England is even more discomfiting for Unger's assumptions. He proceeds throughout as if the US Constitution were prototypical for the West as a whole, assailing a supposed standard model of rigid checks and balances for stymieing decisive political initiative. The complete lack of any such pattern in the UK, with its virtually untrammelled executive power, appears to have escaped him. Decisional capacity is the last thing missing here. Who would argue the results are nearer a 'radical democracy'? Ironically, the most devastating critique of the Westminster State to be produced from the Left, Tom Nairn's great polemic *The Enchanted Glass*, looks on the contrary to the American Constitution as an inspiration of republican liberty. Not for the first time, socialists reciprocate in finding foreign virtues where their neighbours see domestic vices. In general, Unger pays too much attention to the legal framework of the state, and too little to its bureaucratic machinery and party outworks.

The central theme of his economic argument, on the other hand, is compelling. The disaggregation of consolidated property rights – Unger points out that these can be nominally collective as well as private – would surely be one of the basic principles of any socialism worth the name. The lexicon of leasing is likely to become greatly amplified and diversified in the transition towards one, as it is already starting to do in the East today. Unger, on the whole a shrewd observer of the Communist experience, anticipates not a few of the notes struck in *perestroika*. In the West the potential of the lease as a contractual devolution of public facilities to independent groups of producers, so 'cutting the knot tied by the speculator and the bureaucrat', was early seen by Raymond Williams as an alternative to state monopoly or commercial dominance of the means of communication. For the origins of his own conception, Unger invokes the contested name of Lassalle – as corrected by Rodbertus and Marx. His general formula of the 'rotating capital fund' suffers, however, from a noticeable vagueness about the delicate question of rotation itself – that is, how and when capital would be reallocated between enterprises, short of insolvency or takeover. The word planning does not appear in the text, although the idea is clearly present – perhaps a gesture of tact. Nor is much said about self-management, beyond an effective criticism of the Yugoslav version of it. The emancipation of labour is entrusted more to flexible work organization than to industrial democracy. Nevertheless these lacunae do not really detract from the novelty of the main proposals.

Finally, of course, Unger's emergent cultural agenda is one that is deeply shocking to liberal assumptions. Its basic claim, that 'the ultimate stakes in politics are the fine texture of personal relations',[20] warranting revolutionary transformation of psychic identities and affective ties alike, is a manifest affront to the principle of a private realm shielded from public intrusion. Unger justifies it with the argument that no society is ever in practice institutionally neutral between all possible styles of personal interaction or modes of association. But selection is not the same as determination – the fact that some forms (varying according to the social order) are always excluded does not necessarily mean that others are therefore enforced. The liberal claim is

---

20. See FN, pp. 397–401.

simply to maximize the range of allowable choice; Unger would be on stronger ground querying that. He describes his own position as 'super-liberalism'. Despite the apparent paradox, the term is not entirely misleading insofar as he shares with the classical variety an intrinsically asocial model of human beings – since the 'negative capability' vested in every individual precedes all common ties between them. The difference is that this is an individualism without human nature. Only the fugitive capacity of the self for transcendence, and an ominous longing for others, define it. The first provides the passage to modernism, interpreted by Unger as a dissolution of traditional conceptions of personal character and social roles, rather than of the idea of the subject itself, as in post-structuralist versions. This is the strong sense of empowerment – the throwing off of the masks of false necessity, by individual defiance of all self-expectation or exterior convention. The second leads to the strained sense of empowerment, as 'mastery over the conditions of self-assertion', through the enhanced mutual exposure of a community enfolded not in consensus but in conflict. The connexion between the two is as forced as was Sartre's vast conjugation of the term 'freedom' in *Cahiers pour une Morale*, heroically stretched from an ontological indicative to a political imperative for just the same reason – the desire to reconcile a metaphysic of nihilation with an ethic of generosity. Unger's programme for a cultural revolution combines 'role-jumbling' with 'solidarity rights'; but whereas the former is evoked vividly enough, the latter remain impalpable – even unimaginable, as entitlements declared 'unenforceable'.[21]

Critics have not failed to point out, with justice, the omission from Unger's preoccupations of a great deal of the ordinary agenda of politics in the West. There is little about the issues of poverty or unemployment, race or gender, armaments or environment. Although these are real limitations, perhaps their main significance lies in the detachment from the actual chequerboard of political forces they suggest. The universal endowment of negative capability generates no specific calculus of collective action – either of social interests or of social abilities to realize them. The result is that Unger can on occasion argue, in all apparent seriousness, that his overall programme should appeal to conservatives, centrists, social democrats and radicals alike![22] At

---

21. FN, p. 539.
22. FN, pp. 379–395.

other times he concedes that it has a 'far better chance of taking root in the reform, labour, socialist, and communist parties', or identifies certain social groups – unemployed or unskilled, petty-bourgeois or professionals – as more likely adherents to it than others.[23] At others again, he argues that the escalation of political conflict is typically characterized by not a polarization but a disintegration of class allegiances, giving way in revolutionary situations to a struggle between pure 'parties of opinion' – moments of great historical decision, in their intensity, do not reveal but consume the logic of class.[24] What these vagaries amount to is a basic indeterminacy of political agency in Unger's thought. Its most telling sign is the absence of any category of the adversary. There is no equivalent to the figure of the 'foe' in Carl Schmitt. The opponents of a radical democracy remain without shape or name. Do they even exist? At most, it might seem, in the risk of an obstructive civil service.

If the subjective forces for, or against, fundamental social change remain in the end largely inscrutable, its objective conditions are little less elusive. Unger looks for the opportunities of democratic empowerment in what he calls middle-level crises today, in which the border between routines and contexts may be most readily crossed. Excluding the impact of wars or the overthrow of tyrannies, superseded in the West, he finds them in the dictates of economic growth and the pursuits of self-fulfilment. These he terms respectively the 'humdrum and ethereal' springboards for institutional reconstruction.[25] To the tough-minded, who might be tempted to call them trite and vaporous, Unger would no doubt reply by invoking the contrasted crises in Czechoslovakia and France of the year 1968. But whatever the validity of such a description, Unger does not in fact put much weight on the notion of structural crises at all. For on the one hand the formative context is always more or less arbitrarily stitched together in the first place, and on the other the pressure of negative capability can always burst it apart at the seams anyway. Again and again Unger insists that 'society, no matter how impregnable it seems to its inhabitants, always stands at the edge of the cliff' – since it is an order 'subject to an endless stream of petty disruptions that can escalate at any moment into more subversive conflicts'.[26] If the possibility of explosion is perpetual, there is little call for the work of a Richter. At the same time, and in part for

---

23. FN, pp. 409, 549.
24. ST, pp. 153–54; FN, pp. 241–43, 547.
25. FN, p. 546.
26. ST, p. 205; FN, p. 215.

the same reasons, there is not much need for a theory of transitions either. *False Necessity* skirts all discussion of the actual social processes – national turmoil, international reaction – that any bid to implement its programme would unleash. Instead Unger merely offers a menu of preliminary institutional measures, as if his scheme of radical recon-struction had no losers. Intimations of harmony discount consider-ations of strategy, in a reminder of the other side of the utopian tradition.

That side belongs to the character of the work as a whole. For the enormous edifice of *Politics* undeniably possesses a dream-like quality. Unger himself freely describes his enterprise as speculative, and much of it lies at a visible remove from the realities of history or politics. Yet unlike nearly all others today, the dream is a salutary and emboldening one. Unger is entitled to say, as he does at one point, that its realization 'would mean reversing the defeat of the revolutionary movements and leftist experiments throughout Europe in the aftermath of World War I' – would represent one version of 'the victory of which they were robbed'.[27] Where else have past and future been so temerariously joined? For a long time intellectuals from the First World have been diagnosing the condition and prescribing the treatment of the Third – still the dominant mode of all writing on the subject. Here something new has occurred: a philosophical mind out of the Third World turning the tables, to become synoptist and seer of the First.

1989

---

27. FN, p. 508.

7

W.G. Runciman:
A New Evolutionism

Under a flat, anonymous title and in serial guise one of the most exotic – even flamboyant – intellectual projects of recent years is coming to fruition. The first volume of W.G. Runciman's *Treatise on Social Theory*, devoted to the dry topic of methodology,[1] set out in reasonable and moderate tones an agenda for social understanding combining – in so many words – the ambitions of a Ranke, a Comte, a Proust, and a Hart: to report accurately, to explain scientifically, to recreate imaginatively, and to judge impartially and benevolently. Perhaps the most striking feature of this programme was its association of two aims normally reckoned antithetical: an explanatory structure continuous with the natural sciences and an imaginative recapture modelled on literary fictions. Few practitioners of the social sciences have the confidence to invoke the ideals of Herbert Spencer and Henry James simultaneously.

In his second volume, Runciman proceeds to his own substantive social theory. He remarks at the outset that he will here be concerned only with the explanatory segment of his overall prescriptions. But this involves no shrinkage of horizon – on the contrary. For the two questions he seeks to explain are nothing less than these: what kinds of society are possible at any given stage of human development, and why any given society became the kind it did, in the course of it. The answers he arrives at, Runciman goes on to argue, have profound intellectual consequences, offering 'a very great deal' more for our general understanding of history than can be found in the contributions of Marx or Weber, or anyone else.[2] For Volume II of *A Treatise on Social Theory*

---

1. *A Treatise on Social Theory*, Vol. I, *The Methodology of Social Theory*, Cambridge 1983.

2. *A Treatise on Social Theory*, Vol. II, *Substantive Social Theory*, Cambridge 1989, p. 47. Henceforward TST.

proposes a novel account of social structure and an original theory of social evolution. It is the integration of these two conceptions, Runciman contends, that marks a fundamental advance in our ability to grasp the pattern of the past.

What is the import of each? For Runciman, power is as basic a concept to sociology as energy is to physics. Societies are to be conceptualized as so many different ways of allocating power. Such power comes in three, and only three, sorts: economic, ideological and coercive. These are always interdependent, but none is ever reducible to the others. Runciman's principal early debt was to Weber, from whom this axiom derives. He reformulates it, however, in terms designed to effect a bridge to Marx. Societies are modes of distribution of power, founded on differential control of the means of production, persuasion and coercion. It is the variations in these three dimensions of power that furnish the key to a scientific classification of societal forms. At the same time, each of them is composed of a specific set of social *practices*; and these practices are perpetually subject to selective pressures, generated either within or between the societies concerned – above all, from the competition of alternative practices. The process of this selection in turn constitutes the essential mechanism of social evolution.

Runciman's calm, considered commitment to an evolutionary theory of history is a gauge of his independence of mind. Nothing could be less in fashion today. For some time now evolutionism has been a disreputable term for many sociologists – one of the cardinal, egregious errors of earlier generations, since generally repudiated. The last major thinker to attempt a systematic theory of social evolution was Talcott Parsons, in his final years.[3] It is significant that Runciman, amidst a vast bibliography, never mentions him. Moreover, the discredit into which evolutionism has fallen has attached principally to variants of Marxism which assert no more than some directionality to historical development. Runciman's evolutionism, however, is far more specific and stringent. It is a sociology literally sculpted after modern biology. Natural selection serves throughout as the model of social selection. Runciman is well aware of the fate of previous versions of social Darwinism. But he is undeterred by the failure of every previous bid to map *The Origin of Species* onto the genealogy of social forms, because he believes he has corrected the root mistake common to them. All such theories took as their unit of selection – the basic materials out of which

---

3. Talcott Parsons, *Societies: Evolutionary and Comparative Perspectives*, Englewood Cliffs 1966.

only the fittest survived – either whole societies or social groups. Runciman substitutes particular practices. These, he maintains, are the true counterpart of genes. Like DNA, they display random mutations, in the sense that their origins are extraneous and irrelevant to the process of selection itself. The bodies on which they confer advantages in the competition for power are roles – and these in turn are attributes of social groups or societies, which form the equivalent of species.

Armed with this analytic equipment, Runciman then directly broaches the historical record. His purpose is twofold: to establish a Linnaean taxonomy of all societies known to us, and to demonstrate the Darwinian mechanisms of their speciation – how and why success-ive forms evolved from their predecessors. The result is a dazzling display of erudition. On this showing, Runciman's command of the comparative historical record has few, if any, rivals. Old Babylonia, tribal Africa, archaic Greece, pre-Columbian America, stone-age Mela-nesia, classical Rome, dark-age Lombardy, mediaeval Japan, imperial China, feudal Poland, republican Venice, caliphal Islam, absolutist France, industrial Britain, revolutionary Mexico, Stalinist Russia, populist Argentina, social-democratic Sweden, racist South Africa – all these and many more parade across what astonishingly remains a compact, middle-sized book, each deftly and economically captured for the purposes at hand. There are a few gaps: Egypt or Assyria from the ancient world, the Third Reich from the modern; and the sources drawn upon could be thought too consistently Anglophone (about ninety per cent of the modern citations: certainly more than the balance of scholarship). But these are trivial limitations. Runciman handles the enormous range of his evidence with a precision and assurance that are deeply impressive. Vaulting in global ambition, his survey is unfailingly sober and careful in local execution. It is difficult to think of a single obvious lapse or extravagance of historical judgement in the whole account, where stray instances could readily be pardoned. An even, scrupulous, dispassionate voice controls what might otherwise appear an inordinate enterprise. The tone is one of imperturbable suavity.

How should the completed theory be assessed? The comparative testing of Runciman's hypotheses yields a historical inventory of great richness and fascination. But there are a number of difficulties with the theoretical framework itself. The first of these concerns Runciman's preliminary move – the definition he adopts of society itself. Can societies be satisfactorily envisaged simply as so many intertwined networks of power? Runciman is not alone in thinking they can. The same assumption can be found in the work of Michael Mann, of which Runciman has been a severe critic, but whose scale and focus invite comparison.[4] The common source of this bias is Weber — the dominant influence on this cohort of British sociologists. Fixation with power has, of course, gone much further elsewhere, in France and the United States, under the spell of Foucault. The excesses and absurdities of the metaphysic now current in much literary theory, even cultural history, are generally foreign to the more prosaic world of English social science. But they have their warning for it. Whether in its Weberian or Foucauldian version, engrossment with power appears hard-headed: in fact, it is naive. (Weber's own illusions in Ludendorff, Foucault's in Khomeini, are the fitting emblems of each.) Societies are not just power-stuff. Three very large domains of collective life resist such ingenuous reduction. These are the production of persons, of goods and of meanings. Demographic, economic and cultural systems are never mere transcriptions of power relations between human actors: for they always involve transactions with nature that surcharge or overflow these. The sociology of power characteristically seeks to avert this objection by extending its central concept, in a direction originally indicated by Parsons, towards positive-sum usages. Mann, for example, distinguishes between 'distributive' and 'collective' power – the former exercised by some agents over others, the latter shared between agents as a common enhancement of their capacities. For Runciman, similarly, the notion of power encompasses both 'domination' and 'cooperation'.[5] This doubling of the term is not a mere artifice. Technological invention or economic progress can legitimately be entered under it, since these directly involve an increased social power over the natural world. But this is not true of most recorded demographic regimes, of major world religions, or significant art forms – to name only them. It is no accident that these virtually disappear from Runciman's conspectus. Even economic activity, in principle more amenable to his treatment, gets short shrift. Indeed, it is noticeable that he makes much less of his 'cooperative' than Mann does of his 'collective' forms of power. After a perfunctory initial mention, they are all but forgotten thereafter. Symptomatically, Runciman – himself a leading industrialist, who must know more about modern economic realities than most of his peers put together – can nevertheless write that 'the fundamental economic practice is the exchange of goods or services':[6] as if production did not exist. The ellipse is dictated by the

4. *The Sources of Social Power*, Vol. I, Cambridge 1986.
5. TST II, pp. 65–66.
6. TST II, p. 71.

parti pris of the theory as a whole, where to all intents and purposes power *is* 'distributive' domination.

The same inflection recurs in Runciman's account of the ideological dimension of social structure. Once societies are conceptualized as so many practices of power, competition between these must be anchored in the dispositions of the individuals who compose them. Runciman postulates universally effective, and equivalent, strivings for the possession of wealth, force and prestige. The pursuit of ideological power is a quest for the latter, and the 'fundamental practice' of ideology is deference. Noting that some might doubt whether the wish for prestige is really a historical force on a par with the desire for command or riches, he replies that honour is a profound and ubiquitous value, Locke even holding 'credit and reputation' to be the most important of all springs of human action.[7] But this is a non-sequitur. For reputation, which can just as well be moral, intellectual or aesthetic, need have – normally does have – nothing to do with power: of Locke's contemporaries, what ideological sway was exercised by Aubrey or Spinoza, or Vermeer? Even where real ideological systems are at work, moreover, in such massive structures as the great religions, is their principal function usually just to instil social deference? Plainly not: Christianity as a cultural meaning-complex cannot be reduced to the mere authority of priests. Its world-historical role, across successive forms of social order, is not to be squeezed into any such straitjacket. Runciman is right to distinguish between economic, ideological and coercive forms of power, and to insist that the variable relations between them need to be studied empirically, in their different historical settings. But he is wrong to suggest that history itself consists simply of their interplay. Neither labour nor faith, to say nothing of birth or death, is ever just an adjunct of power; and the changes in their regimes – affecting technology, reproduction, belief – cannot simply be assumed to have less causal weight for social evolution than the practices of domination. That has to be shown.

The strains that Runciman's restrictive optic imposes on his own enquiry become apparent as soon as he moves to develop a concrete taxonomy of societal forms. Since these are identified with modes of distribution of power, each a specific combination of separate modes of production, persuasion and coercion, their number should be determined by the actual range of variation of the latter. Runciman proceeds to enumerate these: eight forms of economic power (serfdom, tenancy,

---

7. TST II, pp. 70, 34.

smallholding, debt nexus, corvée, caste, wage-labour, slavery); eight of ideological power (purity-pollution, hereditary status, sacred rank, ethnicity, age-set, genealogy, occupation, charisma); and seven of coercive power (conscript army, warrior aristocracy, civilian militia, magnate levies, servile troops, volunteer professionals, alien mercenaries). That yields a Linnaean grid of some 450 possible kinds of society, as he points out – without considering hunter–gatherer bands or communities prior to the emergence of a state. He then immediately adds that empirical overlaps are possible in each column, and that not all combinations are conceivable, so that the historical gamut of realized forms will necessarily be less.[8] The proviso is reasonable enough. But nothing in it could prepare one for the eventual figure Runciman arrives at: no more than *ten* distinct kinds of society in all, from the dawn of civilization to the present. (Another four, prior to the emergence of the state, are later subjoined.) In other words, less than three per cent of those theoretically called are empirically chosen. The discrepancy between the potential and actual typology is so large that it cries out for explanation. In effect, either the initial classification of variants is misguided and redundant, or there is some intermediate mechanism capable of a drastic transformation of profusion into parsimony. Runciman, however, does not appear to register the anomaly of his own conclusions. Here, if anywhere, the issue he announces at the outset – what kinds of society are historically possible? – is unambiguously posed. But the promise of an answer is not kept, the question itself seemingly forgotten.

There is a further anomaly within the taxonomic outcome itself. For the fourteen separate forms ultimately classified as discrete modes of distribution of power, are themselves aligned in a developmental sequence which commands their order yet remains external to their identity. Runciman, in effect, lists them as follows: limited-power; dissipated-power, shared-power, obstructed-power; patrimonial; citizen, warrior, bureaucratic, feudal, bourgeois; liberal-democratic capitalist, authoritarian, state-socialist, racist. Each of these kinds of society is defined in terms of the configuration of power within it. But at the same time each is de facto situated within a larger set organized on a very different principle. Limited power obtains in hunter–gatherer societies. Dissipated, shared or obstructed power is characteristic of horticultural, nomadic pastoral or primitive agricultural societies. Citizen, warrior, bureaucratic and feudal forms belong to agrarian

---

8. TST II, p. 59.

civilizations proper – bourgeois to early commercial capitalism. Liberal-democratic, authoritarian, state-socialist and apartheid societies are specific to industrial nation-states. These correlations are not merely deducible from Runciman's account; they are conceded by him, in so many terms. In effect, behind the apparently static classification of power, lies a surreptitious dynamic based on an economic periodization.[9] There is no reason to quarrel with the latter. But its discreet presence inevitably throws the rationale for the taxonomy itself into question. Can human societies really be conceived just as patterns of power, if their overall development answers to another – presumably a more fundamental – logic? Should not a theory of social evolution address itself in the first instance to the series of basic historical modes of livelihood, rather than to the various crenellations of power supported by them? Another way of saying this is that while Runciman's taxonomy purports to classify *societies*, its operative units are for the most part actually *states*. This is the level at which his concentration on power is in fact appropriate.

Here, however, the denomination of his distinct 'botanical' species is not wholly consistent. Having argued that any given mode of distribution of power is always composed of separate modes of production, persuasion and coercion, which can vary independently of each other, Runciman goes on to say that a classification of societies along these lines must therefore take a Linnaean 'polynomial' form – that is, must spell out the particular combination of economic, ideological and coercive power in each case, as in 'liberal-democratic-capitalist' to describe Western societies today.[10] But this rule is waived in the larger part of his enumeration. No attempt is made to apply it to early proto-states or semi-states. The five pre-industrial state forms are captured not by polynomial categories, but essentially by designation of their dominant strata (Runciman calls these 'systacts' to avoid preemption of their character): citizens, warriors, lords, bureaucrats, bourgeois. This is certainly one reason why the number of forms drops so precipitously – the criteria for them have tacitly reduced. It is really only with the industrial species that polynomials come into play, yielding such alternatives as 'authoritarian-nationalist-capitalist' and 'liberal-democratic-socialist' (nowhere yet realized, but in Runciman's view a possible future for Sweden).[11]

Yet a certain casual ease with his own formal scheme is in another

---

9. TST II, pp. 149–168.

10. TST II, pp. 49, 57.

11. TST II, pp. 165–66, 260.

sense an attractive quality of Runciman's writing. There is no trace of the manic attachment to pet minutiae so often characteristic of those with a taste for taxonomy. On the contrary, what is striking is the largeness of mind with which Runciman puts his categories to work – depth of learning, one might say, precluding rigidity of construction. His actual depictions of the many societies that he discusses to illustrate his argument are a chief instruction and pleasure of the book. If they stimulate disagreement on occasion, it is nearly always because of their placing within the logic of classification, rather than any error in their representation. How important are the demurrers indicated on this score?

If we start with the transition to statehood itself, there is one curious spot of uncertainty within Runciman's account. He describes the earliest proto-states as 'patrimonial' – rudimentary forms in which those who hold civil or military office stand in a purely personal relationship to the ruler. As such, patrimonialism does not figure in his fivefold typology of pre-industrial constellations of power, species which he locates on a plane 'over and above' it.[12] Categorized as a simple beginner, it would appear to be structurally – in general also chronologically – superseded with the advent of these higher forms. But later on patrimonialism re-emerges as a state form proper, of notable range and potential sophistication, including such diverse structures as the Greek tyrannies and the Carolingian empire, not to speak of the Tudor monarchy or the Portuguese kingdom in the Age of the Discoveries.[13] These contradictory emphases are never really reconciled. This may have something to do with the fact that some of the *Hochkulturen* often regarded as archetypes of the patrimonial state – Pharaonic Egypt or Shang China – are among the few major historical experiences Runciman bypasses in his survey. The exception is Hammurapi's Babylon, to which he devotes a special attention. But the purpose of this is to argue that Old Babylonia was a kind of sport: an unclassifiable hybrid of different forms of the distribution of power, whose only counterpart was – Anglo-Saxon England. The two societies are judged *sui generis* on the grounds that 'they cannot be fitted into any of the five modes just listed'.[14] But why should they not be assigned to the patrimonial mode – where Runciman elsewhere locates Sumerian, Lombard or Merovingian societies, neighbours in time and space? The only reason discernible, from a single stray aside, seems to

---

12. TST II, p. 155.
13. TST II, pp. 190–91; 412; 446.
14. TST II, pp. 239–243.

be that for Runciman the royal administration of Hammurapi or Edward the Confessor exceeded that of a patrimonial ruler. This is scarcely persuasive. Was the staff at the disposal of Henry VII, or the House of Avis really less? Patrimonialism, one is forced to conclude, the least anchored of modes in the subjacent economic narrative, remains a relative black hole in Runciman's spectrum of forms.

There is, of course, another obvious objection to be made to the way this first of state structures features in the survey as a whole. This is simply the enormous historical spread between the cases Runciman adduces. Can the societies of Peisistratus, Ashoka, Chilperic I and Henry the Navigator be in any regard sensibly grouped together under a common label? The difficulty is rendered particularly acute in this case by the brevity and sketchiness of Runciman's initial definition of patrimonialism itself. But the same problem recurs within his more carefully worked out forms as well. Three examples will suffice here. In his very interesting discussion of the 'citizen mode', about which he writes with the authority of an accomplished classicist, Runciman applies the concept alike to Greek cities and the Roman republic, Swiss cantons, North Italian towns, and the Icelandic commonwealth.[15] Here the institutional resemblances, as well as differences, do indeed constitute a productive field for comparison. But however cognate the political fact of a free citizenry, is it plausible to claim that Rome in the epoch of Cicero and Iceland in the time of the Njalasaga were historically the same kind of society? One was a wealthy multi-continental empire, controlling a population of some 50 million from a capital city of 750,000, with massive social stratification, large standing armies, heavy taxation, high levels of monetization, advanced literary culture; the other a desperately poor, tiny pocket of perhaps 30,000 peasants, without mint, militia, trade, administration or written culture. The decisive structural difference, commanding all others, was that the principle of Roman civilization was urban from the outset, whereas Icelandic society was more completely rural than any other sovereign polity on record – there were scarcely even villages, let alone towns, in the heroic age of the commonwealth. A socio-economic contrast of this magnitude surely breaks any bracketing apart. Runciman is able to minimize its import only by deciding that 'for the purposes of sociological theory' towns can be regarded simply as 'institutional expressions of power' (a view close to that of another Cambridge sociologist,

15. TST II, pp. 197–202.

Anthony Giddens, who terms them 'power-containers').[16] The limitations of this way of looking at the historical significance of cities need no labouring.

Feudalism as a form of society provides a set of similar paradoxes. Here there is a considerable existing literature, going back at least to Bloch, that has tried to grapple with the taxonomic problems it poses. Opinion has generally divided into two camps: those who restrict the term to areas where the institution of the fief, as conditional landed property deriving from the nexus between benefice and vassalage, involves jurisdiction over a dependent peasantry, and those who extend it to any pre-capitalist regime of large landowners extracting customary rents from the direct producers. For the first, mediaeval Europe and Japan tend to exhaust the field; for the second, India, Africa, China, the Near East, Mesoamerica all had their examples of feudalism. Runciman takes up an intermediate position, by defining as feudal any regime of decentralized magnate power, where landlords extort a surplus from dependent cultivators. This looks like a reasonable compromise. Nevertheless, its application leads to some curious results. For on the one hand, he excludes mediaeval England from the range of feudal societies, on the grounds that the Angevin and Plantagenet monarchies were too centralized. On the other hand, he includes the Latin American states of the nineteenth century.[17] The resistance this proposal arouses is not just to do with an erratic use of the criterion of 'decentralization' itself – though that is certainly relevant: by no standard could governments like those of Roca in Argentina, Guzmán Blanco in Venezuela, or for that matter the Empire in Brazil, be deemed weaker than Lancastrian rulers, even at their height. More important, however, is the sheer developmental distance between the sword and lance world of Capetian or Ashikaga knights, to take two original cases of feudalism accepted by Runciman, and the railway and carbine universe of Latin American presidents.

Something of the same difficulty is visible in the discussion of 'absolutism' as well. Runciman identifies this with the bureaucratic mode of distribution of power, in which there is a strong central administration composed of salaried state servants without patrimonial ties to the ruler. He then takes as two paradigm examples the Roman Principate and the Bourbon monarchy. But so much had

---

16. TST II, p. 85; cp Giddens, *A Contemporary Critique of Historical Materialism*, London 1981, pp. 144–46.
17. TST II, pp. 214–15; 378; 381.

changed, materially and culturally, between the two that the pairing
loses analytic force. Without considering the wider society, the two
state structures themselves were qualitatively distinct in ways that
Mann – contrasting the 'territorial empire' with the 'organic
monarchy' – has graphically shown.[18] Louis XIV could raise an army
larger than Trajan's from a realm an eighth of the size. In Asia,
Runciman treats among his major instances of absolutism both Imperial China, from Sung times onwards, and Tokugawa Japan.[19] But the
dissimilarities between the two societies and their respective states are
so large as to form a virtual *topos* in Far Eastern scholarship – not least
because of the dramatically divergent outcomes of their common
collision with the West. To refer only to the structural profiles of the
holders of power: mandarin and samurai differed in recruitment to
office, focus of allegiance, relation to land, role in war, function in
learning. Nor was the machinery of power at all alike. The Heavenly
Kingdom commanded, in principle and in normal times in practice, an
effective monopoly of armed force. The Shogunate did not even control
a majority of the military levies in Japan, where the combined troop
strength of the outlying *han* always outnumbered its own – a weakness
brought home in the hour of its overthrow. Can a state of this kind be
usefully termed absolutist? A final quirk of Runciman's discussion
here, it may be noted, concerns England. Having contested that Angevin or Plantagenet rule was ever feudal, he goes on to deny that Stuart
government was ever absolutist. 'England alone evolved from a patrimonial to a bourgeois monarchy', he writes: 'there was no genuinely
feudal stage any more than there was ever a genuine absolutism.'[20]
This seems categorical enough. Yet elsewhere, in a rare moment of
apparent inadvertence, he paradoxically classifies the *Norman*
monarchy after the Conquest as absolutist.[21] There have been so many
perverse claims for English exceptionalism in this period that it would
be churlish to make too much of this particular contradiction. But it
nevertheless points to a more general problem.

   The tacit modulation from society to state in the typology as a whole
unbalances the triad that was intended to govern it. For virtually all
pre-modern states devoted the bulk of their resources to the mode of
coercion, in Runciman's sense: the administration of force was nearly
always much the most costly and most vital of their functions.

---

18. *The Sources of Social Power*, I, pp. 250ff. and 450ff.
19. TST II, pp. 225–26; 220.
20. TST II, p. 412.
21. TST II, p. 218.

Concentration of focus on states thus necessarily tends to relegate modes of production and persuasion to the margins of this field of vision. The result is twofold. On the one hand, economic disparities between the states assembled under a common rubric are largely disregarded, once their type has been positioned in the understated background sequence. But the sheer developmental distance between many of Runciman's cases strains to breaking-point the attempt to yoke them together conceptually. Technology in its widest sense, which is always in part specific to ecological setting, cannot be factored out so easily from historical comparison. France *circa* 870 and Argentina or Brazil *circa* 1870 were separated not just by a millennium, and a hemisphere, but an industrial revolution capable of material transformations across the world. Even on Runciman's own criteria they should be allocated to different modes of distribution of power, since serfdom predominated in the first, wage-labour in the second, and slavery in the third. Closer settings, or epochs, should put less burden on common definitions. But even here acute problems arise. The England of Edward I and of Elizabeth I was one country; but was it really the same kind of society, within the terms of the taxonomy itself, when villeinage had disappeared between the two? Sung China was a contemporary of Norman Sicily, and Runciman judges them absolutist alike. But where were the free peasant tenants, and high commercial agriculture, in the latter – to say nothing of industrial skills and teeming urban radiance?

In such classifications, culture fares no better than economy as a marker of substantive difference. The same double attrition of it occurs. In effect, Runciman first confines his 'mode of production' to what Marxists would call relations of production – excluding forces of production from it; and then often sets aside these relations themselves in constructing his typology. Similarly, he restricts his 'mode of persuasion' to the formal figures of deference – excluding all larger meaning-systems; and then gives only intermittent attention to these figures themselves. By his own criteria, for example, the form of legitimation of power was hereditary in the Poland of the sixteenth-century *szlachta*, but charismatic in the Bolivia of the nineteenth-century *caudillo* – each of which, however, he qualifies simply as feudal.[22] Despite their role in the theory of social variation, distinctions of this kind are absent from the taxonomy of pre-industrial forms that issues from it. Yet they constitute only one particular sort of 'persuasion' – the justification of rule. Differentiation here is, in other words, ideo-

---

22. Compare TST II, pp. 373–74 with p. 381.

logical rather than cultural. Runciman's solution to the problem of material productivity is to displace it into a generic chronicle outside the typology. His solution to the problem of cultural diversity is to trim culture itself to the typology, by treating it as no more than the *content* of the institutional rules of power, whose *pattern* composes a social structure.[23] This definition then allows him to abstract structure from culture for the purposes of historical classification. This is the operation which yields such startling juxtapositions as the twinning of Old Babylonia and Anglo-Saxon England, which depend on the elimination of central empirical features of each – cuneiform script or Christian belief – from the picture. Given the eloquence of Runciman's own case for the capture of cultural interiority, in Volume I of his *Treatise*, there is something wry in this procedure. Runciman himself remarks that in practice structure and culture never vary independently of each other, but this is a maxim whose consequences he never follows through. He observes at one point, for example, that Muslim societies were generally either warrior or patrimonial in structure, in part because Islam was inimical to feudalism.[24] But the reasons why, and extent to which, religious culture may have contributed to delimit the range of political structures in the Middle East – that is, potentially to select their form, rather than merely supply their content – is left quite unexplained. Questions like this fall beyond the ambit of the enquiry. One result is that Runciman can repeatedly assert that the diversification of human societies has greatly increased over time,[25] a thesis that is remotely defensible only if they are identified with structures in his sense (although even then the argument seems curious, since no more than four modes are held to exist today). In fact, it is the opposite process that is surely striking – the enormous reduction in the number of discrete forms of society under the impact of modern capitalism: above all, from the extraordinary variegation of primitive cultures, to the lesser number of religious civilizations, down to the global uniformities of industrial living today; but also from the formidable diversity of pre-capitalist relationships of production and power, to the relatively stark simplicity of the institutional map of the contemporary world.

In the spirit of *Economy and Society*, Runciman's typology is resolutely oriented to formal comparison – in diametric contrast to Mann's single-track narration. Each contends that the one excludes the other, Mann denying the possibility of a comparative macro-sociology,

---

23. TST II, p. 9.
24. TST II, p. 382.
25. TST II, p. 39.

Runciman scouting the prospect of an inter-societal history.[26] But although the *Treatise* is faithful to Weber in its taxonomic drive, pursued with a lucid rigour that leaves the sprawling mass of *Economy and Society* well behind, Runciman has no time for the teleology of rationalization that is the other side of Weber's inheritance. His theory of social evolution is designed to supersede it and all its counterparts, including Marx's dialectic of class or any other. This second moment of the enterprise occupies the long concluding part of the book, where Runciman tests the theory against a gamut of empirical cases. The originality of the evolutionary account put forward here lies, as has been seen, in its focus on practices rather than societies or groups. But Runciman's evolutionism also differs from its most recent predecessor in another way. For Parsons, the principal mechanism determining evolutionary change was adaptation – of societies to their environment. For Runciman, this mechanism is selection – or competition between practices. This is a sharp change of emphasis, which brings his sociology much closer to the neo-Darwinian leitmotif that the dynamic element in evolution is not the adjustment of species to an environment but the warfare of species with one another – Dawkins's 'arms races';[27] and which also, of course, marks a return to the earlier tradition of evolutionary social thought that gave pride of place to the 'survival of the fittest', in the nineteenth century.

The central objection to the Parsonian notion of adaptation – lately levelled most scathingly by Anthony Giddens[28] – was always its vacuity: for it never defined what it was that societies were adapting to, as they evolved, or what adaptation itself, taken as a nebulous 'reduction of uncertainty', actually meant. Does Runciman's alternative avoid these pitfalls? Certainly the idea of social selection is much more precise than that of adaptation, and specific practices more plausible as units for it than whole societies. But there is still a difficulty. The process of selection, in Runciman's account, turns on *competition*. How does he envisage the workings of this competition? The answer, if one looks at the test-cases he presents, proves to be oddly elusive. One of the most extended treatments is his discussion of the origins of European feudalism in France, Northern Italy and Germany, whose purpose is to show the 'selective pressures' that picked each end-result in the three regions – why the monarchy eventually achieved dominance in the first, towns in the second, magnates in the third; whereas

26. Compare *The Sources of Social Power*, I, pp. 30, 503, with TST II, pp. 60, 309.
27. Richard Dawkins, *The Blind Watch-Maker*, London 1986, pp. 178–193.
28. *The Constitution of Society*, Cambridge 1984, pp. 263– 274.

in the different context of the Byzantine state, there was a stand-off between monarchy and magnates.[29] Runciman's account of these variants is succinct and sensible. But is it more than an intelligent inspection of the respective balance of forces in each zone, of a kind that historians without evolutionary equipment make all the time – indeed to which he appeals later? The explanatory bonus yielded by the idea of competitive practices is unclear. Its effect seems more like a redescription.

The same could be said of Runciman's analysis of the ending of Japanese feudalism, as he sees it – the emergence of the *bakuhan* order under the first Tokugawa rulers. Here he advances the unusually strong claim that the isolation of Japan from exogenous pressures made its evolution from a feudal to an absolutist mode 'as near to inevitable as any such shift can be'.[30] The crucial practices that permitted it, he suggests, were those which involved the transformation of *bushi* from armed retainers into salaried officials. But how these were *competitively* selected remains unstated: Runciman contents himself with saying that this was the trend of the time. So far as the larger thesis goes, it is surely more plausible to argue the reverse – that the Shogunate never developed into an absolutism precisely because there was no external danger to impose true military (or administrative) centralization. This was why, in part, it proved so easy to overthrow from within once a threat did materialize from without. What an example like this indicates is that for the notion of competitive selection to have force, there must be some unambiguous medium or *Kampfplatz* in which rival practices can conflict, for one to triumph over the other.

Revolution would seem to form one major kind of arena for such a shock. Runciman contests the use of the term for the armed movement that created the Meiji state, which he views rather as the ideal-typical model of a (successful) reform. His own discussion of revolution, rebellion and reform – to which a substantial excursus is devoted – is full of ingenuity and interest. But it is Linnaean rather than Darwinian in emphasis, an illuminating typology more than an integral moment of the account of evolution. In fact, Runciman shows a consistent scepticism about the importance of revolutionary change for social selection. The two examples he analyses at length are the Mexican and the French.[31] He concludes that the first merely restored the Porfirian *status quo ante* in more centralized and secular guise; while the second

---

29. TST II, pp. 370–73; 299–301.
30. TST II, p. 388.
31. TST II, pp. 355–367.

was accidental in origin and irrelevant in outcome, leaving the evolution of French society unaffected. The Russian Revolution, by contrast, was truly transformative, but it too was historically an 'improbable' occurrence, let loose only by the hazards of the Great War.[32]

For classical theories of social evolution, the prime arena of social selection was, of course, precisely war. It was the battlefield that provided the supreme medium of decision, between alternative forms of collective life. Paradoxically, however, Runciman also shows the utmost reticence towards this kind of test, which acquires little or no salience in his survey. The reason he gives, revealingly, is one that recurs in his treatment of revolutions. Wars are dramatic events, which may indeed 'divert the whole course of human history'. But their 'outcome is so often a matter of chance', the product of 'accidents of fortune', that they frequently 'cannot be grounded in an evolutionary theory concerned only with the sociological causes of differences in modes and sub-types of the distribution of the means of production, persuasion and coercion.'[33] Empirically, the claim that the issue of military conflicts tends to be especially fortuitous is quite unsupported here. Runciman's only illustration is the Second World War – in many ways a particularly unhappy one, given the huge disparity in material resources between the victorious Allies and the Axis powers. Theoretically, however, what is significant is the apparent downplaying of war, as the regular terrain of competitive selection that might be expected within a quasi-Darwinian framework. Here it looks as if Runciman may be over-compensating for Spencer's notorious stress on it, in a wish to put as much distance as he can between their two accounts of evolution.

There is, finally, one other medium of competition which does not feature as prominently as might have been imagined in Runciman's theory of social selection. This is simply the market itself. The most widespread version of an evolutionary outlook today is the belief that the Cold War is coming to an end as the superior economic practices of the West visibly prevail over those of the East, portending the rapid elimination of an alternative societal form that has been proved historically uncompetitive. This has, of course, long been the prediction of von Hayek, a thinker for whom the truths of economics have always been continuous with those of biology, in a neo-Darwinian synthesis of his own.[34] It is noticeable that Runciman's reserve extends to this

---

32. TST II, p. 422.
33. TST II, pp. 433–34.
34. See *The Fatal Concert*, London 1988, pp. 11–28.

diagnosis as well. His treatment of Communist societies, cool and judicious throughout – it contains a remarkable shaft of observation on Stalin's purges – gives no hint of such a prospect. Perhaps he is just suspending judgement.

These uncertainties all concern the mechanisms of social selection. But biological evolution, of course, has another and prior side to it – the genetic variation that furnishes the raw materials for natural selection. It is here that the real, insurmountable weakness of any theory of social, or for that matter cultural, evolution lies. For all analogies break down at this crux. The mutation of genes is a strictly random element within the process of natural evolution. That is, the causes of misprints in DNA have no relation whatever to the filter that selects these: they belong to another order of determination altogether. The origin of mutations is in this sense completely irrelevant to the origin of species. They belong to two separate planes of intelligibility. But does this hold in social or cultural life? The formal counterpart of genes in Runciman's explanation of social evolution are practices of power. His biological model then commits him to the claim that the origin of these practices – the mutations which are selected or eliminated – is *also* random. Innovations consequently become 'intrusions from another causal sequence', which can be treated simply as 'acts of God' for the purposes of social explanation.[35] The structure of argument is the same in Franco Moretti's splendid *Signs Taken for Wonders* (with Gould rather than Dawkins in the background), which proposes a theory of literary evolution where genres play the role of species, and individual works furnish the random mutations.[36]

Human history, however, exhibits no such Darwinian dualism. For in the process of its unfolding, innovation belongs to *the same plane* as selection. There is no split-level causation here. For both the genesis, and the generalization, of social practices always involve the common material of conscious human agency. The origins of institutional (or aesthetic) forms are thus never divided by an epistemological abyss from their stabilization. The two rather compose one continuous flow of intentional action. They are thus, contrary to Runciman's suggestion, amenable to the same kind of social explanation. There is no sense in which major social innovations can be treated as 'random inputs' for a plausible theory of historical development. Some of the finest Marxist work of recent years has, in fact, been devoted to elucidating the origins

---

35. TST I, pp. 199–200; TST II, pp. 42–43.
36. *Signs Taken for Wonders*, London 1988 (revised edn), pp. 262–278.

of such momentous new practices as: the emergence of the Greek *polis* from the debris of the Mycenaean palace-kingdom (Ellen Wood), of feudal relations from the involution of late-imperial Roman society (Chris Wickham), of capitalist farming from the unravelling of English manorialism (Robert Brenner) – all innovations of central importance to Runciman's own account of social evolution.[37] But there is nothing specific to historical materialism in such enquiries. Perhaps the greatest modern example of one is Peter Brown's masterpiece *The Body and Society*, which explores the emergence of sexual ascesis in Early Christianity, a far-reaching practice of the kind Runciman's theory leaves aside.

Beginnings such as these can all be reconstructed as intelligible patterns of intentional action, typically yielding unintentional consequences – in this no different from their ongoing sequels. But there are, of course, historical episodes which bear the impress of a much more deliberate kind of will. The practice of social insurance, with all its long-term significance for the construction of the contemporary welfare state, was inaugurated by Bismarck for specific political ends. Can the initiative of the Iron Chancellor really be treated as an Act of God? Were the reforms by the Meiji oligarchs of rank-order or land-tenure mere 'random inputs' into the evolution of modern Japanese society? Should the inception of international monetary coordination by Keynes and White at Bretton Woods be regarded as belonging to a cognitive world different from the one governed by the workings of the gold-dollar standard? Social engineering of this kind is a central, pervasive fact of the modern world. Runciman compares it to stock-breeding – no disproof, he insists, of natural selection from random genetic mutation. But no rancher or pigeon-fancier has ever produced a new species. Yet what, in Runciman's own typology, was the birth of the Soviet state other than a true speciation – and who would care to deny the prior purpose of Lenin and the Bolsheviks in bringing it about? In all these cases, the skein of historical causality is one. The reasons why Bismarck, Kido, Keynes or Lenin made their innovations – response to the rise of the socialist movement, the threat of foreign takeover, the memory of pre-war slump, the opportunity of revolution – are no different in kind or level from the reasons why these practices 'took' as institutions thereafter, as their authors approximately intended – say: moderation of popular insecurity, contribution to

---

37. Chris Wickham, 'The Other Transition: from the Ancient World to Feudalism', *Past and Present* 103, 1983 ; Ellen Meiksins Wood, *Peasant-Citizen and Slave*, London 1988, pp. 84–98; T. Aston and C. Philpin, eds., *The Brenner Debate*, Cambridge 1985.

national growth, stabilization of foreign exchanges, social promotion of labour. Just because that is so, historical development shows not the slightest similarity to natural evolution in the tempo of its innovations. The whole force of Darwinian biology lies in its stress on the implacable slowness with which natural selection necessarily works, since the only variations offered to it are infinitesimal modifications – whose gradual cumulation alone, in an unimaginable series of tiny steps, produces evolution. The social innovations that are Runciman's topic are utterly different in both the scale of the variation they represent, and the speed of the changes they unleash. It is a far cry from the reign of Monera, lasting three billion years, to the rise of Islam in fifty.

Undeterred by these disparities, Runciman concludes his work with a grand restatement of his major themes, and claims. 'However much further refinement and elaboration is called for, the fundamental idea that the evolution of human societies and their constituent roles and institutions proceeds through a continuing struggle for power whose outcome is determined by the competitive selection of practices in the three mutually irreducible dimensions of social structure is no less demonstrably superior to its rivals – or so I believe – than Darwin's was.'[38] Social evolution, like natural, is directional in the sense that both reveal a cumulative increase in complexity. Yet each buries every teleology beyond hope of resurrection: the history of humanity, as of life itself, has no pattern, goal or meaning. The one significant difference between the two is that in society 'power, not survival, is the criterion of success'.[39] That was the shift made by Nietzsche, critic of the generalized notion of a 'struggle for life' in *The Twilight of the Idols*: 'where there is a struggle, it is a struggle for *power*'.[40]

Nietzsche himself is a reminder, however, that to repudiate teleology is not necessarily to renounce metaphysics. His will to power was resolved out of a – fabulously – speculative instinctual psychology. For all the distance in temperament and outlook, there is a trace of the same temptation in Runciman. He looks forward to the day when advances in psychology will provide a more complete underpinning for his sociology. Meanwhile, it can be said with assurance, in social evolution there are only people 'competing with one another for economic, ideological and coercive power, as they will continue to do as long as the species survives'.[41] The agonistics of this vision are close to

---

38. TST II, p. 449.
39. TST II, p. 291.
40. *The Twilight of the Idols*, Harmondsworth 1968, p. 75.
41. TST II, p. 448.

fortune-telling. Should we say, with Nietzsche, that competition for power will be perpetual between the sexes too? A doctrine of Eternal Rivalry belongs with that of Return, outside any rational social science. This gesture aside, the seriousness of Runciman's commitment to such a science is never in doubt. He explains that it was his conviction of the essential unity of scientific method, eloquently defended in Volume One, that helped him reappropriate evolution as the *idée maîtresse* of Volume Two of his treatise. The result is a theory of history that, by any standards, amounts to a large intellectual sum.

1989

8

On Emplotment – Andreas Hillgruber

Of the literature involved in the historical dispute that broke out in West Germany four years ago, one work stands out in retrospect. Andreas Hillgruber's *Two Kinds of Ruin* not only poses what is likely to be the most persistent substantive problem, it also raises the most significant formal issue to emerge from that debate. The text comprises two essays, whose respective subjects are designated by the sub-title, *The Dismemberment of the German Reich* and *The End of European Jewry*.[1] In their original versions these were written separately; the latter, much shorter than the former, concluding a colloquium on 'The Murder of European Jews in the Second World War'. But both essays are terse, their economy not unusual in this historian.

The first question presented by the text is an obvious one. The two accounts that make up the work are not interwoven, but remain at a distance from each other. What, then, is the force of their juxtaposition? A dissociate double narrative is a rare form of historical composition. Plutarch's *Lives*, a biographical undertaking, is perhaps the only sustained use of it. What is its function here? If we adopt the vocabulary of *Metahistory*, the figural ground of the text is the trope termed in classical rhetoric *collatio*[2] – in which two objects are set in parallel, without being identified, by means of a metaphorical projection across them. Hayden White does not discuss this particular device, but his claim that tropes typically govern the narrative strategies of historians[3] – whatever its general validity – undoubtedly holds good here.

---

1. *Zweierlei Untergang. Die Zerschlagung des Deutschen Reiches und das Ende des europäischen Judentums*, Berlin 1986. The original version of the first essay was published in 1985; that of the second essay was written in 1984.

2. Quintilian, *Institutio Oratoria*, 5.11.23, 8.3.77.

3. *Metahistory*, Baltimore 1973, p. 427: 'A given historian will be inclined to choose one or other of the different modes of explanation, on the level of argument,

In this case the initiating trope commands the emplotment in a quite precise sense. The conventional narrative of the Second World War represents it as a gigantic ordeal that nevertheless ends with the reconciliation of a fortunate victory – that is, in the technical terms used by Frye and White, plots it as comedy. Hillgruber's figure reverses this representation, by the gesture of an apposition which draws the fate of Germany into the orbit of that of Jewry, an area of incontestable tragedy. He insisted on the category of tragedy, expressly, in a significant passage on the German beginning and ending of the war. 'Whether the concept of the tragic can be applied to the events that culminated in the Second World War, may be left open; guilt and fate, legitimate demand and blatant injustice, tyranny and entanglement, were here inextricably mixed. But in the case of the German East in 1944–45 we ought indeed to speak of tragic processes, for there it is clear that there was no way out for the soldiers and inhabitants of those provinces.'[4]

In *The Content of the Form* White has argued that narrativity always involves moralization – historical emplotments invariably embodying ethical judgements.[5] Plutarchian parallelism is certainly a case in point. What is the moral effect of Hillgruber's construction? In the historians' controversy, it was assimilated by his critics to arguments of Ernst Nolte. Both were charged with relativizing the Nazi extermination of the Jews, by extenuating comparison – in other words, a banalization of evil. The procedures of the two were nevertheless distinct. Nolte's work fully meets the charge. Its direct effect is to diminish the enormity of the Judeocide, in two ways; by arguing that it was typologically – in quantity and quality – no worse than other great massacres of the twentieth century; and that it was causally precipitated by the fear and example of Communist terror, within a European civil war. Hillgruber's text makes neither of these claims. His essay on the Final Solution asserts it to be historically unique, and ascribes it essentially to Nazi racial doctrines.[6] Within the spectrum of scholarly interpretations of the extermination programme (as of the war aims) of the Third Reich, Hillgruber was an intentionalist, who stressed Hitler's fanatical pursuit of biological purification and territorial expansion in

---

emplotment, or ideological implication, in response to the imperatives of the trope which informs the linguistic protocol he has used to prefigure the field of historical occurrence singled out by him for investigation.'

4. *Zweierlei Untergang*, p. 64.

5. 'Narrativity in the Representation of Reality', *The Content of the Form*, Baltimore 1987, pp. 21–25.

6. *Zweierlei Untergang*, p. 98 ('historische Einmaligkeit').

the East, as the central goals – the nucleus – of Nazi ambitions at large.[7] A certain intentionalism, by concentrating overwhelmingly on the demonic figure of the Führer himself, can tacitly exonerate any wider sections, or longer traditions, of German society from responsibility for the crimes of the regime. Hillgruber, who went out of his way to reject any view that would put Nazism into a realm of pathology outside history, was not of this kind. He dated the origins of both the turn to virulent anti-semitism and the drive for an immense empire in the East to the year 1916, when Hindenburg and Ludendorff took command of the Third Army on the Russian Front.[8] When the fatal opportunity of limitless conquest and killing came twenty-five years later, he stressed, responsibility for them was very widely shared. In the party and state apparatus, apolitical functionaries as well as zealots organized the extermination of the Jews; much larger numbers carried out their deportation; while 'the mass of the German population', preoccupied with the pressures and hardships of the war, predictably accepted the *unvermeidlicherweise nur unzulänglich verschleierten Vorgangs* – 'a process that could never be more than inadequately concealed'.[9] It would be difficult to find a stronger statement of far-ranging moral responsibility than this. The officer corps too, Hillgruber argued, was deeply implicated in the practices of exterminism unleashed by Operation Barbarossa. The traditional tension within it between an ethos of corporate honour and a duty of strict obedience had shifted steadily towards unconditional fulfilment of orders from the Wilhelmine epoch onwards; and when that ended freebooters outside the service knew no law but violence anyway. After 1918, German soldiers could take the path of the Freikorps or that of the Reichswehr under Seeckt. 'These roads seem to have divided', Hillgruber grimly observes, but in the collaboration of the SS and Wehrmacht elites in the Russian campaign of the 1940s, 'they ran more or less closely back together again'.[10] Without the active or passive collaboration of a large part of the traditional military leadership of the country, in whom all moral substance had been lost, Hitler could never have waged his unprecedented war of annihilation in the East, which from the start had combined territorial expansion and racial

---

7. See his fundamental essay, 'Die "Endlösung" und das deutsche Ostimperium als Kernstück des rassenideologischen Programms des Nationalsozialismus', in *Deutsche Grossmacht und Weltpolitik*, Dusseldorf 1977, pp. 258–261.

8. *Zweierlei Untergang*, pp. 81–83; *Germany and the Two World Wars*, Cambridge Mass. 1981, pp. 41–44.

9. *Zweierlei Untergang*, p. 98.

10. *Deutsche Grossmacht und Weltpolitik*, p. 270.

extermination.

It cannot therefore be said that the purpose of Hillgruber's dual narrative is to normalize the Final Solution, by assimilating it to other mass killings. Its function is rather to solemnize the German Expulsions as a tragedy too, albeit of another kind, historically adjacent to it. The distinction is not a mere artifice. It corresponds, as we have seen, to two quite different treatments of the Judeocide. Nevertheless, it remains to be asked: within the generic category of tragedy, which in principle might allow of any number of illustrations, what is Hillgruber's specific justification for associating the fate of the Germans in the East with that of the Jews? His foreword asserts more than the formal characterization of both as national catastrophes, of which there have been many. It argues that this particular pair 'belong together'.[11] What reasons does Hillgruber give for this commonality? He stresses, in the same sentences, that the pre-history of and responsibility for each differed. 'The murder of the Jews was exclusively a consequence of the radical racial doctrine that in 1933 became the ideology of the state in Hitler's Germany.'[12] The expulsion of the Germans, on the other hand, was not simply a response to the crimes of the Nazi dictatorship, but also answered to independent war aims of the Allies, formulated in ignorance of the full measure of these crimes. Later in the text Hillgruber argues that in a longer-term historical perspective, the fatal idea of *völkische Feld- und Flurbereinigung* – ethnic clean sweeps – can be seen to have spread practices of organized mass killing and forcible population transfer from the European periphery, when Armenians and Greeks were their principal victims, to the whole of Europe under Nazi domination, not leaving even the British or American record intact by the end of the war.[13] Critics have objected to this contextualization, but it is difficult to deny it all validity. Hillgruber does not here equate the Judeocide with the massacres and deportations that preceded it, but views it rather as the finalized absolute of an inhumanity of which they were initial or relative versions. The argument, however, is not pressed. Hillgruber's linkage of the destiny of Germans of the East with that of the Jews does not essentially depend on either the proximate causes or precise character of the disasters which overtook them; it rests instead on the ultimate *consequence* that issued from them. They belong together, above all, for their common effect, which was to destroy the

---

11. *Zweierlei Untergang*, p. 9.
12. Ibid.
13. *Zweierlei Untergang*, p. 67.

'Europe of the Centre'. Once the middle of the continent was broken to pieces in the cataclysm of war, Europe as a whole was the loser. Division and subordination to the two Great Powers on its wings inevitably followed.[14]

How is this construction to be assessed? Much of the discussion of it has treated Hillgruber's text as if it were more homogeneous than it is. In fact, it contains a number of different arguments, which require a more discriminating response. We may look at four of them. The first is in a sense the most obvious. Because Hillgruber never directly compares the two processes of which his title speaks, but simply juxtaposes them under a runic adjective *zweierlei* (two kinds), the parallel narrative cannot accord them their due disproportionate weight. The result is inevitably to scale down, however inadvertently and *in*directly, the nature of the Judeocide. The effect of this oblique reduction is then aggravated by the register in which the end of the German East is described. Notoriously, Hillgruber declared that the – presumptively German – historian was obliged to 'identify' with 'the concrete fate of the German population in the East' and therefore also with 'the desperate and sacrificial efforts' of the German armed forces to protect it from the vengeful advance of the Red Army, with its train of savageries and deportations.[15] The notion of identification, often at work in the practice of historians, but rarely so ingenuously professed, belongs to a certain traditional canon of tragedy. Hillgruber's appeal to it has been emphatically and rightly dismissed by Wehler and Maier, in particular.[16] Behind it, almost certainly, lay biographical experience. Hillgruber grew up in Königsberg, where his father was a schoolteacher dismissed by the Nazis, and as a young man fought in the Wehrmacht's defensive campaign in East Prussia in the winter of 1945, which he describes as allowing two million refugees to escape across the Baltic to Denmark or Schleswig– Holstein. Had Hillgruber simply noted this personal background, as a subjective basis for his account of the situation confronting German civilians and troops in the eastern provinces, rather than declaring identification with them objectively mandatory, few could have quarrelled. But in making this false move, Hillgruber slipped in one step from the understandable to

---

14. *Zweierlei Untergang*, pp. 10, 73–74.

15. *Zweierlei Untergang*, pp. 23–25. Note the subject-specification: 'Dies is das gerafft zusammengefasste und mit einigen deutlichen Akzenten versehene Geschehen des Zusammenbruchs im Osten 1944/1945, *wie es sich aus deutscher Sicht darstellt*': p. 42.

16. See the commentaries of each in Hans-Ulrich Wehler, *Entsorgung der deutschen Vergangenheit?*, Munich 1988, pp 49–53; and Charles Maier, *The Unmasterable Past*, Cambridge Mass. 1989, pp. 21–23.

the indefensible. His construction is immediately compromised. For identification with the fate of the Jews is not demanded of the historian in the companion essay. Perhaps he thought that otiose.

The procedural fallacy of Hillgruber's plea for identification, nevertheless, does not in itself dispose of the substance of his analysis of the collapse of the German East. Hillgruber makes three fundamental claims here. The first concerns the final year of the German military effort against Russia. In June 1944 the Wehrmacht had suffered its decisive defeat of the war, when the strongest of its forces, Army Group Centre, was suddenly overwhelmed and broken by a Soviet offensive in Belorussia that cost it 350,000 casualties – four times the number at Stalingrad – and drove a huge breach through the German front, exposing East Prussia to immediate attack. A month later, the military opposition led by von Stauffenberg attempted to kill Hitler and overthrow the Nazi regime. How does Hillgruber judge the *Attentat* of 20 July? He argues that by that date, after so many previous opportunities had been missed, the conspiracy was too late. The war was by now lost anyway, and even if the coup had been successful, it would only have led to strife and chaos in the German leadership, accelerating the debacle on the Eastern front. The motive of the Resistance plotters was an ethic of expressive intention, designed to show the world that another Germany than that of the regime existed. By contrast, he suggests, many of those soldiers and officials who fought on did so out of an ethic of responsibility, seeking to lessen the consequences for the German population in the East of looming Soviet conquest and vengeance. Hillgruber in effect validates their choice. The continued resistance of the Wehrmacht permitted, he argues, the escape of two million people across the Baltic, and the eventual surrender of some 60 per cent of the troops in the East – close to another two million – to the Western Allies rather than to the USSR, so saving large numbers of further lives. From a strictly German standpoint, then, the prolongation of the war for another ten months appears from Hillgruber's account as if it were the lesser evil. It is this suggestion, more than any other in *Zweierlei Untergang*, which lacks any historical warrant. Here the full strength of the moral reaction against Hillgruber expressed by Habermas and Wehler was justified.[17] For in those months, German military and civilian casualties alone amounted to between one and a half and two million dead – half the total killed in the fighting of the

---

17. See, in particular, *Entsorgung der deutschen Vergangenheit?*, pp. 51–58.

entire war: not to speak of the continuing victims of Nazi terror, and Allied casualties on the other side. If a counter-factual calculation is to be made, the overthrow of Hitler in July 1944, by shortening the war, would without question have saved far more lives that were actually lost than the continuation of the fighting hypothetically saved, before Germany surrendered. Moreover, the surrender itself would all but certainly have been partially negotiated – as, despite the principle of unconditional surrender, was in practice that of Japan, in a far weaker position vis-à-vis the Allies in August 1945 than a Goerdeler government would have been in August 1944; not to speak of the peace concluded by Finland in September. Post-war suffering and loss for Germany would thus also have been curtailed.

For the terms of the peace in turn play a central role in Hillgruber's second argument. One of the major themes of his text is that the truncation of Germany, by the transfer of East Prussian, Pomeranian and Silesian lands to Poland in 1945, cannot be regarded simply as geopolitical retribution for Nazi criminality in the East. For it had already been projected as a strategic goal by leading Polish politicians in the inter-war period, and was then adopted by Britain and the United States during the war, with the aim of eradicating what was widely supposed to be the driving-force of Prussian militarism, and putting an end to Germany as a major European power. These plans, Hillgruber argues, envisaged the expulsion of up to six million people from their homes, in the name of *raison d'état*, not of commutative justice. In the event, the number of those expelled at the end of the war was eleven million, of whom probably two million perished in the process. These deportations were – it follows from Hillgruber's account that he does not even need to say so – unjustifiable. Herein lay the final German tragedy of the war.

The most extended attempt to rebut this case has been undertaken by the English historian Richard Evans, in his recent general review of the German controversy, *In Hitler's Shadow*. Evans argues that the role of the German minorities in Poland, Czechoslovakia and elsewhere before the war had revealed their subversive potential, convincing the Western Allies of the need to remove them; that Poland had to be compensated in the West for its loss of territories to Russia in the East; and that in any case, however they were brought about, 'forty years of uninter-rupted peace add up to an unanswerable defence of the arrangements reached in 1945'. Evans concedes that the expulsions were accom-plished with 'appalling harshness', but maintains that 'the wholly unacceptable means by which the expulsions were effected can and must be distinguished from the end sought by the expulsions themselves.'[18] The distinction, however, does not convince. What are the acceptable means of forcibly dispossessing millions of people from their homes and driving them from their native lands? Sudeten irredentism did provide the pretext for Hitler's aggression against Czechoslovakia; but did it therefore warrant the wholesale deportation of the German communities of the area after the war? On the authority of the current Czech president himself, it did not. Was Poland's extension to the Oder–Neisse Line in the West a compensation of equivalent nature to its contraction behind the Curzon Line in the East? In the territories lost, Poles were a minority of perhaps thirty per cent of the population – which was why the Entente had originally awarded them to Russia after the First World War; in the territories gained, Germans were a majority of nearly ninety per cent of the population.[19] Is the fact of subsequent peace in itself justification of these events? Both ethically and logically, it is quite insufficient. Peace has reigned for seventy years along Turkey's Eastern frontier, over the graves of the Armenian community: is that a defence of them?[20] The population of the German East was expelled, not massacred; but is it really the case that peace depended on such expulsions – that no alternative settlement was conceivable? Allied calculations precluded any other outcome, it may be said; that, however, is to confirm the force of Hillgruber's observation that traditional imperial interests, as well as (and capable of overriding) universal values, determined the fate of Germany in 1945. The violences committed then were in no way commensurate with those inflicted by the Nazi state. But for the millions who lived through them,

---

18. *In Hitler's Shadow*, London 1989, pp. 99, 95.

19. The ethnic composition of Poland's eastern *kresy*, in which Ukrainians and Belorussians formed a large majority, may now be beyond detailed reconstruction. Of a total population in these regions of some 13 million in 1939, over a million Poles were deported east by the Soviet Union, of whom large numbers perished, while after the war some two million made their way west.

20. Evans is mistaken in asserting that 'Hillgruber's account [of the political background to the expulsions] is contradicted by recent research both in its detail and in its overall thrust' (*In Hitler's Shadow*, p. 95). The most scholarly recent work on the origins of the Oder–Neisse Line, Sarah Terry's study of Sikorski's wartime aims and their prewar background, *Poland's Place in Europe*, Princeton 1983, makes it clear that Polish annexation of East Prussia, Pomerania and Silesia was an objective entertained by the exile government without reference to the *kresy*; and that Churchill, within a few months of signing the Atlantic Charter, was assuring it that principles of self-determination would not stand in the way of measures to break the power of Prussia: pp. 3–10, 272–286. It should be said that Hillgruber's account is not directed only at foreign powers: it does not spare the rulers of Germany either, from the Second Reich through Weimar to the Third, whom he charges with an increasing disregard for the safety of the inhabitants of the German East: *Zweierlei Untergang*, p. 69.

they were suffering enough.[21] When Hillgruber was asked in a questionnaire what was his fondest dream, and ironically replied – 'to live a
life in Königsberg', his answer commands respect. It did not mean he
thought the disappearance of his native province reversible; but he
recalled for explanation, and criticized, the expulsions which had
brought it about. Although Hillgruber's reflection is here at its most
nationally self-absorbed, the issues it raises are paradoxically of most
contemporary concern to Jews too – as Israeli historians recover,
against official legends, the complex and painful realities of the Arab
flights involved in the birth of their country, at a time when some voices
envisage their repetition in the West Bank today.

Finally, beyond the dilemmas of German soldiers or the expulsions
of German farmers, there was in Hillgruber's view a third tragic
element in the collapse of 1945. The obliteration of the German East,
he argued, broke Europe itself in two; for it had historically been
Germany, the 'Land of the Middle', which had been the principal
bridge between the Western and Eastern halves of the continent –
mediating, in innumerable economic, cultural and political, as well as
military ways, influences from beyond the Rhine into the vast area
between the Baltic and the Black Seas. Once this bridge was destroyed,
Europe's centre could not hold, and the continent was doomed to
scission and subjection by the rival Great Powers on its flanks. The
dismemberment of Germany thus also spelt the overthrow of Europe as
a whole in world politics. It remained to be seen whether a common
German nationality and a Europe of the centre could be reconstructed
anew.[22] These reflections were bitterly attacked by Habermas, who
charged them with threatening 'the only reliable basis of our connexion
to the West', and by Wehler, who declared that they subverted loyalty
to the West 'far more effectively even than the foolish talk of the
Greens'.[23] For Habermas and Wehler the very idea of Germany as a
'Land of the Middle', indeed of a 'Europe of the Centre', was to be
rejected, as incompatible with the anchorage of the Federal Republic in
the West – not just Western Europe, but the Western world headed by

---

21. There is a lexical echo in the closing lines of the two most famous poems inspired
by the events described in *Zweierlei Untergang*, Celan's *Todesfuge* and Solzhenitsyn's
Prusskie Nochi. The blue eyes of *Der Tod is ein Meister aus Deutschland sein auge is blau*
are those of a camp guard, seen by their Jewish victims; of *s bledno-sinimi glazami/
neprivychno blizko sblizyas'* those of a peasant girl, seen by the Russian soldier who has
forced her.

22. *Zweierlei Untergang*, pp. 72–74.

23. Jürgen Habermas, 'Eine Art Schadensabwicklung', in Piper Verlag, '*Historiker-
streit*', Munich 1987, p. 76; Wehler, *Entsorgung der deutschen Vergangenheit?*, p. 210.

the US. Modern German national identity, Habermas maintained, could take only one legitimate form: a constitutional patriotism centred on Bonn. Anything else was a dangerous lure.

How are we to judge this exchange? Strangely, in their haste to repudiate Hillgruber's whole problematic, such critics overlooked what is in fact the main reproach to be made against his treatment of it. Hillgruber starts by linking – programmatically – the Jewish and German catastrophes as interlinked dimensions of the collapse of Central Europe. But in what follows, whereas the role played by Germans in the history of the region is directly touched upon, more than once, that of the Jews is not. Logically, Hillgruber's argument requires some rendered account of the contribution of European Jewry to the binding of the two halves of the continent. That role merits the term mediation much less ambiguously than the German, since it was always essentially economic and intellectual, free of the stains of political and military domination that marked the latter. The consequences of its removal are evident enough – there are few more vivid illustrations of the disappearance of what a Europe of the centre once meant than the culture of, say, post-war Austria. Hillgruber found no words for this. To register it is not to deny, but to accept, the validity of the notion of peoples and places located in the middle of Europe, on whose fate the linkages between its western and its eastern ends historically depended. Hillgruber's own concern with this theme was, of course, not simply a scholarly but also an avowedly political one. Despite the catastrophe of the Second World War, he maintained, Germany's role in the centre of Europe was not inevitably cancelled for all time. German national identity could not be divorced from the spatial setting of an undivided nation. Replying to his critics, he wrote that it was necessary always to keep in mind the prospect – the hope – that one day Germany would be reunited again on the basis of self-determination.[24] In however unforeseeable a way, the possibility of a reconstruction of Central Europe was still open.

Hillgruber died in May 1989. In November the Berlin wall was breached. Today, less than a year later, German unification is at hand. Hillgruber, a conservative, saw things here more lucidly than his liberal critics. One might say that his equations are taking shape before our eyes. The reunion of Germany will indeed involve the reemergence of a Central Europe – already *in statu nascendi*; and the reconstruction of Central Europe will all but certainly restore independence to Europe as

---

24. 'Für die Forschung gibt es kein Frageverbot', *'Historiker-Streit'*, pp. 240–41.

a whole, in the wider theatre of the world. To have asserted these connexions so clearly, on the eve of their historical realization, was not an inconsiderable achievement. Two years ago, Charles Maier described Hillgruber's emphasis on Germany's mediating role between Western and Eastern Europe as 'the geopolitics of nostalgia'.[25] The phrase looks less appropriate now. Maier's discussion of the problems of national identity raised in the course of the German historians' debate nevertheless remains the most interesting exploration of the issues at stake. Criticizing conceptions of the 'land of the middle', he argued that national identity should in any case not be viewed simply as a deposit of successive historical experiences. It ought perhaps rather to be rethought as something closer to the older idea of national character – one especially strong, he notes, in America, from the time of Crevecoeur onwards: a character in good part amenable to non-historical, quasi-anthropological analysis. To this end Maier invokes Lévi-Strauss's well-known denial of any special value to history.[26] The character or identity of an individual is, of course, always something relatively plural and unstable – so how much more so is that of any nation. But if the concept of a national identity is at all negotiable, and its elements be held to exceed the imprints of historical time, what are the most plausible further constituents? Surely not the biological substrata of race detected by Gobineau, nor the involuntary uniformities of the human mind divined by Lévi-Strauss, but the coordinates of geographical space. These are durable and material enough, in most cases, to possess an obvious specific efficacy. The logic of Maier's argument thus paradoxically points back to the very thematic he initially discounts. German national identity, if it exists, must in part be a function of German territorial position. It is because the idea of the 'land of the middle' corresponds to certain objective realities that it was a polemical mistake of the liberal Left in Germany to allow conservatives to make it their own. There the Greens showed better sense.

Scrutiny of *Zweierlei Untergang* reveals, then, a series of complexities. Hillgruber was a nationalist historian, but he was not an apologist of National Socialism. The device of *collatio* did not in itself dictate a diminution of the Final Solution. Nor did Hillgruber's treatment of the destruction of European Jewry as such contribute to one. But any juxtaposition of Jewish and German fates demanded an exceptional – moral and empirical – delicacy that was beyond the compass of this

25. *The Unmasterable Past*, p. 23.
26. Ibid., pp. 151–56.

historian. In its absence, the laconic could not but seem the insensible. For its part, coloured by personal memory, Hillgruber's obituary of the German East was of divided validity too: its counter-factual assessment of the conspiracy of July 1944 groundless, its factual verdict on the expulsions of 1945–47 well-grounded. Finally, Hillgruber's projection of Central Europe as the common scene, and victim, of the tragedies he related, signally failed to situate the Jews historically within it; but, political in impulse, it captured the current position of the Germans, and some of its possible consequences, remarkably well. All of this, in its mixture of acuteness and obtuseness, fallacies and foresights, is quite normal for a historian.

Abnormal, however, is the subject. If we ask, what are the limits of a historical representation of Nazism and the Final Solution, through the prism of Hillgruber's work, the answer is surely this. Firstly, certain absolute limits are set by the evidence. Denial of the existence of either – of the regime, or its crimes – is plainly ruled out. No such issue arises in this case. Counter-factuals are also subject to control by the rules of evidence, which will eliminate some of them, as they do in this case. Narrative strategies, to be credible, always operate within *exterior* limits of this kind. Secondly, however, such narrative strategies are in turn subject to a double *interior* limitation. On the one hand, certain kinds of evidence preclude certain sorts of emplotment – the Final Solution cannot *historically* be written as romance, or comedy. On the other hand, any generic emplotment has only a weak determinative power over the selection of evidence. Hillgruber could legitimately depict the end of East Prussia as tragic; however, that choice, permitted by the evidence, did not in itself dictate the series of particular empirical judgements that make up his account of it. There is a large gap between genre and script. Other, divergent, tragic accounts could be written of the same events – and these would not be aesthetically incommensurable forms, or so many fictions, but epistemologically discriminable attempts to reach the truth. The typical measure of such discrimination is not the presence of *suggestio falsi*, very rare in modern historiography, but the degree of *suppressio veri* – that is, representation omitted rather than misrepresentation committed. In history, as in the sciences, the depth of a truth is usually a function of its width – how much of the evidence it engages and explains.

Narratives, then, are never plenipotentiaries over the past. The modern scepticism that would reduce history to rhetoric has a number of sources. It would be a mistake to read these selectively – as if, for example, one could trace in them principally a fascist ancestry or a leftist progeny. That would be to satisfy oneself too easily. American pragmatism, a liberal philosophy, was earlier and more influential than Italian activism in diffusing an instrumental conception of what today are sometimes called 'truth-effects'. It was Claude Lévi-Strauss, on the moderate Right, who was the first theorist of the incommensurability of historical codes, each of them arbitrary in relation to the others.[27] There is good sense in Gramsci's remark that in intellectual battles, the only lasting victories are those won over the adversary at his strongest. For those who conceive representation as a responsibility, rather than a velleity or (as in the successor doctrine of Michel Foucault) an impossibility, the advice remains sound.

1990

---

27. 'What makes history possible is that a sub-set of events is found, for a given period, to have approximately the same significance for a contingent of individuals . . . the dates appropriate to each class are irrational in relation to all those of other classes' – 'history is therefore never history, but history-for.' *The Savage Mind*, London 1966, pp. 257, 260.

9

Max Weber and Ernest Gellner: Science, Politics, Enchantment

The two addresses given by Max Weber on 'Science as a Vocation' and 'Politics as a Vocation' occupy a special position within his work. In a body of writing often intractable and diffuse, they stand out as masterpieces of literary economy and passion, sudden distillations in a few glowing pages from the sprawling mass of Weber's scholarly thought. Here the themes of rationalization, religion, value-freedom, power, bureaucracy, charisma, ethical responsibility are all present, with a rhetorical intensity that has made these texts two of the most influential intellectual statements of this century. Yet it is as if their classical status has tended to shield them from close inspection. For beneath their surface clarity, each reveals signs of a turbulence that escapes logical control, generating a series of aporia which form a significant pattern.

Weber delivered his lecture on 'Science as a Vocation' on 7 November 1917, the day the Bolsheviks seized power in Russia. To his student audience in wartime Munich, he explained the sternness and strangeness of the scientific enterprise. Quite apart from its external drawbacks, in the lottery of academic life, it afforded no inner satisfactions of a traditional sort either. Irremediably specialized, it excluded any possibility of general cognitive achievement; inherently impersonal, it forbade temperamental self-expression of the kind normal in art; perpetually developing, its progress ruled out any lasting achievement. Nor could it acquire meaning from any other sphere of life. For modern science had stripped the world of those fictive harmonies where it was once believed to be united to eternal truth, or to nature or divinity or happiness. Structurally disappointing for the scientist and disenchanting for society, what value then attached to it? At least, Weber argued, it was the indispensable means of technical efficacy and conceptual clarity – of practical control or clear thinking, to whatever purpose. The vocation of science, so understood, had nothing to do with politics – the principles of the two were absolutely separate, permitting of no mixture.

Pronounced to the same audience just over a year later, on 28 January 1919, in the midst of the Bavarian Revolution, 'Politics as a Vocation' spelt out the differences. The role of the politician was to exercise independent leadership in the conquest of state power, defined by its monopoly of legitimate violence. Such legitimacy, assuring the obedience of those subject to it, could be traditional, charismatic or legal in character. Its enforcement required a permanent administrative staff, in whose historical development lay the origins of the modern professional politician. Unlike the functionary, however, the statesman takes personal responsibility for his political action, initially as a leader among notables, later as plebiscitary commander of a popular following organized in a mass party. Where such figures failed to emerge, electoral machines operated by mere officials over the heads of equally passive constituencies were the only alternative – leaderless democracy. The true politician, by contrast, not only relished the exercise of power for its own sake, but was distinguished by a combination of passion, judgement and sense of responsibility. Such passion could be for any cause – the choice of a faith was unarguable. But once made, the vocation of politics imposed its own rules. Since the decisive medium of politics was violence, with its peculiarly unpredictable consequences – force breeding force, the only appropriate code to guide it was a secular ethic of responsibility, judging actions by their consequences not by their intentions.

In outline, such is the substance of the two lectures. The connexion between them is at first paradoxical. For the theme they most conspicuously share is also that which Weber intended to separate them – the idea of the vocation as such. In the formal organization of Weber's discourse, whatever else the term may come to mean, it always denotes the exclusive pursuit of *one* goal – be it science, art, business, politics – at the expense of all others. What makes it serious is *specialization*. The central message of the two addresses appears to be that politics and science obey distinct laws, which must on no account be commingled or confused. The term *Beruf* is, of course, pervasive in Weber's sociology. But what has been insufficiently noticed is its extreme semantic instability – the drastic shifts in its meaning from one context to another. Its original sense was, of course, a religious calling; as Weber himself noted, it was first introduced into German by Luther, in his translation of the Bible.[1] *The Protestant Ethic and the Spirit of Capitalism* freely mines this usage for its account of the high spiritual purpose and rigid moral discipline of the early Calvinist merchant. It is this register, now detached from its religious background, which dominates the Munich addresses – science and politics conceived as strenuous existential callings. But by Weber's time, the normal German meaning of the term was quite different: *Beruf* was simply a profession. That sense too recurs in the lectures, and Weber occasionally senses the difference, but without at any point theoretically fixing it, or realizing its consequences for his construction as a whole. Thus, in a famous passage, he spoke of 'two kinds' of *Berufspolitiker* – those who lived for politics, and those lived from them. The former could devote themselves to public life in economic independence from it, typically as rentiers or landowners; the latter, without major property of their own, derived their income essentially from offices of party or state. This would seem a clear-cut enough contrast. No sooner is it made, however, than it is undone, when Weber goes on to remark that politically dominant strata invariably exploit their power for private economic ends, while the most unconditional political idealism is normally displayed by the propertyless.[2] The antithesis of 'living for' and 'living from' is incoherent here in part because it does not coincide with an opposition that is more important to the argument. For Weber starts by defining the vocation of the politician 'in its highest expression' as pure charismatic leadership – *hier wurzelt der Gedanke des Berufs in seiner höchsten Ausprägung*.[3] After tracing the rise of various kinds of administrative staff, he then proceeds to a catalogue of political roles in which the idea of *Beruf* finds, so to speak, its lowest expression. These include the party official and the machine boss, parliamentary herds (*Stimmvieh*) or municipal cliques: in short 'professional' politicians in the pejorative sense of the word. To these Weber finally applies the disgraced term *Berufspolitiker ohne Beruf* – in effect, a *reductio ad absurdum* of the contradictions in the concept.[4] For what Weber had yoked together under the single rubric of his title were three completely

---

1. *Wirtschaft und Gesellschaft*, Tübingen 1972, p. 344; *Economy and Society*, Berkeley and Los Angeles 1978, p. 569. Henceforth WG and ES.

2. 'Politik als Beruf', *Gesammelte Politische Schriften*, Tübingen 1971, pp. 513–15; H.H. Gerth and C. Wright Mills, eds., *From Max Weber*, New York 1958. pp. 84–86. Henceforth GPS and FMW.

3. GPS, p. 508; FMW, p. 79.

4. GPS, p. 544; FMW, p. 113, which renders this as 'professional politicians without a calling'.

opposite meanings: charismatic leadership in the pursuit of high ideals, bureaucratic service under orders in the state, and mercenary competition for spoils of office.

In *Wissenschaft als Beruf* the oscillation of meaning is scarcely less severe. On the one hand, the vocation of science is to serve the moral purpose of 'self-reflection' – *Selbstbesinnung* – by instilling 'a sense of duty, clarity and responsibility' in the individual who answers to its intellectual standards. On the other hand, it simply furnishes the techniques for 'calculable control of external objects and human behaviour', much as a Mid-West grocer's wife supplies cabbage across the counter.[5] The second function is in fact more plausibly presented by Weber than the first, which would not seem to require any specialized scientific knowledge at all. Here too the notion of *Beruf* dilates and fissures in the course of the argument. This process is not confined to the formal exposition of the lectures. The same pattern can be observed in Weber's informal accounts of himself. Explaining his refusal late in life of the compromises demanded of a politician, he could declare proudly: *Ich bin von Beruf: Gelehrter.* But he could equally express thorough contempt for the whole notion, as too narrow for him: *irgendeinem Respekt vor dem Begriff des 'Berufs' habe ich nie gehabt,* he wrote as a young man of his attitude to his prospects.[6] Ironically, the great final peroration of 'Politics as a Vocation', climactically conjuring up once again the mission of 'the leader and the hero', also involuntarily lets out that same dreary underside of the concept. What will become of you? he challenged the students before him, listing their possible life-failures: *Verbitterung oder Banausentum, einfaches stumpfes Hinnehmen der Welt und des Berufes?*[7] Here, with the further connotation of philistine routine, the fall – across the same term – of 'calling' into 'career' is complete.

There are a number of ways of seeing this particular strain in the structure of the two lectures. It can be related to Weber's more general

5. 'Wissenschaft als Beruf', *Gesammelte Aufsätze zur Wissenschaftslehre*, Tübingen 1922, pp. 550, 549 – henceforth GAW; FMW, pp. 152, 150.

6. Letter to the Chairman of the German Democratic Party, explaining his withdrawal from it, of April 1920: Wolfgang Mommsen, *Max Weber und die deutsche Politik*, Tübingen 1974, p. 334 – English translation *Max Weber and German Politics*, Chicago 1984, p. 310, rendered as 'I am a scholar by profession' – henceforth MWDP and MWGP; letter to Marianne Schnitzger of 1893: Marianne Weber, *Max Weber – ein Lebensbild*, Tübingen 1926, p. 197 – English translation *Max Weber – A Biography*, New York 1975, p. 185, rendered as 'I have never had any respect for the concept of a "vocation"' – henceforth MWL and MWB.

7. GPS, p. 560; FMW, p. 128 – which gives: 'Will you be bitter or banausic? Will you dully accept world and occupation?'

difficulty in negotiating the relationship between the 'ideal' and 'material' elements of his social theory, where the actual balance or connexion between the two is rarely if ever confronted. Typically, rather, the former acquires a tacit predominance through the formal volume of its elaboration, suddenly interrupted by uncompromising reminders of the weight of the latter – often all the more brutal, as if by way of compensation for steadier treatment. Something like this occurs with the notion of vocation. There are other striking instances in the Weberian theory of politics as well. In them *Herrschaft* undergoes a duplication comparable to that of *Beruf*. After asking how political domination is secured – why do men obey a given state? – Weber proceeds straightaway to discuss the ideal-types of legitimation, as the forms of its 'inner justification'; then recollects briefly that 'in reality' obedience is conditioned by 'very solid motives of fear and hope', and material 'interests of the most varied sort'; thereafter reverts once more to the eminent powers of charisma. In similar fashion, he explains that the obedience elicited by legitimation can then be used to obtain the means of administration – staff and matériel – necessary to enforce a monopoly of coercion: and then undermines this causal sequence by remarking that the 'ultimate and decisive basis' for the loyalty of administrators to power-holders is 'fear of losing their wages',[8] so rendering the argument circular. The material means of rule become at once product and precondition of the ideal operations of legitimacy.

But there was another, and more specific, reason for the anomalies in Weber's treatment of the concept of vocation. The term had one unambiguous force, common to its ideal and material registers alike. It spelt specialization – whether as higher calling or lowlier profession. It was this which rendered the notion a fire-break between science and politics. What was then its antonym in Weber's vocabulary? The answer is readily to hand. Strewn throughout his political writings is a set of obsessive references to 'literati' and 'dilettantes'. These function as nearly interchangeable imprecations. However indiscriminate in their polemical application, they always contain at least one fixed charge: the slur of amateurism. Over against the man of a vocation or profession, there was the dabbler and the dilettante. The *Literaten* against whom Weber so tirelessly thundered varied over time. They included the sycophants who enthused over Bismarck's mere violence and cunning, as well as the carpers who impotently resented them; the parasites who advocated a relaxation of German diligence after the

---

8. GPS, pp. 507–509; FMW, pp. 78–80.

war, and the demagogues who demanded too many territorial annexations during it; the dreamers of democratized industry, alongside the confectors of new religions.[9] But by the time of his second lecture in Munich, in its dramatic political setting, previously diffuse referents had narrowed to one overwhelming target. The German Revolution had put power into the hands of 'absolute dilettantes', whose only claim to it was 'their control of machine-guns'; all that distinguished the rule of Bolshevik or Spartacist ideologues, workers' or soldiers' councils, from that of any military dictatorship was their 'dilettantism'.[10] Eisner was a prize example in Bavaria. Another was Trotsky, who had displayed 'the typical vanity of the Russian literati' in questioning the good faith of Germany at Brest-Litovsk, forcing the Reich to impose its own peace.[11] In these years, the familiar terms of earlier dislike become fused into a figure otherwise elusive or absent in Weber's sociology of modernity – the 'intellectual'. In the talk he gave to Austro–Hungarian officers on socialism in July 1918, he told them that 'the Bolshevik government consists of intellectuals, some of whom studied here in Vienna and in Germany; among them there are certainly only a few Russians.'[12] In Munich a few months later, he declared that the 'sterile excitation' of the worst Russian intellectuals had now spread to their German counterparts 'in this carnival tricked out as a revolution'.[13] Such fevers, typical of the 'mere political dilettante', were the antithesis of the disciplined passion of the true politician – not to speak of the disinterested research of the scientist. Identified with revolutionary socialists of all persuasions – USPD, Spartacists, Syndicalists, Bolsheviks – the figure of the intellectual, lacking the specialized aptitudes for either science or politics, bespeaks generic irresponsibility and incompetence.

This theoretical contrast, at least, seems hard and fast enough. Yet the notion of what it is to be an intellectual, too, suffers a curious sideways disturbance in Weber's writing. For one of the central themes of his later thought – unforgettably developed in 'Science as a Vocation' – is what he termed the 'intellectualization' of modern life. By this he meant just that process of specialization which divided life into separate and incompatible spheres of value, draining meaning from it as a

---

9. GPS, pp. 311; 189, 217–18; 249; WS, p. 314.
10. GPS, pp. 521, 550; FMW, pp. 91–92, 119.
11. 'Der Sozialismus', *Gesammelte Aufsätze zur Soziologie und Sozialpolitik*, Tübingen 1924, pp. 513–15 – henceforth GASS.
12. GASS, p. 514; was Weber referring to Jews? It seems hard to credit, but the remark otherwise seems inscrutable.
13. GPS, pp. 545–46; FMW, p. 115.

whole. 'The fate of our age, with its characteristic rationalization and intellectualization – above all disenchantment of the world – is that the ultimate and highest values have withdrawn from public life.'[14] In other words, here the character of the process is the very opposite of the figures who should logically embody it. Intellectualism portends just what intellectuals forego. Crucially, moreover, Weber deplored the consequences of the process as he described it. After invoking the 'unending and inconclusive struggle' between different outlooks on life in the disenchanted world, he told his audience that he too 'hated intellectualism as the worst evil' of modern times.[15] The strongest expression of that dislike is, of course, the scathing final verdict of *The Protestant Ethic*: 'Of the last stage of this cultural development it might truly be said: "Specialists without spirit, sensualists without heart; this nullity imagines it has attained a level of civilization never before achieved." '[16] The Nietzschean scorn for the *Fachmensch* here was one that could extend to the *Berufsmensch* – the two indeed being equated as products of the bureaucratization of power and culture, whose long-run effects threatened something like an Egyptian bondage of the spirit.[17] Weber, who was sure that he himself 'could in some measure perform in rather a large number of positions', had reason to say that he detested this kind of intellectualism.[18]

On the other hand, however much he disliked it, Weber never formulated an alternative. In part, that was certainly because he regarded specialization as the unalterable condition of modernity, whatever its cultural by-products. But it was probably also because he feared the actual historical forms such an alternative might take. Before the war, he had observed two intelligentsias that refused a separation of value-spheres. In Russia, a revolutionary intelligentsia rejected capitalism from the left, in the name of what Weber saw as the 'last great movement' in history 'to approximate to a religion'.[19] In Germany, a conservative intelligentsia doubted 'if the dominion of capital would give better or more lasting guarantees to personal liberty and to the development of intellectual, aesthetic and social culture than the aristocracy of the past', and so – 'a serious fact' – 'the representatives of

14. GAW, p. 554; FMW, p. 155.
15. GAW, pp. 550–51; FMW, p. 152.
16. *Gesammelte Aufsätze zur Religionssoziologie*, Tübingen 1934, p. 204; *The Protestant Ethic and the Spirit of Capitalism*, New York 1958, p. 182 – henceforth GAR and PE.
17. WG, p. 576; ES, p. 987.
18. MWL, p. 197; MWB, p. 185.
19. WG, pp. 313–14; ES, pp. 515–16.

the highest interests of culture turn their eyes back, and with deep antipathy oppose the inevitable development of capitalism, refusing to cooperate in rearing the structure of the future.'[20] The social order that Weber defended, even if at times as no more than a relative brake on the growth of bureaucracy, was thus under pincer attack from left and right by the most prominent groups of intellectuals in his line of sight. It is not surprising he was so hostile to the category when capitalism entered the most dangerous crisis of his lifetime.

Yet the problem posed by the bane of 'intellectualism' – value-disintegration – remained. It was the strong sense of vocation that was uppermost in Weber's mind when he gave his Munich addresses. Science and politics were callings – a summons to the right conduct appropriate to each. But how was an ethics possible in either, once the process of intellectualization had divested the world of all objective obligations? Within the texts themselves, two kinds of response can be found. The first attempts to formulate a morality proper to each calling in terms of the immanent logic of its practice. The pursuit of science assists or forces individuals to confront the logic of their life-choices, 'to render account of the ultimate meaning of their actions', even while it cannot prescribe it. In so doing, Weber declared, it served the *sittliche Mächte* – social-moral forces – of 'duty, clarity and responsibility'.[21] The practice of politics, for its part – because its principal means was violence – required sober reckoning of what might come of any action contemplated: not the morality of pure intention preached on the Mount, but the civic responsibility defended by Machiavelli. In each field the ethic enjoined – one of intellectual clarity, the other of practical consequence – is of a technically formalist type, stipulating no substantive ends. Moreover, Weber conceded, neither could motivate their own adoption.[22] A decision external to, and unwarrantable by, each was necessary for that. This decisionism, with its markedly Nietzschean background, has been sharply criticized by Habermas and others: its irrationalist cast is obvious enough. What has been less noticed is the incoherence of each of the formal prescriptions them-selves. After defining contemporary science as inherently *specialized* knowledge, Weber has ruled out in advance any possibility of arguing that it can perform the completely generic task of logical clarification he eventually ascribes to it; and, in fact, there is a predictable slippage at this point in the text to *philosophy* as the indicated help-meet – i.e.,

---

20. St Louis Address,'Capitalism and Rural Society in Germany', FMW, pp. 371–72.
21. GAW, p. 550; FMW, p. 152.
22. GPS, p. 558; FME, p. 127; GAW, pp. 550–51; FMW, p. 152.

just the opposite of the sciences as depicted by him, or the most general of intellectual disciplines. Similarly, his case for an ethic of responsibility in politics centres essentially on the claim that in the world of power it is the case that good ends can be achieved by bad means – that is, the use of force prohibited by the Sermon on the Mount. It is on 'this problem of the justification of means by ends that an ethic of convictions inevitably founders.'[23] But since for Weber the decisive means in politics, as he never tires of repeating, is violence, the means are by definition *always* bad: they therefore cease to be discriminative – so that within this schema policies can paradoxically only be judged by their ends, in other words precisely the maxim of an ethic of conviction. At the same time, in remarking that the 'tragedy of all political action' is that 'as a rule' – in other words, whatever ethic is adopted – outcomes not merely fail to coincide with intentions but contradict them, he renders ends themselves incalculable, and the lessons of statecraft he adduces from Chandragupta onwards irrelevant. In a remarkable non sequitur, Weber draws the conclusion that 'precisely because' of this unreckonability, political action 'must serve a cause if it is to have inner strength' and not 'bear the curse of creaturely nullity'. But 'what cause the politician adopts in his drive for power is a matter of faith'.[24]

If Weber's endeavours to deduce a morality specific to the pursuit of science or politics lack much cogency, there is a more consistent theme that is partly screened by them. This is a psychology of practical success, which provides the real voltage of the account. What is striking is the similarity of its formula in each calling. The first requirement of the scientist, Weber explained, was passion – 'a strange frenzy' that was the condition of inspiration. The second was hard work, which normally prepared the ground for it.[25] Intoxication on the one hand, application on the other, were the keys to scientific insight. In politics, likewise, the first essential quality of the statesman was passion – devotion to 'the god or demon' of a cause. The second was detachment, the capacity for a cool gaze at the world and the self, which demanded a 'firm taming of the soul' that set the true politician apart from the dilettante.[26] The duality is echoed in the concluding flourish which evokes the 'immeasurably moving' spectacle of the 'mature man' at a crossroads of conscience whom Weber represents – ignoring an earlier

23. GAW, p. 550; FMW, pp. 151–52; GPS, p. 553; FMW, p. 122.
24. GPS, pp. 547–48; FMW, p. 117.
25. GAW, pp. 530–32; FMW, pp. 135–36.
26. 'Jene starke Bändigung der Seele': GPS, pp. 545–46; FMW, p. 115.

claim of their incompatibility – as suddenly synthesizing the ethics of responsibility and of conviction in his person: 'that is truly human and affecting'.[27] The recipe for the two vocations is thus basically the same – a combination of intense passion and iron discipline. The recurrence of this trope, across the separation of science and politics, had deep biographical sources. For it corresponded, of course, to Weber's sense of himself. In the resonant words of his marriage proposal to Marianne: 'High breaks the tidal wave of passion and it is dark around us – come with me, my high-souled comrade, out of the quiet harbour of resignation, onto the high seas, where growth comes from the struggle of souls and the ephemeral falls away. But *reflect*: in the head and heart of the mariner there must be clarity, when all is surging beneath him. We must tolerate no fanciful surrender to turbid and mystical moods within us. For when feeling rises high, you must chain it to be able to steer with sobriety.'[28] On that bridge, the scientist and politician are already at the helm.

Weber's portraits of them are not quite exhausted by the projection of what might be called his own vulcanism. Beyond this common stock, they have features of their own. The scientist is a teacher, and his work is necessarily impersonal. The politician is a leader, whose authority can only be personal. Vanity in the former, however frequent, is innocuous; in the latter, ruinous. These contrasts are designed to underwrite the segregation of the two activities. But in Weber's account, the fundamental difference between the two lies elsewhere. Science is the main force for that rationalization of the world which has denuded it of objective values, and must itself abstain from the expression of subjective preferences. Modern politics operates within the disenchanted world created by science, but necessarily pits subjective causes against each other. The cardinal error for the scientist is to stray across this line into value-judgements on public life. 'Politics has no place in the lecture-room.' The proper duty of a public speaker on democracy, Weber declared, is to use words not as 'ploughshares for loosening the soil of contemplative thought' but as 'swords against opponents, instruments of struggle'. Such language would, however, be 'an outrage in a lecture'.[29]

The most cursory glance at the two addresses reveals how far Weber was from practising these precepts. Value-judgements abound in each,

---

27. GPS, p. 559; FMW, p. 127.
28. 'Denn wenn die Empfindung Dir hoch geht, Musst Du sie bändigen' – MWL, p. 190; MWB, p. 179.
29. GAW, p. 543; FMW, p. 145.

giving them their peculiar rhetorical force. The whole structure of 'Science as a Vocation' builds up to an impassioned final warning against the 'swindle or self-deception' of new religious cults fabricated by intellectuals 'without a new and genuine prophecy' – as distinct from the 'sublime values' to be found in the transcendental realm of 'mystical life' or in the intimate realm where the 'pulsations' of immediate community recall the sacred *pneuma* of old.[30] What could be the scientific criteria for demarcating these, on Weber's own terms? The polemical ends of 'Politics as a Vocation' are still more insistent and overt. Far from being the neutral survey promised by Weber in his opening sentences, in which all advocacy would be 'completely excluded' – *ganz ausgeschaltet* – it is filled with furious attacks on the revolutionary socialists of the time, in Russia and in Germany. In a typical passage, Weber could accuse Bolshevism in the same breath of disarming and dispossessing all 'bourgeois elements' and of accepting 'everything it had fought as bourgeois institutions'; of building its power on a network of informers that stripped the Tsarist police of their positions, and using the agents of the Okhrana as 'the main instrument of its state power'. The German Revolution was a 'vast collapse' into successive 'mob dictatorships'. The attempt to create socialism in conditions of modern class struggle was bound to appeal to 'predominantly base ethical motives' – 'the satisfaction of hatred and the slaking of revenge', 'power, booty and spoils'.[31] Pronouncements like these, within days of the killing of Luxemburg and Liebknecht, were swords indeed.

Weber's inability to separate science and politics in his practice, radical though it was, matters less than the nature of the relationship actually at work between them in his thought as a whole. The central themes of his sociology of modernity are disenchantment and bureaucratization – the loss of meaning and the loss of freedom paradoxically brought by that process of rationalization which gave Western civilization its lead over the rest of the globe. Science is the principal author of the demystification of the world. But what is the nature of the waning of enchantment it causes? In perhaps the best-known of all his passages, Weber described it as a new polytheism in which 'the many gods of old, no longer magic but become impersonal forces, rise from their graves and contend for power over our lives in unending mutual struggle.'[32] Which are these deities? Weber amalgamates two answers

---

30. GAW, pp. 553–54; FMW, pp. 154–55.
31. GPS, pp. 505, 529, 556; FMW, pp. 77, 100, 125.
32. GAW, p. 547; FMW, p. 149.

in his account that are logically independent of each other. One is that they represent, as in the pantheon of Antiquity, rival ideals of wealth, power, art, love, knowledge – in other words a *multiplicity* of value-spheres. There might then exist binding norms specific to each, inherent in the nature of their domain. This is the version, derived from Mill, on which Weber relies in arguing for an ethic of responsibility in politics – whose morality he contrasts with those that govern the spheres of eros, commerce, family or administration. 'We are placed into various life-spheres, each of which is governed by different laws.'[33] But there is, of course, a second answer: that the strife of the gods means – not because there are many of them, but because they have lost their magic – a general *indeterminacy* of values within each sphere. This is the more radical version, derived from Nietzsche, to which Weber would revert when discussing the general logic of modern culture, whose 'every step leads to an ever more devastating senselessness', a 'meaningless bustle in the service of worthless, self-contradictory and mutually antagon-istic goals'.[34] In other words, the intellectualization of the world could lead to either ethical pluralism or nihilism.

What were the consequences of this conception of the impact of science for Weber's politics? He was an early twentieth-century liberal, of a distinctively German kind. Civic rights, electoral competition and private enterprise were conditions of individual freedom. If universal male suffrage had probably come too early in Germany, the censitary franchise in Prussia was an obstacle to national unity. Parliamentary responsibility was needed, but did not have to extend to the choice of Chancellor. Academic life should be free from political control, and trade unions encouraged. Neither natural rights nor free trade entered into this liberalism, whose basic concern was the formation and expression of the free personality. Before the war, Weber believed that strong leadership was best nurtured by competitive selection of inde-pendent elites in parliamentary settings; after the war, by plebiscitary mandates over-riding parliamentary divisions. He identified himself with the German bourgeoisie from which he came, but was an uncom-promising critic of what he held to be its cowardice in the Wilhelmine order. He assailed the conservatism and egoism of the junker class, but much of his outlook was markedly aristocratic: few terms are so cherished in his political vocabulary as honour. Wounds to that, he told his audience in Munich, a nation could never forgive.

---

33. GPS, p. 554; FMW, p. 123.
34. 'Zwischenbetrachtung', GAR, p. 570; FMW, pp. 356–57.

For his deepest political commitments were, of course, national. Weber never retracted his inaugural address at Freiburg, which announced at the outset of his scholarly life that the 'power interests of the nation are the ultimate and decisive interests' for the study of economic policy, 'a science in the service of politics' for which '*raison d'état* is the final measure of value'. In famous phrases, he declared: 'it is not to peace and human happiness that we must show the way to our descendants, but to the endless struggle for the preservation and higher breeding of our race' – 'in the hard and clear air in which the sober work of German politics flourishes, yet pervaded too by the serious splendour of national emotion.'[35] Critical of the diplomatic ineptitude of the Wilhelmine regime, he was a strong advocate of German naval and colonial expansion. When the First World War broke out, he greeted it with jubilation: '*Whatever* the outcome, *this war is great and wonderful*.'[36] It had led to 'the inner rebirth of Germany', for the country had a '*responsibility before history*' to become a great power, as a nation of seventy million whose 'calling as a master people' was to 'turn the wheels of world development'. The cause for which Germans were fighting was 'not changes on the map or economic profits, but *honour* – the honour of our nationality'.[37] If 'our state has to be an armed camp', it was because it had a duty to prevent 'world power – that is, control of the culture of the future – from being divided between the regulations of Russian bureaucrats and the conventions of Anglo-Saxon "society", perhaps with a dash of Latin *raison* thrown in.' Only German military might could protect the small nations of Europe, and command the role that befitted the Second Reich in 'the shaping of the culture of the earth'. Here lay the 'tragic historical duty of a people organized as a power state', without which the German Empire would be 'an idle, culturally inimical luxury'.[38] Weber never repented these exultant visions. His nationalism survived the defeat of 1918 intact – 'the war had to be fought because German honour demanded it.' He ended his life looking forward to another great General Staff, confident that 'history, which has already given us – and us alone – a second youth, will give us also a third one'.[39]

35. 'Der Nazionalstaat und die Volkswirtschaftspolitik', GPS, pp. 14, 25.

36. 'Gross und wunderbar' – he repeated the phrase like a refrain: MWL, pp. 527, 530, 536; MWB, pp. 519, 521–22, 528.

37. 'Deutschland unter den europäischen Weltmachten', GPS, pp. 170, 176; 'Parlament und Regierung im neugeordneten Deutschland', GPS, p. 442.

38. 'Zwischen zwei Gesetzen', GPS, pp. 143–44.

39. Speech of January 1919, MWDP, p. 347. – MWGP p. 323; Letter of 24 November 1918, in Eduard Baumgarten, ed., *Max Weber – Werk und Person*, Tübingen 1964, p. 538.

Weber's nationalism was more important to him than his liberalism. But the two were connected, since for most of his life he believed that only a liberal political order could equip Germany to play its appointed imperial role. If they conflicted, however, within the horizon of his own experience nationalist principles came first. He declared that for him 'the German nation and its future in the world towers above all questions of state organization', and at the hour of the Freikorps had no hesitation in urging 'revolutionary violence' in the service of German irredentism: 'he who is not willing to risk scaffold and prison will not deserve the name of nationalist.'[40] Although Weber was outspoken for his generation, this hierarchy of values had been characteristic of the main tradition of German liberalism in the epoch of unification, exemplified in the career of the National Liberals. But by Weber's time, the stakes were higher – no longer national unity, but world power. How did he justify these? There are two basic themes in his bellicist writing. One is the cultural mission of the German people to save the world from Russian diktat and English etiquette, equally stifling of inner authenticity. This was a standard *topos* of wartime literature, capable of a number of individual variations. By comparison with the extended constructions of Thomas Mann or even his brother Alfred, Weber's use of it is quite cursory: unlike them, he never spelt out the contrasting virtues of German *Kultur* – on the contrary, conceding that small nations often produced better art and displayed more community than large ones – and never opposed Anglo–French *Zivilisation* to it, Russia always remaining the most dangerous enemy for him.

The real mandate for Germany's world-historical embrace of war lay elsewhere. It was fate – *Schicksal* – that decreed it. Since 'the mere existence of a great power, such as we have become, is an obstacle in the path of other great powers', the European conflict was inevitable. 'The fact that we are a people not of seven but seventy millions – *that* was our fate. It founded an inexorable responsibility before history, which we could not evade even if we had wished. We must make this clear again and again, when the question of the "meaning" of this endless war is now raised. The magnetic force of this fate drew the nation upwards, past the perilous abyss of decline, onto the steep path of honour and fame, from which there could be no turning back – into the clear hard air of the realm of world history, to look its grim majesty in

---

40. GPS, p. 439; MWDP, pp. 335–37 – MWGP, pp. 312–13.

the face, as an imperishable memory for our remote descendants.'[41]

The significant crux here is the linkage of *meaning* and *fate*. It recurs again, in a particularly revealing way, when he compares the life of the masses in peace and war, speaking of 'that loveless and pitiless economic struggle for existence, which bourgeois phraseology calls "peaceful cultural labour", in which hundreds of millions wear out body and soul, sink under, or lead a life infinitely more devoid of any perceptible "meaning" than the engagement of all (including women – since they too "wage" war, when they do what they must) in the cause of honour, *that is* – the historical duties of the nation decreed by fate.'[42] For Weber, in other words, nationalism was above all meaning regained. It is no accident that in this text, devoted to Mars, he should have invoked the theme of the new polytheism. The purpose of his argument was to dismiss pacifism as a Gospel mentality incompatible with any action in this world. That world included not only 'beauty, dignity, honour and grandeur', but also 'the inevitability of wars for power', and the different laws binding each of these domains. He who enters the world 'must *choose* which of these Gods he would serve, or when one and when another'.[43] Fate and Choice are thus exploited side by side, in the same rhetorical construction. The oscillation between them corresponds, one might say, to the two poles of Weber's political outlook. The idea of a free choice between the locally valid codes of this world, allowing for temporal negotiations between them, answered to Weber's liberalism. It followed the logic of the mild version of disenchantment. The idea of a sheer fate imposing one value, without appeal ('we could not evade if we wished'), inspired his nationalism. In a paradoxical way, it followed the logic of the strong version of disenchantment. For if there are no specifically valid codes, in any sphere of life, there are no grounds for selecting or negotiating between them. Choice that is purely arbitrary then swivels into another form of facticity. A pure decisionism is thus always liable to be shadowed by a radical fatalism. Nietzsche had already displayed this paradox, as he moved from the death of god to *amor fati* – the will to power operating simultaneously as metaphysical challenge and physical destiny. So it was with Weber. If choice between values is rationally impossible, the chance of nationality becomes unanswerably valuable. The intellectualization of the world which strips it of meaning here prompts just that

---

41. GPS, pp. 143, 177.
42. GPS, pp. 144–45.
43. GPS, p. 145.

sacrifice of the intellect Weber otherwise scorned, in the discovery of supreme meaning in fate, and its moral decoration as duty. Weber, of course, was not alone in the headlong rush to the Great War. But it is striking how unconscious he was, sociologically, of his own solution to the disenchantment he feared. The extent of his self-reflection was the solitary sentence at which the few scant paragraphs on the 'nation' in the vast mass of *Economy and Society* peter out: 'Intellectuals are in some degree predestined to propagate the "national" idea.'[44] The most powerful political force of his day, and central passion of his public activity, is all but absent from his theoretical sight. It is as if nationalism had to be exempt from the light of science, as the consolation for what it wrought. It was immune, too, to the maxims of politics Weber ostensibly defended. The sermons to the Left on the ethics of responsibility have their irony. For it was Weber who welcomed the carnage of the First World War 'whatever the outcome' – with a cult of expressive community and a pathos of military power heedless of all consequences. The cost of those ethics of conviction was about seven million lives.[45] But on the battlefield, such deaths were enchanted. 'War grants the warrior something uniquely meaningful: the experience of a sense in death that consecrates it' – 'the community of the standing army today feels itself a community unto death: the greatest of its kind.'[46] The *Sinnlosigkeit* of the world dissolves in the modern sublime, the *Sinnhaftigkeit* of national destiny.

*   *   *

To move from the pages of Max Weber to those of Ernest Gellner is a large change in atmosphere. It is not just that the two belong to such different epochs. Their temperaments and tones are so contrasted – what could be more antithetical than Weber's heroically elevated pessimism and Gellner's deliberately plain-man optimism: the high rhetoric of the one, and the low jokes of the other? The distance between the cultivated middle classes of Berlin under Bismarck and

---

44. WG, p. 530; ES, pp. 915–16.

45. At the end of it all, Weber could still speak of the war in the language of the gaming-table, applauding Ludendorff as a *wahnwitziger Hasardeur*. Only 'old women' could ask who was responsible for massacre and defeat, for it was 'the structure of society that produced the war': MWDP, p. 317; GPS, p. 549 – FMW, p. 118.

46. GAR, p. 548; FMW, p. 335.

those of Prague under Benes have their part in this – Czech manners, in the absence of a nobility, were no doubt always more egalitarian. But there is also a marked opposition of philosophical background. Where Weber was deeply affected by German vitalism, above all the legacy of Nietzsche, Gellner comes out of British empiricism and utilitarianism as it culminated in Russell. The gulf between the two traditions speaks for itself: Gellner is a shining example of the 'eudaemonism' Weber scorned. Ironically, on the other hand, Weber professed a variety of methodological individualism for the social sciences, even if his practice – to its advantage – ignored it; whereas Gellner has been a trenchant critic of the doctrine, which for obvious reasons has rarely appealed to anthropologists. Last but not least, of course, there is the striking divergence in the forms of their corpus: the massively detailed scholarship of the one, monuments of historical erudition and taxonomic improvisation, compared with the insouciantly reconnoitred forays of the other, travelling light over the most variegated terrain to unexpected theoretical effect. In all these respects, the two are evident antitheses.

Yet there is another sense in which, of all the sociological thinkers of the subsequent epoch, Gellner has remained closest to Weber's central intellectual problems. Some have sought to develop his formal analytic of action, building it into large new systems theories. Others have taken up the unfinished tasks of his historical encyclopaedia, giving it a superior narrative direction or typological consistency. But none has addressed themselves with such cogency to the core cluster of his substantive concerns. If we take Weber's great terminating themes of science and politics, this becomes readily apparent. Gellner's account of the 'structure of human history', like Weber's, is essentially one of the pilgrimage of reason through the world, from magic through religion to science. It is, of course, more tightly – also more selectively – focused: not 'rationalization' as a whole, which in Weber is a process differentiating and transforming all the domains of life from the economic and administrative to the aesthetic and erotic, but 'cognition' as such – that *Reich des denkenden Erkennens* which forms only the last, if most important, of Weber's reflections in the *Zwischenbetrachtung* – is the leading theme of *Plough, Sword and Book*. Philosophy and science are foregrounded in this version with greater overall force. But the new situation created by the advent of modern science is the same in both accounts – a decline of meaning. For Gellner, consistently with his starting-point, this is however in the first instance an epistemological crisis, where for Weber it was unmediately ethical and existential. In the general problem posed by *Legitimation of Belief*, 'What can

I know?' logically commands 'What should I be/do?'[47] Here there are two problem-areas to which Gellner returns again and again: the original validity-basis of modern science, and the contemporary forms of philosophical relativism. The former, he has argued, can best be seen as a – not wholly natural or easy – union of an empiricist sense of the self and a mechanist view of the world: an atomism of evidence, and structuralism of explanation. The fit between them is never quite sealed in Gellner's writing, which tends to fall back on professions of faith for the autonomy of the first – the ghost always rattles somewhat in the machine. When Gellner treats of the classical tradition of modern philosophy, the scientific universe is the cold mechanical environment of impersonal causation, scoured of value as Weber held it to be. But when Gellner tackles the lax conceptual relativism of so much late twentieth-century culture, science – the precipitant of the crisis of meaning – *reverses out to become its solvent*. This is the basic intellectual move which distinguishes him from Weber. It is one that in part reflects their different historical situations. Where Weber jousted no more than briefly with Spengler in the last months of his life, Gellner confronted the luxuriance of his descent forty years later, as it was mediated through Wittgenstein. Gellner's reaction to the doctrine of the incommensurability of the 'forms of life' embodied in different communities was to emphasize the universal cognitive and *therewith moral* power of science. In substance, his argument has consistently been that science – and science alone – brings modern industry, that yields mass prosperity, which permits effective morality. It is the material affluence afforded by scientific reason that is its epistemological trump-card.[48] No community, once exposed to the benefits of industrialization, has ever resisted them; and once gained – hunger and disease overcome – ethical decency for the first time becomes generally possible. This is the change of thought of *Thought and Change*, in which – one might say – premises derived from Weber somersault into conclusions close to Holbach.[49] The political force of the argument is

---

47. *Legitimation of Belief*, Cambridge 1974, p. 30.

48. *Cause and Meaning in the Social Sciences*, London 1973, pp. 71–72.

49. Thanks to science, 'for the great majority of mankind, current politics is a transition from the certainty of poverty, short life, insecurity and brutality, and the strong likelihood of tyranny, to a condition containing the near-certainty of affluence and at least a reasonable possibility of security and liberty'; so that whereas moralizing in the past was a rather sterile exercise, 'today the situation is different. A fairly modest "annual rate of growth", sustained over time, can do more to alleviate human misery than all the compassion and abnegation that past ages could muster': *Thought and Change*, London 1964, pp. 46, 219.

entirely sympathetic; but its philosophical form is one Gellner himself criticizes in others. To rest philosophical truth on technological success is to veer towards the pragmatism he rebukes in Quine;[50] while to tie moral decency to material ease is to assume more than to found its content. The role of industrial progress in Gellner's thought is rather like that of human rights in the world at large: a value whose only normative foundation lies in the extent of its *de facto* acceptance. The distance between this position and Weber's is not just a question of temperament. It also reflects the immense transformation of life-conditions brought by industry since the Second World War, creating levels of popular consumption in the advanced countries – and promising them to the backward – unimaginable at the time of the First. It is difficult to imagine Weber, relaxed before a television set, greeting the festivities of the time as a new Belle Époque.[51] But his sociological realism would have respected the empirical strength of Gellner's case.

Where does this leave disenchantment? Among the most striking of Gellner's ideas is, of course, the thesis of the Rubber Cage. Industrial modernity, far from constructing houses of an iron bondage excluding all meaning, provides open ground for constant new flowerings of it. Reenchantment, indeed, becomes an industry in its own right with a multiplication of self-indulgent fads and subjectivist creeds, from the Oxonian cult of ordinary language to the Californian mysteries of daily conversation.[52] The disciplines of industrial production prove more than compatible with these fantasies of ideological consumption – both increased leisure, and the effortless technical aids to it, actually encourage them. Gellner likes to invoke Weber's contempt for the sham spiritual furnitures of his time, while pointing out that he never conceived they could become so widespread. But, of course, in Gellner's scheme of things, the proliferation of bogus meanings can occur because *real* meaning has already been restored. Science provides the grid of all our effective beliefs, leaving us the luxury of symbolic creeds that can be retracted as easily as a video-cassette.

Or so it would seem at first sight, from Gellner's main doctrine. In fact, it is part of the interest of his work that it contains certain contra-indications. In his final reflections on the crisis of meaning, Weber

---

50. See *Spectacles and Predicaments*, London 1979, pp. 234–37, 253–54.

51. Gellner's term for the era 1945–1973: *Culture, Politics and Identity*, Cambridge 1987, p. 111.

52. Gellner's earliest statement of this idea is perhaps to be found in *Cause and Meaning in the Social Sciences*, pp. 132–33; the formal treatment of it is in *Spectacles and Predicaments*, pp. 152–65; its most coruscating application is the essay on ethnomethodology: ibid, p. 41–64.

showed particular concern with two domains of value: the religious (artificial or authentic) and the inter-personal (erotic or convivial).[53] It is no accident that Gellner should have devoted major studies to each of these. The results are not entirely consistent with the ironic harmonies of his general theory of reenchantment. Of the major world religions, Weber wrote least on Islam, and it is this lacuna Gellner has filled to pointed contemporary effect. For all its imaginative brilliance, it is true that his sociology of actual Muslim societies models them too heavily on the Maghreb, the backward Wild West of the Islamic world, rather than the core zones of settled agriculture in the Middle East. But this limitation is less significant for his more general theoretical programme than his contention, often reiterated, that Islam is so soberly mono-theist, scriptural and egalitarian that of all the world religions it is most compatible with the requirements of an industrializing age, and will perhaps alone survive intact into it. Khomeini himself – certainly the nearest recent approximation to a 'prophet' in Weber's sense – is presented as theologically true to this singular Muslim modernity.[54] Here Gellner, scathing about ersatz religions, is curiously uncritical about the original article. The claim that Islam is uniquely egalitarian forgets entirely the position it accords women (always something of a blind spot for him). More generally, it overlooks the obvious fact that precisely because it is a traditional religion – that is, a set of dogmatic beliefs about a supernatural order – it is bound to be decommissioned by contact with modern science and mass consumption, like every other such faith, for just the reasons Gellner elsewhere insists on, ending up like them in the symbolic rather than effective economy of belief. Intercontinental hysteria over blasphemy expresses not unusual congruence with modernity, but exceptional fear of it. With good reason: there will be no special reprieve for the integrity of the Koran.

Gellner's treatment of the realm of the inter-personal is very different in character. If *The Psychoanalytic Movement* is the most wittily sustained of all his polemics, it is also his most serious and searching: arguably his finest single book. In conditions of material security, social fluidity and moral anomie, it suggests, traditional fears and anxieties projected onto the natural world become concentrated on the social, at the sensitive points of the individual's most intimate relationships with others. Here, where the greatest share of life's happiness or misery is

53. GAR, pp. 556–563 – FMW, pp. 343–350; GAW, pp. 553–54 – FMW, pp. 154–55.

54. *Muslim Societies*, Cambridge 1981, pp. 4–5, 62; *Culture, Politics and Identity*, pp. 145, 148.

now decided, all seems unpredictable, yet often unfathomably pat-terned, an arena of tension, mystery and danger. Freud's doctrines owe their success to a combination of ostensibly scientific explanation of this domain of experience, with covertly pastoral ministration to it, condensed in the unique confessional mechanisms of transference. Of all the modern forms of reenchantment psychoanalysis, offering perso-nal salvation through an austere theoretical medication, is the strong-est. In a considerable adversary literature, Gellner's critique of it is unmatched. His principal concern, however, is less with its intellectual shortcomings than with its cultural influence. If he exaggerates this – psychoanalysis has never been a 'movement' in the normal sense of the term, with a mass following – the error paradoxically stems from an acknowledgement of the scale of the distress it promises to relieve. For the other main theme of the book – vindicating Nietzsche against Hume – is the intrinsic crookedness and unruliness of the human psyche, contorted in so many involuntary directions by multiple unconscious forces that Freud naively simplified, assimilating them to the workings of the conscious mind.[55] Weber, expressing interest in psychoanalysis as a new field of research, found its clinical material still 'alarmingly thin', and looked forward to the development in two or three decades of an 'exact casuistics' of the instinctual dynamics it had started to explore.[56] These are essentially the demands that remain for Gellner still unsatisfied today – more and better evidence, more precise and complex theory, for the study of what is not conscious. The stress that falls on the painful precariousness of this zone of experience, and intensity of the need to wrest meaning from it, nevertheless contradicts the portrait of the Rubber Cage. On Gellner's own showing, here the bars are truly cold and hard; and it is desperation, not distraction, that shakes them in search of escape.

If such are the sequels of Weber's view of science in Gellner's work, what of politics? Much more straightforwardly and unreservedly, he too has been a liberal. That liberalism is a primary commitment, unaffected by dreams of imperial power. But the view of democracy that issues from it has sociological points in common with Weber's, and might be described as a benignly updated version of it. Popular will can only exist within a concrete social structure that cannot be willed: democracy reposes on principles that are not based on consent, but

---

55. *The Psychoanalytic Movement*, London 1985, pp. 99–107.
56. MWL, pp. 379–380; MWB, p. 376.

limit it. Parliamentary government therefore is most effective where decisions to be taken are relatively marginal. The essence of democracy is perhaps no more than civic rights garnished with symbolic participation in the Durkheimian community – the ballot essentially limiting the life of governments, and so indirectly cautioning their conduct.[57] The Western exemplars of it should inspire no smugness: they overlook unnecessary enclaves of poverty and preserve archaic areas of hierarchy. But can they really be much improved? Egalitarian in mores, if perhaps less so in structure, they can allow reveries of yet greater equality because the danger of these being implemented is so small that their compatibility with liberty is unlikely to be tested. No one has yet shown how power might be more diffused in an industrial society.[58] Compared with Weber, there is a much more central attachment to the openness of liberal institutions to criticism and reform as values in their own right; and much less (scarcely any) interest in the leadership presiding over them, a difference that follows from the tasks of the epoch: the mission of the state is not to conquer world power, but to manage growing affluence.

With this sanguine outlook, Gellner reacted to the upheavals of the late sixties with sardonic good humour, treating student rebellion as little more than the obverse of establishment conservatism – both equally facile ideologies, the one rejecting all general ideas in the name of common sense, the other trumpeting any number of them as a *dérèglement des sens*;[59] each comfortably ensconced in a costless realm of make-belief typical of advanced industrial societies. Uncharacteristically, his serenity briefly deserted him in the seventies, when industrial unrest and oil price rises seem to have disproportionately agitated him. Texts of this period strike an apocalyptic note found nowhere else in his writing: the horizon suddenly becomes menacing, civilization undermined by rot and betrayal, England itself doomed – all, apparently, because of the blackmail of miners and sheikhs. These addresses are his modest version of Weber's forebodings at Munich: a liberalism under threat of social unrest, at home and abroad, fearing if not a polar night, at any rate a 'dark and lowering sky' before it.[60] One imagines a Conservative vote in 1979. Return to normal service, with

---

57. *Contemporary Thought and Politics*, London 1973, pp. 29–39.
58. *Contemporary Thought and Politics*, p. 172; *Thought and Change*, p. 119.
59. *Contemporary Thought and Politics*, pp. 8–19, 84– 85.
60. *Spectacles and Predicaments*, pp. 39, 280; *Culture, Politics and Identity*, pp. 111, 123.

the boom conditions of the eighties, has restored Gellner's natural *sang froid*. Other and more lasting preoccupations have since dominated.

The main one, of course, has been nationalism. Here lies the most significant and paradoxical of all the relationships between the two sociologists. For Gellner has made good Weber's central omission, with a vengeance. His work contains the boldest and most original theory of nationalism to date. Prompted by his field-work in the Third World, it explains the emergence of nationalism as a breakwater of differential industrialization. Modern technology demands occupational mobility. But the more fluid the social structure, the more unitary is the culture it requires of its agents, as they shift and intermesh across its positions in an increasingly complex and mutable division of labour. This is a universal imperative of industrialism. But its advent is not only histori-cally staggered; it hits a world already ethnically and linguistically divided. On the one hand, no single culture is yet powerful enough to encompass the globe; on the other, the later a region comes to indus-trialization, the more it risks subjugation to those which arrived earlier, and exclusion of its inhabitants from the local fruits of the process. The result is nationalism: or the spread of the drive to create states whose political frontiers roughly coincide with ethnic boundaries. Nationalist movements are typically recruited from a disaffected intelligentsia and an uprooted proletariat – the former standing to benefit from mono-poly of public office in an independent state, the latter at least to be exploited only by fellow-citizens. Contrary to received prejudices, the diffusion of nationalism throughout the globe is a salutary process, which has certainly improved the lot and perhaps bettered the conduct of humanity. For the nation-state, however fortuitous its original demarcation (there are far fewer than the possible linguistic candi-dates), is the necessary general framework for the unitary culture – also preliminary protection – required by modern industry, which is in turn the only passport to prosperity for individuals, and equality between peoples.

This explanation of the nature of nationalism is an outstandingly powerful one on its own ground. But that ground is self-confessedly less than the whole phenomenon. Gellner's theory can account for the rise of nation-states in Eastern Europe, and the decolonization of Asia and Africa, even if it runs into difficulties with the earlier liberation of Spanish America. But what it completely skirts is the really spectacular manifestations of twentieth-century nationalism – not the indepen-dence of Czechoslovakia or Morocco, but World War and Nazism. Such catastrophic processes cannot be blandly tidied away as anoma-lies, with the discreet assurance that 'exceptionless generalizations are seldom if ever available'.[61] It is difficult not to sense a *parti pris* here, as if Gellner has over-reacted to previous depictions of nationalism as a destructively irrational, atavistic force – producing something like a mirror opposite, in which it becomes to all intents and purposes a wholesomely constructive and forward-looking principle. The huge world-historical ambiguities of nationalism are not captured by either; they call for an account that is temporally and spatially more differentiated. But what Gellner leaves out casts into a sharp light what he puts in. The most arresting feature of his theory of nationalism is its single-minded economic functionalism. 'The economy needs the new type of cultural centre and the central state; the culture needs the state; and the state probably needs the homogeneous cultural branding of its flock . . . The mutual relationship of a modern culture and state is something quite new, and springs, inevitably, from the requirements of a modern economy.'[62] Gellner early on defined his sociological position as a 'multiform materialism', with a clear-sighted insistence on the general (not invariable) priority of the (several) physical and material determinants of social existence.[63] Whatever its variability over time, this moderate materialism has generally distinguished him from Weber, to whom such clarity of outlook was foreign. Ironically, however, there is a sense in which Gellner's theory of nationalism might be described as immoderately materialist. For what it plainly neglects is the overpowering dimension of collective *meaning* that modern nationalism has always involved: that is, not its functionality for industry, but its fulfilment of identity. Here, in effect, only the rational is real: the irrational, underlined in his critique of psychoanalysis, is set aside – economy and psyche do not join. The result is that, in his tour of reenchantments, Gellner has paradoxically missed far the most important of all in the twentieth century. There are surely reasons of sensibility for this. That same Enlightenment optimism which made him avert his gaze from the threat of nuclear war during his own Belle Epoque, as 'not easily amenable to rational consideration', has also probably stopped it before the Great War of the original one: the founding episode of the century simply seems 'in retrospect sheer madness'.[64] Whereas Weber was so bewitched by the spell of nationalism that he was never able to theorize it, Gellner has theorized nationalism without detecting the spell. What was tragic fate for the

---

61. *Nations and Nationalism*, Oxford 1983, p. 139.
62. Ibid., 140.
63. *Cause and Meaning in the Social Sciences*, p. 127.
64. *Culture, Politics and Identity*, pp. 113, 11.

one becomes prosaic function for the other. Here the difference between idealist and utilitarian backgrounds tells.

But if Gellner's view of nationalism focuses so calmly – at times blithely – on cause at the expense of meaning, there is a sense in which it also does so consistently with the structure of his sociology as a whole. For as we have seen, the serious business of *Sinnstiftung* has already been taken care of, in the scientific provision of affluence. Nationalism is a means to the values of abundance, not a value-force in its own right. There is a political prejudgement behind this. Gellner's liberalism has been resistant to any crossing of the division between public and private spheres – critical of all hopes of a more expressive community than we now have, in which individuals would find a larger share of their identity in collective life. That for him, it would seem, is dangerous romanticism.[65] The public realm is instrumental, for the management of prosperity – the more marginal its meanings (he takes monarchy as an ideal) the better. Private life, where the fruits of ease are to be enjoyed, is the proper sphere of self-expression.

It would look as if with this, Gellner's universe has – at any rate potentially – solved all its major problems, save those mishandled by psychoanalysis. But there is a serpent in the garden. Science may unexpectedly have brought peace among Weber's warring gods – by installing Pluto as unchallengeable master over them. But what if its progress should move on from triumphant transformation of the world to that of the self?[66] The rickety fit of the ghost in the machine, noticeable at the epistemological start of Gellner's enterprise, returns as a sociobiological shiver at its end. Perhaps genetic engineering might one day cancel the illusions of the empiricist ego, leaving only mechanist laws for its manipulation. Loss of meaning affected the objective world, and proved curable – or tolerable – with the de facto appearance of subjective consensus about the one major meaning after all. Loss of self could attack the stability of subjective agreement about anything – prosperity, liberty, knowledge – at all. In these moments, it is as if Gellner is caught wondering whether Weber did not under- rather than over-estimate the long-term problems of science for public and private life alike.

1990

---

65. *Spectacles and Predicaments*, pp. 38–40.
66. *Plough, Sword and Book*, pp. 267–68.

10

Nocturnal Enquiry:
Carlo Ginzburg

Carlo Ginzburg has many claims to be considered the outstanding European historian of the generation which came of age in the late sixties. Certainly few have equalled him in originality, variety and audacity. He made his début with a spectacular discovery: the first, and still only, documented case of a magical fertility and funerary complex in the countryside of early modern Europe, the trances of the *Benandanti* in Friuli, stumbled upon unawares by the Roman Inquisition. Next, he transformed the genealogy of religious dissimulation in the age of the Reformation, by tracing the origins of Nicodemism – theological doctrines sanctioning public concealment of private faith – to the defeat of the Peasants' War in Germany and milieux close to Anabaptism, well before the rise of Calvin whose attacks on it coined the term. There followed his famous, vivid portrait of the autodidact Italian miller Menocchio, whose cosmology of spontaneous generation – the world born as cheese and worms – he related to a subterranean peasant materialism. Changing terrain again, Ginzburg then suggested a new iconographic explanation of Piero della Francesca's greatest paintings, linking them through an unnoticed Aretine humanist to the abortive union of Greek and Roman Churches, and the crusades projected around the fall of Constantinople. The intellectual unity, and novelty, of these different enquiries can best be grasped in the essays that make up the recent collection *Myths Emblems Clues*. Its centre-pieces are two long methodological reflections, the first on the Warburg tradition of art history, and the second on the general heuristics of attribution, from ancient divination to modern connoisseurship or the psychopathology of verbal slips.[1]

---

1. *I Benandanti – Stregoneria e culti agrari tra Cinquecento e Seicento*, Turin 1966; *Il Nicodemismo – Simulazione e Dissimulazione Religiosa nell'Europa del Cinquecento*, Turin 1970; *Il Formaggio e i Vermi – Il Cosmo di un Mugnaio del Cinquecento*, Turin

Ginzburg's new book, *Storia Notturna*, more than keeps the promise of this record.[2] It is by far his most ambitious work to date. Subtitled 'A Decipherment of the Sabbath', it advances a vast, dramatic reinterpretation of the central image of the European witch-craze. Far from being simply a phobic invention of the persecutors, confected from fixed stereotypes of heretical diabolism and garbled scraps of rural magic, the witches' sabbath reflected the deepest mythological structures of popular culture of the age – a network of beliefs and practices rooted in Eurasian shamanism, stretching from Ireland to the Bering Strait, and running back across millennia past the Ancient World to the darkness of Indo–European and Ural–Altaic origins. In a polemical introduction Ginzburg criticizes those historians who have concentrated on the authorities and procedures that set European witch-finding in motion, at the expense of research into the beliefs of those persecuted as witches – Trevor-Roper in the first instance, but also Keith Thomas, charged with reductionism and functionalism. Against this tradition, Ginzburg sets what he sees as the superior progamme of Lévi-Strauss's structuralist treatment of myths as symbolic systems, whose hidden meaning is generated by unconscious operations of the human mind – even if Lévi-Strauss's anthropology has given insufficient weight to historical research proper. By contrast, Ginzburg's aim is to combine the morphology and history of the Sabbath – its synchronic significations and diachronic development – in a single, comprehensive reconstruction.

The argument of *Storia Notturna* is divided into three parts. The first opens dramatically, with a staccato account of the French pogrom against lepers and Jews in 1321, accused of poisoning wells in a plot against Christendom orchestrated by the Muslim 'king of Granada'. It then moves to the massacre of Jews in 1348, as agents of a conspiracy spreading the Black Death, which unfolded further east towards the Alps. In each case, confessions of a phantasmagoric iniquity were extorted from the victims, under pressure of torture. By 1380 inquisitors were ferreting out Waldensian heretics on the southern flank of the Alps. Soon afterwards, Ginzburg suggests, the obsessive fears at work in these persecutions of successive marginal groups were condensed and displaced into the spectre of a new sect practising witchcraft in the

---

1976; *Indagini su Piero – Il Battesimo, il Ciclo di Arezzo, la Flagellazione di Urbino*, Turin 1981; *Miti Emblemi Spie – Morfologia e Storia*, Turin 1986. In English, respectively: *The Night Battles*, London 1983; *The Cheese and the Worms*, London 1980; *The Enigma of Piero*, London 1985; *Myths Emblems Clues*, London 1990. The latter henceforward NW, CW, EP, MEC.

2. *Storia Notturna – Una Decifrazione del Sabba*, Turin 1989: henceforward SN.

Alpine regions. With this, other dread themes surfaced, absent from the earlier confessions. By about 1440, the full nightmare of the Sabbath – diabolism, anthropophagy, animal metmorphoses, supernatural flight, promiscuity – had been incubated in Christian imagination.

Ginzburg does not pursue the consequences. Breaking off his historical account here, he switches directly to the meaning of what he terms the 'folkloric nucleus' of the Sabbath – identified with the motifs of nocturnal flying and animal transmogrification. The second part of *Storia Notturna* pursues the archaeology of these. It picks out three cultic origins behind the popular beliefs that went into the compound image of the Sabbath: ecstatic experiences (by women) of a night goddess surrounded by animals, and (by men) of a night battle to ensure fertility or prosperity; and ritual processions (of males) masked as animals. Ginzburg tracks each of these across formidable temporal and geographical distances, starting out from Archaic Greece and Gallo–Roman Gaul: the first in Lombardy, Scotland, Sicily, the Rhineland; the second in Latvia, Dalmatia, Hungary, Romania, Finland, Corsica, the Caucasus; the third in Germany, Bulgaria, the Ukraine. Through every kind of exotic variation, however, all betray a common source – the voyage to the dead undertaken in the shaman's trance. The journey of the living to the land of death, symbolized in such practices over thousands of years, constituted the clandestine core of the Sabbath, as it took shape at the end of the Middle Ages.

In the third part of the book, Ginzburg explores possible explanations for the morphological unity of a folklore extending far into Siberia and Turkestan. He starts by suggesting that it could have derived from the nomadic migrations that spilt out of Central Asia in the eighth century BC, which brought the Scythians – an Iranian people – into the Caucasus and the steppes to the north of the Black Sea, where Greek traders and colonists encountered them, absorbing certain shamanistic features of their culture. In the sixth century, Scythian contingents penetrated south, establishing themselves in the Dobrudja, where they ruled over a local Thracian population, subsequently joined by Celtic settlements. Could this Scythian region have been the original scene of a cultural synthesis, fusing mythological elements from all three peoples into a millennial substratum of beliefs and customs, capable of spreading across the continent and surviving in the depths of folk memory from the age of Herodotus to that of Galileo, if not beyond? Does the remarkable similarity of 'Animal Style' art, whose decorative forms stretch from China to Scandinavia in a continuum where the Scythian achievement was outstanding, testify to comparable historical connexions? After dwelling on the plausibility of these hypotheses, Ginzburg then points to the limitation of all diffusionist explanations – which leave unanswered the question of why external contact between societies should lead to the internal reproduction of the forms of one in another. The problem posed by the persistence over time and dispersal in space of shamanistic motifs can only be resolved, he concludes, by postulating the existence of general structural characteristics of the human mind.

To demonstrate these, Ginzburg proceeds to examine – in another sudden shift of focus – myths and rites involving lameness. This motif had already been discussed by Lévi-Strauss, who related it to the change of seasons. Rejecting this interpretation, Ginzburg scours (in the first instance) Greek mythology for every manifestation of a deeper category, in which lameness is only one variant, along with the wounded leg, the perforated foot, the vulnerable heel, the missing sandal, which he dubs 'asymmetrical deambulation'. Oedipus, Perseus, Jason, Theseus, Heracles, Achilles, Philoctetes, Empedocles and a host of other figures display this motif – as does Cinderella, the most far-flung of all folk tales, or the Chinese crane-dance. Its symbolic meaning is a journey to the world of the dead. But if the pervasive recurrence of this motif belongs to a unitary Eurasian mythology, it is anchored in a universal human experience, 'the self-image of the body'. Asymmetrical deambulation is the privileged signifier of contact with death, because all living beings are symmetrical in form, and among them humans are specifically biped. The impairing of walk amounts to putting a figurative toe in the waters of extinction. There is thus in the end an ontological foundation for the symbolization of the voyage beyond human experience, to the world inhabited by the dead. Myths dictate the limits of their own variation, because they are constrained by the formal structures of the imagination.

Storia Notturna ends with a brief 'Conclusion' that is in fact more like a coda. Here Ginzburg suggests that if the image of the Witches' Sabbath could fuse so effectively clerical obsessions from above and folk myths from below, it was in part because they shared a common fear of conspiracy – whose popular form was the belief that those who had recently died were moved by hostile resentment towards those who were still living. Perhaps too, he speculates, there was a psychotropic element in the trances which either in fact contributed or were projected onto the whole complex – the use of hallucinogenic rye or mushrooms. However that may be, the myths which flowed into the Sabbath all converged on the notion of a journey to the beyond and back again, crossing over to the world of the dead and returning from it. Ginzburg ends by arguing that the permanence of this theme, through hunting, pastoral and agricultural societies alike, has perhaps a simple but fundamental explanation: the voyage to the dead is not just one narrative among others, but the original matrix of all possible narratives. In the cauldrons of Walpurgis Night are concocted the ingredients of every human tale.

By any standards, this is a bravura performance. It is difficult to think of any other historian who combines such polymathic cultural erudition, grasp of textual or visual detail, and high theoretical aim – not to speak of literary skill. The result is a work of vertiginous effect. There can be little doubt of the audience it is destined to win. To do it critical justice, however, may not prove so simple. For with all its extraordinary gifts, *Storia Notturna* poses a series of difficult problems, concerning the methods it adopts, the conclusions it reaches, the outlook it suggests. It is best to begin with the first of these. Ginzburg tells us at the outset that the procedure of his book was inspired by a comment of Wittgenstein on Frazer's *Golden Bough*, to the effect that mythological materials did not need to be set out historically, as Frazer had done (situating them in an evolutionary sequence), but could equally well be presented 'perspicuously' – that is, he explained, 'just by arranging the factual material so that we can easily pass from one part to the other' and therewith 'see the connexions'. Hence, Wittgenstein went on – here is the motto Ginzburg took for his research – 'the importance of finding *intermediary links*', 'as one might illustrate the internal relation of a circle to an ellipse by gradually transforming an ellipse into a circle'.[3] For Ginzburg this was the charter for the kind of morphology he was seeking. A more formalized version of it was to be found, as it happened, in an essay by the English anthropologist Rodney Needham, on 'Polythetic Classification', which Ginzburg duly uses.[4] Needham too was much impressed with Wittgenstein's insights, although he relied rather on the familiar text from the *Philosophical Investigations* which describes the notion of a game as indicating no more than a 'family resemblance', without any common feature in the set of which it is used, just as 'the strength of a thread does not reside in the fact that some one thread runs through its whole length, but in the *overlapping* of many fibres'.[5] Whereas monothetic classification requires the presence of at least one common trait in the class identified, polythetic classification – Needham argued – merely demands that each member

---

3. *Remarks on Frazer's 'Golden Bough'*, Retford 1979, pp. 8–9.
4. 'Polythetic Classification: Convergence and Consequences', *Man*, 10, 1975, pp. 349–369; now in *Against the Tranquillity of Axioms*, Berkeley–Los Angeles 1983, pp. 36– 65.
5. *Philosophical Investigations*, Oxford 1978, p. 67.

of the set display a large number of the range of relevant traits, and that these traits are displayed in a large number of the members. He illustrated the basic idea with three descent systems, the first exhibiting features p/q/r, the second r/s/t, and the third t/u/v: such was the type of overlap that sufficed for polythetic purposes.

In urging the importance of this kind of classification for the social sciences, Needham nevertheless entered two cautions. It was the example of the natural sciences, where it was first employed, that lent weight to the validity of the method; yet there the findings of bacterial taxonomy suggested that it did not, after all, make much difference, since a monothetic core of common properties appeared in polythetic classes anyway. On the other hand, whereas in nature there are discrete empirical particulars – elements and particles – from which classes can indisputably be built, no such readily isolable units exist in society. To meet this difficulty, Needham later went on to postulate certain 'primary factors of human experience' as basic elements underlying the possibility of polythetic classification in anthropology.[6] But he warned that the latter remained a vague notion, since it lacked any rigorous definition of what counted as 'a large number', either of features or members.[7] Ginzburg, for his part, rejects Needham's primary factors of experience, as a conception too close to Jungian archetypes. But he provides no alternative elements of a formally comparable character in lieu of them; and he neglects the problem of defining the acceptable range of a class altogether. The result is effectively a hermeneutic blank cheque, drawn from an uncritical reliance on Wittgenstein. This a slender reed to rely on. Generally innocent of the social sciences, Wittgenstein was attracted to just one dabbler in them – Oswald Spengler. It is no accident that in the very note on *The Golden Bough* used in *Storia Notturna* the only specific example Wittgenstein gave of the method he was recommending should have been, precisely, Spengler – one that Ginzburg tactfully omits in citing it as a credo. The naiveté of Wittgenstein's morphological recipes is thus what might be expected. Family resemblance: who has not winced at the fatuities of its discovery in any improbable infant feature – or for that matter adult, by doting uncle or gaga grandparent? Intermediate links: by the method of gradual changes, circles can be geometrically transformed not just into ellipses, but into any number of oval shapes – or indeed into hexagons, triangles, or squares, at will. As

---

6. *Circumstantial Deliveries*, Berkeley–Los Angeles 1981, pp. 1–3.
7. *Against the Tranquillity of Axioms*, p. 58.

a principle of comparison, the procedure licenses approximations without end.

Myths have always formed treacherous ground for morphological analysis, at once apparently hospitable in their formal variations, yet actually intractable in their lack of natural segmentation. The kind of structural analysis practised by Lévi-Strauss always depends on a series of analytic fiats which break up their narrative unity into so many semantic units at the convenience of the analyst, for rearrangement into putatively underlying patterns. In the absence of independent criteria for selection of the features so translated, the results are notoriously contestable: scarcely one of Lévi-Strauss's exercises has ever enjoyed a general consensus. Seemingly insensible of the objections of method so often raised against them, Ginzburg's only real criticism of Lévi-Strauss is that he is insufficiently faithful to himself. *Plus royaliste que le roi*, he taxes him with a relapse into a humdrum Frazerian interpretation in viewing lameness as a mere seasonal, rather than lethal, motif – or, as he grandly puts it, 'my Frazer has read Wittgenstein'.[8] The consequences are what might be expected. If polythetic classification is to be operationally defensible, it requires a reasoned demarcation of the features bounding the set in question, and an unambiguous specification of the proportion of them that counts for membership of it. Unless each of these – features and proportions – amounts to a *dominant* cluster, the class will be more or less arbitrary. Ginzburg does not attempt to show either. Instead, he picks out those elements in successive myths that interest him, and then connects them as so many 'intermediate links' in a chain that confers a common meaning on them. His single-minded quest through classical mythology for asymmetric deambulation is a brilliant feat of imagination. But for all its ingenuity, it rests on a series of calculated extrapolations from the narrative contexts of the myths concerned.

The story of Oedipus is clearly centred on sexual and familial issues. Sophocles paid little attention to his lameness, as Ginzburg himself admits. But he discounts the evidence of Athenian tragedy with the 'supposition' that 'in the oldest version of the myth of Oedipus', pierced feet were the first stage in a tale concerned with travel to the world of the dead.[9] The portrait of Achilles in Homer does not even mention his heel – which is a late accretion first registered under the Roman Empire. Undeterred, Ginzburg tells us that behind the hero depicted by Homer, and unknown to him, a prior god of the dead 'has been

8. SN, pp. 261, 184.
9. SN, p. 208. The supposition comes from Propp's essay on Oedipus.

discerned', of Scythian stock.[10] The figure of Theseus, pervasively connected to the sea, exhibited no physical defect at all. Ginzburg nonetheless enlists him for his construction on the grounds that he lifted a rock to find his father's sword and pair of sandals – a case of the circle cartwheeling from triangle to square indeed, since there is not even asymmetry in the deambulation here. The legend of Prometheus is incontestably focused on issues of knowledge. There is not even a hint of a hobble in the 'fore-thinker', in any of its variants. Ginzburg, however, adduces first a Caucasian parallel, in which a hero stealing fire sacrifices some part of himself to a rescuing eagle, who restores it, and then an Italian folk tale in which another hero, without discovering fire, loses a heel to the redeeming bird. From this graphic example of the method of intermediate links – he casually notes that the theme of intelligence plays no role in either fable – he confidently concludes that in all probability it is 'pure chance' that Prometheus suffers no asymmetry of deambulation in the versions that have come down to us.[11] Classicists might well retort that the only thing lame about the Greek hero is this explanation of him.

In his enthusiasm, Ginzburg dubs such parallelism between Ancient Greece and modern Georgia or Modena with the same epithet that he once used to describe the convergence he found between Menocchio's cosmogony and Vedic or Kalmuck mythology: *stupefacente*.[12] With the 'perspicuous' method of 'arranging the factual material', Wittgenstein promised, 'we can easily pass from one part to another.' Just so. The passages are much too easy, as the morphology cascades swiftly from one myth to another in an accelerating torrent of identifications – the local evidence for which often consists mainly of variations on the formula 'it has been suggested', which recurs with tell-tale insistence.[13] Eventually, Greek gods and heroes flow – 'all but inevitably' – into the great estuary of Cinderella tales. Here Ginzburg singles out as especially significant those versions which include the collection by the heroine of the bones of an animal who has helped her. He then goes on to argue that 'the most complete version' of the fable involved the

---

10. SN, p. 212.
11. SN, p. 239.
12. SN, p. 239; *Il Formaggio e i Vermi*, p. 68; CW, p. 58.
13. The preferred construction is an impersonal passive: see SN, pp. 207, 208, 211, 212, 213, 217, 220: *sono stati interpretati – si è identificato – si è supposto – è stato attribuito – è stato individuato – è stata accostata – si suppone – si è proposto – è stato accostato*, etc. Supporting references are in each case to be found in footnotes, but these are rarely accompanied by indications of alternative or contrary readings of the same myths.

subsequent resuscitation of the dead animal from its bones.[14] But of the three hundred and more stories accounted as versions of Cinderella, from across the globe, less than ten per cent include the gathering of bones, and less than one per cent – just three cases – involve resuscitation. In such defiance of distributional frequency, it is difficult not to see a preconceived conclusion. The resuscitation of an animal from its bones is, of course, a shamanistic representation of the voyage to the dead.

In his influential essay 'Clues', which can be taken as a general historical manifesto, Ginzburg argued for an epistemological paradigm attentive to small traces and discrepancies as the signs of hidden truth, whose great modern pioneers were Morelli and Freud. The kind of 'circumstantial' knowledge to be wrested from minor clues went back to the first hunters peering at hoof-prints in the ground; it was practised by ancient medicine and divination; inspired jurisprudence and paleontology; before acquiring exemplary modern form in connoisseurship and psychoanalysis. Unlike the quantitative, generalizing knowledge pioneered by Galilean physics, it sought qualitative individuation of its objects. As such, it was the appropriate paradigm not only for history, but for the ensemble of the human sciences, which over time have ever more assumed it as their model. More generally indeed, we witness the decadence of systematic thought, after the unwise pretensions of Marx, and the rise of aphoristic thought, associated with Nietzsche – illumination in the fragment.[15] Although this argument recalls the familiar neo-Kantian division between nomothetic and idiographic disciplines, since Ginzburg too appeals to subjective experience for his circumstantial paradigm, the heuristic emphasis it gives to the vestigial and the anomalous sets it apart. But, of course, these can prompt enquiry in any field of the natural or social sciences, just as they never exhaust any. They provide no special model for the latter, which – contrary to Ginzburg's suggestion – are certainly not closer to the model of 'diagnostic' as opposed to 'anatomical' medicine, as a glance at the procedures of economics or sociology would show.

What is more striking, however, is that in arguing for the 'circumstantial paradigm', Ginzburg does not discriminate between his illustrations of it. Necromancy and science, empirical lore and speculative fantasy, jostle side by side in his catalogue of the arts of decipherment. Perhaps this is because Ginzburg assumes there has been a historical winnowing of them, leaving only certified candidates today for what he

---

14. SN, p. 228.
15. *Miti Emblemi Spie*, pp. 158–209; MEC, pp. 96–125.

calls the 'elastic rigour' specific to them. But the oxymoron says enough. Mentioning at one point Sebastiano Timpanaro's devastating work *The Freudian Slip*, Ginzburg says he would reverse its judgement – 'while Timpanaro rejects psychoanalysis because intrinsically close to magic, I try to show that not only psychoanalysis but most of the so-called human sciences draw their inspiration from an epistemology of divination.'[16] Timpanaro concentrated his attack, conclusively, on the association of ideas as a method of interpreting the *lapsus*, showing that it was incapable of *not* disclosing the meaning Freud assigned them. In analogy with that method, Wittgenstein commended approaching myths and rituals as an 'association of practices'.[17] This would be one way of describing what Ginzburg has done. The price, however, is the same. Just as at the level of the paradigm, there is no way of identifying what is not a valid form of divination, so at the level of the morphology there is no point at which the associations need ever stop – falsifications never feature.

The end result is similar too. Freud's interpretation of slips and dreams insisted – contrary to the most obvious, and overwhelming evidence – that the meaning of every diverse case of displacement, substitution or condensation lay in repressed sexual desire. Lévi-Strauss once compared psychoanalysis to shamanism. But his own interpretation of mythologies reproduces the same schema. Beneath the inexhaustible proliferation of myths across the world, with their luxuriance of every kind of local vocabulary, lies one great invariable theme: mediation between nature and culture. Propp, who pioneered the morphological analysis of the wonder-tale, producing the thirty-one functions of its hundred and seventy-seven variants, likewise found just a single master-fable underlying them all. In his case, it was the rite of initiation as a journey to the land of death, transmitted from shamanism.[18] Ginzburg has now taken over Propp's conclusion, and generalized it beyond the wonder-tale, to the farthest-flung corners of Eurasian mythology as a whole. The fascination of the data he assembles is beyond question. But once again, what is striking is the contrast between the richness and variety of the materials, and the paucity of the meaning to which they are reduced. Seeing the mote in the folklorist's eye, the anthropologist complained of the procedure,

---

16. *Miti Emblemi Spie*, p. 199; MEC, p. 205.
17. *Remarks on Frazer's 'Golden Bough'*, p. 13.
18. *Morphology of the Folktale*, Austin 1968, p. 23; *Theory and History of Folklore*, Manchester 1984, pp. 117, 122.

while reproducing it on a grander scale.[19] The historian, criticizing each, goes further, joining fable and myth together in a cosmic one-liner, encompassing all the narratives ever told.

In venturing this final step, Ginzburg moves beyond the formal bounds of his own enquiry. The outline of a unitary Eurasian substratum of beliefs and rituals dissolves into universal categories of the human mind. In fact, the latter part of *Storia Notturna* continually hesitates between these two. Ginzburg poses this as a dilemma between two kinds of explanation of the regularities he finds: cultural diffusion (alternatively common descent) or psychic uniformity. Declining to opt for one or the other, he exploits both possibilities. It is their combination that affords the 'interweaving' of history and morphology at which he aims. But their simultaneous presence in the text looks more like tactical reinsurance than theoretical synthesis, for they cannot logically be reconciled. On the one hand, there is the hypothesis of a specifically Eurasian mythology based on the practices of shamanism. This line of thought has its own history. In the Russian emigration between the wars, 'Eurasianism' was an Orientalizing version of the Slavophile tradition, whose leading theorist was N.S. Trubetskoy, the founder of structuralist phonology. The 'Presentiments and Subversions' of the Eurasian Manifesto, which were already preoccupied with unitary folk culture,[20] have an involuntary echo in the 'Conjectures' of *Storia Notturna*. Shamanism, for its part, received heroic exploration from Mircea Eliade, in a study tracing it far from its North and Central Asia homelands, to Germans, Greeks, Scythians, and many other peoples. It was Eliade who emphasized the difference between the ecstatic states of shamanism and possession – the shaman controlling communication with the spirits of the dead, the possessed controlled by them.[21] Ginzburg adopts this opposition, and makes of it a cultural frontier. Eurasia is characterized by the ubiquity of shamanism, sub-Saharan Africa by possession. The Cinderella cycle and scapulimancy,

---

19. 'La Structure et la Forme: Réflexions sur un Ouvrage de Vladimir Propp', in *Anthropologie Structurale Deux*, Paris 1973, pp. 158–161.

20. *Utverzhdenie Evrazintsev – Iskhod k Vostoku: Predchuvstviya i Sversheniya*, Sofia 1921. Trubetskoy's contributions, on 'True and False Nationalism' and 'Heights and Depths of Russian Culture', stressed the importance of common Eurasian motifs in folksong, dance, ornament and popular character, for the needed *perestroika* of Russian culture after the disaster of the Bolshevik Revolution.

21. *Shamanism*, New York 1964, p. 6. For some qualifications of the contrast, see the judicious discussion in A. Hultkrantz, 'Ecological and Phenomenological Aspects of Shamanism', in V. Diószegi and M. Hoppal, eds., *Shamanism in Siberia*, Budapest 1978, pp. 41–49.

likewise, are common to the former and unknown to the latter.[22] But if this is so, appeal from correspondences between Indo–European and Ural–Altaic ecstatic forms to universal categories of the human mind is ruled out.

On the other hand, Ginzburg states unambiguously: 'Long ago I set out to demonstrate experimentally, from history, that human nature does not exist; twenty-five years later, I find myself maintaining the exact opposite.'[23] Although his Eurasian conjectures provide no support for it, the claim itself may of course be independently valid. Certainly there is nothing outlandish about it. Ginzburg's way of construing the notion of human nature, however, is quite particular. Loyal to his structuralist inspiration, he interprets it in a strictly intellectualist sense. By human nature here is understood the mechanisms of the human mind. Needs and emotions, which might be thought prime candidates, do not figure. Lévi-Strauss has announced: 'I cannot give these turbulent forces primacy; they erupt onto a stage already constructed and patterned by mental constraints.'[24] Needham, seeking the primary factors of human experience, goes out of his way to deny that affects count among them – no inner turbulence is universal: ' "anger" in another civilization is not equivalent to anger in our own.'[25] What is universal is a common repository of 'collective representations', derived from the properties of the cerebral cortex, which can be viewed as close to Jungian archetypes.[26] Ginzburg rejects even these as too concrete, for transcendental operations of the mind whose symbols are not so readily intelligible. But he too toys with the idea of fitting Jung with a materialist pediment – that is, giving universal myths a somatic foundation.[27] In the end, the deathly meaning of asymmetric deambulation is traced to an exigency of the self-representation of the body. At first sight, the case Ginzburg makes here looks plausible. But it rests on the slenderest of documentary evidence: one possible interpretation of a single myth from the Moluccas is the only empirical referent supporting it. The general argument depends, moreover, on the identification of humanity with the capacity to walk on two legs – a gait that is shared, however, by various animal

---

22. SN, p. 231.
23. SN, p. xxxvii.
24. *La Potière Jalouse*, Paris 1985, p. 264.
25. *Circumstantial Deliveries*, p. 63: 'More generally, the outcome is that inner states are not universals and do not in this sense constitute natural resemblances among men.'
26. *Circumstantial Deliveries*, pp. 25, 51.
27. SN, p. 262.

species (not just apes and bears, mentioned by Ginzburg, but more generally by birds). The human species is more frequently identified with language, and one has only to think of the ease with which the same case could be made for (let us imagine) myths involving 'irregular articulation' — muteness, hoarseness, stuttering, lisping, whispering, mumbling and so on — to see how inconclusive it is likely to be. The problem is not the conviction, eminently reasonable, that there is such a thing as human nature: but where to locate and how to define it. Collective representations, however they are conceived, are unlikely to be the main road to an answer. Asymmetric deambulation, for all the ramifications it acquires, will not support the anthropological weight put on it.

What then is its more specifically historical relevance to the original theme of the book, the Witches' Sabbath? It must be said, rather little. Many fantastical elements went into this Christian–pagan brew, but one thing it did not include was this. The only connexions Ginzburg is able to offer between the ostensible subject and actual climax of the book is one limping boy in a (third-hand) version of memories of a Livonian werewolf and a lame Aegean bogey.[28] Neither has any direct relation to the Sabbath. Even by the method of intermediate links, this is a tenuous thread. The first part of the book must be regarded as an effectively independent enquiry, to be judged on its own merits. How are these to be assessed?

Ginzburg's 'decipherment of the Sabbath' involves two principal claims. The first concerns the configuration of the image of the Sabbath itself. Where Trevor-Roper, following a long tradition, viewed this as essentially a theological fabrication incorporating jumbled fragments of peasant gullibility, Ginzburg in effect reverses the order of importance within the mixture, indicating popular belief rather than learned fantasy as the core of the phenomenon. This judgement is never quite spelt out as such. But it is insistently conveyed by the use of the term 'nucleus' to describe the folkloric elements of the Sabbath. The grammatical ambiguity of such pronouncements as 'here lies the folkloric nucleus of the Sabbath'[29] is unlikely to be casual: Ginzburg employs the notion to suggest both coherence and centrality. What is his case for them? Here the problem of methodological imprecision returns. For the criteria required to decide what is dominant (and what is subordi-

---

28. SN, pp. 134, 153–54, 147. A German woodcut of a Long John Silver-style devil is also offered: an illustration equally remote from the subject.

29. SN, p 78; or more categorically: 'the primary nucleus of the phenomena considered here is constituted by the voyage of the living to the world of the dead', p. xxxviii.

nate) in a composite formation are missing. So too, in fact, are criteria for defining the composition. For Ginzburg there are essentially two layers to the Sabbath: satanism on high – the pact with the devil; and shamanism below – the voyage to the dead. The latter is the organic substratum of the phenomenon, whose originally beneficent meaning (the shaman as warrior of the good) is converted into a fearful ceremonial of evil (the witch as servant of satan) by the artifice of the former. What this dualism, of sanguine folk myth deformed into vicious elite craze, omits is popular fear of witchcraft itself. General and intense belief in *maleficium*, the sorcerer's curse, as the agent of every kind of material injury or misfortune, was a fundamental condition of the witch-craze. Massively documented by Keith Thomas and others,[30] it is virtually ignored by Ginzburg. But it has much more obvious claims to be regarded as the folk soil of the phobia than anything to do with ecstatic trances or monosandalism. In Hungary, a region where the presence of a shamanistic element in village life was probably stronger – certainly better documented – than anywhere else in sub-arctic Europe (the well-known figure of the *táltos*), it played a discernible role in only about two per cent of witchcraft trials.[31] The malefice, on the other hand, was everywhere; even the *Benandanti*, it has been pointed out, were involved in the transactions of the curse.[32] In other words, Ginzburg's account of the Sabbath paradoxically tends to forget the witches – in the most familiar sense of the term. Sociologically, this is an absolutely central lacuna of his study.

How far, on the other hand, does Ginzburg's historical narrative sustain his ethnographic view of the Sabbath? Tracing its genesis to the French pogrom of 1321, he stresses more than previous historians the role of deliberate machinations by municipal, royal and noble authorities in fanning a popular hysteria against lepers and Jews from which

---

30. *Religion and the Decline of Magic*, London 1971, pp. 436–37, 441 ff., for the case of England: subsequent research has showed how pervasive and persistent was belief in the malefice in continental Europe as well.

31. Gabor Klaniczay, 'Hungary: the Accusations and the Universe of Popular Magic', in Bengt Ankarloo and Gustav Hennigsen, *Early Modern European Witchcraft*, Oxford 1990, pp. 248–49. An authority on Magyar shamanistic traditions, Klaniczay stresses the extent to which there existed in Hungary 'a set of popular witchcraft beliefs largely independent of this archaic background', capable of unleashing persecutions even in the absence of intervention from above: 'The popular universe of magic could ruin itself in this way, even without the active pressure of an "elite culture" wishing to reform it': pp. 249, 255.

32. See the fundamental essay by Robert Rowland, ' "Fantasticall and Devilishe Persons": European Witch-Beliefs in Comparative Perspective', in Ankarloo and Henningsen eds., pp. 161–190, the best general theory of the structure of confessions, which includes a critique of Ginzburg's treatment of the Friulian material.

they stood to benefit economically.[33] 'Plot' there was, but on the part of Christian magistrates rather than against them. Here, at the outset, initiative is firmly imputed to those above. But by the time of the Alpine witch-trials of the next century, with which Ginzburg's narrative concludes, he goes out of his way to emphasize that in the emergent image of the Sabbath 'anti-heretical stereotypes' unleashed from above were 'only a secondary element'.[34] Norman Cohn is taken to task for exaggerating their importance. The claim is unpersuasive. Cohn's demonstration of the constancy of the stereotype of the secret sect – practising promiscuity, blasphemy, anthropophagy – from pagan accusations against the early Christians onwards, loses no relevance with the arrival of the Sabbath, since these were always the capital iniquities ascribed to it. The folkloric themes of nocturnal flight and animal metamorphosis were picturesque embroidery on this background – in themselves moral small change, dismissed as no graver than idle fancies by the *Canon episcopi* in the Dark Ages. If any elements were secondary in the Sabbath, it would logically and functionally be these. As it happens, it is Cohn who provides the best explanation for a fusion of motifs: the inclusion of nocturnal flying in the anti-heretical stereotype allowed for multiplication of suspects, by magical assembly of a host of secret evildoers.[35]

Beyond these structural considerations, there are also chronological difficulties in Ginzburg's reconstruction. His opening account of the pogrom of 1321 is a masterpiece of laconic narration, displaying all his exceptional gifts as a writer. Much of the power of his story-telling, here as in *The Cheese and the Worms*, lies in the understatement of its spare, concise prose. But this very conscious art is also, in another and less obvious way, highly theatrical. Ginzburg's narratives proceed by short, numbered paragraphs, with minimal connectives between them. The device of enumeration, typically used since Spinoza to suggest rigorous logical deduction, here evokes rather dramatic sequence: scenes or takes for stage or screen. This is a very effective way of unfolding a story. But it has a particular drawback as a method of writing history: it too often depends for its effects on *withholding* information. Ginzburg's way of recounting events militates against providing their context, which might slow the speed and diminish the

---

33. Ginzburg criticizes Malcolm Barber's account, from which he takes the title of his chapter (there is an oversight in his reference), 'Lepers, Jews and Moslems: the Plot to Overthrow Christendom in 1321', *History*, Vol. 66, No. 216, February 1981, pp. 1–17: see SN, pp. 23–24, 28.

34. SN, p. 49.

35. Norman Cohn, *Europe's Inner Demons*, London 1975, p. 205.

surprise of the tale. We are told very little, in the end, about the *Benandanti* beyond their fabulous adventures, or the Friulian society that enclosed them, about the village life that harboured Menocchio, or the Inquisitors who cross-examined him. So too France in 1321 is presented *ex abrupto*, shorn of all socio-political perspective. The lack of any informational frame – general features of France in the early fourteenth century, immediate situation of the kingdom, policy and personality of Philip V, position of lepers and Jews – quickens the sinister drama, but also deprives it of depth. One effect of this is especially relevant, and questionable. In representing the French mass-acre of that year as the starting-point of the fuse leading to the European witch-craze, Ginzburg neglects the *cause célèbre* that pre-ceded it – the extermination of the Templars unleashed by Philip IV in 1307. The charges made, and confessions extracted, in this political repression were in certain respects closer to the phantasmagoria of the Sabbath than the accusations against lepers and Jews. Conforming to the 'anti-heretical' rather than 'folkloric' nucleus, however, they play no role in Ginzburg's account – despite the fact, critical for a local aetiology, that the chief leper confession of 1321 borrowed from the show-trial of the Templars thirteen years earlier.[36]

The more general problem posed by the timing and trajectory of the witch-craze, however, remains. What generated the new persecutory hysteria that came to be driven by the image of the Witches' Sabbath? Ginzburg criticizes Cohn for focusing on a single long tradition of anti-heretical phobia from the time of Roman Emperors to that of Renais-sance Popes, at the expense of the 'evident cultural discontinuity' introduced by the idea of a sect of witches.[37] But his own concen-tration on a substratum of shamanistic trance-beliefs enduring far longer, across many thousands of years, raises even more sharply the question of what it was that suddenly precipitated the Sabbath out of them. The explanation he offers is conventional and cursory – little more than generic reference to the socio-economic crisis of the four-teenth century.[38] But reliable evidence for the crystallization of the Sabbath starts about a hundred years later; the witch-craze first reached its height in the relative prosperity of the late sixteenth century; persisting through the depression of the early seventeenth century, it then eventually subsided in the main regions infected before economic recovery was in sight. Moreover, its geographical incidence was very

---

36. See Barber, 'Lepers, Jews and Moslems', pp. 16–17.
37. SN, p. 50.
38. SN, pp. 54–55.

uneven. In Western Europe, England – lacking inquisitorial procedures and addiction to torture – was largely exempt from the obsession with the Sabbath; also relatively unaffected were the United Provinces. In Eastern Europe (where so many of Ginzburg's examples of shadow shamanism come from), the Orthodox Church paid little attention to it, and major persecution was confined to Catholic regions, particularly Poland. Between these zones, the real epicentres of witch-hunting were Germany, Switzerland and France, where Brian Levack has estimated perhaps 75 per cent of all prosecutions occurred.[39] The fundamental enigma of the European witch-craze is the pattern of its development in time and space – why it erupted when it did, whom it attacked, why and how it affected certain zones yet passed by others, why and when it petered out. In the answer to these historical questions must lie the key to deciphering the Sabbath. For all the steady gains of later research, the intellectual firmness and clarity with which they are posed in Trevor-Roper's great essay has yet to be equalled.

If Ginzburg's approach is so different, his aversion to this precedent so marked, the reason lies in the most constant conviction of his work. *Tout ce qui est intéressant se passe dans l'ombre* ran the epigraph to *The Cheese and the Worms*, from Céline. The hidden side of history is where the truth resides. In one of the essays in *Myths Emblems Clues*, Ginzburg maintains that no cultural opposition is so universal as the values ascribed to the positions of High and Low – the former being always equated with what is better, the latter with what is worse.[40] He overlooks another pervasive opposition in our culture, which reverses it: the Superficial and the Deep. Here, what is below inherently excels what is above. But the surface covers the depths, and must be parted to get to the bottom of things. If there is a single assumption that unifies all of Ginzburg's versatile work, it is this: that the deeper something lies, the more significant it must be. Nowhere has this belief acquired such writ as in *Storia Notturna*. The meaning of the Sabbath that matters is to be found in a subterranean level of human imagination stretching back from European fertility or funerary cults through Greek myths and Scythian ornaments to Siberian or Mongol shamans, perhaps to Paleolithic bands before them – whose evidence is everywhere symbolic traces of the voyage to the dead. However hazardous some of Ginzburg's interpretative connexions may be, his general argument for the

---

39. *The Witch-Hunt in Early Modern Europe*, New York 1987, pp. 176–182. Levack's work, the major comparative synthesis to have emerged from the new generation of research, is not mentioned in Ginzburg's otherwise copious bibliography.

40. *Miti Emblemi Spie*, pp. 109–110; MEC, pp. 62–63.

persistence of motifs of shamanistic origin over a very long span of time can readily be accepted. But persistence is in itself no warrant of significance. What is missing from Ginzburg's account is that erosion of meaning which is such a large part of any cultural history – the familiar process whereby customs or beliefs once centrally active become in altered conditions sporadic or marginal, and then lose their sense altogether as they are surcharged with further developments that incorporate or efface them, ceasing to be understood by any current agents at all.

Ginzburg himself notes often enough that classical authors failed to see the significance of asymmetrical deambulation in their myths; indeed he complains of their 'rationalistic' reconstructions of the mysteries that interest him.[41] But he does not draw the obvious conclusion, of a symbolism gone dead. As facts of cultural history, the realistic explanations of the single sandal attempted by Thucydides or Servius are in many ways more interesting than its aboriginal sense – since they obviously tell us more about Greek and Roman society. Shamanism in its Siberian or Lapp homelands was a central institution of rudimentary hunter–gatherer or pastoral tribes; whatever might have passed from remote social backgrounds, possibly akin to these, down to the Mediterranean city-states would necessarily have assumed a different weight and meaning in them – still more so, if there were such continuity, in the societies of late mediaeval or early modern Europe. Ginzburg insists on the parallels between shamanism and ecstatic trances of the kind he found among the *Benandanti*. Yet all of these were clandestine, whereas – in Eliade's words – 'every genuinely shamanistic séance ends as a *spectacle* unequalled in the world of daily experience':[42] a fundamental difference. Ginzburg finesses it with a structuralist flourish – a homology nevertheless holds by inversion: if shamans were public, their dreams were individual battles for the good, where the oneiric combat of the *Benandanti* was collective, even if its performance was private.[43]

Whatever the merits of this argument, the salient point it avoids is that the historical function of ecstatic experience had changed completely in the interim – from socially enacted drama to furtively secreted reverie; so too would have its subjective meaning. Likewise, the paraphernalia of broomsticks and toads resemble dim vestiges of a half or wholly mislaid past more than living emblems of the 'primary

---

41. SN, p. 207.
42. *Shamanism*, p. 54.
43. SN, p. 150.

nucleus' of the Sabbath. In social life, what is older and in that sense deeper is often more trivial – which has survived just because it has been reduced to insignificance. In a famous retort to Lévi-Strauss, Jack Goody once remarked that the persistence of certain dishes might be explained not by their symbolic meaning, but their indifference to it, as simple pegs of existential continuity.[44] The same could, of course, be said of many features of dress. This is the general phenomenon of buttons on the cuff. Words and myths, unlike objects of material use, are inescapable signifiers. But they too are always liable to *de-significa-tion*, the process Ginzburg's morphology consistently forgets. The only difference is that in their case it typically involves the cancellation of one meaning by the superimposition of another, which can easily contradict the first. To seek to determine the essential meaning of a classical legend or a mediaeval phobia by appeal to a shamanistic origin is not unlike the attempt to demonstrate the contemporary significance of a philosophical concept by recourse to the etymology of its pre-Socratic roots, a procedure favoured by Heidegger. But just as the words of a language can survive and evolve through the obliteration or reversal of their earlier meanings, so may the elements of myth: in neither does what come first have any semantic privilege. The temptation, however, to equate persistence with significance has its own promptings. Appropriately, Wittgenstein's commentary on Frazer gives revealing expression to one of them. Lamenting the 'narrowness of spiritual life we find in Frazer', Wittgenstein deplored his rationalist analysis of magical cult or ritual, whose mystery was better left to reverent contemplation: 'even the idea of trying to explain the practice seems to me wrong-headed' – 'we can only *describe* and say, human life is like that'.[45] Above all he rejected the idea that there had been any basic change, let alone for the better, in human sensibility with the development from magic through religion to science, as Frazer assumed. The simplicity of Wittgenstein's argument is unmatched: 'I wish to say: nothing shows our kinship to those savages better than the fact that Frazer has at hand a word as familiar to us as "ghost" or "shade" to describe their views' – 'a whole mythology is deposited in our language.'[46] Here the ideological drift of the fallacy of continuity is ingenuously clear.

Ginzburg tells us that his first and most enduring ambition was to

---

44. *Cooking, Cuisine and Class*, Cambridge 1982, p. 152.
45. *Remarks on the 'Golden Bough'*, pp. 5, 1, 3.
46. Ibid., p. 10.

supersede the alternatives of rationalism and irrationalism.[47] Similar hopes are often expressed of the opposition between materialism and idealism, or Left and Right. It is rarely difficult to see which term of the two pays the cost of the operation. Ginzburg ends his introduction to *Storia Notturna* with the claim that: 'the immensely ancient myths which flowed, for what was after all a short time (three centuries) into the composite stereotype of the Sabbath, survived its disappearance. They are still active. The inaccessible experience which humanity has for millennia symbolically expressed in myths, fables, rites, ecstasies, remains one of the hidden centres of our culture, of our mode of being in the world. The attempt to know the past is also a voyage to the world of the dead.'[48] This declaration of faith in the perennity of the nocturnal region of twisted gait and swaying trance is, of its nature, unadorned with evidence. It is doubtful whether Ginzburg would welcome occult magazines and palmistry stores as witnesses. He prefers instead the self-enclosing gesture with which Lévi-Strauss designates his own analysis of myth as itself another, thought by the common substance of the human mind.[49] So the sign of the hidden centre becomes the enterprise of the historian himself – in this place of concealment, mage and scholar are one. There is no need to dwell on the weakness of the conceit in either case. It functions less as argument than as index of an outlook. In Ginzburg's case, as we have seen, what defines that outlook is the call of the deep.

Paradoxically, however, the very consistency with which he has pursued underground cultural continuities provides its own antidote to them. The *Benandanti*, peasants practising somnambulist magic to better the harvest or propitiate the dead, were bearers of a 'genuinely popular stratum of beliefs', 'with roots stretching far back into time', to an 'antiquity when they must once have covered much of central Europe'.[50] The *Nicodemiti*, intellectuals justifying religious dissimulation in the name of Christian detachment from outward rites, in a time of confessional wars, betokened a 'deeper and more homogeneous stratum' of faith, beneath 'the conflicts agitating the surface of European religious life in the sixteenth century'.[51] The miller Menocchio, village philosopher expounding a materialist cosmogony without magic or Christianity, expressed views and aspirations whose 'roots

47. *Miti Emblemi Spie*, pp. ix, 158; MEC, pp. vii, 96.
48. SN, p. xxxviii.
49. 'Thus this book on myths is itself, in its fashion, a myth' – *Le Cru et le Cuit*, Paris 1984, p. 14.
50. *I Benandanti*, pp. xii, xv, 47; NW, pp. xviii, xx, 39.
51. *Il Nicodemismo*, p. xv;

were sunk in an obscure, all but unfathomable stratum of remote peasant traditions'.[52] Diana, Cinderella, Cordelia, heroines of myth, fable, drama alike, spring from a 'subterranean stratum of unitary Eurasian mythology', a 'stupefying dissemination of shamanistic traits', in which are deposited 'a history of thousands of years'.[53] Behind Freud diagnosing a disorder or Berenson telegraphing an attribution, can be glimpsed 'perhaps the oldest gesture in the intellectual history of humanity: the hunter crouched in the mud peering at the tracks of his prey'.[54] The vocabulary of depth and diuturnity is unvarying: but its objects are so various that they cancel each other. How probable is it that *both* ecstatic voyages to the beyond, *and* robust materialist denials of the divine, were ancient peasant traditions in the same Friulian hills – existing beneath the surface of a European Christianity, whose own divisions were *also* traversed by a clandestine movement profounder than Catholic or Calvinist confessions? Each of these research programmes has yielded fascinating empirical fruits. But it is a metaphysical predisposition that projects their results repeatedly downwards or backwards. The decipherment of the Sabbath suffers from it. Ironically, perhaps the most unanswerable objection to the thesis that its 'primary nucleus' derived from popular ecstatic myths is supplied by Ginzburg's work itself. For the only investigated case of such cultic trances, the *Benandanti*, was actually treated with offhand indifference by the Inquisition. So little alarmed were the witchfinders by the quaint beliefs of the night-walkers that not a single prosecution was ever concluded against them. It is difficult to avoid the conclusion that the crux of the phantasm lay elsewhere.

Ginzburg once wisely remarked that an ideological option may both vitiate the documentary findings of an author, and yet also be the condition of them. He was speaking of Georges Dumézil, one of the great pioneers of comparative mythology, in whom he detected possible pre-war sympathies with Nazism.[55] Mircea Eliade's *Myth of the Eternal Return*, another landmark in the field, was born of the defeat of the Iron Guard in Romania, he observes elsewhere.[56] What of Ginzburg's own options? Reflecting on its pathos of human nature, the distinguished Italian critic Franco Fortini has termed *Storia Notturna*

---

52. *Il Formaggio e i Vermi*, p. xxii; CW, p. xxiii.
53. SN, pp. 240–41.
54. *Miti Emblemi Spie*, p. 169; MEC, p. 105.
55. *Miti Emblemi Spie*, p. 233; MEC, p. 145.
56. 'The pathos of defeat inspired Eliade, who had a fascist and anti-semitic past behind him, to his theorization of the flight from history': SN, p. 183.

the work of a liberal conservative.[57] This is certainly unjust. Ginzburg's original inspiration, from which he has never departed, lay rather in a kind of populism, as he himself has noted.[58] But it is true that populism lends itself to a number of timbres, according to its perception of the people. Ginzburg's early work reflected the insurgency of the late sixties, whose mass character was more pronounced in Italy than in any other European society. It spoke of class culture and repressive tolerance, peasant war and social utopia. With the subsidence of the eighties, the tone has changed. Ginzburg now declares: 'Growing doubts about the efficacy and outcome of revolutionary and technocratic projects oblige us to rethink the way in which political action is inserted into deep social structures, and its real ability to alter them.'[59] *Storia Notturna* is still dedicated, in the spirit of Walter Benjamin, to the history of the vanquished. But now the accent is on the simple perdurance of popular beliefs, across any number of social structures and through every kind of historical and civilizational change, because of their anchorage in the operations of the human mind. In the process, an immense cultural halo is swung round the gyrations of the shaman, in which we read imprinted as in a *trecento* image the glowing letters of Greek Legend and Universal Fiction. Thus are the folk shards of witching hour and animal familiar – Trevor-Roper's 'mental rubbish of peasant credulity'[60] – redeemed, as they enter into and yet pass beyond the Sabbath.

The earlier Ginzburg warned against just such idealization. Commenting on a contemporary Italian cult near Salerno, in which a local woman periodically assumed the personality of a dead nephew, he did not evoke the grand continuity of Eurasian ecstatic traditions, but wrote: 'In wretched and disintegrated conditions, religion helps men and women to bear a little better a life in itself intolerable. It may not be much, but we have no right to despise it. But precisely because they protect believers from reality rather than prompting or helping them to become aware of, and change it, such popular cults are in the end a

57. 'Il Corpo e la Storia', *L'Indice*, No. 10, December 1989, p. 10.

58. *Miti Emblemi Spie*, p. x; MEC, pp. vii–viii.

59. SN, p. xxvi.

60. 'The European Witchcraze of the Sixteenth and Sevententh Centuries', *Religion, the Reformation and Social Change*, London 1972, p. 116. It is appropriate that Trevor-Roper should have used a memorably different imagery of depth in his concluding lines on the myth of the Sabbath: 'It remained at the bottom of society, like a stagnant pool, easily flooded, easily stirred . . . To destroy the myth, to drain away the pool . . . the whole intellectual and social structure which contained it, and had solidified round it, had to be broken. It had to be broken not at the bottom, in the dirty sump where the witch-beliefs had collected, but at its centre, whence they were refreshed' (p. 192).

mystification: to overvalue them in populist fashion is absurd and dangerous.'[61] It would be good to hear that voice once again. For one, needed word has disappeared from the vocabulary of *Storia Notturna*: superstition. It is salutary to recall that a Hungarian scholar, describing the poor, sparse societies in which it once dominated, could speak of 'the misery of shamanism'.[62] That judgement is too strong for what was once a coherent set of beliefs, giving moral shape to a world. But superstitions are the scrambled relics of belief, no longer comprehended: their role in the history of the Sabbath surely merits it. The perspective of – should we, in tune with the times, call it? – postrationalism forbids the thought. Yet what is true of Dumézil and Eliade holds here too. The ideological option may affect the empirical materials, but without it they would not in all probability have come to light. *Storia Notturna* may overshoot its resources. But these are more than rich enough to justify the enterprise. Readers of virtually any persuasion will find Ginzburg's latest history a gamble to admire, a pleasure to read, a provocation to think.

1990

---

61. 'Folklore, Magia, Religione', *Storia d'Italia*, Vol. I, Turin 1972, p. 675.
62. A. Voigt, 'Shamanism in North Asia as a Scope of Ethnology', in *Shamanism in Siberia*, pp. 65–66.

The Pluralism of Isaiah Berlin

Intellectual hero to Noel Annan, whose political heroine is Margaret Thatcher, should Isaiah Berlin be left to the – 'unfashionable' – enthusiasms of *Our Age*? Or consigned to the dutiful plaudits that have broken out for his latest volume from the *Spectator* to the *New Statesman*? He himself strikes a more modest note. 'I talk about other people. I examine their views. But what about me?' he said recently, disclaiming any large notions of his own. His opinions, he told Richard Ingrams, were just local currency. 'My ideas are very English. I've thrown in my lot with England. It's the best country in the world.'[1] Such loyal self-deprecation is scarcely less suspect. An accurate view of Berlin should start elsewhere.

The Crooked Timber of Humanity is more an elegant restatement than a substantial addition to his characteristic themes. Three quarters of the book consist of essays from the same fund of texts out of which the four volumes of his *Selected Writings* were assembled at the end of the seventies, and their topics for the most part retrace familiar ground – Machiavelli, Vico, Herder; Pluralism, Romanticism, Utopianism. Even the longest piece, on Joseph de Maistre, is an enlargement of a portrait already sketched in an earlier comparison with Tolstoy. In a sense, however, this is the interest of the collection: it serves to bring the unity of Berlin's thought sharply into focus.

A philosopher by training, Berlin's main work has lain in the history of ideas – a field which, he maintains, has traditionally been neglected in England. Between the time of Leslie Stephen and, say, Quentin Skinner, that was certainly true. Even today, this branch of studies has far less elbow-room in English than American universities. But since the seventies the situation has been changing, and the rise of a new kind

---

1. *Observer*, 14 October 1990.

of intellectual history, originated at Cambridge, provides the appropriate background for assessing Berlin's contribution to the field. No other living practitioner has his European zest and range, encompassing Russian and German, Italian and French, not to speak of Ancient literatures, or his capacity to throw out bold generalizations across them. There are two poles to this imagination. On the one hand, Berlin is fascinated by individual – often idiosyncratic – personalities, men like Belinsky or Hess, whom he has depicted in a series of inimitable cameos. On the other hand, he constructs and pursues very general notions, broad *idées maîtresses* like monism or positive freedom, through swooping pedigrees down time. Perhaps these were the natural units of attention for an analytic philosopher of strong humanistic bent. The contrast, at any rate, with the practice of current historians is marked. Pocock, Skinner or Ashcraft, in treating the ideas of Harrington, Hobbes or Locke, have concentrated on detailed textual analysis of a corpus of work, and its setting in (especially) the discourses and (optimally) the practices of the age, overturning many received interpretations in the process. Berlin has rarely given his thinkers the same kind of systematic scrutiny or contextual depth.

This is not the result of oversight. Rather it is because, as he has often remarked, he believes the specific arguments of a theorist less important than their general outlook, and the origins of ideas less interesting than their echoes.[2] As much as statement of a method, this is the expression of a temperament. Its fruit is an approach best suited to unsystematic, intuitive thinkers who do not require, perhaps resist, close conceptual reconstruction. Berlin's most memorable essays deal with writers like Sorel or Tolstoy, rather than with the major political philosophers of the modern period. The sympathy for the informal and undoctrinal they reveal is one of the attractive features of his work. But it has its costs. Where there are elements in a particular corpus of ideas which for one reason or another are uncongenial to Berlin, his characteristic procedure can free him from the need to accord them proportionate attention. The risks of selective emphasis exist in even the most systematic of treatments, as the controversies in recent Harrington or Locke scholarship demonstrate. But they are greatly enhanced, once specific arguments are discounted for general outlooks, documented origins for presumed effects. Berlin's accounts of – for example – Tolstoy's view of history, or Herzen's brand of politics, or

---

2. *Against the Current*, London 1979, p. 298; *Vico and Herder*, London 1976, pp. xiv–xvi, xx.

Mill's conception of value, understate central aspects of each: the simple chauvinism of *War and Peace* or mysticism in *Anna Karenina*, the agrarian socialism of *The Bell*, the declared utilitarianism of *On Liberty*. The result is to make each sound subtly closer to their commentator than they are. His readings of Vico and Herder, the major subjects of his later work, show the same proprietary impulse. Seeing them essentially as precursors of cultural pluralism, the tradition in which he situates himself, Berlin is disinclined to pay much attention to the themes of mental identity and emergent universality in their respective writings, which point in another direction. Machiavelli plays a rather similar role in Berlin's vision, becoming the stepping-stone to a tolerant liberalism.[3] In this interpretation, the scandal his work provoked lay not in Machiavelli's counsels of princely crime, but in his equable observation of contrasting civic and Christian virtues. The only evidence for this claim, abundantly disproved by centuries of polemic, is the autobiographical illumination Berlin reports in these pages – the intellectual discovery he himself made on reading Machiavelli.[4] In such annexations, philosophical advocacy visibly takes precedence over historical balance. Detached from their context, ideas are gracefully *umfunktioniert* for present purposes.

The title of this volume provides a graphic illustration of the point. 'Out of the crooked timber of humanity no straight thing was ever made': Immanuel Kant *dixit*. By dint of repetition – it is cited once in *Russian Thinkers*, twice in *Against the Current*, three times in *Four Essays on Liberty*, and twice more in *The Crooked Timber* itself – Berlin has virtually made of this a saw.[5] Here, we are given to understand, is a signal expression of that rejection of all perfectionist utopias which defines a humane pluralism. But what was the actual force of the text from which the sentence is taken? The *Idea for a Universal History in a Cosmopolitan Perspective* is a terse, incandescent manifesto for a world order still to be constructed, and a world history yet to be written. If there is a single prophetic vision of the political agenda now apparently unfolding before us two centuries later, it is this. Fukuyama might have done better to appeal to Kant rather than Hegel. The message of the *Idea* is not the diversity of values, the imperfectibility of institutions, or the contingency of history. What

---

3. *Against the Current*, p. 79.
4. *The Crooked Timber of Humanity*, London 1990, pp. 7–8.
5. *Russian Thinkers*, London 1978, p. 202; *Against the Current*, pp. 148, 353; *Four Essays on Liberty*, Oxford 1969, pp. 39, 170, 193; *The Crooked Timber of Humanity*, pp. 19, 48. The phrase duly reappears in *Our Age*, London 1990, p. 279.

Kant celebrates is the driving force of competition – the mutual 'antagonism' implanted in the human species by nature, as the motor of social progress. It is the dynamic of the rivalry for honour, riches and power that has generated every step of civilization. Social advance has at length reached the point where the task for humanity can be the realization of a civil society under the rule of law, guaranteeing freedom for all. But this can only be complete when external relations between states obey the same principles of peaceful union as the internal relations between their members. Humanity will have to endure many devastations and upheavals before such a league of peoples comes to pass. But the natural laws which govern the development of our species, engendering a productive common order out of colliding individual wills in the form of a competitive economy, which strengthens the state, should in the end also lead to a world society out of the conflicting states, in which the full potential of the human race would come to fruition. Then, in the fullness of time, nature will bring forth the Kepler or Newton capable of explaining the scientific mechanisms of this universal history.

Meanwhile, the greatest difficulty in achieving civic union within a state derives from the fact that 'man is an animal that needs a master', to 'break his own will and oblige him to obey a generally valid will whereby each may be free'[6] – but can only find such a master among other men, who are also animals that need to be mastered in their turn. It is this problem, of the unruliness of the ruler, that occasions the comment Berlin has taken for his motto. Kant, however, is referring not to humanity as a whole, as unfittable into any symmetrical scheme, but to the fallibility of any *individual* as sovereign. *Das höchste Oberhaupt soll aber gerecht für sich selbst und doch ein Mensch sein* – 'The highest magistrate should be just in himself and yet be a man.'[7] It is *this* task, as Kant puts it, that is beyond fulfilment. He makes the distinction immediately clear, in a way that brings home sharply the distance between Kant's argument and Berlin's inference. The inhabitants of other planets may be able to perfect themselves in their individual lives. But 'with us it is otherwise; only the species can hope for this' – 'but if we accomplish nature's mission well, we can certainly flatter ourselves that we may occupy no mean rank among our neighbours in the cosmic order.'[8] In other words, the collective destiny of humanity, working

6. Immanuel Kant, 'Idee zu einer allgemeinen Geschichte in weltbürgerlicher Absicht', *Werke*, Vol. IV (ed. Cassirer), Berlin 1922, p. 157.

7. Ibid., p. 158.

8. Ibid., p. 158.

through the deficiencies of its individual members, reveals what Kant calls 'the hidden plan of nature to bring into existence an internally and externally perfected political constitution'. The naturalism and final-ism of this vision are at the antipodes of Berlin's outlook. So far from Kant insisting on the irremediable crookedness of humanity in general, he uses the self-same term – *krumm* – to describe the kind of timber humanity need *not* become in a well-ordered civic union, where something straight – *gerade* – is just what can indeed be made. 'Only in such an enclosure as civil unification offers can our inclinations achieve their best effects; as trees in a wood which seek to deprive each other of air and sunlight are forced to strive upwards and so achieve a beautiful straight growth [*einen schönen geraden Wuchs*]; while those that spread their branches at will in isolated freedom grow stunted, tilted and crooked [*krüppelig, schief und krumm*].'[9] The imagery of the bent and the straight, in other words, tells the opposite story from its proverbialization.

However frequently invoked, only a catchword is at stake here. But it pinpoints a procedure whose dangers become more acute in the vast genealogies of leading ideas that make up the other side of Berlin's *oeuvre*. The famous contrast between positive and negative freedom in *Four Essays on Liberty* derives, of course, above all from Benjamin Constant's lecture under the Restoration comparing Ancient and Modern Liberty. But where Constant sought to ground the difference between the two in a comparative sociology of the classical and contemporary worlds, Berlin treats them largely as normative concep-tions floating free from determinate social contexts. Constant's portrait of Greek democracy as a society of martial conformists, contrasting with the peaceful and commercial individualists of modern liberty, is one-sided and polemical: ignoring the extent to which *isonomia* included ideals of diversity within the community – 'liberty in', rather than either 'from' or 'to', in Pocock's phrase. But it is more worked through than Berlin's chain of associations, which link the most disparate figures – Locke momentarily cheek-by-jowl with Fichte, Burke arm-in-arm with Robespierre – into rapidly constructed align-ments for the purposes of contrasting his two concepts, in which paradoxically even Constant himself, who in his fashion hoped to combine them, is scarcely done justice. The textual basis of the enterprise is very scanty – citations of a sentence or two from most of the roll-call; elsewhere stylized utterances in an anonymous first per-

---

9. Ibid., p. 157.

son, as if attributed to a timeless tradition, illustrate the argument.[10] The risks of mistreating individual thinkers with this method are obvious, even if substantiation of each case might in principle still be possible in some larger compass. But it is the general upshot of the procedure that is often most disconcerting. In Berlin's conjuring of ideas, they appear at times to lose any specific gravity as they hurtle towards the most unexpected and perverse destinations, or shuttle back again with scarcely less ease. Kant's 'severe individualism' issues into virtually 'pure totalitarian doctrine', and the combined efforts of – at one time or another – Locke, Spinoza, Montesquieu, Rousseau, Fichte, Hegel, Comte, Marx, Green, Bradley and Bosanquet pave the way for the 'great, disciplined, authoritarian structures' in which positive freedom eventually came to be pursued.[11] The evidence for these connexions is essentially circular: modern despotism proves the dangers of the ideal of positive liberty, so that ideal must have contributed to the rise of despotism.

However captious this claim may be in the case of particular thinkers – or exaggerated in the general importance it confers on philosophy in history – it is straightforward. The trajectory it postulates has one direction, pointing downwards. In *The Crooked Timber of Humanity* still larger claims of historical consequence are tacitly entered for the ideals of romanticism, which is credited with 'breaking the foundation-stone' of millennial belief in one objective truth by which men should live, and thereby 'creating the modern outlook'[12] – that is, the acceptance of a pluralism of values. For Berlin this represents the crucial emancipation from the past, permitting the ultimate advent of a liberal society. But although this romanticism born in Germany liberated Europe by proclaiming the free creation of values, its cult of subjective will later fostered autocrats bent on suppressing liberty, when its aesthetic ideals were transferred to politics under Napoleon, reinterpreted by Hegel and Marx, and eventually instigated the furies of fascism and communism. But the unconquerable spirit of resistance to totalitarianism has also been inspired by 'this same untamed German spirit', the 'conception of man inherited from the romantic movement'.[13] The power of ideas as prime causes of political change is a not uncommon belief; what is striking here, however, is their alarming volatility – the same doctrines exercising diametrically oppo-

---

10. For example, *Four Essays on Liberty*, pp. 135–36, 141, 143–44.
11. *Four Essays on Liberty*, pp. 152, 171.
12. *The Crooked Timber of Humanity*, p. 182.
13. Ibid., p. 199.

site effects in sequence, or even concurrently. On occasion, Berlin speaks of the kind of connexions he draws between concepts and consequences as not logical, but historical and psychological.[14] The evidence for these, however, whose demonstrations would be a major agenda, is missing. In their absence, any number of speculative moves become possible. In an earlier text, the sources of totalitarianism are found not in the ideals of positive liberty or the values of romanticism, but in the arrival of sociologies of knowledge, undercutting faith in the possibility of rational argument.[15] The compatibility of the different culprits is not pursued.

Talking about the ideas of other people, then, Berlin can be a wayward *raconteur*. What of his own – are they really English commonplaces? There is a clear sense in which the avowal of adoptive identity is relevant and valid. Politically, Berlin has in many ways been a liberal of a specifically English stamp – socially humane, empirical, sceptical. If we compare him with the two other great liberal thinkers of émigré background who left their mark on this country in the period of the Cold War, Hayek and Popper, these traits stand out. The Austrian duo have their own important differences, as Ralf Dahrendorf has recently suggested.[16] But the common features are plain. The specialized work of each, in the fields of economics and philosophy of science, has been radically original and systematic in a way Berlin's contribution to the history of ideas is not. Their ideological record, on the other hand, has been marked by a stridency and imbalance foreign to Berlin. Unlike Hayek, he never saw Attlee as involuntary cousin to Goering; or felt, like Popper, soiled at the mental touch of Hegel.[17] Mill, object of lurking suspicion or overt rebuke for them, receives his unqualified admiration. Equality was an ideal for him, as well as liberty, which might on occasion take precedence over it, as Popper denied it might[18] – for example, by the abolition of private education, anathema to Hayek. Berlin's oblique description of himself as a man of the moderate Left[19] is ratified by the sniping he has drawn from the radical Right. No doubt deeper personal immersion in English culture – arrival here

---

14. *Four Concepts of Liberty*, p. 152.
15. 'Political Ideas in the Twentieth Century', in *Four Essays on Liberty*, pp. 18–27.
16. *Reflections on the Revolution in Europe*, London 1990, pp. 25ff.
17. See *The Road to Serfdom*, London 1986, pp. 86–88, 148–49; *The Open Society and its Enemies*, Vol. II, London 1952, p. 79.
18. *Unended Quest*, London 1980, p. 36.
19. See *Russian Thinkers*, pp. 297, 301.

as a child, rather than as an adult – explains some of this distance from his Viennese counterparts.

But differing backgrounds in East and Central Europe must also have had much to do with it. The Habsburg Empire, autocratic though it in many ways remained to the end, was not a repressive despotism: legal procedures, civic liberties, freedom of the press and political organization, if not effective assemblies or responsible government, existed. After the Metternich epoch, opposition was rarely driven to revolutionary responses. On the other hand, politics in the later Empire were always more national or social than constitutional; and when it fell, the Austrian Republic divided between the Catholic and socialist traditions that dominate the country to the present. Paradoxically, the society which has produced the most powerful school of modern theoretical liberalism has less tradition of liberal politics than virtually any other democracy in Europe. Even today, the principal alternative to the Grand Coalition in Vienna is a party rooted in Germanic nationalism (some would argue: national-socialism), rather than liberalism. Behind Popper or Hayek is an original background gone dully, or eerily, blank. The formulaic, doctrinaire tendencies in their work probably come in part from this uprooting.

The Tsarist Empire, by contrast, remained an unregenerate absolutism throughout the nineteenth century, a police regime that suffocated any space for legal opposition. It thereby engendered a revolutionary tradition like none other in the continent: one that extended from its original centre in the intelligentsia to the working class and the peasantry, and – what is often forgotten – in the end even affected significant sections of the liberal bourgeoisie. After two great upheavals against the *ancien régime,* bureaucratic dictatorship followed in the twentieth century, plunging the best of the Russian intelligentsia, after the briefest of intervals, back into persecution and moral opposition. The continuity of this background sets off Berlin's liberalism from the Viennese variants. Democracy installed, Hayek could brood on its dangers. Corporatism, eroding the freedom of the market, and flourishing (so it happened) as nowhere else in post-war Austria, became the main enemy. Tyranny renewed, Berlin's concern was for political and intellectual liberties, in the setting of a tradition where their greatest historical champion had been a revolutionary socialist. *Russian Thinkers*, whose central hero is Herzen, gives touching testimony on every page of this engagement with his culture of origin. The warmth of Berlin's accounts of the Russian radicals of the last century, recreating the historical context of their lives in Moscow or St Petersburg in a way unique in his work, the delicacy and wit of his portrait of their troubled observer Turgenev, the controlled intensity of his memories of Pasternak and Akhmatova, make this body of writing his *Hauptwerk*. It is good to think of its appearance in Russia today.

There was a second allegiance that distinguished Berlin as well. From boyhood onwards, he was committed to the creation of a Jewish homeland in Palestine. Many of the intellectuals from Eastern or Central Europe who had such an impact on English culture in this century were of Jewish origin, but few assumed it as a primary identity. (Wittgenstein was an extreme example of dissociation, to a point of anti-semitic aberration.) Convinced and articulate Zionism was still rarer. Berlin and Namier were the two great exceptions. A generation older, Namier was the more active; but Berlin has been no less eloquent. Reviewing his current collection, John Dunn has wondered whether Berlin was not always in some ways a deeply unpolitical person, only driven into politics by the threats of Nazism and Communism.[20] The suggestion cannot survive a reading of his essay on Weizmann and the foundation of Israel, the most powerful and personal of all his *éloges*; or his reflections on Einstein in Jerusalem. The World Zionist Congress was certainly an earlier and probably a greater value for him than the Congress for Cultural Freedom. Berlin's attachment to Zionism is not a separate compartment, without connexion to the rest of his thought or sensibility; it is central to an understanding of his outlook. In an obvious way, it crossed over into his Russian world, where it formed what he tactfully records as his one point of tension with Pasternak.[21] For in Berlin's view, it was only from the Russian Empire that the historical chance of Israel sprang. 'The more rational, but more exhausted – the thinner-blooded – Jews of the west' (included here are German and Danubian lands) were 'not the stuff from which a new society could be moulded overnight. If the Jews of Russia had not existed, neither the case for, nor the possibility of realising, Zionism could have arisen in any serious form.'[22] There is some shorthand here – there were Jews in Galicia and the Bukovina, outside Tsarist frontiers, who played a part too: Namier was one of them. But in a curious way, the loyalties of Berlin and Namier reflect the reality of the regional distinction he was making: of the major Jewish émigrés in English intellectual life, they were the two who did not come from Central Europe, however broadly defined. But whereas Namier, who came from Podolia, put a detested Germanic world and all its works behind

20. *Times Literary Supplement*, 5–11 October 1990.
21. *Personal Impressions*, London 1981, pp. 179–180.
22. *Personal Impressions*, p. 40.

him, the Russian and the Jewish sides of Berlin's imagination, responding to historically nested situations of oppression, have gone naturally
together.

The specific character of Berlin's philosophy has emerged out of
these conditions. It is less reassuringly English than it appears. At first
sight, it looks like a classical liberalism centred around the defence of
individual freedoms – the negative liberty of non-interference from the
state. This was certainly the polemical force of his oration of 1958. But
it is noticeable how ready Berlin was to correct over-interpretations of
it. In an altered climate of 1969, he found no difficulty in conceding
that positive freedom was, after all, a 'valid universal goal', and that the
ideal of negative freedom too could foster 'great and lasting social
evils', among them 'the blood-stained story of economic individualism
and unrestrained capitalist competition'. Simply, the dangers from
ideological misuse of the former were now much greater than of the
latter – 'liberal ultra-individualism could scarcely be said to be a rising
force at present.'[23] The *mise au point*, which underlines his distance
from the vision of a beneficent catallaxy that soon became a rising
force, involved no lessening of his personal preference. Negative freedom remained the superior value for Berlin. Significantly, however, it
has never become the focus of a constitutionalist philosophy. Berlin is
quite unlike Constant in this regard. He has not shown much interest in
the juridical framework for the safeguarding of negative liberty, the
classical object of much liberal thinking – rather a certain indifference
towards the machineries of law and government. In Great Britain, he
remarks, 'legal power is, of course, constitutionally vested in the
absolute sovereign – the King in Parliament. What makes this country
comparatively free, therefore, is the fact that this theoretically omnipo-
tent entity is restrained by custom or opinion from behaving as such. It
is clear that what matters is not the form of these restraints on power –
whether legal, or moral, or constitutional – but their effectiveness.'[24]
Such pragmatic insouciance is the specifically English element in Berlin's liberalism. But by the same token, it indicates why this is in a sense
a secondary feature of it. The patriotic conviction that Britain is 'the
best country in the world' is also a kind of exoneration. If our island
story is so satisfactory, what more is there theoretically to add? So
indeed, Berlin has not had all that much to say about the politics or
thought of his adopted country. A tribute to Churchill and a lecture on

---

23. *Four Concepts of Liberty*, pp. xlv–xlvii.
24. Ibid., p. 166.

Mill – each impressive in its own way – are virtually the sum of it. Relieved of major duties at home, his imagination has essentially been drawn elsewhere.

The theme which Berlin has really made his own is, famously, pluralism. The term, of course, has more than one meaning in current usage. 'How the imagination droops at the mention of that dingy word!' exclaimed his admirer Annan, agitated by the disagreeable clamour of pressure-groups in the Winter of Discontent.[25] Berlin's conception, concerned with values rather than interests, owes nothing to American political science. Its thesis is that Western thought from Antiquity to the Enlightenment was historically dominated by the belief that a single ideal way of living existed, in which all ultimate ends achieved harmony – an assumption still informing every kind of utopian or totalitarian thought. Pluralism is the break with this superstition: the acknowledgement that human values are inherently multiple and conflictual, rendering any attempt to model society on one goal alone, capable of synthesizing them, a path to despotism. The presence of this case is all-pervasive in Berlin's work. The contrast between positive and negative freedom is in the end resolved into the opposition of monism and pluralism, in which 'Two Concepts of Liberty' culminates. The plea for moral judgement in 'Historical Inevitability' insists on the need for awareness of pluralism. The gallery of historical portraits is selected and arranged for the contributions of its subjects to the advent of pluralism. The importance of Machiavelli, Montesquieu, Vico, Herder, Herzen – every one of Berlin's favoured theorists: even such a disfavoured figure as Maistre – lies primarily in their rejection, to one extent or another, of the assumptions of monism. With unstaunched eloquence, *The Crooked Timber of Humanity* once again addresses the theme. In a celebrated judgement Berlin described Tolstoy as a fox, which knows many things, who took himself for a hedgehog, knowing only one big thing. The reverse might ironically be said of Berlin. Behind the guise of the fox, the darting variety of his gifts and interests, lies the gaze of a hedgehog, staring forever at a single all-absorbing verity.

What is the nature of this truth? Berlin's accounts of pluralism characteristically involve a stark before and after. Up to a given historical moment – whose precise location can vary, but roughly falls between Machiavelli and Fichte – monism prevailed: the existence of a single normative standard was affirmed by all traditions, however

---

25. 'Introduction', *Personal Impressions*, p. xv.

much they disagreed over what it was. Beyond this time, understanding of the diversity of legitimate values gradually dawned. However often this contrast is repeated, there remains something puzzling about it. Can ancient, or mediaeval, or early modern society really have been so ideologically monolithic that the possibility of alternative conceptions of a good life was never seriously entertained? At the very outset of his story, Berlin seems to have mislaid Mount Olympus. What was classical polytheism but the personification of many and contrary values? Below, among the mortals, a well-known eulogy congratulated the city on its tolerance of different individual choices of life. Constant himself noted that Antiquity allowed for more than one ideal – the practice of philosophy demanded virtues other than those of war, of equal dignity to them.[26] He could, of course, have added poetry. What else is the pastoral tradition founded on, but the consciousness of such discrepancies – *neglegens ne qua populus laboret*? Mediaeval society confessed a range of values too – according to the most established doctrine, fighting, praying and working were separate vocations, each blessed in the eyes of God. Chaucer hardly conveys the sense of a single type of human value. As for the Renaissance – Montaigne, Shakespeare . . .

There is no mystery about all this. What Berlin has overlooked is the simple sociological fact that any society with a moderate division of labour is virtually bound to develop discourses justifying different roles within it. Out of them, literary or moral conceptions of the world, of greater or less sophistication, will emerge – normally, however, continuous with the common wisdom of the society. Popular lore has long incorporated the insights of pluralism, to the point of sententious parody. It was Le Bas who instructed Nicholas Jenkins in the adage 'It takes all sorts to make a world', about the time Berlin was going up to Oxford. A few years later, a wide-eyed Wittgenstein found it 'a very beautiful saying'. Unlike him, the author of *Personal Impressions* and *Against the Current* has made an imaginative reality of it. Berlin's sympathy for the most dissimilar figures, going well beyond the conventional English liking for the mildly unconventional, has a Russian largeness, capable of responding equally to the most powerful and the least assuming, Roosevelt or Moses Hess. But this personal gift

---

26. *Les 'Principes de Politique' de Benjamin Constant*, ed. Etienne Hofmann, Geneva 1980, pp. 432–33. After making an exception for Ancient philosophy, Constant characteristically went on to say that: 'The independence of the philosophers in no way resembled the personal freedom we think desirable. Their independence consisted in renouncing all the joys and affections of life; ours we value for securing and allowing them.'

leaves the intellectual problem intact. Can such a familiar evidence as the variety of commendable lives explain the construction of an entire philosophy of civil existence – is this the sufficient motivation of the doctrine of pluralism?

Plainly not. In principle, individual lives might embody widely differing values, yet each contribute to an overall social harmony. That, after all, is the claim of the traditional adage: the world is a mosaic of complementary temperaments. This is just the kind of conclusion Berlin's philosophy sets out to deny. Although it appeals to our intuitive sense of the rewards of human difference for much of its persuasive force, it is actually not a theory of individual identity at all, but of social choice. Valid human goals are indeed diverse, but they do not admit of collective composition. Berlin again and again emphasizes that the ends of life are often irreconcilable and indeed incommensurable.[27] No arrangement of society can ever satisfy all of them. The kick in his pluralism comes from this equation. What is different is conflictual, and what is conflictual is unrelatable. Logically, as we have seen, there is no reason why the identification of the first two – diversity with incompatibility of values – should not hold of individual existences, but be tractable in social structures. Berlin never directly addresses this possibility, no doubt assuming it to be empirically implausible. But it is the elision of the second two – the incompatible with the incommensurable – that is the weakest link in his position. His own writings make it clear that Berlin cannot sustain it. The one political experience of reform of which he has written with real admiration – significantly no British episode, but the New Deal in America – he extols precisely for demonstrating the *reconcilability* of apparently opposing public values. 'Roosevelt's greatest service to mankind consists in the fact that he showed that it is possible to be politically effective and yet benevolent and human . . . that the promotion of social justice and individual liberty does not necessarily mean the end of all efficient government; that power and order are not identical with a straightjacket of doctrine, whether economic or political; that it is possible to reconcile individual liberty – a loose texture of society – with the indispensable minimum of organizing and authority; and in this belief lies what Roosevelt's

---

27. *Four Concepts of Liberty*, pp. 168–171. 'We are faced with choices between ends equally ultimate, and claims equally absolute.' Vico and Herder are regularly described, and praised, for holding that cultures are incommensurable: *Against the Current*, p. 12; *Vico and Herder*, p. 188; *The Crooked Timber of Humanity*, p. 76.

greatest predecessor once described as "the last, best hope of earth".'[28]

This is not an isolated outburst of enthusiasm. In this latest volume, he writes that 'claims can be balanced, compromises can be reached . . . priorities, never final and absolute, must be established' – 'we must engage in what are called trade-offs.'[29] In other words, the major goods *are* commensurable after all: how else can claims between them be weighed? Beneath the surface radicalism of Berlin's assertion of irreducibly discrepant norms lies a tacit ecumenicism willing, after all, to compound them. The unspoken value that arbitrates between them is happiness; or rather its shadow, as Berlin speaks more reticently of avoidance of suffering. Utilitarian calculation, disavowed in Mill, discreetly reappears in its negative form as the best broker available. Berlin's pluralism is not ultimately agonistic. The difference is very clear if we compare him with the great theorist of modern polytheism, Max Weber. In Weber, the gods that have risen from their graves in a disenchanted world are truly warring – there is no common standard of value, no conceivable truce, among them, any more than in the world of the great powers. The hope of a eudaimonist mediation between rival deities was the paltriest illusion of all. This Nietzschean note is wholly missing in Berlin. It is no accident that he should scarcely ever have alluded to Weber's work, for all its absolute centrality to his theme. According to Annan, such silence bespeaks a dismissal even he finds ill-judged.[30] It is more likely to have been discomfort.

If pluralism is simple byword between individuals, and sensible compromise in society, what explains the distinctive intensity of Berlin's concern with it – his manifest conviction that at stake here are no anodyne truths but a novel and controversial doctrine? The answer can readily be seen from the focus of his historical work. The pluralism that matters, which differentiates Berlin's thought from other kinds of liberalism, is the one that obtains not within but between societies. What Vico and Herder, the magnet of his philosophical interests, essentially stand for is the exploration of contrasting *cultures*, understood in a holistic sense that Berlin paradoxically commends. The multiplicity of such cultures is the real proving-ground of pluralism: it is here that the notion of incommensurability cuts deep. How is one collective form of life to be historically judged against another? The

---

28. *Personal Impressions*, p. 31; see also *Four Concepts of Liberty*, p. 31: 'this great liberal enterprise, certainly the most constructive compromise between individual liberty and economic security which our own time has witnessed'.

29. *The Crooked Timber of Humanity*, p. 17.

30. *Our Age*, pp. 254–55.

logic of a pluralist anthropology appears to point to a relativist ethics. Neapolitan scholar and Prussian pastor alike, in Berlin's account of them, move towards the frontier of just such a relativism. They do so because, in tendency if not in letter, their thought denies (as does Mill's) the existence of any permanent human nature. Variable cultures so shape the different needs and dispositions of their members that no common moral standard is applicable to the species. But after affirming – even applauding – the intransigence of this rejection of 'the central concept of the western tradition from the Greeks to Aquinas, from the Renaissance to Grotius, Spinoza, Locke',[31] Berlin then typically mitigates or retracts it. If *The Crooked Timber of Humanity* strikes one new note, in fact, it is in the strength of its assurance that Vico and Herder were not after all relativists: 'this *idée reçue* seems to me now to be a widespread error, which, I must admit, I have in the past perpetrated myself.'[32] The reason, Berlin explains, is that however diverse or incompatible cultures may be, 'their variety cannot be unlimited, for the nature of men, however various and subject to change, must possess some generic nature if it is to be called human at all.'[33] Values can thus be plural and conflictual, yet at the same time perfectly objective, because a common human nature does exist despite everything, in which they all ultimately come to rest.

The intention of this solution is clear – to bar the path from the liberal notion of pluralism to the nihilist consequences of relativism. But it falls short of accomplishing it. The human species could exhibit a range of common characteristics, including a capacity for mutual communication (on which Berlin lays special stress), without these necessarily having any moral import; and if the social codes it develops conflict, value-choices between them will on any definition be subjective. In one of his most acute essays, Berlin taxed Montesquieu with a central inconsistency. On the one hand, *De l'Esprit des Lois* showed that human laws and morals vary according to material and cultural circumstances, while on the other it upheld the existence of an absolute justice independent of time and place. Berlin comments that 'the only

---

31. *Against the Current*, p. 100. 'It was a stroke of genius to deny, as Vico did in the face of the highest authorities of his time, and of Aristotle, Seneca and the central Western tradition, the existence of an unaltering human nature': *Vico and Herder*, p. 39. The conviction that 'there exists a basic knowable human nature, one and the same, at all times, in all places, in all men', for Mill too, 'is mistaken': *Four Concepts of Liberty*, p. 188.

32. *The Crooked Timber of Humanity*, p. 76.

33. Ibid., p. 80.

link between the two doctrines is their common libertarian purpose.'[34] This is a good description of his own construction. For the best of motives, Berlin wishes to defend cultural pluralism without renouncing moral universalism. But this is a more demanding task than he appears to believe. He tries to meet it in two ways. Ontologically, he maintains, 'a minimum of common moral ground is intrinsic to human communication'[35] – anyone who rejects it ceasing to belong to the species. The claim has a Habermasian ring. But it confuses sharing with comprehending: the Allies and the Axis had no difficulty following each other's communiqués. The facts of language will not yield the morals of the race, however minimally conceived. More historically, Berlin speaks of returning to 'the ancient notion of natural law, in empiricist dress' – founded on the factual ubiquity of certain basic principles, 'long and widely recognized' which may be reckoned 'universal ethical laws'.[36] But that universe regularly turns out to be smaller than it seems. 'The central human values conveyed are those which are common to human beings as such, that is, for practical purposes to the great majority of men in most places and times.'[37] The specification can be refined further, in time and place: 'There does exist a scale of values by which the majority of mankind – and in particular western Europeans – in fact live.' Indeed, when 'I say "our" conduct, I mean by this the habits and outlook of the western world.'[38] The universal shrinks with every step back to the local. The more empirical, the less natural the law within reach. There are other ways of trying to untie this knot – Hayek or Popper, for example, could square the facts of historical variety with the needs of moral unity by evolutionary theories of cultural progress towards common standards. This kind of route Berlin has always declined.

The result is curiously a modern reprise of the original contradictions

---

34. *Against the Current*, p. 157.
35. *Four Concepts of Liberty*, p. xxxii.
36. *The Crooked Timber of Humanity*, p. 204.
37. *Four Concepts of Liberty*, p. xxxii; for another version of the same contraction, see p. liii. Berlin, following William James, has often criticized the contradictions of what he calls 'soft determinism' (roughly, the view that we are free to choose, but our choices are governed by our character or other forces). Formulations like these amount in effect to a soft relativism. Its contradictions are best expressed in Berlin's claim, at one point, that choice between values 'is not a matter of purely subjective judgement: it is dictated by the forms of life of the society to which one belongs, a society among other societies, with values held in common, whether or not they are in conflict, by the majority of mankind throughout recorded history': *The Crooked Timber of Humanity*, p. 18. Rarely have the parochial and the universal been so awkwardly soldered.
38. *The Crooked Timber of Humanity*, pp. 203, 205.

in Vico and Herder themselves. The burden of *The New Science* was actually an amalgam of historicism and innatism: the cultural diversity on which Vico insisted was also the expression of an underlying mental uniformity, of which his work set out to provide the dictionary. Whatever the variety of local customs, providence had ordained a natural law for all nations in the three universal principles of religion, marriage and burial – 'uniform ideas originating among entire peoples unknown to each other must have a common ground of truth.'[39] But Vico too showed himself less than completely confident in the scope of this moral code, with an equivocation nicely prefiguring that of his commentator. 'Since the criterion it uses is that what is felt to be just by all men *or by the majority* must be the rule of social life, these must be the bounds of human reason. Let him who would transgress them beware lest he transgress all humanity.'[40] Herder's theory of cultural particularism was much stronger than Vico's – it was not just an intellectual tenet, but a political commitment to ethnic difference as a value in its own right. Radically egalitarian, Herder attacked Kant not only for his claim that man was an animal that needs a master – 'say rather: the man who needs a master is an animal'[41] – but also for his belief in the racial inferiority of Blacks and others to Europeans. Yet after declaring in the most emphatic terms that every nation has its own cognitive, moral and aesthetic standards, valid for its habitat – 'each nation bears within itself the symmetry of its perfection, incomparable with that of others'[42] – he held out the prospect of each developing the potential of a common humanity, lodged in the original dispositions of the species. 'Reason and justice rest upon one and the same law of nature, in which the stability of our being also has its ground.'[43] That law would find its accomplished form in the 'beautiful dream of a future life', incorporating the best of the cultures of the past as well as the present: a league of humanity gathering all the treasures of time and

---

39. *The New Science*, Ithaca 1948, p. 57, § 144.

40. Ibid., p. 94, § 360.

41. *Ideen zur Philosophie der Geschichte der Menschheit*, Vol. I, Berlin–Weimar 1965, p. 367.

42. *Ideen*,Vol. II, p. 233.

43. Ibid., p. 240. Even more directly: 'Weary and faint with all these changes of region, time and nation, can we find no common property and excellence in our brotherhood upon the globe? None but our disposition to *reason, humanity and religion*, the three graces of human life.' Vol. I, pp. 370–71. 'The tendency of human nature makes up a universe whose motto is: "none for himself alone, each for all, so may you all be mutually valued and happy" – an endless diversity, striving for unity, that lies in everything and advances everything': *Briefe zur Beförderung der Humanität*, Vol. II, Berlin–Weimar 1971, p. 312.

space. But this heady vision of a 'universal conformation of all ranks and nations'[44] also sobers into something more prosaic, as the measure of progress towards it proves, after all, to be the advances of just one civilization. The *Outline for a Philosophy of Human History* ends with the question Western historians have been asking ever since: 'How came Europe by its culture, and therewith the rank it has properly won above other peoples' – as the progressive embodiment of a 'reason and humanity that in time should embrace the planet'?[45]

Berlin's pluralism reproduces these oscillations instead of resolving them. The result is that even on the plane where value-conflicts look most intractable, the doctrine seems on inspection to lose its sting, as the challenge of cultural diversity is neutralized by the insurance clauses of human identity. Here too radical premises appear to yield reassuring conclusions. The classical charge against pluralism as a theory of competing interests was always that it was less plural than met the eye, since political power was exercised within structural constraints set by one ultimate interest. However unlike it in other ways, pluralism as a theory of values is open to a similar kind of objection – in effect, that it is rather more discreetly monist than it suggests. What is the explanation of this paradox? In part, it clearly stems from a general difficulty. Where is the dividing-line between a stress on the multiplicity of cultures that enlarges our sense of humanity, and one that dissolves it? For entirely honourable motives Berlin wants to check any slide towards an agnosticism of values, on ethical grounds. This is the function of a semi-occidental human nature. The danger his pluralism seeks to avoid can be seen from another version that forms the most instructive contrast with it, Michael Walzer's *Spheres of Justice*. Unlike Berlin's, Walzer's pluralism is designed to reconcile differing values within any society by allocating separate regions of jurisdiction to each – consumption, welfare, office-holding, art – in a normative division of labour which in principle allows for a reasonably harmonious demarcation of the spheres. Although there will always be border frictions, 'good fences make just societies'.[46] On the other hand, each society as a whole makes up an autonomous form of life that can be judged only by its own standards – a caste system is just to those who live within its traditions. Internally, values are

---

44. *Ideen*, Vol. II, pp. 255, 485. *Briefe*, Vol. I, pp. 8 ff.
45. *Ideen*, Vol. II, pp. 484, 478. 'Let savage nations break upon Europe: they will not withstand our art of war – no Attila could range from the Black and Caspian Seas to the Catalaunian Fields once more': p. 247.
46. *Spheres of Justice*, New York 1983, p. 319.

complementary; externally, they are incommunicable. This is just the combination, with corrosively relativist consequences, that Berlin rejects.

Yet however different their solutions, it may be significant that these should be the two principal philosophers of pluralism. For one particular commitment unites them. The first focus of Berlin's political interests was Palestine. He subsequently often sought to distinguish between legitimate national sentiment, to be cherished, and nationalism as an ideology, to be condemned.[47] To separate the two, however, would be difficult enough over much of the world in the twentieth century, and certainly impossible in the case of Israel; as Weizmann said, 'Zionism is built on one and only one fundamental conception and that is Jewish nationalism.'[48] In practice, Berlin knows this. It is fitting that his major move beyond the history of ideas towards history *tout court* should have been two striking essays on nationalism.[49] In these, he may overstate the degree of its neglect in the prophesies of the previous century, but what stays in the memory is the depth and intimacy of his insight into it in this one. Reading them, it is easy to see why the culturally driven Herder, bored by constitutions and fascinated by nations, should have interested him more than the juridically minded Constant, whom even his contemporaries found somewhat *apatride*.[50] National sentiment, indeed, is the point of turbulence in which the clear-cut oppositions of negative and positive freedom buckle and dissolve, towards the end of 'Two Concepts'. At one moment not to be confused with either kind of liberty, at another representing a hybrid form of freedom with elements of both, national self-determination visibly undermines the stability of their meanings.[51] If anything, it tends to rehabilitate the positive sense put under suspicion. When Berlin elsewhere describes Chaim Weizmann as 'the first totally free

---

47. *The Crooked Timber of Humanity*, pp. 176, 245.

48. See Norman Rose, *Lewis Namier and Zionism*, London 1980, p. 207. Berlin could see that the term applied to Namier, whom he describes, in his memorable portrait of his friend, as 'an out-and-out nationalist', who 'did not disguise his far from fraternal feelings towards the Arabs in Palestine, about whom his position was more intransigent than that of the majority of his fellow Zionists': *Personal Impressions*, p. 72. This was written in the sixties, of the situation in the thirties.

49. 'Nationalism: Past Neglect and Present Power', *Against the Current*, pp. 333–55, and 'The Bent Twig: On the Rise of Nationalism', *The Crooked Timber of Humanity*, pp. 238–261, which date from 1978 and 1972 respectively.

50. In Constant's view, 'the division of Europe into several states is more apparent than real', since 'a mass of human beings now exists that under different names and under different forms of social organization are essentially homogeneous in their nature': *Political Writings* (ed. Biancamaria Fontana), Cambridge 1988, p. 313.

51. *Four Concepts of Liberty*, pp. 158, 160.

Jew in the modern world',[52] we can be sure he is not referring to the absence of civic constraints in Britain, or the position of the presidency in Israel. Emancipation can release a higher self after all.

The attractive force of national identity, the tug of belonging about which Berlin has written so acutely, is the joker in his pack of freedoms. It may also provide another clue to the specific character of his pluralism, its liveliness and its limits. For the universe of nationalism is by nature always a dialectic of the other and the same. The rationale of every nationalism is cultural difference: but the nationalist ideologies exalting it tend to be remarkably alike – few rhetorics have been more repetitively general in this century than claims for the ethnically particular. The structure of Berlin's pluralism has an affinity with this formal scheme. Values, like nations, are diverse; conflicts between them are inevitable; but in the end nations, like values, share a common discursive universe.

The realities of the international arena have always, of course, been very different. Berlin often sombrely evokes them.[53] But they still do not figure with the force they should, as a special problem for his theory. Within the nation-state, he has an answer to the conflict of ideals: competing values can be traded off into principled outcomes in the framework of a liberal constitution. But between nation-states, there is no authorized trader – when objectives conflict, the stand-off has historically been the rule. It was just this problem that prompted the composition of the *Idea for a Universal History*. Rather than raiding Kant for a phrase, Berlin would have done better to address himself to his theme. The disasters of the twentieth century began, not as Berlin has sometimes suggested,[54] with obscure eddies in tiny circles of socialist émigrés, but in the blaze and carnage of the Great War, when a liberal civilization broke Europe in to modern barbarism. They look like ending with the collapse of the last empire of that time in national strife and communal violence. Russian and Jewish fates are criss-crossing once again, amidst many echoes of the past. In London,

---

52. *Personal Impressions*, p. 62. For a more general concession that moral freedom from 'psychological impediments to the full use of human powers' can 'indeed bring liberation from obstacles, some of the most formidable and insidious in the path of human beings', see *Concepts and Categories*, London 1978, pp. 190–91.

53. For example, *Against the Current*, pp. 343–44; *The Crooked Timber of Humanity*, p. 252.

54. For the vision of a metaphysical watershed – 'an event which marked the culmination of a process which has altered the history of our world' – when delegate Posadovsky rose to speak at the Second Congress of the RSDLP in 1903, see *Four Concepts of Liberty*, p. 16.

Brodsky denounces Solzhenitsyn; in Moscow, a Duma is promised and black-gold-white colours fly again; in Jerusalem, generals debate where best to plant the forthcoming exodus along the Jordan. This is the world from which Berlin's most original impulses came, and to which they remain most relevant – not that of the Reform Club or the British Academy. The upright figure at the Albany may seem as much of an ornament of the British Establishment as his panegyrist, and that of the Prime Minister. This is a mistake. Even where his answers for it are least conclusive, it is in this other setting that his work merits greatest critical respect.

1990

12

Fernand Braudel and
National Identity

The most renowned historian of his time, Fernand Braudel owed his international reputation to the two great volumes on the Mediterranean in the age of Philip II which he published in 1949, and to his trilogy on the material civilization of world capitalism, which appeared between 1967 and 1979. He died a few months before the first volumes of his incomplete final work came out in 1986. More local in topic, and limited in execution, *The Identity of France* has generally been treated as a charming but diminuendo coda to his achievement as a whole. In fact, this concluding project – on which Braudel embarked in his late seventies – was conceived on a cyclopean scale. The torso that survives, two volumes devoted to geography, demography and production, is nearly a thousand pages in its English edition. They were to be followed by two sequels: one concerned with French politics, culture and society, the other with external relations. This quartet on Identity was then to be completed with two further works, respectively on the Birth and the Destiny of France, in which Braudel planned to retotalize the structures analysed separately in the first four studies into an integrated narrative history of his country.[1] Perhaps incredulous of such ambition, Siân Reynolds has taken the liberty of suppressing the full extent of it in her graceful English translation.

What were the aims of this vast design? Braudel's previous themes were virtually invented by him – strikingly original quarries from the past little mined before. Here he chose the most traditional of subjects, on which an abundant literature already exists, much of it distinguished. Why then a new history of France? Because, Braudel contended, 'the profession of historian has changed so utterly in the last

---

1. *L'Identité de la France*, Vol. I, *Espace et Histoire*, Paris 1986, pp. 19, 21. On occasion, I have modified the translation to remain closer to the original.

half-century' through the encroachment on its poorly fenced territory of the 'various social sciences – geography, political economy, demography, political science, anthropology, ethnology, social psychology, cultural studies, sociology'.[2] Braudel's claim was that these innovations made possible a much profounder exploration of the continuities shaping France, a speleological descent to the depths of 'an obscure history, running along under the surface, refusing to die – which this book proposes, if possible, to bring to light'.[3] The subterranean *longues durées* so discovered could then permit the comparative capture of what was historically specific to France; for only structures that are durable over time, as opposed to events that foam and fade away with it, allow meaningful contrasts between national experiences.[4] Tacitly (it is never quite spelt out), this is the double force of the term 'identity' in the title of the book – it denotes what subsists and what singles out, and suggests that they are the same. The premise of Braudel's multi-disciplinary enquiry is that the particular and the permanent in France have been one.

Braudel called his enterprise a gamble. How far does it succeed? The work we possess has a quizzical attraction of its own, which to some extent comes from its unfinished state. Braudel always aspired to totalities, but his forte was details. Here, in a book confessedly personal, these are more wayward than elsewhere; but also often more delicate, and warmer. The first volume offers a physical description of the major regions of France and the tiers of its settlement; moving from general analyses of its villages and towns, to particular reflections on the commercial role of the Rhone corridor, the agrarian primacy of the Parisian basin, the strategic fortresses of Metz and Toulon. The second traces a demographic profile of the populations who have lived in the area of the hexagon; explores the setting and range of their agricultural activities – livestock, wine, cereals; and ends by looking at the historical character of trade, industry and credit in France. The casually vivid, flowing style and bright jetsam of examples carry the reader effortlessly along, through terrain that might with other vehicles seem arbitrary, perhaps sometimes even arid. It is easy to understand why so many reviewers have dwelt on the pleasures of the text. But also why they

---

2. *L'Identité de la France*, I, p. 11; *The Identity of France*, Vol. I, *History and Environment*, London 1988, p. 17 (henceforward IF–I).

3. *L'Identité de la France*, I, p. 14; IF–I, p. 20.

4. See his explanation in *Une Leçon d'Histoire de Fernand Braudel*, Paris 1986, p. 70, the proceedings of a colloquium at Châteauvallon in October 1985, at which Braudel discussed his work with colleagues and critics just before he died.

have complained that Braudel seems to have lost sight along the way of his initial aim. For the work as a whole lacks any sustained – even fitful – comparative dimension. The differing European contexts which ought logically to have given relief to the specifically French experience are virtually all missing. The result is that much of Braudel's book is taken up with extended accounts of settlement patterns, agrarian practices or commercial procedures that were often quite general to Western Europe as a whole, rather than peculiar to France. If its focus moves freely back and forth from remotest prehistory to contemporary times, it also slips seemingly unawares across large ranges of commonality more than identity, as what was distinctively French recedes into what was mediaeval or early modern at large. Braudel says at the outset that his theme was seductive but elusive, and so it proves to be.

Nevertheless, amidst the sunnily digressive mass of this history, unenclosed as he wished it, there are certain claims that do in principle indicate a special position of France within the continent. The first of these is the contention that of all the countries of Europe, France has always been most various in its physical endowments. This is the most insistent thread of the work. For others, space would only be weakly historical as a feature. But Braudel's empirical claim for France reflected the theoretical primacy he accorded geography at large in social causation. Spatial determinations, he declared elsewhere, are 'the most ancient and important of all – what counts in any deeper history.'[5] Here the privilege of France is to be such a happy illustration of the principle. For its regional variety, Braudel argues, meant material and cultural plenty – a wealth of contrasted settings and resources without equal among its neighbours. France has always been 'the dazzling triumph of the plural, of the heterogeneous, of the never-quite-the-same'.[6]

In celebrating French diversity, Braudel had many predecessors. He cites his immediate master Lucien Febvre. But the theme ultimately derives from Michelet, whose history of France lyrically depicted the contrasts between its provinces, 'diverse in climate, customs and language', yet bound in mutual understanding and affection;[7] and most directly from Vidal de la Blache, whose *Tableau de la Géographie de la France* of 1903 declared that 'the word which best characterizes

5. *Une Leçon d'Histoire de Fernand Braudel*, pp. 208–209.
6. *L'Identité de la France*, I, p. 29; IF–I, p. 38.
7. 'Tableau de la France', *Histoire de France*, Vol. II, Paris 1885, p. 161, which declares at the outset: 'History is first of all geography.' This was written in 1833.

France is variety'.[8] For Vidal the 'harmony' of its constituent parts and the 'goodness of its soil, the pleasure of living there' created an ambience that was 'a beneficent force, a *genius loci*, that prepared our existence as a nation and imparted something healthy to it'.[9] In other words, Febvre's phrase 'diversity is the name of France' was already a long-standing trope before him. Braudel affectionately embroiders it. But he makes no effort to substantiate the claim in the way that Vidal did, who pointed out that France alone of European countries combined a Mediterranean, an Atlantic and a Continental zone. Such climatic contrasts are real enough, but whether they suffice for greater regional diversity than anywhere else is another matter. Germany too contains three major geographical zones, between the Rhine, the Baltic and the Alps, with subdivisions that – contrary to Vidal's assertion – rival or exceed those of France. The *Länder* are a lot more vigorous in their regional profiles than today's emaciated *provinces*.

In point of fact, it seems more plausible to argue that France was historically distinguished from its neighbours not so much by its geographical variety as by its early political unity. This is in effect the case made by another *Annales* historian, Pierre Chaunu, who likes to dwell on the singularity of the French 'super-state', by the age of the Renaissance four times the size and population of the only comparable unified monarchy, its English rival.[10] At times Braudel himself seems to concede as much, when he suggests that provincial diversity in France was actually a forcing house of royal centralization. In the actual triumph of the unitary state, in truth, probably lies the clue to the popularity of the motif of national variety – the one functioning as symbolic compensation for the other in the French Ideology. Confirmation of this is suggested by the reversal of the relationship in an Italy that lacked any unitary state. There Manzoni vehemently rejected the patronage of a well-meaning Lamartine, during the revolution of 1848: 'Do you not realize that there is no harsher word to throw at us than that of *diversity*, which epitomizes for us a long past of misfortune and abjection?'[11] It may be less the fact than the cult of regional diversity

8. Paul Vidal de la Blache, *Tableau de la Géographie de la France*, Paris 1903, p. 40.
9. Ibid., pp. 50–51.
10. Pierre Chaunu, *La France*, Paris 1982, pp. 30, 205. Compare *L'Identité de la France*, I, p. 279; IF–I, p. 309.
11. Lamartine, as Foreign Minister of the Second Republic, had urged the Italians to constitutional reforms reflecting the different kinds of state in the peninsula. Manzoni, writing from insurgent Milan, told him 'the word you have uttered is the opposite' of the deep desire of the Italians: Alessandro Manzoni, *Tutte le Opere*, Vol. VII/2, Milan 1970, p. 435.

that tells us something specific about the history of France.

There is a second claim for French specificity in Braudel's account, less prominent or pursued, but comparable in kind. Turning from geography to demography, he argues that the great challenge for historical imagination today is to overcome the artificial divide between prehistory and history, as traditionally conceived – one that the advances of archaeology have rendered anachronistic. Once this is done, he maintains, a striking phenomenon comes into view. France knew a greater antiquity of dense continuous settlement than any other part of the continent. It was the site of the first known human cluster, in the Alpes-Maritimes, a million years ago. It was the crossroads for the spread of neolithic agriculture some six thousand years ago. Towards 1800 BC it supported perhaps as many as five million inhabitants. The basic 'biological combination' making up the population stock of France was thus already in place some four millennia ago.[12] In developing this case, Braudel appeals to the notion of a 'national neolithic civilization' proposed by a leading French prehistorian, Jean Guilaine, author of a recent work entitled *La France d'avant la France*. But here too, the theme itself is by no means new. Introducing his tableau of French spatial diversity, Vidal stressed that its complement was temporal continuity. 'The relationships between land and man are marked, in France, by a distinctive character of antiquity and conti-nuity. Very early in time human settlements appear to have become fixed . . . It has often been remarked of our country that its inhabitants have succeeded each other from time immemorial in the same sites.'[13] Fascination with prehistory is widespread today. On this side of the Channel some of the same impulses behind Braudel's interest in it can be sensed in Raymond Williams's multi-secular fiction of place. But transposed into proto-national register, the distance to myth is short. Braudel's claim for five million neolithic farmers closes it. Guilaine himself allows no more than two to four hundred thousand. Here too the attributes of identity prove to be less specific than specious.

The claims of diversity and of continuity share, however, a common structure. They should be read not as the findings of empirical history, but as fixed points of national ideology. All ethnic mythologies, it has been pointed out, are either territorial or genealogical in character – tracing the identity of the group to an original location or a primordial

---

12. *L'Identité de la France*, Vol. II/1, *Les Hommes et les Choses*, pp. 60–61; *The Identity of France*, Vol. II, *People and Production*, London 1990, pp. 70–71 (hencefor-ward IF–II).

13. *Tableau de la Géographie de la France*, p. 3.

ancestry.[14] Later nationalist ideologies reworked these basic myth-emes into their own forms of 'poetic space' or 'heroic memory', as Anthony Smith terms them in his fundamental study *The Ethnic Origins of Nations*.[15] In a moving passage, Braudel confessed his passion for France, but promised to put it aside in his book. He characteristically added: 'It is possible that it will play tricks on me and catch me out, so I shall keep it under close watch.'[16] It bamboozled him just the same. But it was also typical of him that, found out, he could concede his errors with disarming bonhomie. At the end of his second volume, he reports that an audience at Göttingen would not let him get away with the thesis of France's superior diversity, and that he had no answer to their claims for equal German variety; and just before his death, he ruefully yielded to more modest estimates of France's genetic continuity.[17] Although he was at times the creature of a national self-image, he was never a captive of it.

Where do these retractions leave the quest for the identity of France? In the last and longest part of his work, Braudel develops the elements of another approach to it, more serious and less congenial to collective *amour propre*. The title of this part sums up its message: 'A Peasant Economy down to the Twentieth Century'. Here Braudel dwells on the extraordinary stability of French agrarian life, with its inveterate routines of cultivation and sluggish levels of productivity; the early adoption of birth-controls, checking population in the countryside; the peripheral pattern of urbanization – all major towns save Paris and Toulouse scattered round the edges of the country, leaving a 'hollow interior', yet without stimulating major foreign trade; the lack of new industrial complexes comparable to the Ruhr or the Midlands; the hoarding of coinage and weakness of domestic credit; the failure to take effectively to the seas. France, Braudel concludes, was margina-lized within the history of capitalism, which developed in a circular movement around it from the later Middle Ages onwards, from Italy to the Low Countries to England to Germany, without ever transforming the slow metabolisms of the hexagon between them. The peculiar identity of France derives from this fate – or fortune. 'Is it perhaps both France's tragedy and the secret of its charm that it has never really been

---

14. John Armstrong, *Nations before Nationalism*, Chapel Hill 1982, pp. 12 et seq.
15. This remarkable work was published in the same year as Braudel's book: London 1986, pp. 183–200.
16. *L'Identité de la France*, I, p. 9; IF–I, p. 15.
17. *L'Identité de la France*, II/2, p. 423; IF–II, p. 670; and *Une Leçon d'Histoire de Fernand Braudel*, p. 207.

won – what is called won – over to capitalism?'[18] The French Revolution, contrary to received opinion, was not responsible for the economic misfiring of the country – any more than for its political unification. The die was cast much earlier. France enjoyed a brief period of economic leadership in the thirteenth century, when the Champagne fairs were the commercial hub of the continent. Thereafter, bypassed by sea routes linking the Mediterranean and North Sea economies, 'France was no longer a partner in the most advanced economic activities of Europe.'[19] From now on it would be a covetous spectator of other people's successes, on occasion tempted to annex them – fifteenth-century Italy or seventeenth-century Holland – by force of arms, in vain forays to offset the peasant stillness at home.

This is a memorable description. But what were the causes of the web of inertias that made up this French identity? Braudel has rather little to say about them. The luxuriant foliage of documentation surrounds a very slender trunk of explanation. The nearest he comes to a comparative hypothesis is to wonder, at a number of points, whether the very size of France was not an essential handicap to integrated economic development in the early modern epoch, preventing the emergence of a national market and creating an exorbitant state to hold it together – where England, by contrast, was small enough both to form a single market centred on London, and to maintain political unity with a modest state.[20] The observation is in itself a reasonable one. But it will hardly do as a central explanation of the French path of development. What Braudel's whole account of France's 'peasant economy' significantly ignores is the peculiar dynamic of its smallholder *property*. The omission is all the more arresting in that it was here, precisely, that Marc Bloch located the originality of French agrarian history. The pivot of his great work on the subject is a comparison of the differing fates of the peasantry as their lords sought to resolve the crisis of feudal rents in late mediaeval Europe.[21] In Eastern Europe, the outcome was the spread of demesne farming and a new serfdom – the loss of personal freedom and security; in England, it was the transformation of perpetual leases into tenancies at will – personal freedom and insecurity. In France alone, it was the widespread conversion of customary leases into heritable property – personal freedom and security. The consolida-

---

18. *L'Identité de la France*, II/2, p. 420; IF–II, p. 666.

19. *L'Identité de la France*, II/1, pp. 146–150; IF– II, pp. 163–66.

20. *L'Identité de la France*, II/2, pp. 225–26; IF–II, pp. 458–59.

21. *Les Caractères Originaux de l'Histoire Rurale Française*, Paris 1931, pp. 126–29.

tion of this smallholder agriculture, never completed but never rolled back, became the key to the social stability and the technological backwardness of the French countryside down to Bloch's own time.

Some fifty years later, Robert Brenner was to develop the kernel of Bloch's insight into a magisterial comparative analysis of the variant property relations thrown up by class struggles on the land across Europe, and their consequences for development of agrarian capitalism – deploying the same three-way contrast between Eastern Europe, England and France in a fully systematic framework. Brenner's account was widely seen to be a landmark, and set off perhaps the most important international debate among historians since the war.[22] The absence of any reference to it in Braudel's book is astonishing. More than an individual foible, however, may be discernible here. For this controversy – focusing centrally on France, in which leading French historians participated – has never been translated into French. Perhaps the illustrious figure of Emmanuel Le Roy Ladurie, inescapable on all channels, felt uneasy about an exchange in which his own ideas were among those at issue. But could this have amounted to an embargo? The explanation seems to be wider, touching on the evolution of the *Annales* tradition itself. One of the most striking features of its latter-day development is the extent to which it has relinquished two of the central legacies of Bloch's work: his insistence on a fully comparative history, and his concern with social relations of property and dependence. The overwhelming bulk of recent *Annales* output has been devoted simply to France – the contrast with Anglo-Saxon production is quite startling. Within this newer literature the place of property has in practice increasingly been taken by demography, often posed in theory too as an alternative to it.[23] Much of the Brenner debate, of course, hinged on the rival importance ascribed to these as explanatory mechanisms of historical change.

In the version made famous by Le Roy Ladurie, the demographic interpretation of French agrarian history stresses the long-range Malthusian cycles of the countryside. Population increase among the peasantry would push up rents and sub-divide plots, so precipitating subsistence crises that led to decline of population and concentration of

---

22. After their original appearance in *Past and Present* between 1976 and 1982, the collected contributions were published as *The Brenner Debate* (eds. T.H. Aston and C.H.E. Philpin), Cambridge 1985.

23. For an *outré* example, see Hervé Le Bras, *Les Trois Frances*, Paris 1986, which purports to derive virtually the whole economic and electoral geography of the country from a set of regional family-types, themselves interpreted as so many rational choices in response to French centralism.

land, which eventually triggered a renewed upswing of prices and population that in due course hit the same limits as before. The result, Le Roy Ladurie maintained, was a 'homeostatic' system that imposed iron constraints on pre-capitalist economic growth. Tested out in the Languedoc, between the late fifteenth and mid eighteenth centuries, this model was then generalized across Western Europe, no longer – at any rate in principle – distinguishing French experience as such.[24] Against this background, another *Annaliste* then picked out a much more striking and specifically French phenomenon. In a series of professional and popular works, Pierre Chaunu focused on the preco- cious spread of contraception in the French countryside during the eighteenth century – birth controls that no longer took the 'ascetic' form of late marriage, traditional in the downswings of the Malthusian cycle, but the new 'hedonistic' form, to the scandal of contemporary preachers, of the *saut de l'ange* in the marital bed. Here something exceptional certainly did occur in France, as Braudel emphasizes: a sexual pattern that set the country apart from the rest of Europe, resulting in much lower population growth in the nineteenth century. What were its reasons? He suggests a combination of long-standing rural density with a new-found moral scepticism, after-effect of the peculiar short-circuiting of both Reformation and Counter-Reforma- tion in France. Chaunu's version is more lurid: the dry tinder for 'the revolution against life' lay in the hyper-individualism of the small proprietors, in an overcrowded countryside, suddenly ignited by the rupture with traditional religion in the 1790s.[25] But in either case, there is no doubt that the stability of the French peasant economy down to the last days of the Third Republic was to be secured by a biological self-regulation unique of its kind; and that if there was a single structural complex which defined the character of modern French society more than any other, it was this configuration – what, in Weberian terms, might be called tradition-bound production and rationalized reproduction.

What, on the other hand, has become of these features since the Second World War? For some two decades after 1945, France suddenly reversed its past and experienced high birth rates – a surge Chaunu

---

24. Emmanuel Le Roy Ladurie, 'A Reply to Robert Brenner', *The Brenner Debate*, pp. 102, 104.

25. Compare *L'Identité de la France*, II/1, pp. 181– 185; IF–II, pp. 199–202, with *La France*, pp. 273–74, 279. Curtius noted the cultural significance of this French pattern in his perceptive pre-war study of *The Civilization of France* (1930), now dated but still perhaps the best short essay in the literature.

attributes to the 'suicidal' self-elimination of the secularized majority in the inter-war years, when two-fifths of French adults produced only one out of ten children, while a minority (nearly all Catholic) of about one-thirteenth produced one out of four children. This miraculous redressment, as Chaunu sees it, did not last long. By the 1970s, the faithful too had been struck by the 'White Death' of negative rates of reproduction. But this was now a catastrophic general pattern in the West, which France had rejoined, as Christian apologetics everywhere fell silent.[26] Meanwhile, in the countryside the peasantry was carried away by 'a deluge Bloch could never have imagined', writes Braudel, as modernization finally engulfed the old rural order, leaving a mere seven per cent of the labour force in agriculture. 'The spectacle that over-shadows all others, in the France of the past and even more of today, is the collapse of a peasant society', a balanced way of life so long sustained by its virtues – hard work, practical wisdom, modest comfort.[27] Although on occasion he suggests these may survive in the small towns where half of the French still live, Braudel's book ends on a note of regret at the landslides that have buried the village world in which he grew up. The sense of loss is tempered by the stoical creed which separated him from Marxists and liberals alike: 'Men scarcely make their own history, it is history that rather makes them, and therewith absolves them from blame.'[28] But the conclusion of the work can only put its title into question. If the historical complex most distinctive of modern France has disappeared, what is left of its identity? Normalized to a standard pattern of advanced capitalist production and reproduction, how far has France simply lost the numen Braudel was seeking?

The answer is, of course, that what differentiates one country from another is not only social structure but culture. Although these are never independent of each other, there is a wide range of possible relationships between them. At one extreme, the Hindu caste system – specifying divinely-ordained hereditary roles for all incumbents in the division of labour – could virtually fuse the two. At the other, modern capitalist societies can resemble each other very closely in all structural features – distribution of the labour force, degree of urbanization, demographic profile, size and functions of the state – while remaining significantly dissimilar in culture: no one would confuse Belgium with

---

26. See *La France*, pp. 276–77, 359–361; for Chaunu's impassioned natalism see his alarm cries *Le Refus de la Vie* (1975), *La Peste Blanche* (1976), *Un Futur sans Avenir* (1979).

27. *L'Identité de la France*, II/2, pp. 427–430; IF– II, pp. 674–77.

28. *L'Identité de la France*, II/2, p. 431; IF–II, p. 679.

Japan. Insofar as Braudel took up what he called 'the perspective of the present' in his historical reflections, one might say that he was looking for the identity of France in the wrong place. For the underground streams of long-term population and production that occupy his two volumes have tended to converge with those of other countries. It was the sequel he did not live to write on politics and culture that might have yielded answers less subject to contemporary erosion.

This was in effect the assumption, in its own fashion, of the traditional literature on national character. Today, this is a notion that has largely fallen into intellectual disgrace. One suspects that few readers of this journal, if asked point-blank, would assert their belief in it. But how many scruple over the familiar judgement: 'typically ——', of foreigner or friend, in daily conversation? There are no generalizations that seem in principle so indefensible, yet in practice so unavoidable. The shadow of prejudice that falls across them was felt already in the Enlightenment. The first major writer on the subject, David Hume, introduced it with the caveat that 'the vulgar are apt to carry all national characters to extremes.' But that was not a reason to deny their existence. 'Men of sense condemn these undistinguishing judgements; though, at the same time, they allow that each nation has a peculiar set of manners, and that some particular qualities are more frequently to be met with among one people than their neighbours.'[29] Hume's aim was to show that national character, so understood, was not a product of fixed geographical environment but of changing political, economic and diplomatic circumstances – 'the nature of the government, the revolutions of public affairs, the plenty or penury in which people live, the situation of the people with regard to their neighbours'.[30] The most he would concede to climate was perhaps the greater inclination of Northern peoples to alcohol and of Southern to sex ('wine and distilled waters warm the frozen blood' , whereas 'the genial heat of the sun exalts the passion between the sexes').[31] Otherwise, it was moral not physical factors that counted. The English were the most various in individual temperament of any nation in the world, displaying 'the least of a national character, unless this very

---

29. 'Of National Characters', *Essays, Moral, Political and Literary*, Indianapolis 1987, p. 197; the essay was written in 1742.

30. *Essays*, p. 198.

31. *Essays*, p. 213. Allowing that 'the passion for liquor be more brutal and debasing than love', Hume observed that 'this gives not so great an advantage to the southern climates' as might be imagined, since 'when love goes beyond a certain pitch, it renders men jealous, and cuts off the free intercourse between the sexes, on which the politeness of a nation will commonly much depend.'

singularity may pass for such'.[32] This variety owed nothing to the uncertainty of their weather (shared by the more conformist Scots), and everything to the mixed nature of their government (a blend of monarchy, aristocracy and democracy), the composite make-up of their rulers (joining gentry and merchants), the number of their religions (every sect could be found), and the personal freedom these pluralisms made possible. With the substitution of temperament for territory, diversity here becomes the hallmark of England rather than France.

Its flattering function did not escape notice then, any more than it might today. Kant retorted that it was precisely the English affectation of individuality that expressed their collective contempt for foreigners, an arrogance born of the illusion of self-sufficiency. Character, in any case, was not so much a mere factual disposition as a normative unity only achieved by coherence of ethical conduct. 'The man of principles has character.' Fortunately, the Germans were well-known for their good character – combining honesty, industry, profundity, modesty (if with a touch of undue deference and pedantry).[33] A century later, Nietzsche reverted to the higher ground. Compared with the English, 'a herd of drunkards and rakes who once learnt moral grunting under the sway of Methodism, and more recently the Salvation Army', the Germans might deserve their share of sarcasms, yet they were more intangible, more ample, more incalculable than any other people – the nation that above all escaped definition.[34] The adaptability of the figure is striking. Beyond the Alps, Vincenzo Gioberti could weave it no less deftly into his explanation of the *Moral and Civil Primacy of the Italians*. First in the world of action through the role of the Roman Church, and in the realm of thought through leadership in philosophy, theology, science, statecraft, literature, painting, Italy was 'the mother nation of the human race' whose civilizing mission was to foster the unity of the continent, for after all Italy's variety made it 'the mirror and synthesis of Europe'.[35] Among so many self-addressed comple-

---

32. *Essays*, p. 207.

33. *Anthropologie in pragmatischer Hinsicht* (1798), in *Werke*, Vol. 10, Darmstadt 1983, pp. 659, 625, 667–670. For his part, Voltaire in the *Encyclopédie* had found the French to be the envy of Europe for their gallantry and urbanity, their genius perhaps equal to the English in philosophy and supreme in literature (Vol. XV, 1779 edition, pp. 338–342). The main theoretical discussion of national differences occurs in the substantial entry on *moeurs* written by Marmontel, which discusses the impact on them of – in succession – government, climate, economic activity, town and country, and class.

34. *Jenseits von Gut und Böse*, Leipzig 1896, pp. 222, 209; *Beyond Good and Evil*, London 1967, pp. 211, 197.

35. *Il Primato Morale e Civile degli Italiani*, Brussels 1843, Vol. II, pp. 399–401.

ments, one requisitory stands out in relief. Leopardi, at least, was proof against the conceit. Brooding on the character of his compatriots under the Restoration, he came to the conclusion that their outstanding trait was not diversity but conformity – their unfailing display of a cynicism immune from mediaeval superstition yet incapable of modern socia-bility, the product of a broken-backed history combining the wrong kinds of sophistication and backwardness.[36] The customs of the Italians called for reform rather than indulgence. These bitter reflec-tions remained unpublished till the early twentieth century.

By then, in the new world of industrial armaments and academic scholarship, national character had become the object of major theore-tical treatises in the competing powers. Three cases exemplify this change. In France, Alfred Fouillée – a colleague of Durkheim and fellow spokesman for the Solidarist cabinets of the nineties – published his *Esquisse Psychologique des Peuples Européens* in 1902, the first comprehensive tour of the different temperaments of the continent. His patriotic aim, he explained, was to inform the French more thoroughly about their neighbours so that they should not fall dupe or prey to them. Fouillée distrusted the Russians and admired the English, although he was critical of their colonial egoism – the book contains a plea for the Entente Cordiale that was negotiated soon afterwards. The French themselves were preeminent for their amiable vivacity, their critical wit, their passionate logic, their fraternity and generosity to other nations – even if they did drink too much and have too few children ('losing a battle each day' against the Germans).[37] In Fouil-lée's gallery of types, the static factors of race or milieu were – contrary to materialist suppositions – less important in forming national char-acter than the dynamic *idées-forces* transmitted by each elite to the masses.

Fouillée was, as this suggests, exercised by the dangers of Marxism. Five years later, Otto Bauer published his massive work on *The Question of Nationalities and Social Democracy* in Austria. At its centre, often forgotten today, was a full-tilt theoretical construction of

---

36. *Dei Costumi degl'Italiani*, Venice 1989, pp. 141–49. Italy was thus morally inferior both to nations that were more cultivated and sociable than it – France, England, Germany – and to nations that were less so – Russia, Poland, Portugal, Spain – because these at least retained an ethos of the past, however barbarous this might be. (Leopardi proceeds to a magnificent denunciation of religious intolerance and feudal oppression: pp. 151–52). These reflections were set down in 1824 and first published in 1906.

37. *Esquisse Psychologique des Peuples Européens*, Paris 1902, p. 331. Another political aim of the book was to refute current theories of the decadence of the 'neo-Latin races', prompted by the defeats of France, Spain and Italy at Sedan, Manila Bay, Adowa.

the idea of national character – a concept which Kautsky and other Marxists held heretical, but Bauer considered essential to rescue from the ode, the *feuilleton* and the tavern if nationalism was to be combatted effectively. That could never be done by denying the self-evident specificities of each nation, but only by explaining them rationally as so many different products of history – which Bauer sought to show by a comparative analysis of the social origins of English empiricism and French rationalism as salient national traits, very much in the spirit of Hume.[38] Such traits were always mutable, as could be seen from the quite recent decline of traditional German *Gründlichkeit* – still valued by Engels – into a dreary cult of fact and force. National character was a descriptive term for a community of culture that included the arts and sciences, public life and social customs of a people; but in a class-divided society the toilers were always in some measure excluded from it. Socialism would mean for the first time its full extension, and its free self-determination. Contrary to the expectation of many Marxists, that would lead to increasing rather than diminishing differentiation of national characters. For while the material dimensions of culture would certainly become more cosmopolitan once the working class gained power, their spiritual appropriation would also become more democratic – in other words, naturalized through millions more individual minds and sensibilities than in the past, preventing that convulsively rapid assimilation of foreign fashions typical of restricted elites, like the Meiji oligarchs.[39] The more popular a culture, the more national it would be, without prejudice to the international solidarity of labour.

In England, it was a liberal who gave the subject the most systematic treatment of all. In his work on *National Character*, published in 1927, Ernest Barker provided both a careful theoretical framework for its analysis and an empirical application of his schema to England. Employing a distinction often mistakenly attributed to Marx (and nervously discarded by Marxists – it in fact goes back to Harrington), Barker divided the factors in its formation into a material base, comprising genetic stock, geographical setting and socio-economic composition, and a cultural superstructure, embracing law and government, religion, language and literature, and education. The second set

---

38. *Die Nationalitätenfrage und die Sozialdemokratie*, in *Werkausgabe*, Vol. I, Vienna 1975, pp. 57–60. Kautsky, in particular, had taken Bauer to task for employing the un-Marxist notion of national character, arguing that nations were defined not by a common culture but merely by a common language. Bauer had no difficulty replying.

39. Ibid., pp. 166–170.

was both more significant than the first, and more amenable to conscious alteration. The national character so formed was best understood as a transmitted 'tradition', if opaline in the number of its hues.[40] Barker was interested in regional contrasts within England, noting the importance of the division between South–East and North–West from Anglo-Saxon times onwards. But he thought that the small size of the country had helped to keep the different facets of this tradition more congruent with each other than elsewhere. The key determinants of the tradition, he believed, were clear-cut sea frontiers dispensing with the need for a strong executive; the evolution of common law, more important even than parliament for a spirit of legality and compromise; the divided legacy of the religious reformation, generating the two-party system and a pioneering strain of puritanism; the ethical and social bent of so much of the national literature, and its aversion to speculation; the concern of schools with character rather than learning. The outcome was a predictably, if never artlessly, benevolent portrait of the native temper. Empire scarcely features. Nations ought to coincide with states, Barker thought, yet the United Kingdom does not: he registers its ambiguities with a delicate prefix – Scotland is a nation that is something like a quasi-state, Britain a state that is at least a quasi-nation.[41] The besetting English weakness was their religion-derived, class-divided, state-retarded educational system, a major international handicap. This sounds contemporary, and Barker sensed difficult economic times ahead with the decline of Britain's traditional exports. But he thought schools should be training citizens not for more efficient work, but for more creative leisure. Nothing dates his project more than that.

In fact, these were the last ambitious attempts to analyse the constituents of national character. Not that the idea disappeared; but it gradually subsided back into the undergrowth of folklore and *feuilleton* from which Bauer had wanted to extricate it. Popular tracts like Orwell's *Lion and Unicorn* or radio addresses like Pevsner's *Englishness of English Art* continued to minister to conventional kinds of self-esteem, while public libraries came to be filled with works of reportage on *The Russians, The Germans, The Italians, The French,* a well-

---

40. *National Character*, London 1927, pp. 9, 270. In his generally shrewd treatment of geographical setting, Barker was influenced by Febvre: he was one of the first English readers of *La Terre et l'Evolution Humaine.*

41. *National Character*, p. 131. Barker was sensitive to the role of Calvinism in forming a separate Scottish culture: pp. 188–194.

established genre for satisfying curiosity about others.[42] But works of a more strenuous and comparative nature ceased to appear. André Siegfried's potboiler of 1950, *L'Ame des Peuples* (English tenacity, French ingenuity, German discipline, Russian mysticism), was the forlorn fag-end of an earlier tradition. By the sixties, national character was no longer serious. What were the reasons for its eclipse? In its heyday, it had always been embedded in the larger idea of a national culture. This term was rarely defined with much rigour, as it entered general currency in the nineteenth century. But it came in time to include four main ingredients: traditional customs, codified values, learned arts, and objects of daily use – roughly, the domains of sociability, morality, creativity and consumption. (Paradigmatically, let us say: Fanny drinking too much negus at the ball in Mansfield Park.) In the age of Hume, the accent fell on the first two – manners and qualities; by the time of Bauer, the third was often regarded as most significant – philosophy or literature; it was not till the domestic ethnography of Mass Observation that the last really came into its own, releasing Orwell's copy for the British bob and bitter.

Since the Second World War, each of these traditional contributions to the nationally distinct cultures of Western Europe has been under pressure. The object-world of all the rich capitalist countries has been relentlessly hybridized or homogenized, as the circuits of multinational production and exchange grow more pervasive. The old signifiers of difference have progressively waned. First, dress – the days of the bowler and beret are long gone; of a once extensive repertoire, only the Austrian *Tracht* survives, perhaps because it always had elements of dressing-up. Then diet – still much more resistant; but the time when hamburger advertisements in the Metro could be surcharged with graffiti like *Français, Françaises, rejetez cette bouffe déshonorante* is also past: fast food and nouvelle cuisine are in principle at home everywhere. Then furniture – with the spreading modules of IKEA. If buildings have been least affected, despite the office block and service flat, it is mainly because so many houses predate the post-war world, rather than display current regional styles. In the spheres of art and communication, the rise of image at the expense of print, and demotic relative to elite genres, increasingly creates a single time-zone of the imaginary, bounded by the optical fibre. Language, still far the strongest of cultural enclosures, has been at critical points bypassed. Mean-

---

42. See, for example, Luigi Barzini, *The Italians* (1964); Sanche de Gramont, *The French* (1969); Hedrick Smith, *The Russians* (1976), David Marsh, *The Germans* (1989).

while, the disciplines of socialization that once inculcated sharply distinct codes and manners have relaxed: school systems no longer embody contrasting educational ideals to the same degree; a common measure of progressivism, out of conviction or demoralization, laps them all. Classrooms formerly conceived as crucibles of national culture bespeak less of the nation, at times of culture.

If national character was the human precipitate of a national culture – the range of qualities and forms of conduct it encouraged – the thinning of the latter was bound to unsettle ideas of the former. But as it happened, the notion of character had fallen independently under suspicion in its own right. If its most powerful version had once been provided by realist fiction, the first radical attacks on it came from literature too, with the widespread rejection of any stable ego in early twentieth-century modernism, even in a transitional figure like Lawrence. The impact of psychoanalysis then further weakened traditional assumptions of individual character as a moral unity. The term had thus already suffered a certain loss of confidence as a personal category by the time that cultural conditions had changed to its detriment as a national attribute. A new situation was created, in which both could be repudiated. The logic of this change has recently been taken to its conclusion by at least one historian, Theodore Zeldin. A tart critic of Braudel's enterprise,[43] his own study of *The French* disavows any notion of national or individual coherence at all, on the grounds that people are becoming more different from each other than ever before, and more disjointed in themselves. The result, he enthuses, is a society in which everyone can customize a happily tatterdemalion life-style of their own: Durkheim laid to rest, anomie becomes luxury as France advances into 'the Age of Whim'.[44] Why the French should any longer even be called such, from the viewpoint of this 'post-pluralism', is not explained – perhaps itself a whim. The only reason left for the book would appear to be that 'all the human passions can be seen at play in France'.[45] Few historians have been willing to *noyer le poisson* quite like this.

What has happened instead is a change of register. Over the past decade, the discourse of national difference has shifted from character to identity. The two terms are often treated as if they were interchangeable. In fact, their connotations are significantly distinct. The concept

43. *London Review of Books*, 16 March 1989: a notice of the first volume of *The Identity of France*.
44. *The French*, London 1983, pp. 510, 342.
45. *The French*, p. 5.

of character is in principle comprehensive, covering all the traits of an individual, or a group; it is self-sufficient, needing no external reference for its definition; and it is mutable, allowing for partial or general modifications. By contrast the charge of the notion of identity is more selective, conjuring up rather what is inward and essential; relational, implying some element of alterity for its definition; and perpetual, indicating what is continuously the same. Talking of individuals, we typically use the term identity in two main ways. One is quasi-ontological, when we want to suggest the deepest core of a personality. The other is social, and customarily refers to roles in the division of labour. There is an obvious tension between the two. Compared with character, we might say, identity appears both profounder and more fragile: metaphysically grounded in one way, yet sociologically exposed and dependent in another. It is no accident that current parlance speaks of a 'change' of character but a 'crisis' of identity: character is not generally held subject to crisis, nor identity amenable to change – save in the cloak-and-dagger sense that disguises rather than alters it. What separates the two conceptions here is not just the difference between an evolution and an upheaval. There is a further important contrast: the second must involve some self-awareness, while the first need not. Identity, in other words, always possesses a reflexive or subjective dimension, while character can at the limit remain purely objective, something perceived by others without the agent being conscious of it.

What obtains for individuals, holds good for peoples. If national character was thought to be a settled disposition, national identity is a self-conscious projection. It always involves a process of selection, in which the empirical mass of collective living is distilled into armorial form. Subjectivity is here inseparable from symbolization. The symbols capture the past and announce the future. Memory is crucial to identity, as it is not to character. So too is mission – the *raison d'être* of a specific contribution to the world, rather than the mere *être* of a particular existence within it. Together these two give the idea of national identity its eminently normative force. The notion of national character had itself never been purely descriptive, for the reason indicated by Kant: that character was also the virtue of self-mastery. Fouillée could say that he would only discuss the good sides of the French character, not to flatter his countrymen, but to spur them to live up to their ideals.[46] Orwell, for whom depicting and extolling his

---

46. *Esquisse Psychologique des Peuples Européens*, p. 455.

compatriots was mostly one, still felt there was a vital task of elevation ahead – his account of them was dedicated to 'bringing the real England to the surface'.[47] Here, as the heraldic title suggests, the work of extraction and sublimation is already closer to the tack of national identity. Orwell's own term hovers between the two notions – the 'native genius'. But his apostrophe of it anticipates many of the themes of the later literature: 'England will still be England, an everlasting animal stretching into the future and the past, and like all living things, having the power to change out of recognition and yet remain the same.'[48] Definitely a unicorn, rather than a lion.

In a more literate, less rawly demagogic way, national identity was to assume something like this guise: fusing the factual and the ideal, the mutable and the eternal. Braudel gives eloquent expression to the protean result. 'What, then, do we mean by the identity of France – if not a kind of superlative, if not a central problematic, if not the shaping of France by its own hand, if not the living result of what the interminable past has deposited, layer by layer, just as the imperceptible sedimentation of the seabed in the end created the firm foundations of the earth's crust? It is in sum a residue, an amalgam, a thing of additions and mixtures. It is a process, a fight against itself, destined to go on indefinitely. If it were to stop, everything would fall apart. A nation can have its *being* only at the price of forever searching for itself, forever transforming itself in the direction of its logical development, unceasingly testing itself against others and identifying itself with the best, the most essential part of itself.'[49] Here the prose, mimicking the accretions it evokes, continually alternates between layers of geology and of deontology – what has immemorially come to be, and what transcendentally ought to be – as principles of definition. *The Identity of France* can in this sense be regarded as a classic statement of the genre, at its most dignified and open-minded.

What has occasioned the rise of the discourse of national identity? Part of the answer lies in the decline of the idea of national character itself. As its reassuring outlines appeared to waver amidst post-war social changes, there was a need for some moral substitute. The narrower conception of identity fitted this role well – suggesting a more intimate, idealized bond than the gross links of daily custom. But there was to be a snag. Identity might be the deeper concept, but it is also – for nations as for persons – the more brittle. The very rigidity of its

47. *The Lion and the Unicorn*, London 1982, p. 123.
48. *The Lion and the Unicorn*, p. 70.
49. *L'Identité de la France*, I, p. 17; IF–I, p. 23.

social projection, into a few cherished images, makes it prey to a kind of structural anxiety. Causes for the latter were not long in coming. The developments that seemed to undermine the supports of national character in Europe sprang essentially from the market. But on their heels have come two changes affecting the state. The first was mass immigration from non-European zones, and the second the consolidation of the European Community. Issues of citizenship and sovereignty touch the nerves of national identity in a way that consumption and diversion do not. The symbolic political plane is its natural habitat. The growth of concern, erudite and popular, with national identity since the mid eighties must be understood against this background.

Braudel's book was one of its products. Of all European nations, France has traditionally been most prolific with historical self-portraits, which from the time of Guizot and Michelet onwards have served successive versions of the country's role in the world – bearer of culture, or liberty, or valour. Braudel rightly situated himself in this descent. But he was writing in an immediate context as well. By the Mitterrand Presidency, France had lost the illusions of *grandeur* revived with de Gaulle's magisterial rule of the Fifth Republic. Economically, it could no longer steer an independent policy in a Community dominated by Germany. Diplomatically, it had rejoined the ranks of the Atlantic Alliance commanded by America. Culturally, its prestige was being sustained wih garish outworks from London or Orlando. Moreover, within its borders it now contained a population of four million North African Muslims, jarring every racial and many republican images of the country. France had once been the great land of European immigration, capable of assimilating Poles, Italians, Jews, Belgians like no other. Maghrebin Arabs have so far proved a different matter. The historical shock they represent to the solaces of narcissism must be measured against the unusual nature of the French nation-state. It is often forgotten that France is the *only* large example of an ancient territorial state coinciding with a national community in Western Europe. Germany and Italy were long territorially divided; Britain and Spain remain nationally composite. In these conditions, the stage was set for the rise of Le Pen. It was the electoral breakthrough of the Front National (20 per cent in Marseille, 15 per cent in the *beaux-quartiers* of Paris) that forced the vocabulary of French identity onto the political agenda. Braudel's book appeared in early 1986, surrounded by opposing volumes across the ideological spectrum on the same subject – *L'Identité Française* mounted by Espaces 89 for the Left, countered by *L'Identité de la France* from the Club de l'Horloge for the Right (wound up by the Mayor of Nice, Jacques Médecin – who wished his fellow-citizens would pay more homage to Apollo than Dionysus, prior to his departure for the casinos of Uruguay).[50] Immigration and education, as one would expect, lie at the centre of these exchanges. Braudel too broaches them, decently and slightly apprehensively, as unavoidable topics of the day. It was in this climate, of communal tension and intellectual bemusement, that his book sold no fewer than 400,000 copies – becoming a public event in its own right.

In the same year, German public life was being shaken by the so-called Historians' Dispute, which broke out in the summer of 1986. Formally, its principal focus was the meaning of the Final Solution. But its substantive political battlefield – perceived as such on all sides – was the future of national identity. The conservatives Michael Stürmer and Andreas Hillgruber argued, in effect, that the crimes of the Third Reich did not cancel the traditional and fateful position of Germany in the centre of the continent. The most historically discontinuous national identity in Europe was still anchored geographically – the Germans continued to be the people of the Middle, as Nietzsche had termed them, and their reunification could not be deferred indefinitely.[51] On the other side of the dispute, Hans-Ulrich Wehler and Jürgen Habermas rejected any geopolitical definition of the nation as a retrograde heritage of the past that had led to the Nazi regime.[52] For Habermas, German – indeed any acceptable modern – national identity could only be 'post-conventional', that is based on a critical reception of universal principles. The theoretical account of identity here was modelled on the psychology of adolescence in Erikson and Kohlberg, a quirk of the German discussion. For Habermas, the political form of collective maturity would be a 'constitutional patriotism' cleaving to the West alone.[53] Events soon revealed the price for this lack of historical sense,

---

50. The leading essay from the Club de l'Horloge, by Yvan Blot, sets the note: 'L'Identité de la France – une Aspiration Menacée'. The opening rubric in the collection from Espaces 89 is 'Les Crises Identitaires'. Commenting on the success of the Front National, Hervé le Bras explained that the motivations of Le Pen's electorate were not merely a superficial xenophobia: 'they also express a crisis of national identity'; *Les Trois Frances*, p. 66.

51. Michael Stürmer, 'Deutsche Identität: auf der Suche nach der verlorenen Nationalgeschichte', and 'Mitten in Europa: Versuchung und Verdammnis der Deutschen', in *Dissonanzen des Fortschritts*, Munich 1986, pp. 201–209, 314–330; Andreas Hillgruber, *Zweierlei Untergang*, Berlin 1986, pp. 72–74.

52. For the principal historical reply, see Hans-Ulrich Wehler, *Entsorgung der deutschen Vergangenheit?*, Munich 1988, pp. 174–189, 210.

53. Jürgen Habermas, *Eine Art Schadensabwicklung*, Frankfurt 1987, pp. 135, 173–74; *The New Conservatism*, Cambridge, Mass. 1989, pp. 227, 261–62.

when its repetition by the SPD three years later left Kohl master of German unity.

If in France national self-examination was a reaction to loss of coherence and standing, in Germany the same concerns spelt a return to power and position in the world. The early eighties had already seen a wave of collections in which leading scholars debated the concept of national identity and its shape in Germany.[54] Behind such probing lay the formidable economic success of the Federal Republic. The dangers of this connexion have since formed the central argument of the spirited study by the young English historian Harold James, *A German Identity*. In a lively sketch, James suggests that historically German conceptions of their identity as a nation moved through a sequence from cultural to political to economic definitions in the late eighteenth and nineteenth centuries (roughly: Herder to Mommsen to Rochau), and then repeated the cycle in the twentieth (Mann to Hitler to Erhard). Relatively benign though current pride in the D-Mark might be, compared with the hubris of the *Gründerzeit*, economic performance was an inherently unreliable basis for a sense of national identity, subject to downswings and disillusionments. What was needed instead was stable political institutions commanding a dense network of traditional allegiances[55] – in other words, what Burke recommended and Westminster supplies. James was to be a trenchant critic of the left-liberal myopia about German unity, but his own prescriptions confuse legitimacy with identity as much as those of Habermas.[56] The German constitution is in fact far more democratic than the British, but it is not

---

54. See, for example, *Die deutsche Neurose – über die beschädigte Identität der Deutschen*, Frankfurt 1980 (sponsored by the Siemens Stiftung); *Die Identität der Deutschen*, Munich 1983 (edited by Werner Weidenfeld); *Die Last der Geschichte – Kontroversen zur deutschen Identität*, Cologne 1988 (edited by Thomas Gauly). The latter contains one of the rare comparative reflections on the form of national identity itself, by the distinguished classical historian Christian Meier, who points out that it is at once less exhaustive than the collective identity which defined the citizenry of the Greek city-state (which lacked a range of other attachments), and more consolatory – not so much conferring power on the individual through active membership of the community, as compensating for lack of power through a highly symbolized adherence to it: pp. 61–62.

55. *A German Identity*, London 1989, pp. 4, 6, 9, 209.

56. 'Die Nemesis der Einfallslosigkeit', *Frankfurter Allgemeine Zeitung*, 17 September 1990. Post unification, James in effect inverts his original argument. Here it is no longer the institutions of constitutional democracy which provide the necessary struts of national identity, but sentiments of national identity which must sustain democracy in Eastern Germany, which otherwise risks discredit from the inevitable economic hardships while capitalism is being introduced.

this national specificity that interests either – merely a generic parliamentary order as such, which of course in no way distinguishes Germany from any other member of the OECD. If economic nationalism is perilous, such constitutional patriotism is vacuous. Amidst the remorseless grinding of regions and classes from the East in the cement-mixer of the new unity, we can be sure we have not heard the end of the quest for German identity.

Meanwhile, over in Oxford, the assembled ranks of *History Workshop* were debating the same issues from a more radical perspective, in a series of conferences from 1984 onwards. The final results were published in three volumes on *Patriotism – the Making and Unmaking of British National Identity* in 1989. In his rich keynote essay Raphael Samuel, their organizer and editor, put his emphasis on the second of these processes. Distinguishing British from English identity at the outset – as harder and more formal, its connotations military–diplomatic–imperial rather than literary or rural, but also more inclusive for newcomers – he argued that attachment to it had notably fallen away since the 1950s. The fading of the Commonwealth, the decline or denaturalization of much of the economy, the discredit of the civil service, the marginalization of the established Church, the disappearance of anti-Americanism, had brought a general loss of respect for its traditional fixed points. What had multiplied by way of compensation were the innumerable efforts of the heritage industry, seconded by popular sensibility, to conserve or counterfeit the material bric-à-brac of the past – from bakelite cups to slag-heaps – and the folk life that went with them. Deadly official bombast had for the most part given way to inoffensively meretricious nostalgia. National identity, Samuel observed, is always a fitful ideal in the lives of individuals; but perhaps, he hinted, its forms were always more variegated in Britain than elsewhere, because of the absence of the binding pressure of invasions[57] – a surmise in which Hume's agreeable fancy is still running.

The most pointed alternative to this vision of patriotic declension to a mildly sentimental pluralism came from Tom Nairn. The monolithic devotion of the British to their monarchy, he suggested, whose cult had intensified in the post-war period, hardly squared with it. Nairn's study of the royal fixation, *The Enchanted Glass*, is in fact far the deepest single exploration of the mechanisms of national identification that we

---

57. 'Introduction; Exciting to be English', *Patriotism – the Making and Unmaking of British National Identity*, Vol. I, *History and Politics*, London 1989, p. xv.

possess. But its thrust is precisely that the Ukanian case is an abnormal one – the monarchy functioning as a fetishized surrogate for an ordinary attachment to the nation-state, blocked by the composite jurisdiction and constitutional archaism of 'Great Britain'. If the construction of any national identity involves projection of a few selected features of historical experience onto an emblematic plane, here – Nairn suggested – the exceptional rigidity of the symbolic investment was to be explained, as in fetishism proper, by the prohibition of the whole for which the magical part stood: 'a democratic and egalitarian nationalism'.[58] The normalcy of the latter may be doubted – the adjectives cling too smoothly to the noun; the ideologies of national unity have just as frequently served to mask social division and inequality. But the central force of the diagnosis is all too compelling. Amidst continuing economic difficulties and looming European integration, Britain has in no way escaped the modern anxieties of national identity, as the Bruges spirit and curricular lobbies testify; it has merely cast them in its own frozen forms.

Such tensions have been most acute in the three leading countries of Western Europe, the large states with a recent hegemonic past. They are significantly less in the two countries in the next rank down. Italy, with its long sense of disconnexion between popular life and public institutions, has seen no comparable output on national identity. Pavese's exchange – 'Do you love Italy?' 'No. Not Italy. The Italians'[59] – still expresses a widespread attitude. In keeping with it, the one major text on the subject is the caustic essay L'Italiano. Il Carattere Nazionale come Storia e come Invenzione by Giulio Bollati, a study of Risorgimento projects of cultural engineering and their sequels, as the successive efforts of a manipulative trasformismo to create a suitable Italian people for the Italian state.[60] In Spain, where once Unamuno and Ortega anguished over the essence of the nation – was its flaw a cult of isolating purity, or a lack of elites to give it backbone? – and where Américo Castro and Claudio Sánchez-Albornoz would later pursue its 'historical abode' back to mediaeval recesses of Judeo–Arab–Christian intercommunion or the origins of its 'enigma' into the mists of a Roman or Visigoth españolía,[61] a robust pragmatism now rules. In no country

58. 'Britain's Royal Romance', Patriotism, Vol. III, National Fictions, pp. 81–84.

59. The House on the Hill, London 1956, pp. 80–81.

60. The text was originally a contribution to the first volume of the Storia d'Italia edited by Einaudi, Turin 1972, and broadly inspired by Annales traditions; it was published in book form in 1983.

are the prosperous and educated so determined to shed everything formerly taken for national characteristics (cult of pride, disdain for work, austerity, fanaticism, etc). Here, as in Italy too, European integration represents upward, not downward, national mobility – an opportunity to rise above traditional identity, rather than a potential threat to it. The only Prime Minister thinking of changing his post for the Presidency of the Commission is in Madrid.

Below this duo there stretch the smaller states, already a majority of the members of the Community, and one that is going to increase.[62] Will their numbers tend to multiply the alarms of national identity, or gradually muffle them? This is the Europe of Hans Magnus Enzensberger's ironic ejaculation. His tour of the continent, composed in these years, circles round the periphery from Scandinavia through Poland to Portugal, in an elegant gesture ignoring the three central powers altogether. The boldness of the selection has its limits: as in the conventional sympathies of the time, the Balkans remain out of bounds. But it was too much for the American publisher, who crassly deleted the longest and most revealing chapter from the book in the English-language editions, perhaps because it was devoted to the smallest country, Norway – the one its author knew best. Enzensberger's reportage proceeds by vignette, anecdote, boutade, skirting comparisons or conclusions for queries and speculations. His wry

---

61. Unamuno's *En torno del Casticismo* was published in 1912, Ortega's *España Invertebrada* in 1922; Américo Castro's *La Realidad Histórica de España* in 1954, Sánchez-Albornoz's *España, Un Enigma Histórico* in 1962. For a tonic reaction to this polemical tradition, see Julio Caro Baroja's *El Mito del Carácter Nacional*, Madrid 1970, which illustrates the formation of stereotypes of Spanishness from the Renaissance onwards.

62. It is these that have inspired the one unquestionable masterpiece of the historical writing on national identity, Simon Schama's study of Dutch culture in the Golden Age, *The Embarrassment of Riches* (London 1987). The distinctive achievement of this work lies in Schama's clear-sighted treatment of Dutch identity as an elaborate normative construct worked up by legend, treatise, image, sermon, from a range of empirical materials – the marine setting and military dangers, the commercial fortune and religious scruples, and some of the household customs of the Republic – which secured its powerful aura of phenomenological reality. The objection that the book minimizes the divisions in Dutch society in a sense misunderstands its object – a social imaginary designed to be proof against them. The size of the Netherlands no doubt has something to do with the success of the study. Perhaps the most lively single contribution to the contemporary literature of national identity deals with another small country: Anton Pelinka's *Zur Osterreichischen Identität*, Vienna 1990, a caustic survey of the variety of projections of Austria, from the post-war years when affirmation of national difference became an insulation against the memory of the Ostmark, down to the uncertainties of the present – Austrian identity as bridge in Central Europe, or suitor to the EC, or extension for German unity, or emulator of Switzerland.

collages of each country avoid any grand claim of portraiture. There is scarcely any mention of national identities, and national character is roundly scouted. 'Could anything be more barren than the study of "national psychology", that mouldy compost heap of stereotypes, prejudices and *idées reçues?*'[63] Yet, he typically adds, 'it is impossible to dislodge these traditional garden gnomes' – who even in his pages make an occasional appearance: the docile Swedes or the tolerant Portuguese. But what *Ach Europa!* really offers is something else: a kaleidoscope of manners discreetly shaken into the glimpse of a politics. Enzensberger's wayward cameos have a definite message: they bespeak detestation of bureaucratic dictatorship, and reserve towards clerical revival, in the East; and suspicion towards the welfare state, social planning, mass production, heavy industry, traditional parties, ideological extremism in the West. The land where these values are most nearly realized is Norway, of which Enzensberger writes with an intimate affection: a nation, he says, at once behind and in front of the rest of Europe, folk-museum and future-laboratory, 'monument to obstinacy and moody idyll',[64] whose social arrangements might yet recapture the utopian ideas of Marx.

Norway was also, of course, the only country to reject membership of the European Community by popular vote. Consistent with his dislike for all that is too big and systemic, Enzensberger shows no inclination to find the antidote to the pretensions of Paris, London or Bonn in Strasbourg, let alone Brussels, as others of his generation on the Left have done. In his imaginary conclusion, depicting the continent in 2006, European unity is sidestepped as nimbly as national identity was in the real accounts that precede it. Communist tyrants overthrown and American troops gone, the Commission is little more than ceremonial, as Europe – the follies of integration forgotten – basks in a congenial cantonalism. A modest *Kleinstaaterei* is welcome to all, save the recidivist French. The peoples of Europe are spared world power, which – as the continuing fate of the US demonstrates – has always made a collective cretin of those who enjoy it.

War in the Middle East has since put this proposition to a test, where it might be thought that its author, forgetting himself, has momentarily illustrated it. Diagrammatically, the opposite political response to the Allied expedition came from Régis Debray, the writer on the Left whose theoretical vision of the future of nations and of Europe forms

---

63. *Ach Europa!*, Frankfurt 1987, p. 105; *Europe, Europe*, New York 1989, p. 76.
64. *Ach Europa!*, pp. 310–14.

the most striking antithesis to Enzensberger's. Pointing out how vener-
able is the tradition of comparing Middle Eastern dictators to Hitler (it
was the standard image for Nasser at the time of Suez), and how deeply
Mitterrand was involved in the Fourth Republic's associated propaganda and repression in North Africa, Debray rejected French participation in the attack on Iraq; the line to which France should adhere was
the contrary tradition represented by de Gaulle.[65] Debray had, as it
happened, just devoted a programmatic book to the General, *A
Demain de Gaulle*, intended to reclaim his inspiration for a contemporary politics of the French Left. For Debray, de Gaulle was the statesman
who best understood that the principal agents of modern history are –
contrary to both liberal and Marxist beliefs – neither ideas nor classes,
but nations. This was not a blinkered or irrational nationalism. De
Gaulle avoided the vocabulary of French chauvinism, never speaking of
native roots or foreign bodies. 'The term national *identity* was foreign
to him.'[66] The General did not believe in any fixed essence of France –
he was an existentialist of the nation, convinced that it could make of
itself what it wanted, within the historical possibilities afforded by its
past. Debray contrasts what he sees as de Gaulle's conception with the
opposing traditions of Enlightenment (American) contractualism and
(Germanic) romanticism: for the leader of the Free French and the
founder of the Fifth Republic, the nation was neither an artificial
juridical pact nor an organic cultural community, but rather a 'symbolic heritage' joining a past and a will, a language chosen by none and a
legislature elected by all. The sign of this synthesis was the peculiar
blend of the romantic and the classical in de Gaulle's appeal to his
people, which combined the warmth of a *rassemblement* with the
coldness of a *Rechtsstaat*. Its fruit was a characteristically temperate
but deliberate realism in the conduct of foreign affairs, that made de
Gaulle the most far-sighted statesman of his time – one which has not
passed away.

The lesson of this experience, Debray argues, is the permanence of
the national passion as a motor force of political life even in the world
of high-tech consumption and international integration that marks
European capitalism today – let alone the outlands just beyond it, from
the Baltic to the Black Sea and the Mediterranean. The advance of
technology does not produce a dream-free mentality. In post-commu-

---

65. 'La Guerre – Lettre Ouverte aux Socialistes', *Le Nouvel Observateur*, 14–20
February 1991; compare Hans-Magnus Enzensberger, 'Hitlers Wiedergänger', *Der
Spiegel*, 4 February 1991.
66. *A Demain de Gaulle*, Paris 1990, p. 96.

nist or post-colonial societies, the arrival of the modern typically triggers the eruption of the archaic as compensation – the queues in Moscow lengthen for McDonald's and St Basil's alike. In post-industrial conditions, the same dialectic can be more benign. Delivered from older material pressures, peoples will above all seek to recover themselves, in new forms of national culture made that much more precious by the global commodity-nexus encompassing them. The more European the Community becomes, the more inventively and consciously distinct its members will want to be, as nations in their own right. The echo of Bauer here is apt: for the other side of Debray's book is a strong statement of what socialism should still mean in the contemporary world, beyond the timid affairism of local governments of the Left.

The differing diagnoses of these writers point to a central ambiguity of capitalist rationalization and its discontents, which only events can resolve. If the preoccupations of national identity are a product of the material erosion of much of what was once thought to be national character, will the further progress of a cosmopolitan modernity dissolve or intensify these? In his recent survey of *Nations and Nationalism since 1750* Eric Hobsbawm concludes that the owl of Minerva has now flown over them.[67] In the skies over the USSR and Eastern Europe, some would more readily detect the petrel; others the albatross. The rival hypotheses are, at all events, going to be tested in two huge experimental theatres – the disintegration of the former Soviet world, and the integration of the western half of Europe. Capitalism and the nation-state are more or less coevals. There were once those who thought they would pass away together, or that the second would outlive the first. Now it is more generally wondered whether capitalism is not final, and nation-states are fated to become nominal. The answers to these questions are not necessarily going to be the same. They constitute the two main incognitos of *fin-de-siècle* politics.

1991

---

67. *Nations and Nationalism since 1750*, London 1990, p. 183.

13

The Ends of History

In the spring of 1989, an arresting work of intellectual history was completed in Germany. Its author, Lutz Niethammer, had hitherto distinguished himself as an oral historian specializing in the reconstruction of popular life from below. The field of *Posthistoire* is virtually antithetical.[1] Its subject is the emergence of a web of speculations on the end of history, at the highest reaches of the European intelligentsia, in the middle years of this century. Drawing on a variety of philosophical and sociological sources, these could stem from a range of distinct intuitions. Niethammer distinguishes three main variants: the idea of a spiritual closure of the repertory of heroic possibilities, derivable from Nietzsche; the vision of a petrification of society into a single vast machine, associated with Weber; and intimations of civilizational entropy, following from Henry Adams. But the focus of his study lies downstream from ultimate origins, in the confluence of such themes into a striking intellectual configuration that he situates, with some precision, in the Franco–German area between the time of the Popular Front and the Marshall Plan.

It was then that an uncanny skein of thinkers started to suggest that history was nearing its terminus. In a brilliant feat of intellectual detection, Niethammer brings to light the hidden links or affinities – cultural or political – within a group of otherwise very contrasted theorists of the period: Henri de Man, Arnold Gehlen, Bertrand de Jouvenel, Carl Schmitt, Alexandre Kojève, Ernst Jünger, Henri Lefebvre, even in their way Walter Benjamin and Theodor Adorno. *Posthistoire,* a French term that exists only in German, adopted in the fifties by Gehlen from a reading of de Man, signifies for Niethammer less a theoretical system than a structure of feeling, the precipitate of a certain common historical experience. These were thinkers, Niethammer argues, who shared early hopes of a radical overthrow of the established social order in Europe, as activists or sympathizers with the

---

1. Hamburg, 1989: the preface is dated May, publication was in November.

major 'parties of movement' of the inter-war period – socialist, fascist, or communist; and then disappointments which crystallized into a deep scepticism about the possibility of further historical change as such. The result was something like a collective vision – glimpsed from many different angles – of a stalled, exhausted world, dominated by recursive mechanisms of bureaucracy and ubiquitous circuits of commodities, relieved only by the extravagances of a phantasmatic imaginary without limit, because without power. In post-historical society, 'the rulers have ceased to rule, but the slaves remain slaves.'[2] For Niethammer, this diagnosis of the time is not without persuasive force: it corresponds to many particular experiences of daily life and local observations of social science. But they who speak of the end of history do not escape it. The pathos of *Posthistoire* is the intelligible product of a political conjuncture interpreted in the categories of a philosophical tradition.

For this is a vision, Niethammer argues, that should be understood as an inversion of the optimistic theories of history of the eighteenth and mid nineteenth centuries, that had once looked forward to universal peace or freedom or fraternity as the end-goal of human progress, in secularized versions of the teleology of sacred history. That serene Enlightenment confidence – shared by Holbach and Kant, Comte and Marx – in the objective course of social development had fallen into discredit by the close of the last century. What succeeded it were tense voluntarist bids to achieve millennial ends by force of subjective will, in the doctrines of Nietzsche, Sorel or Lenin. These acquired a mass following during and in the wake of the First World War, and form the immediate background to the revolutionary ambitions of those who were to become the theorists of *Posthistoire*. Their original expectations cashiered, these did not abandon the metaphysic of a historical transfiguration, but rather reversed its sign. The optimism of evolutionary progress or collective will gave way to an elitist cultural pessimism, that saw only petrefaction and massification in the stabilized Western democracies after the Second World War. Time still arrived at its term: but no longer with the meaning of an end – simply the facticity of an ending, disabling any ulterior aspiration or purpose. In metaphorically projecting their own political experience as a world-history gone blank, these thinkers characteristically paid little heed to the material development which actually threatened to bring history to end, the dangers of nuclear war; still less to the fate of the famished majority of humanity outside the zone of industrial privilege. *Posthistoire*, a discourse of the

2. *Posthistoire*, p. 156.

end of meaning rather than the end of the world, was consistently blind to such questions: *die Sinnfrage verdunkelt die Existenzfrage*.[3]

Evidently critical, Niethammer's treatment of the cluster of writers at the centre of his account is never dismissive. Written from the Left, about a set of figures many of whom were or ended on the Right, its method – inspired by Benjamin's mosaics – is delicate and diagonal. The historical understanding it brings to the reveries of post-history does not seek to diminish them, as significant reflections of their time. Niethammer's conclusions lie elsewhere. These were generally intellectuals who, after their political disappointments, adopted the stance of an elite equally distant from the masses and from the apparatuses of the post-war order, conceiving themselves as isolated seers. From this posture they sought an overarching viewpoint, capable of distilling the substance of universal experience into a single narrative. Against this twofold pretension, Niethammer affirms the creed of a democratic history from below. Socially, intellectuals form in fact one part of the mass from which they like to distinguish themselves, a collectivity that dissolves on reflection into so many individual subjects. Epistemologically, truth lies first of all in the direct life-experiences of these subjects. It is their clarification that is the first duty of the historian, who is best advised to eschew all larger structural interpretations save as limiting surmises. Critical knowledge is to be found, not in the vain filibuster of macro-narratives, but in the modest commonplace books of the multitude – whose measure of freedom and responsibility is the only safeguard against the dangers which the diviners of post-history saw, as well as those they missed.[4] The concluding judgement of Niethammer's study could be taken as an obituary, laying to rest an esoteric doctrine whose creative time has passed.

Two months later, in July 1989, Francis Fukuyama published his essay 'The End of History?' in Washington.[5] There has rarely been a more striking *rebondissement* in the fortunes of an idea. Within a year, an arcane philosophical wisdom had become an exoteric image of the age, as Fukuyama's arguments sped round the media of the globe. Unaware of Niethammer's work (completed in May, published in November), this American reprise was directly linked to the Franco–German nexus studied in *Posthistoire* through the figure of Alexandre Kojève – the declared theoretical source of Fukuyama's

---

3. *Posthistoire*, p. 165.

4. *Posthistoire*, pp. 165–172.

5. *The National Interest*, Summer 1989, pp. 3–18. Fukuyama and Niethammer must have completed their respective texts all but simultaneously.

construction. But the connection represents a paradox for Niethammer's verdict. For the new version of the end of history did not come
from any vantage-point, real or imaginary, in equidistant isolation
from the populace and power, but from the bureaux of the State
Department itself, and its organizing theme was not one of forbidding
pessimism, but of confident optimism. The change of register was also a
shift in plane. In the Franco–German philosophers of history there was
always more philosophy than history, politics glimmering only as
elusive metaphor in the background of the diagnosis. In Fukuyama's
intervention the relations were reversed, history and politics in an
emphatic sense occupying the foreground, with philosophical references forming a tracery behind them. The central thesis of his original
essay was, of course, that humanity has reached the end-point of its
ideological evolution with the triumph of Western liberal democracy
over all competitors at the end of the twentieth century. Fascism, once a
powerful rival, had been durably destroyed in the Second World War.
Communism, the great post-war adversary, was in visible collapse,
surrendering as a system to the capitalism it had once sought to
overthrow. These two global alternatives discredited, there remained
only local residues of the historical past: nationalisms without distinctive social content or universal claim, fundamentalisms confined to
particular religious communities, in the backward zones of the Third
World. The victory of liberal capitalism had been won not only in
Europe, with the defeat of Nazism and the disintegration of Stalinism,
but in the equally momentous battleground of Asia too, with the post-
war transformation of Japan, the current liberalization of South Korea
and Taiwan, the developing commercialization of China. In the industrialized world, competition between national states would continue.
But purged of ideological or military toxins, it would concern mainly
economic issues, within a collaborative framework of which the Common Market perhaps already furnished a model. In this view ethnic
tensions or sectarian passions, terror or insurgency, might still prolifer-
ate in the South. But they do not compromise the deep configuration of
the time. For the end of history is not the cessation of all change or
conflict, but the exhaustion of any viable alternatives to the civilization
of the OECD. Progress towards freedom now has only one path. With
the rout of socialism, Western liberal democracy has emerged as the
final form of human government, bringing historical development to its
close.

This outcome, Fukuyama argues, was foreseen by Hegel. The first
philosopher to transcend fixed conceptions of human nature, his
phenomenology of the restless transformations of the spirit issued, not

into the bad infinity of an interminable process of change, but into the moment of an absolute culmination, in which reason as freedom on earth was realized in the institutions of a liberal state. The merit of Kojève was to have shown that Hegel believed this hour had come with Napoleon's victory over Prussia at Jena, breaking the power of the *ancien régime* in Germany and laying the basis for the universal spread of the principles of the French Revolution. The essential accuracy of Hegel's conviction that history was at its end is unimpaired by the two hundred years that have followed. For the greatness of his philosophy lay in its unambiguous affirmation of the primacy of ideas in history – the truth that the developments of material reality do not determine, but conform to the emergence of ideal principles. What prevailed at Jena was not the completed practice but the regulative principle of a new political order. Massive struggles and upheavals were still in store, from the abolition of the slave-trade to the victory of suffragism, before liberal ideals acquired their full institutional shape in the West, and were then gradually extended beyond it. But the fundamental outline of the liberties Hegel had perceived as the definitive form of modern freedom was never improved upon. 'The state that emerges at the end of history is liberal insofar as it recognizes and protects through a system of law man's universal right to freedom, and democratic in so far as it exists only with the consent of the governed.'[6] Such freedom includes, of course, as it did in the time of Jena, the rights of private property and the operations of the market economy. If liberalism as a political order is inseparable from capitalism as an economic system, however, this is not in the sense that the latter generates the former as its real basis. Rather both reflect an underlying alteration in the realm of consciousness which governs the course of the world. But the consumer abundance that is the unique achievement of capitalist economics unquestionably consolidates the democratic values of liberal politics, stabilizing the change first grasped by Hegel in a way that could be expected at the end of history. For all the deliverance it brings, however, the conclusion of the story of human freedom has its costs. Daring ideals, high sacrifices, heroic strivings will pass away, amidst the humdrum routines of shopping and voting; art and philosophy wither, as culture is reduced to the curation of the past; technical calculations replace moral or political imagination. The cry of the owl is mournful in the night.

In its clarity and boldness, this finalization of history has set off more – far more – public controversy than any earlier version. The most

---

6. 'The End of History?', p. 5.

striking feature of the discussion which followed the publication of Fukuyama's essay was the virtual universality of the rejection which it met. For once, most of the Right, Centre and Left were united in their reaction. For different reasons, liberals, conservatives, social democrats, communists all expressed incredulity or abhorrence of Fukuyama's arguments.[7] Two kinds of objection were consistently raised against Fukuyama. The first was that his construction rests on a basic misrepresentation of Hegel. The second was that it involves a complete misconception of the age – ingenuously apologetic for some, dangerously insouciant for others. Each of these criticisms, made before the publication of Fukuyama's book *The End of History and the Last Man* in 1992 amplified his case, bears examination. Before looking at them, however, one thing should already be plain. Niethammer's profile of the philosophical figure of post-history, penetrating though it is, does not capture all its variations, which have proved richer than he suggests. The concluding cadences of Fukuyama's essay, echoing late reflections in Kojève, belong to the portrait of *Posthistoire*. But here they appear as if an ironic after-thought, in an account whose central theme is a robust affirmation of the democratic prosperity Jünger or Gehlen scorned, and whose function is precisely to mediate between the official worlds of government and popular currents of opinion with a compelling public vision of the time. Such a role suggests a limit not just of Niethammer's description of the discourse of post-history, but of his recommended antidote to it. For his critique of the Franco–German tradition in effect concludes, not with an alternative to its diagnosis of the age, contesting its substantive theses, but with a call to eschew such ventures altogether – rejecting any macro-historical narrative as intellectually and politically overweening. Currently, the effect of such a withdrawal would be to leave the American variant in possession of the field. If this is to be questioned, it can only be on its own – legitimate, even inescapable – terrain. The values of daily experience and local investigation are real; but they are no refuge from the course of the world. In general modern historians have nearly always reacted, understandably, against philosophies of history. But these have not gone away, and are unlikely to, as long as the demand

---

7. Compare, for example, the trend of responses in *The National Interest*, Summer and Fall 1989 (Pierre Hassner, Gertrude Himmelfarb, Irving Kristol, Samuel Huntington, Leon Wieseltier, Frederick Will), with those in *Marxism Today*, November 1989 (Jonathan Steele, Edward Mortimer, Gareth Stedman Jones); or *The National Review*, 27 October 1989 (John Gray), with *Time*, 11 September 1989 (Strobe Talbott), across to *The Nation*, 22 September 1989 (Christopher Hitchens).

for social meaning over time persists. The idea of a closure of history has a more complicated pedigree than is often assumed – one which merits consideration in its own right, for the light it sheds on the political issues posed by contemporary versions.

1. Hegel

In other words, the end of history is best tackled from its beginning. Fukuyama's construction has consistently claimed the authority of Hegel for the form of its reasoning. How far is it entitled to this mantle? Numerous critics have complained of supererogation. There are, in fact, two distinct issues here. Did Hegel maintain that history had come to an end? If so, what kind of an end was it? The answer to the first question is less straightforward than it seems. In the letter of his texts, the phrase is scarcely to be found. Nor is there any single passage in his writing where the idea is directly spelt out and developed as such. But there can be no doubt that the logic of Hegel's whole system virtually required it as a conclusion, and that there is sufficient evidence of something like its assumption in the various ciphers of his work. In its psychological register, the *Phenomenology* already speaks of history as the conscious, self-mediating evolution of the Spirit, through the succession of its temporal forms, to the goal of absolute knowledge of itself.[8] The institutional survey of *The Philosophy of Right* declares that 'the present has cast off its barbarity – what is unjust and arbitrary, and the truth has ceased to be other-worldly – a contingent force', allowing 'true reconciliation, which reveals the state as the image and actuality of reason, to become objective'.[9] In the historical account of the *Lectures on the Philosophy of History*, the actualization of freedom is 'the ultimate goal at which the world-historical process has been

---

8. 'The *goal*, Absolute Knowing, or Spirit that knows itself as Spirit, has for its path the recollection of the Spirits as they are in themselves and as they accomplish the organization of their realm. Their preservation, regarded from the side of their free existence appearing in the form of contingency, is History; but regarded from the side of their comprehended organization, is the Science of Knowing in the sphere of appearance: the two together, comprehended History, form alike the recollection and calvary of absolute spirit, the actuality, truth and certainty of its throne, without which it would be lifeless and alone.' *Phänomenologie des Geistes, Werke* Vol. 3, Frankfurt 1970, p. 591; *Phenomenology of the Spirit*, (ed. J.N. Findlay), Oxford 1977, p. 493. Henceforward W–3 and PS respectively.

9. *Grundlinien der Philosophie des Rechts, Werke* Vol. 7, § 360 – p. 512; *Elements of the Philosophy of Right*, (ed. Allen Wood), Cambridge 1991, p. 380. Henceforward W–7 and EPR respectively.

aiming . . . which alone realizes and fulfills itself, as what is constant amidst the ceaseless change of events and conditions, and their effective principle.'[10] The *Lectures on the History of Philosophy* announce, in the most emphatic key of all, that 'a new epoch has arisen in the world', for 'the world spirit has now succeeded in shedding all alien objective existence and finally grasping itself as absolute' – 'such is the standpoint of the present, and the series of spiritual forms is therewith for the moment concluded.'[11] The terms and referents change, but the gesture of closure is insistently repeated. If the end of history was never thematized by Hegel, it is easy to see how it was deduced from him. But the difference has its importance. For if Hegel himself never actually coined the phrase, or quite fixed the notion, there were two reasons. The ultimate instance of his philosophy was not history, but spirit – and history was only one side of its diremption, the other being nature;[12] the overcoming of the division between the two was conceived as a result, rather than an ending. Hegel virtually never uses the terms *Ende* or *Schluss* in the lexicon of his closures: only *Ziel, Zweck* or *Resultat*. The reason for this is at one level simple. In German, there is no word that combines the two senses of 'end' in English, as terminus and as purpose, and Hegel's essential concern was with the second rather than the first. The distinction between the two can be seen with emblematic clarity in Kant, the original source of the idea of a universal history. Kant's vision of human progress is radically teleological, in keeping with the cast of his philosophy as a whole. History has an 'ultimate aim', the attainment of the highest good – a state in which human happiness and moral perfection tend to coincide. This is the *Endzweck* of creation at large. But this purpose is not an ending. Kant poured a scathing irony on that notion, in one of his most playful texts, *Das Ende aller Dinge,* whose theme – directed against Christian conceptions of the Last Judgement – was the dangerous absurdity of

---

10. *Vorlesungen über die Philosophie der Geschichte, Werke* Vol. 12, p. 33; *The Philosophy of History* (ed. C.J. Friedrich), New York 1956, p. 19. Henceforward *W–12* and *PH*.

11. *Vorlesungen über die Geschichte der Philosophie*, Vol. III, *Werke* Vol. 20, pp. 460–61; *Lectures on the History of Philosophy*, Vol. III, London 1896, pp. 551–52. Henceforward *W–20* and *LHP–3*.

12. 'Spirit produces itself as Nature, and as the State; nature is its unconscious work, in the course of which it appears to itself something different, and not spirit; but in the deeds of life of History, as also of Art, it brings itself to pass in conscious fashion; it knows various modes of its reality, but only modes. In science alone does it know itself as absolute spirit and this knowledge, or spirit, is its only true existence.' *W–20*, p. 460; *LHP*, p. 552.

moral fancies of the end of time.[13] Goal and stop are separate terms in this tradition, as they were in ordinary language itself. The concept of the end of history in its full contemporary ambiguity had to await translation into French. Kojève's *fin de l'histoire* spells something new.

If the actual outcome of Hegel's synthesis is thus a philosophical consummation more than a social end-state, it remains plausible that the one must in principle imply some version of the other. What was then the political system that realized reason for Hegel? Can it be described as a liberal institutional order? Much of the interest of Hegel's political thought lies in the difficulty of giving any simple answer to this question – partly because of chronological shifts within it, but mainly because of its substantive complexity. By the most relevant criteria, however, Hegel's political outlook belonged to the European liberalism of his time. For central to it was the rule of law, as this was understood by his contemporaries – a public order that guaranteed the rights of the individual to personal freedom, private property and unhindered opinion, and a career open to talents in the offices of the state. Such liberalism was not democratic, of course, since it feared popular rule and rejected universal suffrage. Hegel was no exception in this regard. In that sense, it is naturally an anachronism to ascribe any paternity of liberal democracy to him: like nearly every other liberal of his day, he was a constitutional monarchist. On the other hand, in so far as there was to be an evident continuity – both theoretical and institutional – in the subsequent history of capitalism between the *Rechtsstaat* and the *Volksstaat,* as limited government under the rule of law developed into modern representative democracy, Fukuyama's annotation can be treated as if it were an anticipatory shorthand. The distinctive features of Hegel's political thought which his essay obscures do not concern its distance from twentieth-century democratic norms, but the points at which it diverges from mainstream assumptions of early nineteenth-century liberalism.

---

13. See *Werke*, Vol. 8, Berlin 1912, pp. 327–339. Kant wrote this singular document on the eve of his censorship by the Prussian monarchy for undermining religious authority: it concludes by impudently suggesting that official enforcement of orthodoxy would render Christian doctrine so unpopular that the result would be in its own terms the reign of Antichrist, cutting off Christianity's vocation to become a world religion – 'the (perverse) end of all things'. There is no really good commentary on the text. In his *Conjectures on the Beginning of Human History*, Kant does subtitle a section *Beschluss der Geschichte*, but what this signifies is the end of the first steps in social development that are the object of his surmise – leaving humanity simply at a stage when nomads and agriculturalists start to fuse – not of the course of history as such, as has sometimes wrongly been suggested.

The first of these was Hegel's critique of any atomistic notion of citizenry or instrumental conception of the state. Inheriting from the culture of the Enlightenment a deep admiration for the the public life of the Greek city-state, in which active participation in the government and rites of the *polis* was the central meaning of individual freedom, Hegel came to believe that such immediate civic unity was a form that could no longer be recovered in modern conditions: socio-economic differentiation and religious development had created another kind of subjectivity, whose freedom demanded a more complex political structure. His contemporary Constant, the most logical mind of classical liberalism, saw the same kind of contrast between ancient and modern societies, and drew the conclusion that their respective forms of liberty were virtually antithetical. The ancient republics were small warlike states, whose citizens could devote most of their energies to public – mainly martial – pursuits, because production and trade were left to slaves, in a setting of rigid civic conformity. Modern societies, on the other hand, were large-scale nations devoted to commerce, in which individuals had neither chance nor time to engage much in public affairs, but far greater opportunity to choose their own modes of life. The proper role of the state was thus first and foremost to protect the private autonomy of the citizens, even if it was desirable to foster a certain public spirit as well – within the bounds of the modestly possible.[14] For Hegel, on the other hand, the opposition between the two ideals of freedom was not incurable: the task of the modern *Rechtsstaat* was to articulate them in a rational synthesis. The architecture of state and civil society that is the hallmark of his political theory was designed to enable this. Civil society as a system of needs was the realm of particular economic pursuits, in which the atomism of the market and the individualism of the modern subject prevailed, in the characteristic pattern of negative freedom. The state, with its impersonal civil service, by contrast embodied the universal principle of political will, as the positive freedom of the community. But these two were not counterposed abstractions: they formed an interconnected structure. For civil society was neither self-standing, nor simply a domain of commerce and pleasure. Beneath its transactions lay the family as the primary unit of any customary social life; and within its compass fell not only the exchanges of the market, but also the

---

14. For Constant's most influential statement of his contrast, the famous lecture *De la Liberté des Anciens comparée à celle des Modernes*, delivered in 1819 (as Hegel was giving his lectures on the philosophy of right at Heidelberg), see *Political Writings* (ed. Biancamaria Fontana), Cambridge 1988, pp. 309–328.

institutions of the law and – crucially – the provision of public works and the organization of corporate associations. Above these rose the state with its constitutional framework of sovereign authority, executive and legislative powers, and external relations. The three levels of this conception do not form separable zones of society, but compose an ascending structure in which each lower moment is subsumed into the higher. In this conception the nexus between family and civil society is unproblematic. The crux of the scheme lies in the way it envisages the integration of civil society into the state. Here there is a double overlap. On the one hand, public functions now normally imputed to the state – education, welfare, health, communications – are located in the space of civil society. On the other hand, corporate associations originating in civil society are lodged in the political framework of the state, as the elective units of the Estates Assembly.

These interlocking forms are the sign of Hegel's originality as a political thinker. The conventional liberalism of his time straightforwardly divided the private and public spheres, and limited government to instrumental functions as the guarantor of individual liberties. The link between the two was secured by representative institutions, based on a censitary electorate defined by property qualifications. For Hegel, by contrast, the political life of a community was ideally a realm of expressive meaning, in which the subjective freedom of individual agents was translated into a common objective configuration, the *Sittlichkeit* of the nation. The corporations, as occupational associations, consequently become the natural mediations between civil society and the state, as collective rather than atomic, and professional rather than residential, bodies. Hegel did not reject property qualifications for political participation outright, but for him *Gewerbe* commanded *Vermögen* rather than the other way round.[15] Not the abstract, isolate possession of money, but the concrete pursuit of a calling shared by others, was the condition of responsible suffrage. In this conception, work and solidarity become stepping-stones of meaning to the higher sense of the state.

If the device of corporate associations was designed to remedy the atomization of market society, the function of their counterpart – what Hegel called 'policing' institutions – was largely to check its polarization. Unusually among his contemporaries, Hegel had a very strong sense of the exploitative and crisis-ridden logic of early industrial

---

15. W–7, § 310 – pp. 479–480; *EPR*, pp. 349–350.

capitalism, the jagged patterns of accumulation of wealth and over-production at one end of society and of new kinds of misery and dependency at the other. To limit these, some regulation of the unbridled workings of the economy – the system of needs – was necessary, both to moderate the 'dangerous convulsions' of the market and to assure every member of society 'the right to subsistence'.[16] But how was this to be done? If the regulative authorities, or wealthier classes, provided direct relief to the poor, they would undermine the motivation to work; but if they provided work, they would exacerbate the periodic tendency to overproduction. After announcing the need for social intervention to assure the minimum welfare of every citizen, Hegel effectively despairs of it. The only solution to the phenomenon of mass poverty and dependency, which not merely contradict the very principle of subjective freedom but generate a demoralized rabble that menaces social stability, is overseas expansion – the conquest of markets and colonies abroad in which surplus goods can be sold and excess population can be settled.[17] The dilemmas of social security must eventually find their release in imperialism.

If the drive for such expansion springs from the dialectic of civil society, its systematic organization is the work of the state. Hegel assumes a plurality of states arrayed against one other in external competition. Their principle is necessarily particular, as each embodies its own ethical form of life. The *Sittlichkeit* of any given community is specific to it. But it is a strange substance – a particularity without quiddity, so to speak. For while Hegel regularly uses the term *Volk* and not infrequently *Nation* to designate the bearer of *Sitten*, the national character of his states is in retrospect curiously vestigial. For national-ism itself, in the Romantic sense, he had nothing but scorn: there are no passages in his writing so savage, in fact, as his letters on the *Deutsch-dumm* of the War of Liberation and the patriotic antics celebrating the Congress of Vienna.[18] Nor did he set much store by ethnic identity or

---

16. *W–7* § 236, 240 – pp. 385, 387; *EPR* pp. 262, 264. In his Jena texts of 1803–4, Hegel's view of the market yields little to that of Marx: 'Need and labour are raised into this universality, and so create in a great nation an immense system of communality and mutual dependence, a life of death moving within itself, thrashing to and fro blindly and elementally, that like a wild animal calls for continual strict curbing and control': *Gesammelte Werke*, Vol. 6, Hamburg 1975, p. 324; *System of Ethical Life and First Philosophy of Spirit*, Albany 1979, p. 249.

17. *W–7*, § 246, 248 – pp. 391–93; *EPR*, pp. 267–69.

18. In 1813 – 'if there are by chance any liberated individuals to be seen, I will rise to my feet.' In 1814, 'according to a few rumours, the era after the Congress of Vienna is to

linguistic continuity, even in moderate Enlightenment guise: it is striking how unaffected he was by Herder. The idea of a national 'culture' in the modern sense is absent – the term never appears in his work.[19] Religious cult is more significant, from his early writing on Greece to his late surveys of Europe, where Protestantism and Catholicism remain the central dividing-line between Germanic and Latin nations. But since the Roman faith is treated unambiguously as a fetter to be overcome in the contemporary age,[20] even this distinction yields no real content for the idea of a legitimate plurality of ethical forms of life. There is a logic to this paradox. The variety of national states is structurally underdetermined in Hegel's vision of the modern world, because there is only room for one truly rational version at a time. The stages of history form a sequence of natural principles realizing the development of the world spirit, each of which is allotted to a single nation, and confers on it 'fulfilment, fortune and fame' in turn. This nation becomes 'the *dominant* one in world history for this epoch, *and only once in history can it have this epochal role*' – but so long as it enjoys this 'absolute right' as the bearer of the world spirit, 'the spirits of other nations are without rights, and like those whose epoch has

---

be assured by an interesting literary–artistic idea: the erection of the great memorial column dedicated to the Nation along with a comprehensive national archive for the conservation of Old German monuments and patriotic relics of all sorts, including the song of the *Nibelungen*, Imperial jewelry, King Roger's shoes, electoral capitulations, charters of freedom, Albrecht Dürer's woodcuts, Norica and so on. It will be built on a quiet spot, so that its enjoyment will be more secure from the noise of the rest of reality . . . The entire Congress, however, is to be concluded with a great ceremony, a torchlight procession with the ringing of bells and roaring of cannons to the "ultimate rule of reason" in which the German people [*Pippel*] will be trampled in the dirt. Behind Pippel there follow, as valets and attendants, a few tame house cats, such as the Inquisition, the Jesuit Order, and then all the armies with their sundry commissioned, princely, and titled marshals and generals.' *Briefe von und an Hegel*, (ed. J. Hoffmeister), Vol. 2, Hamburg 1953, pp. 14, 43; *Hegel: The Letters*, Bloomington 1984, pp. 299, 312.

19. There is a sketch of 'national characters' in the anthropological section of the *Encyclopaedia*, similar to the survey in Kant's *Philosophical Anthropology*, if less flattering to the Germans. But they are assigned the humble rank of natural qualities of the soul, before free spirit unfolds: *Enzyklopädie der philosophischen Wissenschaften im Grundrisse*, III, *Werke* Vol. 10, Frankfurt 1970, § 394 (*Zusatz*), pp. 63–70; *Hegel's Philosophy of Mind*, Oxford 1973, pp. 46–51 – henceforward *W–10* and *HPM*.

20. *W–12*, p. 535; *PH*, pp. 452–53. Lukács rightly emphasizes the significance of the later Hegel's shift away from the French Revolution towards the Reformation as the real turning-point of modern history – as he points out, the conclusion of the *Lectures on the Philosophy of History* suggests that 'a socio-political upheaval of the sort that resulted in the French Revolution was only possible and necessary in countries where the Reformation had failed to carry the day': *The Young Hegel*, London 1975, p. 458.

passed, no longer count in world history.'[21] The *dramatis personae* of this succession are significantly vaguer than the standard translations suggest: Hegel uses the term *Volk* with a widely fluctuating range of reference, from small city-states to broad civilizations. The Germanic world, with which the *Lectures on the Philosophy of History* conclude their survey of the progress of the spirit, at times extends across most of Europe, at others indicates its Northern region, and elsewhere narrows to the German-speaking lands alone. The indeterminacy is a symptom of the aporia that the multiplicity of states introduces into the unity of reason, once the idea of freedom is realized. Philosophically, variety could now only figure as disgraced contingency. Politically, Hegel's realism forbade such banishment: the array of major and minor powers was too solid a fixture of the post-Napoleonic world. The result is incoherence. On the one hand, 'the European nations form a family by the universal principle of their legislation, customs and education [*ihrer Gesetzgebung, ihrer Sitten, ihrer Bildung*]', but on the other, each retains a particular individuality 'as exclusive being-for-itself' whose welfare necessarily collides with that of others, in conflicts which can only issue into war.[22] No pact for perpetual peace, such as Kant had dreamt of, could ever hold between them, since 'it would always be dependent on particular sovereign wills, and therefore continue to be tainted with contingency.'[23] The contradictions between modern states, in other words, are not dissolved into a higher universality. History is the province only of the objective spirit: the realm of the absolute spirit remains religion and philosophy.

Because Hegel's system closes itself beyond the empirical world, although the course of history is subject to the movement of the spirit, its upshot need not be as conclusive – the drop in level of vision allows for less resolution in the image. Hegel's political thought does not come to rest in any unequivocal summation of his age. In fact, it can be said that each of its three strategic themes issues into uncertainty. The realization of modern freedom requires a state that expresses the life of its citizens, assures their welfare, and conforms to universal reason. This is the programme of the *Philosophy of Right*, but Hegel could not

---

21. *W–7*, § 345, 347 – pp. 505–506; *EPR*, pp. 373–74.
22. *W–7*, § 339, 322 – pp. 502, 490; *EPR*, pp. 371, 359: 'Individuality, as exclusive being-for-itself, appears *as the relation of [the state] to other states*, each of which is independent in relation to the others. Since the *being-for-itself* of the actual spirit has its *existence* therein, this independence is the primary freedom and supreme dignity of a nation.'
23. *W–7*, § 333 – p. 500; *EPR*, p. 368.

deliver it. The corporate structure, designed to repair the anomie of the market and compensate for classic participation in the city, was also calculated to circumvent more direct forms of suffrage and parliamentary government – whose principles broke through European politics in Hegel's last years. No form of public regulation succeeded in checking economic crises or social destitution, as he acknowledged. Colonial expansion and continental war could only yield an international order of radical contingency. Far from his view of the time suggesting a stable end of history, it is striking that Hegel uses just the opposite language when he confronts these outcomes. The July Revolution in France unleashed the kind of liberalism he deplored – 'the atomistic principle that insists upon the sway of individual wills, and maintains that all government must emanate from their express power.' But he did not believe that this turbulence could be lightly stilled: 'Thus agitation and unrest [*Bewegung und Unruhe*] are perpetuated. This collision, this knot, this problem is that with which history is now occupied and whose solution it has to work out in the future.'[24] When he contemplated the spread of misery in the new industrial world around him, his tone was the same: 'The emergence of poverty is in general a consequence of civil society, and as a whole arises necessarily out of it . . . hardship at once assumes the form of an injustice inflicted on this or that class. The important question of how poverty can be remedied is one that is especially agitating and tormenting [*bewegende und quälende*] to modern societies.'[25] So too when he came to describe the mutual relations between states, he stressed that no praetor existed on earth to settle their disputes, and therefore international affairs were inherently unstable [*schwankend*]: 'The broadest view of these will encompass the ceaseless turmoil [*das höchst bewegte Spiel*] not just of external contingency but also of the inner particularity of passions, interests, aims, talents and virtues, violence, wrongdoing and vices, that exposes the ethical whole itself – the independence of the state – to the realm of accident.'[26] Shortly before his death, he was writing to his sister: 'We are for the moment . . . spared all the current unrest; but these are still anxious times, in which everything that was previously taken for solid and secure seems to totter.'[27] Not rest, but unrest

---

24. *W–12*, p. 534; *PH*, p. 452.
25. *Philosophie des Rechts: Die Vorlesung von 1819/1820* (ed. Dieter Henrich), Frankfurt 1983, p. 193, and *W–7*, § 244, p. 390; *EPR*, pp. 266–67, 452.
26. *W–7*, § 339 – p. 503; *EPR*, p. 371.
27. *Wo alles zu schwanken scheint, was sonst für fest und sicher galt – Briefe*, Vol. 3, Hamburg 1954, p. 329; *Hegel: the Letters*, p. 422.

is the consistent note. The terms that recur are *Bewegung* and *Schwankung*. Above, there is the order of 'the higher praetor that is the universal spirit'.[28] Below, it is movement and turmoil that persist.

2. Cournot

It is thus not wholly surprising that in the nineteenth century Hegel was rarely seen as a philosopher who had theorized the end of history. His reputation was identified, understandably, more with his express doctrines of nature or logic or politics. It was these which became the focus of controversy, even for such a committed historical critic as Marx. The original source of what were eventually to become ideas of *Posthistoire* lay, as Niethammer's account makes clear, elsewhere.[29] The philosopher who explicitly developed a coherent conception of the end of history was a very different figure. Antoine-Augustin Cournot, one of the most remarkable minds of his age, still awaits a due rediscovery in our own. He is most often, although not widely, remembered today as one of the ancestors of neo-classical economics. In fact, his *Recherches sur les Principes Mathématiques de la Théorie des Richesses* (1838) was the pioneering work of modern price theory, which not only invented the demand curve that became a standard tool of marginalist analysis in the time of Jevons and Walras, but also anticipated the game-theoretical models of imperfect competition developed in a much later epoch by Neumann and Morgenstern. This founding text of formal equilibrium theory was so much in advance of its period that for a generation it was virtually ignored, until it was acknowledged as a precursor by Walras. By the time Marshall came to write his *Principles of Economics* in the last decade of the century, he explained that it was to Cournot's ideas of interdependent functions that he was most indebted, although he also – surprising as it may seem today – paid tribute to the influence on his thought of Hegel.[30]

For his contemporaries, however, Cournot was above all the philosopher of probability and chance. In 1843 he became the first thinker to

---

28. W-7, § 339 – p. 503; *EPR*, p. 371.
29. See *Posthistoire*, pp. 25–29.
30. 'Cournot's genius must give a new mental activity to everyone who passes through his hands': *Principles of Economics*, Vol. 1, London 1890, pp. x–xi.

advance a systematic theory of the difference between two kinds of probability that had traditionally been assimilated: evidential plausibility and statistical frequency. He called these, respectively, subjective or philosophical probability, and objective or mathematical probability.[31] The distinguishing feature of his philosophy was the way in which it articulated these two. For Cournot, the subjective probability yielded by induction was the primary form of our knowledge of the world – although, contrary to Mill, not the exclusive one, since mathematics afforded certainties that were deductive. Objective probability, on the other hand, was inscribed in the general nature of the world as a principle of the laws of chance. Where for Christian theology chance was no more than divine will in disguise, while for Hume or Laplace it was a mere name for our ignorance, for Cournot it was a positive and fully intelligible reality. In a famous definition, he declared chance events to be those that were produced by the encounter of two independent causal series. Since the universe was not the outcome of a single natural law, but was plainly governed by a variety of different mechanisms, there were both processes governed by more or less linear causal sequences, and occurrences set off by intersections between them. This was the difference between what was regular and what was random, each equally intelligible – the contrast, for example, between the movement of planets and meteors, or of tides and glaciers. Where the conditions of chance events were themselves repeated, as in such standard cases as games of dice or coloured balls drawn from an urn, the likelihood of differing outcomes could be mathematically calculated – out of accidents came order, from contingency probability. If the deductive capacities of the human mind to attain mathematical truths found correspondence in the numerically regular laws of the physical world, so its inductive powers of empirical conjecture – always subject to error – had what could be taken for their counterpart in the distribution of natural probabilities. Human reason was the fitting intelligence of the reason of things.[32]

---

31. Cournot's contribution to the development of this distinction is understated in the standard treatments by Keynes (*A Treatise on Probability*, London 1922, pp. 282–84) and Carnap (*The Logical Foundations of Probability*, Chicago 1950, p. 186), both interested essentially in the logic of induction alone; and with less justification is virtually ignored – under Foucauldian rules of evidence – in Ian Hacking's more historical study *The Taming of Chance* (London 1989).

32. Cournot first formulated this idea in his *Exposition de la Théorie des Chances et des Probabilités*, Paris 1843, § 40 – p. 73; for his distinction between mathematical and philosophical probability in this work, see § 18–20; 231–33 – pp. 35, 425–28. He

Cournot's scientific background (his first publication was in mecha-nics) and statistical interests, his economic modelling and epistemologi-cal prudence, set him far apart from Hegel. In some ways like a last great figure of the French Enlightenment in his combination of mathe-matical, philosophical and social concerns, he also belongs to a much more modern world than that of German Idealism. Yet Cournot shared certain central ambitions, and some assumptions with Hegel, as in its own idiom the title of what might be called his *Encyclopaedia* suggests: *Traité de l'Enchaînement des Idées Fondamentales dans les Sciences et dans l'Histoire*. For Cournot sought to unify a philosophy of know-ledge and a philosophy of history in a single theory, in which a formal exposition of the developmental order of reason – the concatenation of fundamental ideas that has produced the sciences – grounds a substan-tive account of the development of civilization, that accords ultimate primacy to the progress of the human mind. In this sense, Cournot's philosophy of history was as consciously idealist as Hegel's, against which it matched itself. But the theorists of the absolute and of the probable had different kinds of narratives to tell. Cournot expressly disavowed any teleogical conception of history, of the kind embodied in Hegel's succession of *Volksgeister*, that 'sort of epic in which a few elite nations each play their role as the representative of an idea'[33] – not to speak of any cyclical version in the style of Vico, or vision of indefinite progress in the manner of Condorcet. The innovation of his philosophy of history was to be what he called an *aetiology*: a systematic enquiry into the weave of causes that composed the fabric of history. The task of such an enquiry was to trace out the complicated patterns of chance and necessity that had shaped human development, by distinguishing between the threads of 'independence' and 'solidar-ity' within its causal continuum. The combination of the accidental and essential did not render the course of history impenetrable to critical explanation. Statistics had already shown how chance events, repeated

---

restated and amplified his argument in a number of later works – see *Traité de l'Enchaînement des Idées Fondamentales dans les Sciences et dans l'Histoire*, Vol. I, Paris 1861, § 57–68 – pp. 89–108 – henceforward *TE*. Nine volumes of Cournot's works have been published in a modern edition by Librairie Vrin: *Oeuvres Complètes*, Paris 1973–1984: henceforward *OC* – here *OC–1*, 1984, pp. 55, 29–30, 280–82; *OC–3*, 1982, pp. 60–71.

33. *Considérations sur la Marche des Idées et des Evénements dans les Temps Modernes*, Vol. I, Paris 1872, pp. 17–18; *Matérialisme, Vitalisme, Rationalisme*, Paris 1875, pp. 235–36 – henceforward *CM* and *MVR*; *OC–4*, 1973, p. 19; *OC–5*, 1979, p. 136.

sufficiently often, yielded predictable outcomes.[34] Historical experiences could not be so reiterated, but the distinction between contingency and necessity still held. Here, however, the contrast lay
between events occurring with the irregularity of facts and processes
exhibiting the regularity of laws. The former were by no means always
trivial or ephemeral: they could be large realities in their own right,
with indefinitely long consequences – comparable to a natural configuration like that, say, which gave greater land-mass to the Northern than
the Southern hemisphere.[35] For all its significance, a causal sequence
of this kind still remained accidental, in a sense that the tidal movement
of the oceans was not. The aim of an aetiology of history was to
establish the hierarchy of these various kinds of causation in the actual
record of human societies.

In practice, there is a significant drift in Cournot's execution of this
programme. He was resolved to give chance its due role in the skein of
events. But he paradoxically tended to conflate two distinct types of
chance that his own examples constantly illustrated – one that could be
called punctual, the other medial. In the first, a rare event occurs
because of the intersection of unrelated causal chains: in the second, a
recurrent event exhibits a range of unpredictable outcomes. This is the
difference between the meteorite and the roulette wheel. In Cournot's
formal definition of chance the accent falls on the idea of causal
independence, regardless of the scale or frequency of the event so
caused, but in his historical treatment of it, the emphasis lies on the
notion of statistical *compensation* – that is, the way in which a large
number of uninspectably small causes acting within set parameters can
give rise to random variations that cancel each other out to form a
regular distribution. The shift from one to the other passes through the
criterion that governs Cournot's selection of cases – stability of conse-

---

34. Kant, of course, had sketched an account of human development based directly
on this model: 'Marriages, births and deaths do not seem to be subject to any rule by
which their numbers could be calculated in advance, since the free human will has so
great an influence upon them; and yet the annual statistics for them in large countries
prove that they are just as subject to constant natural laws as the changes in the weather,
which in themselves are so inconsistent that their individual occurrence cannot be
determined in advance, but which nevertheless do not fail as a whole to sustain the
growth of plants, the flow of rivers, and other natural functions in a uniform and
uninterrupted course. Individuals and men and even entire nations little imagine that,
while they are pursuing their own ends, each in his own way and often in opposition to
others, they are unwittingly guided along a course intended by nature': *Political Writings*
(ed. Hans Reiss), Cambridge 1991, p. 41. Cournot, without Kant's teleological commitment, wanted to make more allowance for effective contingency than this.

35. *CM–I*, pp. 1–9; *OC–4*, pp. 9–14.

quence.[36] This is what unites the otherwise disparate paradigms of the cosmic disaster and the gaming table. In Cournot's philosophy of history, the contingencies that count are those that yield persistent effects, of duration or repetition. Tacitly, he assimilated the two and assumed they were equivalent to historical significance. In reality, of course, persistence – of either kind – is no guarantee against inconsequence: what lasts longer or happens more often is not thereby necessarily most important for a society. But Cournot's measure of the significance of a cause by the stability of its effect gave a particular shape to his narrative.

For the order of the conditions determining human society underwent a basic reversal in his account. In primitive or ancient times, the philosophical study of history logically started with the ethnographic data of race, language and religious belief, as the structures of greatest longevity; moved to juridical and political institutions, followed by economic life; and ended with art, science and industry. In modern civilization, however – by which Cournot meant the history of Europe since the sixteenth century – the same fundamental criterion imposed the opposite sequence. 'We must give first place to what truly constitutes the substratum of European civilization, what has been least altered or impaired in its progress by elements of more variable nature, what will have most persistent interest for future generations. We will thus treat the positive sciences before philosophical systems, and even philosophical systems before religious doctrines . . . treating last all that has to do more directly with the diversity of origins, genius and customs of the nations that compose our European civilization; and ending with views on the great historical events where accidents certainly play more of a role than elsewhere, though not to the point where we need despair of discerning traces of order and regular concatenation.'[37] The ensuing accounts of each century since the Renaissance in *Considérations sur la Marche des Idées et des Evénements dans les Temps Modernes* obey this protocol: they begin with a survey of the science of the age, pass to philosophy and literature, proceed to religion (sixteenth–seventeenth centuries) and politics, or politics and economics (eighteenth–nineteenth centuries), before concluding with international affairs. The hierarchy runs from the durable to the ephemeral. It was an order that might shock readers, Cournot remarked. The book ended with its most pointed expression. The French Revolution was lifted out of chronological sequence and treated

---

36. See *CM–I*, pp. i–iii; *OC–4*, pp. 3–5.
37. *CM–I*, p. 35; *OC–4*, p. 30.

after rather than before the nineteenth century. The purpose of this experiment, he explained, was to explore how much in the history of his own time was due to general social processes at work in Europe, that would have occurred without any upheaval in France, and how much to specific effects of the Revolution.[38] A philosophical history could only be comparative in method, and must be capable of counter-factual reasoning.

Viewed in this light, the outbreak of the Revolution was indeed all but inevitable within France – given the state of the *ancien régime*, no scenario for its avoidance was retrospectively plausible. But its course was affected by accidents: among them the failure of the flight to Varennes, without which no new dynasty could have been founded, and then the 'incomparable chance' that this was done by a military genius, rather than merely a soldier of fortune of Latin American stamp;[39] and its eventual outcome was at variance with its many vicissitudes. For 'the historical order in which causes and effects unfolded in no way coincides with the order of importance of the conditions and results that finally predominated, as reason conceives it and subsequent events have confirmed it.'[40] The most durable achievements of the French Revolution were those based on the work of science – the cosmopolitan innovations of its metric system. Next came its legal reforms, as they were codified by Napoleon; then its rationalization of civil administration, with the creation of *départements*; and finally the concordat with the Church. The theatre of its most spectacular episodes, on the other hand, had left little behind. For the political legacy of the Revolution was perhaps no more than the endemic instability of governments in France since the Restoration; while economically it had retarded rather than accelerated the industrial development of the country. Looked at within the perspective of the continent as a whole, indeed, the French Revolution delayed more than it promoted the progress of European civilization towards a more rational international order in the nineteenth century. In this framework, it could be regarded as a random perturbation, without which Europe would have reached the same condition quickly and more painlessly.[41] In the coolness of this counter-factual verdict we are a long way from Hegel's judgement of the Revolution, to the end of his

---

38. *CM–I*, pp. iv–vi; *OC–4*, pp. 5–6.
39. *CM–II*, pp. 382–88; 402–403; 392–93; *OC–4*, pp. 513–18; 527–28; 520.
40. *CM–II*, p. 301; *OC–4*, p. 462.
41. *CM–II*, pp. 120–21; 246–47; 395–96; *OC–4*, pp. 346–47; 426–27; 522–33.

life: 'A constitution was now established in harmony with the conception of right, on which all future legislation would be based' – 'That was a glorious dawn. All thinking beings shared in the jubilation of the epoch.'[42] What for Hegel was a change in man's place in the political world comparable to the Copernican discovery that the sun was the centre of the firmament, Cournot could compare to an errancy in the path of a planet around it.

Yet Cournot too could declare that the Revolution was perhaps the last page of epic history that humanity would write. For his aetiology of modern Europe was inserted as a detailed segment within a much vaster theoretical prospectus. The overall development of the species was characterized by a sequence of three phases, that divided social time on earth. In primitive societies, there was no significant order of public events to compose a history proper; social life was the product of instinctual drives, whose play was essentially blind; the train of deeds was the dictate of chance. The records of humanity at this stage of prehistory could yield at best the form of arbitrary annals – a series of curiosities, calamities or prodigies with no relation between them other than mere temporal succession. With the emergence of civilization, instinctual life became increasingly subject to the guidance or control of ideas, leaders arose capable of directing masses beneath them, religions and states were founded, empires battled with each other, the arts and sciences developed. The flow of events now acquired an intelligible order, of which a connected narrative could be written – one dominated by heroes and poets, legislators and prophets, whose principal field of action was politics and religion. The realm of chance was now crossed with that of purpose, yielding a social causation inextricably mingling contingency and necessity. In the course of its development, however, civilization gradually subjected more and more domains of social existence to rational organization. Its tendency, already visible, was therefore towards the advent of a third condition of humanity, which could be termed post-historical. In this stage, the social order would approximate to the regularity and predictability of a natural system, as economic principles became the dominant force shaping collective life, individual greatness declined, popular consumption increased, and politics lost ground to administration. In this 'final state' of civilization, 'society tends to assume, like a beehive, a virtually

---

42. W–12, p. 529; PH, p. 447: 'Never since the sun had stood in the firmament and the planets revolved around him had it been perceived that man's existence centres in his head, that is in thought, out of which he builds the world of reality.'

geometric pattern.'[43] Human actions become so tightly integrated into a set of interconnected social mechanisms that they no longer present the variety of incident and invention of a genuine history: the motions of the resultant structure would merely provide the sort of bulletins recorded in an official gazette. When history comes to an end, it is the realm of necessity that triumphs over chance.

In a century that saw many enterprises in the philosophy of history, this one stands out in the originality of its construction. Cournot's scientific background was, of course, a major influence on it. The general schema is clearly inspired by the trajectory of the natural world as it had been established by the advances of the time. The cosmos had moved from an initial state of chaos, without regular forms or laws, through a period of genesis in which the elements of an emergent order appeared, to a final state of stability, of indefinite duration. Within the solar system itself, which exemplified this curve, the history of the earth repeated it – from original molten mass through fierce convulsions to the tranquil regularity of the quaternary epoch we now enjoy; and in turn the evolution of life on earth reiterated the same movement, reaching relative biological equilibrium among contending species at the term of its development.[44] Cournot's aetiology of human history drew its analytic bias for persistence, as well as its schematic direction, from the prestige of such natural analogies. But if his diagnosis of a post-historical future had only rested on these, it would have been a more fragile and conventional speculation of his age. Its particular force, however, came from the field of his own authority. The basic paradigm informing the vision of a stabilized human condition was the market equilibrium whose mechanisms of price formation he had pioneered. Cournot himself was explicit about this: it was 'the economic idea, the utilitarian principle' that 'pervaded everything' in the contemporary world, providing the standard of social organization.[45] The statistical regularities of the market were the model of the final prevalence of necessity over chance, of rational order over vital impulse. 'The economist considers the social body in a state of division and so to speak extreme pulverization, where all the singularities of

---

43. *TE–II*, § 541 – p. 342; *OC–3*, p. 484. For the whole argument, see *TE-II*, § 528–546 – pp. 324–353, restated in *MVR*, pp. 227–235; *OC–3*, pp. 475–490 and *OC–5*, pp. 131–35.
44. See *TE–I*, § 194 – pp. 305–306; *OC– 3*, pp. 185–86; and *CM-I*, pp. 20–22; *OC–4*, pp. 21–22.
45. *TE–II*, § 619 – pp. 464–65; *OC–3*, p. 552.

individual organization and life compensate and cancel one another. The laws he discovers or thinks to do so are those of a mechanism, not a living organism.'[46]

Atomization – pulverization. Hegel and Cournot use similar terms when they view the market. But what in one was a subordinate system within the configuration of modernity has become for the other a dominant reality, that which defines it as the end of history. What was Cournot's political attitude towards this final state, as he foresaw it? His intellectual independence is striking here too. He spoke of 'the new idea of an administration of social interests, independent of political forms', which 'might be compared to a science or an industry capable of increasing perfection', as characteristic of the coming age.[47] But he was not a technocratic enthusiast for it, like Saint-Simon. Nor, on the other hand, did he express a romantic abhorrence of the mechanical uniformity and symmetry of the society he predicted; the vehement rejection of a long line of *Kulturkritiker* is missing. Cournot's comments on the post-historical future he projected are curiously detached in tone. By upbringing he was a Catholic and a conservative; but by outlook he was a rationalist and by profession a scientist.[48] The combination yielded a peculiar temperamental balance, if with a touch of melancholy. The progressive civilization under way involved the victory of rational and general principles over spontaneous life energies, bringing with it many drawbacks as well as advantages: 'in some respects a lowering and in other respects a perfecting of the conditions of humanity'.[49] The final state would be one in which 'history, absorbed by the science of social economics, would end like some river whose waters disperse (to the benefit of the greatest number) into myriad irrigation canals, losing what was once their unity and imposing grandeur.'[50] The substitution of the world of the gazette for that of the epic would bring well-being and security, as well as anonymity and accidie. For if modernity was a creation of European development,

---

46. *MVR*, p. 219; *OC–5*, p. 46.

47. *TE-II*, § 337 – p. 29; *MVR*, p. 227; *OC–3*, p. 311 and *OC–5*, p. 131.

48. He could be equally dispassionate about the future of his own faith. Christian belief had been virtually synonymous with European civilization, and it was safe to say no extant religion would ever replace it, nor any new one succeed it. But 'objectively, science and religion have nothing in common', and it could not be excluded that one day Europe might astonish the world with its ingratitude and divorce itself from Christianity. Were that to happen, 'humanity would enter a new phase; God would personally withdraw from human societies, abandoning them to the laws of their natural mechanisms, which also form part of his decrees'. *TE–II*, § 589–593, pp. 416–421.

49. *TE-II*, § 332 – p. 22; *OC–3* p. 307.

50. *TE-II*, § 543 – p. 345; *OC–3* p. 486.

what lay beyond it had been prefigured in Asian experience. Unlike Hegel's, Cournot's vision of the direction of world history is not exclusively Western. For centuries Chinese civilization had formed a parallel record to European, equal in achievements but distinct in values. Where Western societies had devoted themselves to the glorification of successive ideals – faith, fatherland, freedom – Chinese realism formed social institutions for the physical and moral improvement of individuals, the utility of men. It was in China, not in Europe, that principles of rational administration and industrial invention were pioneered which only prevailed much later in the West, after the heroic energies of its properly historical phase had flowered and faded.[51] Where for Hegel 'the earth forms a sphere, but history does not describe a circle round it',[52] Cournot envisaged European and Chinese civilizations converging, as the outward movement of their two populations joined on the Pacific shores of America, in a common post-historical order.

Cournot's end of history is a more definitely terrestrial destination than that of Hegel. But at the same time, because it lacks the back-up of a higher movement in the absolute spirit, it is also less categorical. Cournot took pains to stress that while civilization tended towards a final state, it would probably never 'rigorously attain it'.[53] Meanwhile, there remained the problems with which Hegel had grappled: the market, the state, the international order of the time. Cournot's grasp of the structural logic of the market was, of course, much deeper. The economist who anticipated the neo-classical revolution was not, however, a laissez-faire theorist. The *Recherches* stressed that exchange values and use values were not only distinct but could be directly incompatible: the Dutch destruction of spice harvests in the East Indies was 'an act of selfish cupidity, evidently opposed to the interests of society', yet 'this sordid act of material destruction is a real creation of wealth in the commercial sense of the word', the only sense in which value admitted of treatment by political economy.[54] Equilibrium prices could be reached in conditions of monopoly or duopoly, as well

---

51. *TE–II*, § 563–574 – pp. 380–85, esp. 391–92; *OC–3*, pp. 505–514, 511–12. Cournot thought China had missed a heroic phase of history – *TE–II*, pp. 394–95; *OC–3*, p. 513.

52. *W–12*, p. 134; *LPH*, p. 103 – since 'world history travels from East to West, for Europe is plainly its end and Asia its beginning.' This is a rare occasion on which Hegel does use the word *Ende* when speaking of history, but in a spatial sense: the world spirit will not loop back towards its starting-point.

53. *TE–II*, § 543 – p. 344; *OC–3*, p. 485.

54. *Recherches sur les Principes Mathématiques de la Théorie des Richesses*, Paris 1838, §3 – pp. 6–7; henceforward *RP*; *OC–8*, 1980, p. 10.

as perfect competition; and it was not the case that unrestricted free trade was always of benefit to a nation. The unfettered pursuit of private interests did not necessarily result in public welfare, as the ravages of deforestation or the evils of opium traffic had shown: the preordained harmony of the invisible hand was an illusion. The principle of laissez-faire was justified where the complexity of variables was too great for the consequences of intervention to be calculable. This negative rationale could well cover most cases, as a pragmatic rule. But it was not a scientific axiom, and regulation of the market – at the border or at home – might in other cases be preferable. Cournot had little more moral trust in the market than Hegel.[55]

His greater understanding of its dynamic, however, precluded any belief that corporations might be the agents of regulation. The State alone could perform this role. Within its structure, Cournot thought administration was becoming ever more important: it was from its bureaucracy that pressure for intervention typically came. Cournot, who spent the better part of his career as a civil servant under a regime – the Second Empire – in which public functionaries acquired unusual power, naturally had high regard for such administration, without deeming it a universal class. His hostility to representative democracy was no less marked than Hegel's. But in France, where Cournot lived through three revolutions of increasingly radical tenor, no Estates alternative was credible. The result was a political theory in sharp contrast to Hegel's. Freedom was no longer the central ideal of human life. Experience showed that it was of decreasing importance to the men of the nineteenth century: 'the political liberty which once inspired such generous sacrifices and noble impulses will not be such an object of worship to future generations.'[56] Power could not be founded on reason. The social contract was a myth and popular sovereignty a chimera. Universal suffrage and hereditary rule were equally irrational as principles. Political representation was as subjective a practice as artistic representation – there were as many forms of it as of portraiture. If administration served interests, government in the last resort reflected passions. No rational construction of sovereignty was possible: it could only be based on religion, tradition or force.[57] The corrosive scepticism of this doctrine was mitigated only by the assurance that political passions, though never entirely extinguishable, were

---

55. *RP*, §87–94 – pp. 173–196; *TE-II*, § 477–482, pp. 250–59; *OC–8*, pp. 113–125 and *OC– 3*, pp. 433–37.

56. *TE-II*, § 462 – p. 230; *OC–3*, p. 422.

57. *TE–II*, §465–67 – pp. 233–36; *CM– II*, pp. 276–77; *MVR*, pp. 220–24; *OC–3*, pp. 423–25, *OC–4*, pp. 446–47, *OC–5*, pp. 127–130.

now subsiding as industrial civilization progressed. The contrast between this disabused account of public authority and the idea of the state as the realization of freedom marks, among other things, the distance between the two empires under which they were conceived.

If Napoleon could appear to one philosopher as the *Weltseele* on horseback at Jena, his nephew was little more than a pedestrian *pis-aller* for the other, writing just before the Mexican expedition.[58] A decade later, amid the ruins of the Second Empire, Cournot reflected on the international relations of the epoch. Here something of the same antinomy appeared as within each state. The advance of industrialization, creating ever more uniform social and political institutions in Europe, did not thereby cancel the ethnic and cultural differences between nations, which if anything acquired more subjective importance for the peoples concerned – not because they actually increased, but because even though reduced, they gained more relief amidst the larger surrounding commonality. Such ethnic identities gave force to the principle of nationality in contemporary politics, where states still stood arrayed against each other in the traditional balance of powers, and no neutral arbiter was conceivable between them. Could the cosmopolitanism of modern conditions eventually prevail over the rival patriotisms of the continent? Might a federal United States of Europe come into being one day? Only, Cournot thought, if there was a further transformation of society comparable to the changes which had put an end to feudalism.[59]

That was, of course, an idea common – in their own terms – to socialists. If the new scientific culture of the century formed the major difference of intellectual context separating Cournot from Hegel, the emergence of socialism as a threat to the existing order was the great political divide between their worlds. When Cournot came to ask the classical question of his generation of countrymen – was the French Revolution 'over'? – his reply in the wake of the Commune was that another kind of revolution, a social war of European dimensions taking volcanic shape in the First International, had replaced it.[60] Of all the themes in his work that anticipate later problems, none was to be so uncannily clairvoyant as Cournot's response to the revolutionary challenge of the labour movement. The penetration of his insight came,

---

58. See the comment that closes Cournot's memoirs, written in 1859 – if there had to be a dictator after 1848, Napoleon's nephew was more likely to keep the masses in control than any other upstart: *Souvenirs*, Paris 1913, pp. 254–55.

59. *TE–II*, § 543 – pp. 345–46; *CM–I*, pp. 227–230; *CM–II*, pp. 289–290; *OC–3*, p. 486, *OC–4*, pp. 152–53 and 453–55.

60. *CM–II*, pp. 414–420; *OC–4*, pp. 534–38.

no doubt, from the proximity of features in his own vision of a post-historical future to elements in the socialist culture of the time. But already in the ongoing present his own critique of the untrammelled free market posed him with a theoretical problem. If economic regulation by the state was in principle admissible, even desirable, where would it stop – might not its logic lead to, say, public control of woods and arable land, in the interests of better use or greater output? 'That would lead', he warned in 1861, 'straight to what is nowadays called *socialism*, the banner of a new sect of which the world has rightly taken fright, as it realizes the wounds within existing society.'[61] Economically, tariffs were indeed – *pace* Smith – often perfectly sensible; but what was to prevent workers arguing from the validity of measures of protection to laws of redistribution, on the same grounds of a common benefit for the greater number? Modern industrial competition inevitably led to periodic crises of overproduction; capital accumulation to concentration of fortunes; technological progress to mass unemployment. In these conditions of often acute social distress, the eternal conflict between rich and poor, which had always threatened the security of property, took on a new menace. For there now arose the idea of a social order equitably distributing the fruits of nature and industry, capable at once of a high level of output and reduced labour-times for all. The eighteenth century had known utopian schemes, but only as isolated dreams without social resonance. It was a mark of the nineteenth century that such utopias now acquired the force of a mass aspiration in the new working-class centres in the big cities, fostered by the levelling pressures of universal suffrage.[62]

What were their prospects of realization? Cournot argued that politically a proletarian revolution might succeed in doing away with capitalism, although it would run into formidable peasant resistance when it started to tax the countryside, which might overwhelm it. Economically, however, it was quite possible that socialism would be constructed more or less along the lines its theorists envisaged in a particular state – there were so many objective tendencies pointing in that direction. But while a socialist economy might be built internally within one nation, it would inevitably succumb to the pressures of the international environment surrounding it. No matter how authoritarian its state or vigilant its police, such a system could not withstand the forces of commercial competition from abroad. Even its best intentions – say, a desire to conserve natural resources from reckless exploitation

61. *TE–II*, § 481 – p. 258; *OC–3*, p. 437.
62. *CM–II*, pp. 250–56; *OC–4*, pp. 429–433.

– would turn to its disadvantage in foreign trade. Moreover, the world market was not just a system of commodity exchange: all factors of production were mobile within it. These included individuals themselves, who could not be indefinitely penned within single borders, and – above all – ideas or institutions: those that experience proved more efficient were bound to prevail across any frontiers, however closed.[63] The protective barriers a socialist economy would have to erect against the outside world were a sign of weakness, that would undo it.

The prevision of the fate of communism is remarkable. But it did not leave Cournot entirely sanguine. For within capitalism itself, there were trends at work which were inconsistent with the principles of economic freedom. The growth in the scale of public works, the absorption of a major portion of profits on capital by fiscal charges and public borrowing, the spread of progressive taxation, the subventions to social insurance by the state, the legislation on conditions of work, the organization of workers' associations themselves – did not all these developments promise to bring about a sort of gradual, partial socialism? Or, at any rate, a different pattern in the distribution of wealth than would be given by the laws of economic equilibrium alone?[64] By the time of his last work, *Revue Sommaire des Doctrines Economiques*, Cournot had read Marx and had become increasingly concerned to defend the socially beneficial functions of capital. Even if private property, inheritance and inequality were not abolished outright, the trend towards state intervention and redistribution might still discourage individual economic activity to the point where a 'disguised' socialism had the same depressive effects as the 'systematic' sort.[65] Cournot's sketch of processes leading towards social democracy, long before anything like it existed, is scarcely less impressive as a theoretical presentiment – Hayekian forebodings taking shape *ante diem*. But although Cournot feared such a development, he never thought the stark recipes of economic liberalism an effective antidote to it. Market mechanisms did not generate any spontaneous evolutionary order: governmental authority remained the only conceivable *arche* of large modern societies, their essential 'principle of internal coordination'.[66]

---

63. *CM–II*, pp. 258–260; *OC–4*, pp. 434–35.
64. *CM–II*, pp. 256–58; *OC–4*, pp. 433–34.
65. *Revue Sommaire des Doctrines Economiques*, Paris 1877, pp. 323–25 – henceforward *RS*; *OC–10*, 1982, pp. 176–77. Significantly, the image of the beehive is here associated, not with the post-historical society outlined in the *Traité*, but with socialism. The impact of the Commune in unsettling Cournot's late outlook can be compared to that of the July Revolution on Hegel.
66. *RS*, pp. 264–65; *OC–10*, pp. 145–46.

Pure laissez-faire was about as rational in economics as it would be in medicine. 'The cause of property must not be confused with that of economic freedom, nor the idea of socialism with that of regulation.'[67] His own preferences could perhaps be said to anticipate the social market of a later Christian Democracy. But his reservations about the overall logic of unrestrained economic liberalism went deeper than its consequences for national solidarity. They strike an arrestingly contemporary note. What would happen to finite natural resources across the globe, if they were plundered without limit for the profits of the day? The disastrous consequences of deforestation were already evident, and man was a 'concessionaire of the planet' for much else besides – its fossil fuels too. What was the responsibility of one generation to its successors, in the calculus of human welfare – where did the optimum distribution lie between them?[68] For its part, technological progress could in time lead to ever greater substitution of machinery for labour, realizing Bacon's perhaps ominous dream of rendering all natural forces the slaves of man. How then would the consequences of declining employment, within and above all across countries, be handled?[69] Last but not least, what of the international economic order that unfettered capital accumulation would bring – would the mechanisms of global competition not generate a racial hierarchy condemning societies and peoples with fewer comparative advantages to the injustice of crushing inferiority? Such were the troubled questions that Cournot confided to Walras, on the eve of the emergence of general equilibrium theory.[70] Paradoxically, for all its differences, Cournot's legacy contains the same kind of tacit dislocation as Hegel's, between philosophical vision and social observation, the prospect of a historical closure and intimations of political rending.

---

67. *RS*, p. 317; *OC–10*, p. 173.

68. *TE–II*, §477–79 – pp. 250–55; *CM– II*, pp. 239–240; *RS*, pp. 302–303; *OC–3*, pp. 433–35, *OC–4*, pp. 421–22. The last question anticipates concerns only recently raised to full philosophical dignity, in works like Derek Parfit's *Reasons and Persons*.

69. *RS*, pp. 292–99; *OC–10*, pp. 161– 64.

70. 'I tremble at the thought that your curves of "intensive and extensive utility" will lead you to pure laissez-faire, that is to say, in national economies, to the deforestation of the earth, and in the international economy, to the suffocation of plebeian by privileged races in accord with the theory of Monsieur Darwin.' Walras, who had been trying to enlist Cournot's support for the reception of his work in Paris, hastened to reply: 'As for the remote consequences of "pure laissez-faire" which you glimpse beyond my premisses, give me, Sir, a little time and trust and you will see that I shall know how to evade them.' *Correspondence of Léon Walras and Related Papers*, Vol. 1, ed. William Jaffé, Amsterdam 1965, pp. 332, 336: a poignant exchange in other ways as well. For the same themes in Cournot's major treatise, see *TE–II*, § 480 – p. 255; *OC–3*, pp. 435–36.

3. Kojève

By the end of the century, the cultural climate had changed. Conceptions of progress of any kind were now, as Niethammer notes, subject to a surfacing doubt. Nietzsche, its most influential voice, attacked precisely the two versions of historical development that Hegel and Cournot had advanced. In the vocabulary of *The Use and Abuse of History,* Hegelian philosophy was reduced to a variant of grey-headed 'antiquarian history' – but the most dangerous sort, since instead of instilling a crippling modesty before the past, the painful awareness of the epigone, it had prompted the shameless illusion among Germans that they were the peak of the species: 'The belief that one is a late-comer in the world is anyway harmful and degrading; but it must appear frightful and devastating when it raises our late-comer to godhead, by a deft turn of the wheel, as the true meaning and object of all past creation, and his conscious misery is set up as the perfection of the world's history.' Accurately enough, Nietzsche did not tax Hegel himself with having proclaimed the end of history – but rather with *not* having drawn this necessary conclusion from his system, so leaving his successors with the conceit of doing so: 'For Hegel the highest and final stage of the world-process came together in his own Berlin existence. He ought to have said that everything after him was merely to be regarded as the musical coda of the great historical rondo – or rather, as simply superfluous. He did not say it; and thus he implanted into a generation saturated by his influence a worship of the "power of history" that practically turns every moment into a sheer gaping at success, an idolatry of the actual.'[71] A decade later, Nietzsche drew a famous portrait of the quite different ending that modern industry and democracy might bring about, a 'time when man will no longer launch the arrow of his longing beyond man' and 'the earth has become small', without labour or danger, inequality or solitude, rule or passion: a world of human 'ground-fleas', who persist the longest – the last men. 'They have their little pleasures for the day, and their little pleasures for the night; but they are careful of their health. "We have discovered happiness" say the last men, and blink.'[72] Here the imagery of insect life has sunk below the hive: the post-historical vision of a society of

---

71. *Werke* III/1 (ed. Colli-Montinari), Berlin 1972, pp. 303–305; *Thoughts out of Season,* Vol. 2, London 1909, pp. 71–72.
72. *Werke* VI/1, Berlin 1968, pp. 12–14; *Thus Spake Zarathustra,* London 1908, pp. 12–13.

symmetry and utility has become the sphere of universal *Lüstchen*, the final state of mankind 'the most contemptible of all'.

Nietzsche was, of course, unaware of Cournot, whose intellectual isolation during his lifetime was not much less than his own. Unlike the great German, the French thinker never acquired posthumous general renown. But within the universities of the Third Republic, he was not forgotten. The rationalist and solidarist ambience of the emergent social sciences found affinities with him, and in the Belle Epoque he received belated tribute with a special issue of the leading academic journal of the day, and a comprehensive monograph on his thought. This attention continued into the interwar period. It was then that for the first time his views on post-historical stability received extended treatment from a young philosopher whose ontology had been conceived as a modernization of Cournot's work, Raymond Ruyer. His level-headed study *L'Avenir de l'Humanité d'après Cournot* noted at the outset the similarity between Cournot's forecasts and Nietzsche's apprehensions.[73] Writing in 1929, however, he asked whether the novel turbulences of bolshevism and fascism did not contradict the expectation of a secular decline of political energies as the rule of increasingly impersonal administration took hold. Yet since these were one-party regimes suppressing political debate and aiming at complete control of social and economic life, perhaps their destination was ironically the kind of state Cournot had envisaged – though if they did not afford the modicum of civil freedom for individuals he believed inseparable from modern civilization, they would not last.[74] Still, even if they passed, Cournot had probably both overestimated the degree of institutional stability that could ever be achieved by humanity, and underestimated the social costs of the type of stabilization he projected. Any imaginable equilibrium would be more relative, but also on a lower plane, than he had thought. History had hitherto always developed through a variety of human civilizations. Now the European form alone was becoming a universal model imposed across the globe, even as Europe itself was visibly becoming enervated in its own edifice

---

73. 'Cournot announces the birth of a diligent, average, temperate humanity, without nobility or genius, a reasonable species – the "last man" despised by Zarathustra, who in his paltry wisdom says "formerly all the world was mad" ': *L'Avenir de l'Humanité d'après Cournot*, Paris 1930, pp. 6–7. The aim of Ruyer's *Esquisse d'une Philosophie de la Structure*, published in the same year, was to develop a defensible contemporary version of a mechanist view of the world, as close to the truths of twentieth-century science as Cournot had been to those of the nineteenth: p. 11.

74. *L'Avenir de l'Humanité d'après Cournot*, pp. 35–37.

of utilitarian calculation and consumption.[75] The result looked like being an increasingly uniform world, in which humanity no longer had any counter-assurance in alternative cultures. In these conditions, the mechanisms of the future could well become seized by a general rust.

With the onset of the Depression and the victory of Nazism, the conditions in which this judgement was made were struck away. A product of the same professional milieu as Ruyer, Raymond Aron turned sharply against it under the impact of his experience of Germany in 1931–33. Originally formed under the influence of the Gallic version of neo-Kantian rationalism, Aron's exposure to the work of Rickert and Weber, Husserl and Heidegger in the years of Hitler's rise to power led to a strong rejection of what he saw as the complacency and provincialism of the established French philosophy and sociology of the time.[76] His *Introduction to the Philosophy of History* of 1938 was a summons to take the measure of the European crisis that the traditions of Durkheim or Brunschvicg had failed to register – and for which German historicism and existentialism were better preparations. Aron has described the disarray into which the work threw his superiors.[77] Perhaps, however, this was not due only to the unfamiliarity of its themes. For the book is even in retrospect a curious hybrid, whose mixture of claims depends on its discontinuous structure. Significantly, however, Aron's first move was a consideration of Cournot, whose philosophy dominates the *mise-en-scène* of the work. Cournot's view of history, Aron argued, was not so much empirically as methodologically flawed, by its assumption of an end-state whose ultimate order was the only guarantee that the path towards it was a logical evolution, rather than a random becoming – but which the historically situated knowledge of the philosopher could never justify. Cournot could seek to distinguish between chance and necessity in the weave of events only because he had determined their final pattern in advance.[78] Aron rejected not only such metaphysical determinism, but also more specific doctrines of social or economic determination: Durkheim's conception of collective forces, Simiand's preoccupation with bullion flows, or Marx's account of the primacy of infrastructures. All causal relationships in society were at best only partial and probable: there was no first cause or original motor in history, whose processes were irreduci-

75. Ibid., pp. 136–150.
76. See the account in his *Mémoires*, Paris 1983, pp. 67–73.
77. *Mémoires*, pp. 105–106.
78. *Introduction à la Philosophie de l'Histoire*, Paris 1938, pp. 19–24, 178–79. Henceforward *IPH*.

bly plural. 'Neither the reality of local ensembles nor the objectivity of fragmentary determinisms excludes the incoherence of atomic facts or the incertitude of the whole.'[79]

What then were the constituents of a valid philosophy of history, one that had learnt to abandon binding epistemological and political certainties? For Aron, its object emerged in a new light, quite foreign to Cournot. 'The concept of history is not essentially tied to the hypothesis of a total order. What is decisive is rather our consciousness of the past and our will to define ourselves in terms of it. The distinction between truly historical individuals and peoples and those who are ahistorical does not have to do with the pace of social change or the character of institutions. To live historically is to preserve, to re-live and to judge the existence of one's ancestors (and of other societies).'[80] For this programme, Aron invoked the authority of Hegel. But if the idea of an appropriation-internalization of the past by a consciousness in the present could be termed a Hegelian derivation, mediated by Dilthey, the other moments of this agenda – not preserving or re-living, but judging and willing – bear the stamp of Weber and Heidegger. By what value-standards should the past be judged, once a plurality of ethical standpoints was sociologically conceded? How could the subjective adoption of one perspective, among others, be reconciled with the objectivity of historical knowledge itself? Unable to settle for Weber's formalist solution, Aron found himself driven towards its exasperated sequel in Weimar decisionism – arguing, in Heideggerian fashion, that 'man determines himself and his mission by measuring himself against nothingness', with 'the power of he who creates himself by judging his milieu and choosing himself', and so 'surmounts the relativity of history by the absolute of his decision'.[81] Here it is confrontation, not with the complexity of a social past, but with the abyss of the existential present that gives meaning and direction – the void of death rather than the legacy of life. In this key, Marxism itself was to be understood as an existential attitude among others, a practical will independent of the theoretical validity of its claims.

The relativist logic here led to not a rectification but a dissolution of the philosophy of history as Aron had initially conceived it. In the unstable compound of his text, however, it oscillated with its reverse. For elsewhere, Aron sought to anchor his project in permanent disposi-

---

79. *IPH*, pp. 208–225, 276.
80. *IPH*, p. 46. These formulations are expressly directed against Cournot's views.
81. *IPH*, p. 375.

tions of human nature. The historian could not escape the danger of substituting his own preferences for the actual realities of the past, unless he assumed a common standard between them as an 'inevitable vocation in the nature of man and of the mind'.[82] If history was made up of a multiplicity of partial totalities, each of these was nevertheless 'the imperfect work (perfect retrospectively) of a humanity' whose 'unity was equivalent to a goal situated on an infinite horizon: the totality which the philosopher would grasp if man had exhausted his history, by completing his creation and self-creation.' The idea of an end of history, in other words, recurs even in a discourse that seems to set its face against it. In this register, 'only the human species is engaged in an adventure whose goal is not death but the realization of itself.'[83] Here essence unmistakably commands existence. In the *Introduction* the gesture of this ontological reversal is only sketched: it remains without empirical referent. But its inspiration was to become clear elsewhere in Aron's work, and was never disavowed by him: it lay in Kant's notion of reason as the regulative principle of a society governed by law and a world assured of peace. Forty-five years later, reflecting on the political disorders and nuclear dangers of the century, he wrote at the end of his life: 'I continue to believe that a happy ending is possible, far beyond our political horizon, in the Idea of Reason.'[84]

While Aron was composing his *Introduction*, another and more powerful one was under way in Paris at the same time. Kojève had started to lecture on Hegel in 1933. A Russian who had spent his formative years in Germany, Kojève too had absorbed the impact of Heidegger – much more deeply. But in his case it was mediated by the influence of Marx, and led to an interpretation of Hegel that was a genuine intellectual synthesis, of striking coherence and originality. Kojève's fundamental move was to exfoliate the centre of Hegel's system into a double development. The movement of the Spirit through time, in the metaphysical passage of the Absolute to itself, was brought to earth in two complementary figures. The first was existential, and traced the dynamic of human identity as a freedom negating its situation in pursuit of a desire whose fulfilment can only lie in its free acknowledgement by others. The second was social, and traced the pattern of class relations as they developed in successive conflicts from aristocratic domination through bourgeois ascendancy to popular equality. For Kojève, these two figures were interwoven in a single

---

82. *IPH*, pp. 279, 46.
83. *IPH*, pp. 349, 52.
84. 'In the Kantian sense', Aron explains: *Mémoires*, p. 741.

narrative that gave its sense to the history of the world. At its origin, the nihilating action of every consciousness, moved by a desire for what it is not, engages in contest with that of every other, as each seeks to extort the recognition of itself that alone can satisfy it, and in this quest accepts the risk of death to achieve dominance over the other. Out of this battle emerge the first social relations, of master and slave in Antiquity. These are in turn transformed by the labour of the slaves to yield the world of capital, whose formal equality is anticipated in Christianity. That world is then overthrown by the victory of workers over capital, in a revolution assuring the universal recognition of all in substantive equality. Kojève made no secret of the sources of this construction. Heidegger had understood the primordial projection of human existence towards death in Hegel's philosophy, that ensues from the struggle of each consciousness to wrest symbolic tribute – honour or prestige – from its rivals; but he had largely ignored the transformative processes of labour. Marx had grasped the material dynamic of work unleashed by the drive for recognition, but had neglected the struggle to death behind it.[85] Hegel's philosophy united these themes: death, struggle and labour concatenate in one movement as humanity proceeds towards its goal.

In Kojève's reconstruction, this goal acquires a peculiar relief. For the first time, Hegel's philosophy is credited with a full conception of an end of history, as not just the result of human development but also its halting-place. How novel this account was can be seen from the reading of Hegel that prompted Kojève's undertaking, to which he acknowledged his debt. In 1935 Alexandre Koyré, linked to him in the Russian emigration, had published a pioneering essay on the concept of time in Hegel's recently discovered Jena *Logik* and *Realphilosophie*, which had concluded that for all its majesty Hegel's philosophy was a failure because its system was only possible if history was completed, which was just what its dialectic of time, as perpetual negation of the present by the future, precluded. Human freedom and historical finality could not be reconciled.[86] This was just the verdict Kojève sought to overthrow. He argued that Hegel had indeed affirmed the end of history, in perfect accord with the structure of his philosophy and the logic of modernity –

---

85. *Introduction à la Lecture de Hegel* (first edition), Paris 1947, p. 573. Henceforward *ILH*.

86. 'Hegel à Jena', *Revue d'Histoire et de Philosophie Religieuses*, September–October 1935, pp. 457–58: 'The philosophy of history would only be possible if history was finished, and there was no more future – if time had stopped.' But 'if time is dialectical and always constructed as from the future, it is – whatever Hegel says – perpetually unfinished.'

and had identified its arrival with the First Empire. What Napoleon's victory at Jena had represented for Hegel, Kojève maintained, was the advent of a 'universal and homogeneous state', in which the opposition of master and slave is finally overcome in the synthesis of a citizen soldiery combining the traditionally antithetical roles of war and work, in equality under the law. Once the revolutionary armies of this state have vanquished every enemy, and universal equality is realized, the drive for recognition is fulfilled: 'desire thus being entirely satisfied, struggle and labour cease: history is over, there is nothing more *to do*.'[87] All that remains, at the end of time, is the natural existence of man as a biological being – and the contemplation of the historical process of his becoming, in the wisdom of Hegel's philosophy itself.

Kojève's explication of Hegel was at the same stroke a validation. In its essentials, the structure of history was as Hegel had seen it to be. There were only two reservations to be made to his account. Under the influence of Schelling, Hegel had mistakenly extended his dialectic to nature, the domain not of negativity but of identity, to construct a single ontology for the physical and historical worlds that was manifestly untenable.[88] To grasp the truth of Hegel's philosophy, it was necessary to strip nature out of it. The other correction was more local, and affected the historical account itself. Hegel's timetable needed an adjustment. He had miscalculated the hour of the end of history, for Napoleon had not in the event realized it. The universal and homogeneous state had only germinated at Jena, and over a century later was still far from fruition. The political order Hegel had envisaged was not an established reality, but an ideal requiring the negativity of an ongoing action to be brought into existence.[89] The 'perfect state' was a project still to be accomplished. Kojève left little doubt where it was being carried forward. In lectures rife with allusions to the Communist movement of the time, he hinted that Hegel's philosophy already furnished, in advance, the necessary judgements to be made of a virtuous reformism that was no more than a form of bourgeois individualism; of self-indulgent intellectuals incapable of effective socal action; of dreams of permanent revolution that could only lead to anarchy or the destruction of the dreamers. Successful revolutionary struggle required other qualities: among them, the capacity to connect with tradition, and to engage with terror (whose historical necessity

87. *ILH*, pp. 384–85.
88. *ILH*, pp. 483–88.
89. *ILH*, pp. 290–91.

Marx himself had underestimated).[90] It was not difficult to see whose silhouette was being traced here, and Kojève made no secret of it at the time. The role of Napoleon had fallen to Stalin. The end of history was now under preparation in the East.

Kojève's lectures made a deep impression on his listeners – to more various and influential effect than probably any others in France this century. But what was the relation between his vision and Hegel's? Kojève based his reading of Hegel all but exclusively on the *Phenomenology of Spirit*. Neither the early theological texts, which had caused an intellectual flurry in the time of Dilthey, nor the Jena writings that had fascinated Koyré, and still less the *Philosophy of Right* or the *Lectures in the Philosophy of History,* which had dominated discussion in the time of Marx, feature in his account. This choice gave him maximum hermeneutic latitude. For the *Phenomenology,* bearing at once on the formation of the self and the development of the world, in language of opaque passion and elusive intensity, invites the largest interpretive constructions while withholding most of the empirical specifications needed for them. The political background of the text cannot be mistaken, where it nears the French Revolution, and Hegel himself claimed it had foreseen the dénouement of the Napoleonic adventure.[91] But it is entirely lacking in historical or institutional particulars. Not so much as one proper name from the annals of power appears in its pages. Unencumbered by the detailed references and explicit proposals of Hegel's later works, Kojève was free to develop his own formidable variations on the darkling adumbrations at Jena. The result is a decisive political shift. The 'universal and homogeneous state' Kojève ascribed to Hegel could, in fact, be described as an inversion of his programme. For Hegel, at all stages in his career,

---

90. *ILH,* pp. 89–91; 502; 518–19; 555–57; 573.

91. After the final defeat and abdication of Napoleon in 1814, he wrote: 'Great events have transpired about us. It is a frightful spectacle to see a great genius destroy himself. There is nothing more *tragic.* The entire mass of mediocrity, with its irresistible weight of gravity, presses on like lead, without rest or reconciliation, until it has succeeded in bringing down what is high to the same level as itself or even below. The turning point of the whole, the reason why this mass has power and – like the chorus – survives and remains on top, is that the great individual must himself give that mass the right to do what it does, thus precipitating his own fall. I may pride myself, moreover, on having predicted this entire upheaval. In my book [the *Phenomenology*], which I completed the night before the battle of Jena, I said: "Absolute freedom" – which I had previously described as the purely abstract formal freedom of the French Republic, originating as I showed in the Enlightenment – "passes out of its own self-destructive actuality over into *another land* of self-conscious spirit" – I had in mind here a specific *land*': *Briefe,* II, pp. 28–29; *Letters,* p. 307. This retrospective gloss, of course, is completely at variance with Kojève's account of Hegel's expectations in the *Phenomenology*; but given the temptations of hindsight, it should not be overly relied upon.

believed that the state had to be differentiated in structure and delimited in territory: articulated into corporate divisions, and organized
in national forms. This political ideal was to be spelt out most expressly
in the *Philosophy of Right*. But it is unequivocally indicated in the
Phenomenology too, whose allusions to the French revolutionary
experience repeatedly insist on the 'moment of difference' that requires
an 'organic articulation' – *organische Gliederung* – of freedom, dividing the social world into 'stable spiritual "masses" or spheres' into
which 'the plurality of individuals' are assigned as 'specific estates'. The
Terror signifies the abolition of these, but with its passing they take
shape once more, as 'the individuals who have felt the fear of death,
their absolute master, again submit to negation and distinctions
[*Unterschiede*], arrange themselves in their spheres, and return to
apportioned and limited tasks, but thereby to their substantial reality.'[92] Kojève's commentary on Hegel's text moves in exactly the
opposite direction. The post-revolutionary order is constituted by the
definitive reality of the Napoleonic Empire, which is 'a *universal* and
homogeneous State, for it unites the whole of humanity (or at least that
which counts historically) and "suppresses" within itself all "specific
differences": nations, social classes, families.'[93] The state that brings
history to an end is universal because it admits of no further expansion,
and homogeneous since it is exempt from contradiction.

This is a drastic change of definition. Kojève's alteration of Hegel's
agenda is not limited, moreover, simply to the structure of the ideal
state: it involves a transformation of its substance too. For Hegel, the
Rechtsstaat is the rational embodiment of modern liberty. The leading
themes of his whole account of political development are Reason and
Freedom: it is these that are realized in the ethical substance of the
modern state. In Kojève's vision of the end of history, they fade into the
background – references to them become no more than residual, even
vestigial. In their stead, two quite different concepts hold the stage:
Desire and Satisfaction. Kojève drew these from the dialectic of self-
consciousness in the fourth chapter of the *Phenomenology*: human
desire is fundamentally desire for what is not itself – the desiring
consciousness of others. It is this dynamic which unleashes the recipro-
cal contest of subjectivities whose first historical figure is the dialectic of
lord and bondsman, whose stake is recognition. Victory in this struggle
– first one-sided in the pagan–aristocratic world, then mediated in its
Christian–bourgeois sequel, finally generalized among the worker-

---

92. *W–3*, pp. 434, 436, 438; *PS*, pp. 358, 359, 361.
93. *ILH*, p. 145.

warriors of the universal state – is *Befriedigung*: satisfaction. Hegel indeed uses the term to indicate the object of the dialectic of desire: 'self-consciousness achieves its satisfaction only in another self-consciousness.'[94] But this is itself only one episode in the adventure of the spirit. Once Hegel's account reaches the fifth chapter of the *Phenomenology*, the vocabulary of desire and satisfaction falls away: another and higher drama is now played out, whose stage is reason. Beyond that, in turn, lie the vicissitudes of freedom inaugurated by the general will. By the time he came to write his political philosophy proper fifteen years later, Hegel makes little mention of desire or recognition. Satisfaction is still a central category, but its register is now mainly economic – related to material needs.[95] Kojève was thus not wholly unfaithful to Hegel; but he highlighted what Hegel tended to relinquish, or surpass.

The result is a quite distinct historical upshot. Its hallmark is no longer liberty. This is not because freedom as such plays no significant role in Kojève's philosophy of history – but rather because it features so radically at the beginning that it has little left to do at the end. One could call this the characteristic paradox of existentialism. Once human consciousness is defined *ab initio* as non-identity, and freedom as the movement of its nihilation in the world, its essential quest is for *identity* – that is, 'recognition' – not a second liberty. The satisfaction it seeks, in Hegel's original schema, is the fusion of its own self-awareness as for-itself with its presence as an in-itself acknowledged by others. It was Sartre who developed the most famous philosophical construction around this idea. In the phenomenological drama of *Being and Nothingness*, the pursuit by consciousness of a stable transparency in the in-itself-for-itself is an unavoidable yet impossible quest: freedom is a useless passion. The rest of Sartre's philosophy was one long attempt, in different ways, to reinsert freedom as an ethical or political goal still to be attained, back into an ontology which guaranteed it as a necessary burden in the first place. Kojève's version of the dialectic of recognition lacks the self-defeating thrust of Sartre's, but the logic of its relationship to the political realm is much the same. Since in Kojève's equation 'Liberty = Negativity = Action = History'[96] from the start, the output of the last term can add little to the input of the first. Satisfaction lies beyond this series. That is why it, rather than reason or freedom,

---

94. *W–3*, p. 144; *PS*, p. 110.
95. For the isolated references to each, see *W– 7*, § 57 and § 192 (recognition), and § 190 (desire) – the latter here said to be checked by the multiplication of needs: pp. 124, 349, 348.
96. *ILH*, p. 481.

becomes the principle of the perfect state. It was not just Hegel from whom Kojève took his leave here, but also Marx. He noted that his concept of *Befriedigung* is not to be found in Marx's writing. What takes its place, of course, is a concept whose absence is symptomatic in Kojève's: emancipation. The end of history signifies something else for Kojève. So little does its order primarily mean liberation for its citizens that at the limit he could write: 'Certainly, only the head of the universal and homogeneous state (Napoleon) is *really* "satisfied" (that is, recognized by all in his personal reality and value). Hence only he is really free.'[97] But, he went on, the citizenry could nevertheless be potentially satisfied since, with careers now open to talents, all might aspire to head the state. The role of the philosopher was to understand this conclusion of human development with the knowledge of the sage – as Hegel believed he had comprehended Napoleon, with an insight beyond the Emperor himself.

This conception was the occasion of a famous exchange after the war. When the lectures on the *Phenomenology* were finally published in 1947, Leo Strauss, a friend of Kojève from his time in France, and another thinker who had felt the influence of *Sein und Zeit*, greeted them as an extraordinary feat: 'No one has made the case for modern thought in our time as brilliantly as you.'[98] In the same letter, however, he also made a number of penetrating critical observations on Kojève's work. Kojève did not reply directly to these, but when Strauss published his own work *On Tyranny* the following year, Kojève responded with a pregnant restatement of his position in 1950, 'Tyranny and Wisdom'. Strauss's text, a meditation on Xenophon's *Hiero*, had warned his contemporaries that: 'We are now brought face to face with a tyranny which holds out the threat of becoming, thanks to "the conquest of nature" and in particular of human nature, what no earlier tyranny ever became: perpetual and universal.' He left the name of the danger in no doubt – humanity was now 'confronted by the appalling alternative that man, or human thought, must be collectivized either by one stroke and without mercy or else by slow and gentle processes.'[99] Against this menace, the abiding task of the philosopher was more urgent than ever: to expose the threat of tyranny as misrule, and to guard the detachment of philosophy from the city. Kojève's reply was

---

97. *ILH*, p. 146.

98. Letter of 22.8.48, in Leo Strauss, *On Tyranny* (ed. Victor Gourevich and Michael Roth), New York 1991, p. 236 – henceforward *OT*. This revised edition contains the correspondence between the two men, as well as Kojève's essay on Strauss's text, and Strauss's reply to it.

99. *OT*, p. 27.

an extended rejection of both conclusions. Tyranny did not invariably call for condemnation, and philosophers had been natural advisers to rulers, rather than their scourges, from the time of Aristotle onwards. The original relation between the Stagirite and his pupil was, in fact, exemplary. Alexander, the architect of the first universal empire, was not only perhaps the greatest statesman to have arisen within the horizon of Western philosophy, but 'certainly the one whom the great tyrants of our world have imitated for centuries (and who was only recently imitated again by an imitator of Napoleon who imitated Caesar, who was himself an imitator)'. Now, however, the goal pursued by humanity was not only a politically universal state but also a socially homogeneous – that is, classless – society, and once again the linkage of philosophy and power was repeated in the relation of Marx to Stalin. 'The tyrant who here initiates the *real* political movement towards homogeneity consciously followed the teaching of the intellectual', even if in doing so 'the tyrant has falsified the philosophical idea in order to "transpose it from the realm of abstraction into that of reality".' If all the major political enterprises of history had in this sense been guided by philosophical conceptions, 'these two examples effectively exhaust the great political themes of history.'[100]

For Strauss, this was an unabashed apology for Stalin's regime, which – if it did indeed bring a universal and homogeneous state – would represent a universal and final tyranny destructive of humanity as such. No social order could bring the kind of satisfaction Kojève envisaged: as the ancients had always insisted, the weakness and dependence of human nature precluded it. Dissatisfaction, of workers or of thinkers, would break out in any imaginary fulfilment of history. Hence Kojève's tacit admission – inscribed in the notion of a perfect state, rather than its withering-away – of the necessity for continuing coercion to suppress it. Philosophical wisdom pointed away from this, and every other, modern utopia. Political activity was a limited realm within the eternal order, and men were properly held by sacred restraints within it: limited constitutional government by a class of gentlemen – an open or covert aristocracy – was the only alternative to the brutal chaos of permanent revolution.[101] Kojève's prescriptions could only lead to a world of technological terror.

But as it turned out, Strauss's interlocutor eluded him. Kojève's political itinerary awaits detailed reconstruction. But his debate with Strauss revealed only one side of it. During the war, his confidence in

---

100. 'Tyranny and Wisdom', *OT*, pp. 169–173.
101. *OT*, pp. 193–94.

the Soviet state as the advance guard of history seems to have reached its height. In 1943 he wrote what can actually be regarded as his major work, *Esquisse d'une Phénoménologie du Droit*, a remarkable study of Law and the State that is his *Rechtsphilosophie*, which he left in manuscript and was only published in 1981. Here his leading philosophical themes are developed more systematically than in his *Introduction*, as the foundation for a historical typology of justice as the pursuit of recognition: from aristocratic equality to bourgeois equivalence, to their synthesis in socialist equity. The political conclusion of the book is in effect a set of proposals for the civil code of the universal and homogeneous state, which Kojève here straightforwardly terms the Socialist Empire with which history ends.[102] But the outcome of the war, after the Allied landings in Normandy, changed his thinking. By 1945, he had already developed an alternative prospectus. In a memorandum on post-war France, he argued that if the nation-state was now outdated, the universal state had not yet arrived. In this situation, where socialist internationalism and liberal anti-statism were equally impotent, the only effective structure was an intermediate form – the 'imperial union of related states', as both Churchill and Stalin had understood. If France was to overcome the weakness it had so fatally revealed as a nation-state in 1940, it must take the same path as the UK and the USSR. Its task was the construction of a Latin Empire, based on the Mediterranean and embracing Spain and Italy, to counterbalance the Anglo-Saxon and Soviet blocs which otherwise would dominate Europe. Under the leadership of de Gaulle, both the Catholic Church and the Communist parties could be integrated into such a project.[103]

---

102. *Esquisse d'une Phénoménologie du Droit*, Paris 1981, pp. 575–586. It is a paradox, due to the date of its appearance, that Kojève's richest work should still be the least discussed. The influence of Carl Schmitt is visible in it, confirming Niethammer's conjectures of the relations between them. It is here that Kojève explained most clearly the difference between his conceptions and those of Marx or the Utilitarians. 'For Hegel, the act of working presupposes another, that of the struggle for prestige, to which Marx did not give sufficient importance. But there is no doubt that economic man is always doubled by vainglorious man, whose interests can collide with his economic interests . . . To seek "Hegelian" satisfaction is a very different matter from pursuing what is "useful" in the ordinary sense of the term, in other words what is necessary for "happiness" or "well-being". If society is born from the desire for recognition, its supreme goal is the satisfaction and not the happiness of its members. On the contrary, at the limit, in the Ideal State, man satisfied socially is also (in principle) happy individually. But when a choice must be made between the two, it is satisfaction that wins. For it is the desire for satisfaction, not happiness, which determines social life as a whole. Otherwise one could never explain, let alone "justify" the phenomenon of war. Now experience shows that no healthy society ever refuses war when circumstances impose one on it': pp. 196, 202.

103. See the account of Kojève's 'Esquisse d'une Doctrine Politique Française', in Dominique Auffret, *Alexandre Kojève*, Paris 1990, pp. 282–89.

A few weeks after composing this document, Kojève joined the foreign section of the Ministry of Finance under Robert Marjolin, a former pupil in his Hegel seminar, and one of the architects of the Common Market. A year later, in his first publication after taking up official life, Kojève reiterated all the main themes of his pre-war interpretation of Hegel, while noting that the *Phenomenology* lacked a theory of the dialectic between masters that lay at the origin of states. But he ended it by saying: 'If there was from the beginning a Hegelian Left and a Hegelian Right, that is also *all* there has been since Hegel.' History had unfolded within the categorical framework the German philosopher had conceived, even if its exact outcome was still uncertain. 'It cannot be said that history has refuted Hegelianism. At most one can say that it has still not arbitrated between "left" and "right" interpretations of Hegel's philosophy.'[104]

What these were to be was spelt out with great clarity in a letter to Strauss shortly after their exchange. History, Kojève wrote, was moving towards a calculable conclusion, but the roads that led to it were varied, the product of alternative choices. 'For example: if the Westerners remain capitalist (that is to say, also nationalist), they will be defeated by Russia, and *that* is how the End-State will come about. If, however, they "integrate" their economies and policies (they are on the way to doing so), then *they* can defeat Russia. And that is how the End-State will be reached (the same universal and homogeneous State).'[105] As late as 1953 Kojève seems to have suspended judgement as to which alternative would prevail. But the elision in the first parenthesis – capitalism: i.e. nationalism – proved decisive. By the time the European Economic Community, in which he was to play an active role, was formed, the issue was settled : it was the West, not the East, which held the future of the world. The truth of Hegel had fallen to the Right, after all. Kojève died in 1968, dismissing with sardonic scorn the crowds in Paris who had failed to understand it.[106]

A few months earlier, he had written his codicil. In a famous footnote to the second edition of the *Introduction*, he explained that he had realized after the war that Hegel's timing had been correct after all – history had indeed come to an end on the field of Jena, rather than on the banks of the Volga. 'What has happened since is no more than an extension in space of the universal-revolutionary force actualized in

---

104. 'Hegel, Marx et le Christianisme', *Critique*, No. 3–4, August–September 1946, p. 365.

105. Letter of 19.11.50, *OT*, p. 256.

106. See Aron's report of his exchange with Kojève, more confident than he that no revolution was on the cards, on 29 May 1968, in *Mémoires*, p. 481.

France by Robespierre–Napoleon', as backward societies caught up with European principles. The Soviet and Chinese Revolutions were of the same order of events as the independence of Togo or Papua – of greater moment only in so far as they had prompted post-Napoleonic Europe to rid itself more briskly of its anachronisms. American society, now virtually classless in the abundance of its consumption, presented the rest of humanity with the image of its future.[107] Kojève's political reversal could hardly, it would seem, have been more complete. Yet there was a philosophical coherence behind it. He had always defined the end of history as the advent of a universal and homogeneous state. Compared with the ideals of Hegel himself, not to speak of those of Marx, the most striking feature of this description of the good society is its formalism. It lacks, very pointedly, any specification of property regime or constitutional structure. The reason is clear enough: this is an end-state deduced all too rigorously from the original figure of a bare dialectic of consciousness, shorn of social or institutional complication. As such, in its abstraction and simplicity, it was always liable to capsizals of reference. Universality and homogeneity – the all and the same – are categories sufficiently wide to accommodate an ample spectrum of contents. There was thus no conceptual barrier to stop Kojève from switching the end of his story from socialism to capitalism, without major adjustment. There was just one material change that was necessary. Homogeneity might assume any number of guises, but universality at least precluded one – the nation-state. This, which Hegel had upheld, Kojève consistently and vehemently rejected. The condition of his conversion to the West was its supersession of this form. The 'imperial union' advocated in 1945, recast as 'integration' in 1950, became a reality at Rome in 1957, and Kojève could end his days as counsellor to Giscard and Barre, performing the office of the philosopher as he had wished it.[108]

The geopolitical shift in Kojève's construction was thus smooth enough, once the Community was in place. Yet it did not leave its historical substance unaffected. However tacitly, the change of compass altered the meaning of the end of history. In the original conception, the disappearance of wars and revolutions ushered in a world in which politics and philosophy faded away, to leave a humanity at peace with itself and nature, engaged in 'art, love, play, in short everything that makes man *happy*'. This was the prospect Marx had described as

---

107. *ILH*, second edition, Paris 1967, pp. 436– 37.
108. For Kojève's relations with the President and Prime Minister of the seventies, see Aron, *Mémoires* pp. 97–99; Auffret, *Kojève*, pp. 416–423.

the realm of freedom, that lay beyond the struggle between classes and the duress of necessity. But now, with the substitution of the prosperity of capitalism for the promise of socialism, it underwent a transmogrification. The same condition emerges in a different light, as a degraded animality. In the new version, 'after the end of History, men would construct their edifices and works of art as birds build their nests and spiders spin their webs, would perform musical concerts after the fashion of frogs and cicadas, would play like young animals, and would indulge in love like adult beasts.'[109] This could not be described as happiness, but at most as the contentment of a post-historical species whose discourse itself would approximate to the signal-language of bees. The reign of such animality had already begun in the United States.

Strauss had, as it happened, taxed Kojève with just this prospect in his criticism of the *Introduction*, arguing that its projection of a Hegelian–Marxist idyll at the end of history in fact conjured up only the wilderness of Nietzsche's last men.[110] In effectively conceding the case, however, Kojève now turned it against its maker: not the land of the final tyrant, but that of the rule of ostensible gentlemen, was the breeding-ground of the species. The world-historical victory of the West is thus tainted with a philosophical irony. Kojève, who had always believed that wars and revolutions were the driving-force of history, at length concluded that after all it was markets and commodities that decided its outcome. But the heroic stamp of his Hegelianism was never quite effaced. The final mordancy of his image of post-history is the sign of a political nostalgia. It was in character that he added a twist to it. Perhaps the future did not lie in North America after all, but Japan – where for three centuries the ruling class had disengaged from war or work, yet without descending to animality, by transforming the common activities of life into pure exercises of style. A culture of ceremony rather than consumption might be the ultimate resting-place. In this scenario Japan would make over the West, and existentialism survive as formalism.

4. Three Sequels

With this last touch, the three major speculations on the end of history were in place. Hegel's vision of it, as we have seen, was oblique –

---

109. *ILH*, p. 434; and (second edition), p. 436.
110. *OT*, p. 208. It might be said that Strauss's echo of Ruyer found its ironical answer in Kojève's final echo of Cournot.

refracted through the higher medium of the spirit's return to itself in the realm of philosophy; and, partly also for that reason, incomplete – leaving significant contradictions unresolved. But its central theme was unambiguously affirmative: the goal of history was the realization of freedom, whose form would be the modern constitutional state. Cournot's account was a much more explicit conception, taking the form of an overall prediction derived from the trend of human development to date. Here it was the spread of rational administration, enabled by the interdependence of the market, that would bring history to an end, for the greater amenity – but not necessarily liberty – of the race. This vision too had its uncertainties: the rise of socialism as a threat to the market, the blindnesses within the market itself. Kojève's construction was declarative in a quite new way, foregrounding its theme as a philosophical leitmotif and a political guide to understanding the contemporary world. Here the end of history, initially conceived as universal recognition in an egalitarian state, ultimately became a social existence reduced to the routines of consumption, or to the rituals of style: the pursuit of fun or the devotion to form.

Each of these original versions has had its sequels. Cournot's legacy passed, without much attention to its detail or background, into the repertory of the German theorists of *Posthistoire* discussed by Niethammer, as a founding allusion. The conduit here was Henri de Man, in exile from Belgium after the war, whose intellectual formation dated from the time when Cournot's work was still current in French universities. De Man's usage of it is indicated by the title of the work in which he called Cournot's notion of a morphological stabilization of society to his aid: *Vermassung und Kulturverfall*. Written at the height of the Cold War, as it threatened to break out into hostilities, this connected military catastrophe and cultural decline. As the experience of two world wars and the increasing likelihood of a third demonstrated, modern civilization was numbed by an institutional massification in which the sheer scale of large organizations precluded any intelligent human direction. History necessarily lost meaning once social cause and effect became so disconnected, producing the political paralysis of an age of fear.[111] In de Man's version of post-history, rational administration is emptied of its reason, and Cournot's sceptical meliorism turns into nuclear pessimism. Suggestively, at virtually the same moment Aron published the most highly-strung of his writ-

---

111. *Vermassung und Kulturverfall*, Berne 1952, p. 125. Niethammer perhaps understates the military theme in de Man's prognosis.

ings during the Cold War, *Les Guerres en Chaîne*, in which he drew on Cournot's doctrine of independent causal series to analyse the conjuncture that had brought the world to the brink of its third 'hyperbolic war'.[112] But as the immediate danger of hostilities in Europe receded, it was the theme of bureaucratic petrefaction and cultural involution, not military escalation, that was transmitted to the German conservatives who took up the notion of a post-historical society. The most influential of these, Arnold Gehlen – who naturalized the term in the Federal Republic – argued that the sign of *Posthistoire* was a 'crystallization' of culture, in which no new constituents could any longer be generated. Just as the history of religions was to all intents and purposes manifestly over, leaving a range of major faiths to which no further creeds could be added, so now all secular ideological and aesthetic forms had become a fixed inventory. No more general philosophies of the kind once developed from Darwin or Marx or Nietzsche were any longer possible, though the key attitudes they inspired lived on – just as new avant-gardes in painting or literature, with capacity for radical innovation, had ceased to appear. The development of specialized sciences and the administrative structures built around them now precluded any chance of intellectual synthesis. The communist and democratic worlds still staged an ideological confrontation, to the advantage of the latter as more diverse and tolerant; and claimants to aesthetic rupture continued to parade, with varying degrees of talent. But in their basic forms, no further development of politics or art now seemed conceivable, as if the arsenal of historical experience was closed. All that remained was the recycling or crossing of the same elements, hybridization or repetition, great surface variety and deep underlying fixity.[113]

Advanced in 1960, Gehlen's thesis anticipates much of postmodernism twenty years later – was perhaps the first sharp glimpse of it. But if

---

112. The three great series were the unification of the planet as a single field of political force, the rise of Marxism as a secular religion, and the development of a military technology of mass destruction – each containing its own mixture of necessity and chance: *Les Guerres en Chaîne*, Paris 1951, pp. 197–203. Aron himself later expressed discomfort with this work (see *Mémoires*, pp. 284 ff.), but for all its failings of composition and rhetoric, it arguably remains his most imaginative piece of historical writing. It is clear from it that Cournot had left a deeper impression on him than the *Introduction* of 1938 might have suggested.

113. 'Über kulturelle Kristallisation', *Studien zur Anthropologie und Soziologie*, Neuwied 1963, pp. 311–328. Gehlen took the term 'crystallization' itself from Pareto. He ended his address, prophetically, by remarking that if there were two political problems that still loomed, one lay in the pressures building up among students in conditions of massified education, and the other in the call of hunger and overpopulation in the Third World.

there is a single source for the characteristic tone of the exit from history that came to be celebrated by the (mainly) French theorists of post-modernity, it is to be found in Kojève. The intellectual generation of Baudrillard or Lyotard never had any of his original sympathy for the Soviet regime – hostility to Stalinism was a touchstone of its political outlook. But it too originally looked for a social revolution, in quasi-situationist or workerist colours: the year 1968 was its 1942. But the general reestablishment of order which followed the turbulence at the turn of the seventies changed its mind. Capital was here to stay. There was no positive engagement in the enterprise of extending its horizons, of the kind that marked Kojève. But passive acceptance of its victory led to what might be termed a wifully demoralized assimilation of his conclusions. Whether in the variant that proclaimed all grand narratives dead, or which explained the passing of reality into simulation, the hallmark of the postmodern version of the end of history has been a fusion of the two motifs that Kojève had opposed as alternatives: no longer a civilization of either consumption or style, but of their interchangeability – the dance of commodities as *bal masqué* of libidinal intensities.[114] In this space, where aesthetic form and advertising function naturally interpenetrate, and a playful artifice models objects and persons alike, time has lost its strength. Modernity spent, history reaches its standstill in the streamlined whirl of a merry-go-round.

Just this vista is the critical target of the major heir to the Hegelian theme of the fulfilment of reason. In Habermas's work the relationship of philosophical conception to the original source has been much more deeply worked through than in the theorists of post-history or post-modernity, and yields results on quite another scale. *The Philosophical Discourse of Modernity* opens by rejecting both the theory of crystallization and the claims of postmodernism. The dynamic of modernity is not exhausted, Habermas argues. If the Enlightenment idea of a modern epoch can be defined as a present time breaking with the past, not in a single rupture, but in a continuous renewal, towards an elective future, Hegel stands near its starting-point – greeting the dawn of a new period as the sudden flash of lightning over the world, in the first pages of the *Phenomenology*. Hegel's philosophy is seen here as the commanding attempt to develop, out of the disturbing principle of a subjectivity freed from all traditional norms, self-validating structures

---

114. The most uninhibited version is Jean-François Lyotard, *Economie Libidinale*, Paris 1974. An ironic cameo of the post-historical landscape on view after 1968 can be found in Henri Lefebvre, *La Fin de l'Histoire*, Paris 1970, pp. 213–14.

of intellectual and institutional life. For Habermas, Hegel grasped with unmatched profundity the divisions within the culture and society of the Enlightenment, which pitted recently separated forms of thought and belief, and newly antagonistic systems of labour and rule against each other; and he rightly sought to reunite them in a historically grounded reason. But Hegel went astray in locating the site of such a reason. After early coming close to the right answer, his eventual solution was to postulate an absolute already inhabiting the subject, and thereby necessarily capable of overcoming its diremptions, in the passage of the spirit to itself. The result was a reason rendered too powerful: politically in a still authoritarian state, and philosophically in a devaluation of the present. Habermas does not tax Hegel with exalting his own time as the end of history, but rather with rejecting it in his reaction to the emergent demands for democracy in France and England.[115] The first great theoretician of modernity thus failed to remain true to it. But his work posed all its basic problems at such a depth that Habermas insists – echoing Kojève's dictum forty years earlier – we still remain contemporaries of the Young Hegelians.

For every subsequent discourse of modernity has been dominated by the same issue with which they grappled. Habermas defines this as the one-sided development of reason – whether as scientific knowledge, economic exchange, or bureaucratic power – at the expense of social cohesion and human possibility. The quest for a salve has taken many forms: Marx's recourse to production, as the secret of an alienated world and hope of its emancipation; Nietzsche's appeal to the archaic energy of an ecstatic will, against the pretensions of morality and the illusions of individuation; Heidegger's remembrance of an original being, before the arrival of hubristic metaphysics and destructive technologies. None of these critiques of actually existing modernity achieved its objectives. Their failure, Habermas argues, calls for a basic change of paradigm from a subject-centred to a communicative conception of reason, of the kind set out in his earlier work. This alone is proof against both the distortions exhibited by a purely instrumental reason, and the no less dangerous antidotes recurrently proposed for them. Only in such communicative reason can the means of fulfilling the promises of modernity be found. Here Habermas's epistemological revision leads directly to political conclusions. Contemporary societies suffer from two central problems. They are divided into impersonal systems coordinating social action through mechanisms that bypass

---

115. *The Philosophical Discourse of Modernity*, London 1987, pp. 41, 43 – henceforward *PDM*.

intersubjective communication – the steering media of money and power which rule market and state; and life-worlds which are the province of direct communicative understanding between subjects – family, education, art, religion. The differentiation between these forms of social living is a structural necessity of modernity, which cannot be lifted. But capitalist development has led to increasing encroachments of the systems into the life-world – bureaucratic and financial imperatives invading or corrupting its textures, with manifestly damaging consequences. At the same time, the inner coherence of the life-world itself is threatened by a multiplication of expert cultures, without any common vocabulary, weakening the bonds of spontaneous daily understanding between subjects – while the inherited particular identities on which any stable culture depends are undermined by growing pressure from rationalized universal norms. In these conditions, the self-reproducing springs of a free sociability are under threat from within and without.

What are Habermas's remedies? The life-world cannot reclaim the systems that have become detached from it. But the colonization by the systems back into its own space can be resisted by the erection of 'sensors' to detect and check the intrusions of money and power into the fabric of everyday relationships where these do not belong. At the same time, certain 'impulses' from the life-world can be transmitted in the opposite direction towards the systems, to influence their steering.[116] The public sphere is the natural site of such movements, which are strongest when based on collective identities. These always reflect concrete forms of life that cannot be severed from tradition without loss. But communicative reason can mediate between their particular contents and the requirements of a universalist ethics, in such a way as actually to strengthen the skein of customary meanings by lending them reflexive force. 'Critical testing and fallibilist consciousness even enhance the continuity of a tradition that has stripped away its quasi-natural state of being.' In so doing, they preserve 'the context of social integration by the risky means of an individualistically isolating universalism'.[117]

There is an audible echo in these proposals. What they call for, in effect, is a *Neue Sittlichkeit*. For the most striking feature of Habermas's construction is the way in which it remaps Hegel's philosophy of right. Here the division between state and civil society becomes the contrast between systems and life-world; and with the shift of the

116. *PDM*, p. 364.
117. *PDM*, pp. 346–47.

market to the former, and the family to the latter, the relative values attached to them are reversed. But the strict dualism of the underlying scheme, in which each structure has its own zone of competence, not to be infringed by the other, is retained. The same problem is then posed – how are the two domains to be pragmatically or morally integrated? The bridging role of the corporations falls, in Habermas's version, to the 'public sphere', located within the life-world but reaching out towards the systems beyond it. The common ethical substance that then underwrites the whole uncannily reproduces Hegel's own squaring of the circle, in the alchemy of a particular culture that yet displays a universal reason. The correspondence between the two architectonics is indeed more than formal. Politically, adjusting for the elapse of time, there is a curious resemblance in their upshots. Each accepts the market of the epoch as the objective order of any modern economic life, while noting social dysfunctions of it for which there appears to be no structural remedy. Each accepts the state of the day as the necessary form of subjective freedom, and warns against attempts to move beyond it towards more radical forms of self-determination. The Federal Republic is some way from post-Reform Prussia, but Habermas's commitment to parliamentary democracy is historically as conventional for its time as Hegel's was to constitutional monarchy. It leads to no greater hopes for political transformation from below. Popular sovereignty is a fiction: elective governments cannot transpose a collective will. No direct intervention from the life-world into the self-steering systems of the state and the economy is possible – only movements to 'sensitize' them from afar to needs finding their voice in the public sphere. The latter is, however, a somewhat ghostly space in this conception. The corporations which were to bind Hegel's construction together were extinguished virtually as he wrote. The public sphere that mediates social with systemic integration in Habermas's is one whose decline he himself charted long ago.[118] The measure of greater lucidity is part of what explains the lesser confidence of Habermas's scheme. His programme is largely a defensive one, of protection and delimitation, that no longer expects much from public authority. For today the state cannot be deemed the central institution in which 'society brings together its capabilities for organizing itself' – any more than society itself possesses 'capacities for self-organiza-

---

118. See the famous fifth and sixth chapters of *Strukturwandel der Öffentlichkeit*, Neuwied 1962. It is a measure of how beleaguered Habermas's conception of the relations between life-world and systems has actually become that he now typically speaks of the 'sensors' that should be erected by the former against the latter – a term belonging to the world of private security guards and military surveillance.

tion'.[119] The philosophical rejection of Hegel's conception of reason as too powerful issues into a political theory of democracy that is congenitally underpowered. What disappears most strikingly is the original demand that the structure of the state afford not only instrumental liberty but also expressive identity to its citizens. The fundamental need that took collective shape in the *polis* and which Hegel sought to lodge in the modern *Rechtsstaat* has retreated to the quiet conversations of the life-world. Or so it would seem. But there is a gesture that recalls it to a wider stage. Habermas ended his work by invoking the horizon of a European identity beyond the national one, to be constructed in contrast to the dominant American definition of the period, of unfettered military and market competition. The memory of Kojève comes back. But if Habermas's appeal is to the vision of a Europe more radical than that of Kojève – one not to be identified with the narrow institutions of the Common Market – it is also more tenuous. The structural transcendence of the nation-state as a political form, which was decisive for the Russian, acquires no relief in the German. Europe here is rather simply the soil in which 'universalistic value-orientations can take root'.[120] The move beyond Hegel's inter-state system is to that degree weaker. The strength of Habermas's commitment to a politics of solidarity and emancipation is not to be questioned. In a way it is just this that makes the theoretical upshot of his intervention so significant. Against the current of what he has criticized as neo-conservative or neo-anarchist theories of postmodernism, Habermas insists that modernity is a project still to be completed. But it might be said that his recommendations paradoxically amount to a judgement that it already is. For something very like the Hegelian end of history has tacitly arrived, when the limits of the existing liberal state and market economy are held insurpassable, as systems effectively beyond further popular control.

5. Fukuyama

These, then, are some of the principal strands in the intellectual background against which the latest contribution to the theme of the end of history is best seen. There was a substantial and intricate history behind the idea with which Fukuyama startled the world's journalists in the summer of 1989. Fukuyama's own version has developed

---

119. *PDM*, pp. 361–62.
120. *PDM*, p. 366.

significantly between its initial statement as an essay and its subsequent expansion as a book. In considering the merits of his case, it makes sense to look at these separately, since the first was responsible for a public debate that posed some of the issues raised in the second with especial clarity. In his original article, Fukuyama invoked Hegel and Kojève as the philosophical warrants for his intervention. The extent to which this appeal was legitimate should by now be apparent. What Fukuyama actually did here, however, was to combine the legacies of Hegel and of the late Kojève in a novel way. From Hegel he took two strands: the constitutionalism of the *Rechtsphilosophie* – what can, as we have seen, properly be called Hegel's liberalism; and the optimism of his conception of the end itself, as the realization of freedom on earth. The first of these was always foreign to Kojève, for whom liberalism – political or economic – was a relic of the past. The second animated Kojève's original interpretation of his time, when he looked to a socialist road to the realm of freedom, but was abandoned for the irony of his final vision of the spread of capitalism. From Kojève, on the other hand, Fukuyama took the sense of the centrality of the hedonism of modern consumption, and of the caducity of the traditional significance of the national state – themes quite absent in Hegel. The resultant synthesis is an original one, tying liberal democracy and capitalist prosperity together in an emphatic terminal knot.

The great change that has inspired this version of the end of history is, of course, the collapse of communism. When Habermas completed his *Philosophical Discourse*, Gorbachev was not even yet in power. Four years later, *perestroika* was already in agony, and the processes leading to the fall of the Soviet state far advanced. Fukuyama's vision is a product of this moment. Its author was well equipped for it. The classical discourse of conclusion has been the work of philosophers, acutely interested in the politics of their time, but at some professional distance from them. With Fukuyama, this relationship is reversed. A fully political mind is here trained on the structure of history, seen from a philosophical standpoint. That would have been appreciated by Kojève, in his office at the Quai Branly. The functionary of the State Department is – contrary to superficial report – a worthy successor of the *chargé de mission* at the Ministry of Finances.[121] The outcry his

---

121. For an example of Fukuyama's professional skills, see his fluent analysis of the dynamics of the breakdown of apartheid in South Africa, a field far from his original training in Sovietology: 'The Next South Africa?', *The National Interest*, Summer 1991, pp. 13–28.

original thesis provoked was a token, not of its ineptitude, but of its disturbing force.

In the reaction to it, what were the principal objections to Fukuyama's argument that after the gigantic conflicts of the twentieth century, 'the unabashed victory of economic and political liberalism' over all competitors means 'not just the end of the Cold War, or the passing of a particular period of history, but the end of history as such: that is, the end-point of mankind's ideological evolution and the universalization of Western liberal democracy as the final form of human government'?[122] They can be grouped into three categories. The first was a chorus of disapproval at the very idea of a historical conclusion, whatever its character. The great majority of Fukuyama's commentators in the world's press greeted his argument with incredulity – after all, do not common sense and daily news tell us that there are always fresh and unexpected events, and even that their pace is exponentially quickening, as the sensational close of the decade demonstrates? The response is, of course, a non-sequitur. Fukuyama's case allows for any number of further empirical events, as he has pointed out: it simply contends that there is a set of structural limits within which they will now unfold, that has been reached within the OECD zone. Kojève replied to this objection in his time, with characteristic vigour: the movement of history was accelerating more and more, but it was advancing less and less – all that was happening was 'the alignment of the provinces'.[123] Another, somewhat more doctrinal, complaint was that Fukuyama ignored the perennial passions and follies of human beings, which would always ensure instability in human affairs. This had essentially been Strauss's criticism of Kojève and was now typically repeated by conservatives.[124] Fukuyama's rejoinder was entirely Hegelian: human nature no doubt exists, but it also changes historically – today, for example, democracy looks like becoming a need of humanity as much as sleep.

Beyond such generic reactions, of least significance, a second sort of criticism focused on specific problems taken to be unresolved within Fukuyama's vision. It is a tribute to the continuity of his enterprise that the three major issues most consistently identified by his critics should be precisely those that were originally left unsettled by Hegel. The first

---

122. 'The End of History?', pp. 3–4.
123. *La Quinzaine Littéraire*, No. 53, 1–15 July 1968 – Interview with Gilles Lapouge, published just after his death.
124. See the comments by Hassner, Kristol, Huntington, Gray, among those noted above.

of these was war. There was no reason to think that the traditionally hierarchical and rivalrous relations between states would disappear even after a putative generalization of liberal democracy. The Hobbesian logic of the international field would continue to generate violent conflicts between great powers, or small. What was to guarantee that these might not one day explode into nuclear war itself? To this Fukuyama answered, with justice, that modern states have never simply pursued power as an independent goal in itself, but rather as a means to secure particular interests that are always ideologically defined. A world in which all states shared a common normative commitment to free markets and free elections would not be one that generated the classical range of military hostilities. In support of this claim, Fukuyama could point to the evidence that completed representative democracies have not waged war with each other to date: one that a significant independent literature has been insisting on for some time.[125] If Kant's vision of the conditions for a perpetual peace still remains far from reality, a plausible case can be made that with the spread of constitutionally elected government around the world, the trend of development is moving closer towards them.

The second principal criticism of Fukuyama's scheme was to be that it ignored the persistence of inequality and misery within the advanced capitalist societies themselves – not least the United States – which must qualify any liberal triumphalism. There is no doubt that Fukuyama's treatment of social questions in his essay was cavalier to a degree: repetition of Kojève's *boutade* that Marx's classless society had virtually come to pass in America did not help it. Poverty, he conceded, did exist, and inequality might have grown in the most recent period. These, however, were not a function of class, but of culture: black handicaps were a pre-modern legacy of slavery and racism, unrelated to the egalitarian logic of liberalism. The more general phenomenon of under-classes in the West received no mention. Fukuyama's confidence in the consumer abundance of modern capitalism – VCRs for all, as he put it – expresses the outlook of officialdom in the eighties. Hegel's fear that a menacingly destitute and deracinated rabble would be reproduced by the mechanisms of civil society itself, as it generated crises of overproduction and unemployment, has receded. Poverty still lingers, but its causes lie in cultural drawbacks rather than market forces.

---

125. The standard source is Michael Doyle, 'Kant, Liberal Legacies and Foreign Affairs', *Philosophy and Public Affairs*, Summer 1983, pp. 205–235, and Fall 1983, pp. 323–353; and 'Liberalism and World Politics', *American Political Science Review*, December 1986, pp. 1151–1169.

Whether the new explanation assures a readier cure for it was not spelt out. In its original statement Fukuyama's idealism appears to hesitate here, between a belief that liberal principles must eventually carry all before them, bringing cultural laggards up to a common material standard, and a sense that cultures form wider meaning-complexes whose appeal cannot be reduced to the interests of liberty and plenty. In the latter case, no clear-cut solution would be in sight.

The third objection commonly made to Fukuyama's prospect was that it fails to address just those human needs to which a culture in the deeper sense answers. A society built simply on votes and videos lacks *Sittlichkeit*. How stable can it be, in the long-run? Hegel's theory of the State had envisaged a synthesis of freedom and identity – self-determination as both representation and as expression. What comparable moral substance does the contemporary political order in the West have to offer? The most frequent liberal response today is to dismiss the question as misplaced: in a democratic society, the public arena is necessarily no more than the instrumental space in which substantive private goals of diverse kinds may be pursued. The quest for meaning is an individual, not a social affair. One response to this *fin de non-recevoir* is to try to finesse its distinction. This is, in effect, the function of the notion of 'intersubjectivity' in critics like Habermas, which glides back and forth between private and public contexts along a referential continuum – from the conversational to the congressional, so to speak. If such solutions typically deliver less than they promise, the reason lies in their starting-point: the nuclear 'dialogue' between two persons is a domestic, not a civic model. Replying to his critics, Fukuyama neither denied the problem nor floated a solution of this sort. Acknowledging the force of the objection, he suggested that it was a more serious critique of the liberal state than one based upon the persistence of racial or social inequities. Victory over the communist adversary in the Cold War, which did provide the West with a transcendent collective goal, could only accentuate the lurking vacuum within the value-order of liberal capitalism. It was at this, concluding point that Fukuyama's account altered register, and moved towards a Kojèvian irony: for all its vast – definitive – benefits to humanity, the end of history risks being a 'very sad time', as the epoch of high endeavours and heroic struggles becomes a thing of the past.

If the sequel is compared with the original over these three areas, there has been a change of weighting. For Hegel, war persisted as a necessity of the inter-state system, with its bracing effects on the life of societies. Consciously, it posed no problem for him – even if, logically, it contradicted the universality of the realization of freedom. Poverty, on the other hand, was a tare that tormented society, and for which his system confessed its lack of solution. Finally, community posed an acute problem with the new atomism of civil society, but the philosophy of right had an answer in the organic articulation of the state. For Fukuyama, by contrast, poverty was a residue of former times that is subject to attitudinal improvement. War was an evil to be overcome, whose necessity is diminishing as states approach their rational norm. Community, however, has become less imaginable today than in Hegel's epoch, and its absence haunts liberalism even in its apotheosis. But whereas the totalizing claim of Hegel's system as Absolute Knowledge rendered it vulnerable to empirical tensions or puzzles it could not resolve, casting doubt on the implication that history had reached its end, Fukuyama's argument was not subject to the same kind of effect. Quite expressly, his schema did not require the suppression of every significant social conflict or the solution of every major institutional problem. It simply asserted that liberal capitalism is the *ne plus ultra* of political and economic life on earth. The end of history is not the arrival of a perfect system, but the elimination of any better alternatives to this one.

No reply to Fukuyama is of any avail, therefore, if it contents itself with pointing out problems that remain within the world he predicts. An effective critique must be able to show that there are powerful systemic alternatives he has discounted. Were his critics able to do so? Here too three main lines of riposte can be distinguished. The first insists on the tidal force of nationalism, as the most formidable political passion of the century – one whose spread is still gathering momentum, rolling humanity towards unknown destinations. In this line of argument, emphasis can be given either to the boiling of ethnic hatreds between and within newly emergent states – in the Subcontinent, in Eastern Europe, in the former Soviet Union; or to the potential for renewed national rivalries to set in motion Great Power ambitions of the kind that dominated the scene before 1914 – the favourite candidates are Japan, once it becomes the largest economic power, or a more industrialized China, mustering the largest population in the world. Fukuyama's case, however, contained careful consideration of just these possibilities. Neither, he pointed out, amounted to a real contraindication. The spread of small to medium-sized national conflicts in the Third or former Second Worlds would continue, as typical symptoms of regions still trapped in history. But these would be peripheral disturbances, without major incidence on the inter-state system dominated by the large powers – Fukuyama's geographical gesture deliberately recalls Kojève's: 'it matters very little what strange thoughts occur to people in Albania or Burkina Faso.'[126] Competition between the large states, on the other hand, would threaten the new world order only if one or more of them were seized by the kind of nationalism that is global in ambition – that is, which aims at universal empire. Fascism was precisely such a creed, in the Third Reich and Showa Japan. Its destruction throws into sharp relief the limits of the jockeying for national advantage that has followed, now devoid of any universal dynamic of a comparable kind. Even before completing the journey to liberal capitalism, Chinese foreign policy resembles that of Gaullist France more than Wilhelmine – let alone Nazi – Germany. Once within the zone of advanced capitalism proper, the level of antagonisms drops much further – relations between the US and Canada, or within the European Community, providing the emergent standard.

Fukuyama's cool refusal of certain kinds of conventional wisdom is nowhere more striking than in his judgement of this issue. The conflict in the Gulf which excited so many of his critics, igniting enthusiasm on Right and Left alike for the battle to uphold the cause of national independence and democracy in the Middle East against the menace of a new Hitler, he was to compare with the quarrel between a fifteenth-century condottiere and a thirteenth-century clerical seigneurie. Nationalism is virulent where not much counts; where things are of greater moment, innoculation has occurred, or is under way. In neither case is nationalism a serious challenge as a future doctrine. Although provocatively expressed, the underlying judgement here is not out-landish. It substantially concurs, as it happens, with the views of two of the most prominent recent analysts of the phenomenon, one a liberal and the other a socialist, Ernest Gellner and Eric Hobsbawm – whose political attitudes to nationalism differ, but whose historical diagnosis of its future is quite similar. The taming of national passions by consumer pursuits is a common theme of these writers – in effect, the modern version of the role ascribed to *le doux commerce* in the world of absolutism. Its force is unquestionable. Fukuyama's general case is, taken on its own, strong enough. There is a contingency his essay overlooked, however. Nationalist conflicts in themselves may indeed be of less structural significance in world politics; but connected to nuclear weaponry, in the zone of history, they could have greater material consequences even than in the past. Formally speaking, this would not necessarily alter Fukuyama's verdict, since military devas-tation from a Third World exchange offers no prospect of positive

---

126. 'The End of History?', p. 9.

social substitution in the First World. But it is a reminder of the fact that the end of history has another familiar meaning, and that arrival at one kind of terminus in the rich countries does not preclude engulfment in the other kind so long as there are poor countries with modern armaments – that is, of no more than yesterday.

The second potential challenge to the universal hegemony of liberalism to be adduced by Fukuyama's critics was fundamentalism. The Shi'ite revolution in Iran, the growth of Hindu communalism in India, the spread of Sunni rigorism in North Africa – even such movements as the Moral Majority in the US, Komeito in Japan, Solidarity in Poland: do they not reveal the renewed political appeal of revealed religion in today's world? The argument that phenomena like these may presage wider theological enthusiasms to come can draw on sociological speculation about 'the return of the sacred' that dates back to the seventies. A motley cast of figures – Woytila, Solzhenitsyn, Khomeini, Sin, Tutu – is sometimes invoked in support of it. But if nationalism does not provide a credible alternative to Fukuyama's scenario, still less does fundamentalism. Unlike national creeds, religious doctrines are typically – though not invariably – universal in their claims, as truths valid in principle for all of humanity, rather than particular communities within it. But the status of these tenets is also, of course, more vulnerable to the advance of secular culture and technology: faith in supernatural authority may be morally loftier than belief in state power, but the latter is less at risk from the progress of the natural sciences. The actual incidence of religious fervour in the world at large is patchier than that of patriotic zeal. Indeed, it typically catches fire as an additive to inflammable national sentiment, rather than as a combustible material in its own right. The mixture is then nearly always of exceptional potency, as the examples of Poland, Iran, Ireland and elsewhere show. Its price, however, is the limitation of the religious to the national – spiritual faith reinforcing territorial identity rather than transcending it. The one major exception to this rule is to some extent more apparent than real. Islamic fundamentalism at large, as distinct from the Twelver sect of Shi'ism in Iran, is a major cross-national force. It is usually the centrepiece of arguments for the growth in importance of religion in global politics. But here too the intertwining of religious and national strands is very close – the origins of Islam, as a religion of conquest and a doctrine of the sacred, inseparable from the definition of Arab ethnic and linguistic identity as such. For all the intervening differences, Islamic fundamentalism is in this respect a successor to the Arab nationalism that failed. It remains to be seen whether it will prove more effective. But even were it to do so, its appeal would still remain fairly limited, as Fukuyama points out – at most extending into West-Central and South-East Asia, and the Sahel. Fundamentalism, a return to theological origins, is not a serious candidate for prolonging the ideological evolution of humanity beyond the term of liberalism.

Matters are different with the last of the forces to be enlisted as a refutation of Fukuyama's central argument. Communism may have collapsed (even if the final episode has still to unfold in China), but – it was argued – this does not mean that socialism as an alternative to capitalism has disappeared. It is alive and well as the most advanced form of democracy in our time – the variety that calls itself social. In Western Europe, temporary setbacks may have checked its progress in the eighties, when international capital increasingly outflanked national governments; but the proportion of the national product absorbed by public expenditure has not qualitatively fallen, and the coming of a Federal European Union will create the conditions for renewing a forward march. Marxism and totalitarianism finally buried, social democracy emerges in its true colours as the only real socialism from the beginning – its aims now clarified to a responsible regulation of the market, an equitable system of taxation, a generous provision of welfare, within the framework of parliamentary rule.[127] If much still remains to be done, this is because the structures of democracy itself – often the creation of popular movements that had to battle against liberalism for it – are by no means complete in the West: the agenda of socialism is to extend them. A variant of this form of response shares its emphasis on democratic development, but maintains not so much that socialism is a survivor, as that capitalism is a misnomer. Are we not already beyond it, in the increasingly hybrid societies of today, in which the most successful economies – Japan and Korea, or Germany and Austria – reveal high levels of state coordination of the market, or corporatist organization of industrial relations?[128] For Ralf Dahrendorf, the very idea of a capitalist 'system' can be dismissed – in the democratic world today, there are only heterogeneous societies with

---

127. For this general argument, see Michael Mann, 'After Which Socialism?', *Contention*, Winter 1992, pp. 183–192, a reply to Daniel Chirot, 'After Socialism, What?', *Contention*, Fall 1991. Chirot's version of the eclipse of socialism is similar to Fukuyama's, but with greater emphasis on the scale of the problems left outstanding by it, and less confidence that new forms of fascism might not emerge in the poorer countries in reaction.

128. This position is best represented by Paul Hirst: 'Endism', *London Review of Books*, 23 November 1989.

different institutional mixtures; and so it will be in the ex-communist countries tomorrow.[129] Criticisms of this kind have typically, of course, come from the Left or Centre–Left in Europe; although isolated voices from the Right also warned against too facile an assumption that socialism has been finally defeated – since creeping statism has, despite every effort by Thatcher or Reagan, not been genuinely scotched in the past decades.[130] Common to all these objections is the belief that capitalism is less triumphant, because more hedged and blended, than it seems. In the radical versions of this case, the future lies in the continuing expansion of social democracy beyond it, as truly existing socialism.

The impulse behind this rejection of Fukuyama's vision is an honourable one. The desire not to minimize the social gains in human welfare and security that have been achieved against the straightforward logic of capital accumulation, and the hope that these are a pledge of what more might be won, belong to any radical politics of the Left. Progressive loyalty and analytic clarity are, however, two different things. Western Europe as a zone is, of course, distinct in its Social-Democratic – and Christian-Democratic – traditions from the USA or Japan; though the practical effect of these has dwindled over the past two decades, when mass unemployment has actually been higher in the EC. But the economies of the Community are, of course, capitalist on any definition – classical or contemporary – of the term, structurally driven by competition between enterprises hiring wage-earners to produce profits for private owners. Hayekians, Keynesians, Marxists, have no difficulty in agreeing on this. The wish to drape a softening veil over this reality, in the name of local improvements, is idle. The attempt to quit the realm of concepts altogether, by denying the very existence of capitalism – since every advanced society differs from every other – is equally fruitless, a search for a nominalist bolt-hole in the sand. What such postures really represent is a strategy of intellectual consolation. Fukuyama's inventory of the world appears unpalatable: but if it is difficult to find forces capable of altering the world, why not change the inventory? With the wand of a redescription, we can dispose of

---

129. *Reflections on the Revolution in Europe*, London 1990, which develops this theme, contains an uncharacteristic outburst on Fukuyama.

130. See David Stove's comment: 'The welfare state still grows every year at about the same staggering rate as it has done since 1900. Does not *this* process have the genuine feel of irresistibility about it, the irresistibility which Fukuyama's hypothetical opposite thesis so conspicuously lacks?' – *The National Interest*, Fall 1989, p. 98.

capitalism or reassure ourselves of socialism. The truth is that the growth of both economic regulation and social provision were foreseen over a century ago by Cournot, not as disproof of the halting of history at advanced capitalism, but as characteristic of it as a final constellation. Unless a convincing trend-line can be shown, pointing from present welfare arrangements or dirigiste practices towards the threshhold of a qualitatively distinct type of society, neither social democracy nor industrial policy is a witness against Fukuyama; and no critic from the Left suggested one. In the debate which followed Fukuyama's essay, here as elsewhere, the score-card was in his favour. The criticisms made of capitalist democracy – its degrees of material inequality, national rivalry, want of community – are compatible with it as an end-state; the alternatives proffered to it as an end-state – nationalism, fundamentalism, corporatism – lack empirical or conceptual credibility. From this first testing, Fukuyama's case emerged relatively intact.

Some three years later, there has appeared the book-length version. *The End of History and the Last Man* discharges the promissory note of the essay with conviction and elegance. Here, for the first time, the philosophical discourse of the end of history has found a commanding political expression. In a remarkable feat of composition, Fukuyama moves with graceful fluency back and forth between metaphysical exposition and sociological observation, the structure of human history and the detail of current events, doctrines of the soul and visions of the city. It is safe to say that no one has ever attempted a comparable synthesis – at once so deep in ontological premise and so close to the surface of global politics. What are the principal developments in the original argument that it brings? Fukuyama now mounts his interpretation of the dramatic turning-point in world affairs at the turn of the nineties in an overall theory of universal history. Human evolution displays directionality because of the cumulative advance of technical knowledge, perceptible from the dawn of the species, but given decisive impetus with the birth of modern science in early modern Europe. Scientific reason, once unleashed, has over time transformed the world at large by obliging all states to modernize – militarily and socially – if they wish to survive pressure from powers technologically ahead of them; and by opening up unlimited horizons of economic development for the satisfaction of material needs. Fukuyama dubs this process 'the mechanism of desire'. Science supplies the fundamental machinery for the fulfilment of wants. Imposing a rational organization of labour and of administration – factories and bureaucracies – it has raised living standards to previously unimaginable levels. Once its dynamic creates a mature industrial economy, it inexorably selects out capitalism as the only efficient – because competitive – system for raising productivity within a global division of labour.

On the other hand, even a highly successful capitalist economy does not necessarily guarantee political democracy. The path to liberty differs from that to productivity. Its starting-point lies in the contest that Hegel, and Kojève after him, rightly identified – the willingness to risk death to wrest acknowledgement of the self by others, at the origin of the dialectic of master and slave.[131] It is the struggle for recognition that drives humanity towards the goal of freedom: the impulse to self-assertion, rather than self-preservation. Contrasting the Anglo-Saxon tradition of Hobbes and Locke, construing politics principally as the rational pursuit of interest (security or property), with Hegel's vision of it as a quest for existential recognition, Fukuyama argues that this was the opposition originally set out in Plato between *epithemia* and *thymos* – 'desire' and 'spiritedness'. Throughout most of history, as Hegel had seen, thymotic striving was an aristocratic pursuit – the prerogative of lords, doing battle with each other, after subduing their bondsmen. But when modern science eventually brought a commercial society, this warrior ethos declined, as the spirit of greatness – *megalothymia* – yielded to softer comforts, and a newly spirited sense of equality – *isothymia* – sprang up, demanding not particular but universal recognition: the modern ideals of liberty and equality born with the American and French Revolutions. It is the final triumph of these that we witness at the end of the twentieth century. The crowds in Leipzig, the students on Tien An Min Square, step out of the pages of the *Republic* and the *Phenomenology*.

The worldwide liberal revolution of our time, in which capitalism and democracy can be seen sweeping across the globe, is a product of the convergence of the two dynamics, of desire and recognition. The most striking sign, Fukuyama argues, of the irresistible force of the principles of liberal politics (the rule of law, free elections, civic rights) is not just the speed and scale of the collapse of so many dictatorships round the globe – starting in Southern Europe in the mid-seventies,

---

131. Fukuyama is now careful to disclaim any binding authority for Kojève's interpretation of Hegel, and to set his own ideas free from textual issues. 'While uncovering the original Hegel is an important task, for the purposes of the present argument we are interested not in Hegel *per se* but in Hegel-as-interpreted-by Kojève, or perhaps a new, synthetic philosopher named Hegel–Kojève': *EHLM*, p. 144.

spreading to Latin America in the eighties, stretching across the Pacific, then moving to Eastern Europe and the USSR at the end of the decade, before finally reaching Africa – but also the absence of violence that has overwhelmingly marked it. Already inwardly converted to the superiority of their opponents' ideas, the elites of authoritarian regimes of Left and Right have caved in, one after another, without a fight. In these same years, moreover, it was not merely that the central planning of the communist economies proved itself a dead-end. The belief that poor countries could not develop capitalist economies capable of competing with the rich was also shown to be a myth. The astonishing success of the new industrial states of East Asia – Korea, Taiwan, Singapore, tomorrow perhaps Thailand or Malaysia – has destroyed the superstition that late-comers to the world market are fated to penury and dependency. It is now clear that capitalist prosperity is available to all countries that respect the principles of liberal economics. The lesson is rapidly being learnt elsewhere – in Mexico, Argentina, and beyond. A universal consumer culture now beckons all peoples of the world alike, and no underdeveloped region is shut out from the prospect of its bounty.

For Fukuyama it is this double demonstration, of the magnetism of representative institutions and of competitive markets, that has sealed the victory of liberal capitalism. Out of the bloody tumult of the century, an uncontested winner has finally emerged. Today, 'liberal democracy remains the only coherent aspiration that spans different regions and cultures around the globe', and 'we cannot picture to ourselves a world that is essentially different from the present one, and at the same time better' – 'a future that is not essentially democratic and capitalist', and would 'represent a fundamental improvement over our current order'.[132] Many outstanding social problems – lack of homes, jobs, opportunities; need and crime – remain even in the rich countries; and differing solutions can be envisaged to them within the range of trade-offs between liberty and equality that a democratic capitalism affords. If there are outer limits to the range, set by the principles of effective private property, there is no stable optimum along it, and more social democracy can be pressed here and there, without altering the basic parameters of the time. For the central political fact today is that there are no programmes claiming to overcome capitalism left. The liberal revolution is not yet accomplished everywhere. But in the

---

132. *The End of History and the Last Man*, New York 1992, pp. xiii, 46, 51. Henceforward *EHLM*.

absence of any contestants to it, history does indeed appear to have come to its term.

Is that appearance conclusive? Turning to the second part of his title, and now addressing the major problem he conceded was left open by his original essay, Fukuyama points out that the empirical elimination of alternatives does not in itself settle whether this order satisfies the categorical demands of humanity – that is, the enduring aspirations which define our nature as a species. If it does not, then present victory will bring no ultimate stability, since challenges to liberal capitalism will inevitably arise from the structure of human longings themselves. Is there any sign this might be so? Fukuyama's answer is deeply – deliberately – equivocal. The critique of liberal capitalist society from the Left taxes it with failing to realize universal recognition of its members, because of the differences of wealth and status it continually reproduces. The threat to it from this direction lies in the pressure for a 'super-universalization' of rights that would use the vocabulary of liberalism itself to subvert it, by levelling economic property under the mask of assuring juridical equity. But this familiar danger is likely to be less serious than its opposite: the critique from the Right that charges liberal democracy with levelling natural excellence by its constitutional egalitarianism and legal formalism. Reason and desire are satisfied in the technological ingenuity and consumer abundance of this civilization; but spiritedness is not. The *thymos* which achieved modern liberty is not altogether banished once it is established as a normal fact; democracy functions best when there is a public spirit attached to more than prosperity and efficiency – just as capitalism is most successful when pride in work and community exceeds simple calculation of self-interest. But the thymotic elements in contemporary political and economic life are for the most part traces of a pre-modern past: they are not nourished by democratic capitalism, whose logic works against them. Its popular ethos, of immediate wants and civic indifference, lends all too much substance to Nietzsche's vision of the last men. *Megalothymia* has no place here. But a striving for self-assertion, not as an equal among equals, but as an eminence over others, is one of the inherent springs of human conduct. If the modern liberal order should grant insufficient space for it, by denying unequal recognition to superior worth, history will no doubt resume in revolt against its democratic *ennui*. Nietzsche could predict that vast wars would break out even between sated societies. Yet nuclear weapons render this unthinkable. Perhaps, after all, the challenge from the Right too will be contained. Even if capitalist democracy does not fulfil the three parts of the soul in equal measure, it may represent the best available balance between them, beyond which no earthly progress is possible.

With this, Fukuyama's case is complete – the doctrine, in effect, of a liberal *Sprung in der Freiheit*. The charge heard on the Right, of an inverted Marxism,[133] is grounds for tribute on the Left. Any critique which fails to acknowledge this is blind. But if the socialist conception of the leap has fallen into discredit today, is this capitalist version a coherent successor? Fukuyama's work contains a psychology, a history and a politics. For all the force of their assembly, each exhibits its own internal strain. Intellectually, the most striking innovation of *The End of History and the Last Man* is the filling-out of a Hegelian theory of history with a Platonic theory of human nature. What is the fit between the two? Fukuyama's account turns on the role of *thymos* – the spirit that lies between reason and desire in Plato's topography of the soul. Now tripartite models of psychic – or, for that matter, social – reality are in themselves common enough. The Christian division of the subject into mind, will and passions was to be another example of the first; modern sociological theories often exemplify the second – dividing society into forces of cognition, coercion and production, or ideology, polity, economy, etc. Such triads tend to look rather alike, inviting alignment or superimposition. In fact, their merits differ widely, depending on the units of demarcation they employ. In a comparative range, Plato's triad is one of the weakest; and *thymos* is actually its most brittle point. The primary sense of the term was ire – Hegel, in his commentary on the *Republic*, translated it simply as *Zorn*,[134] and Plato himself remarks that infants and animals display it: in other words, anger at frustrated desire. It is motivated into its position within the trichotomous soul, however, as anger at *fulfilled* desire – what would usually today be called 'conscience'. This permutation into its opposite then allows Plato to argue that *thymos* is more closely associated with reason than with desire, and finally to identify it, not with conscience as indignation at the self, but *exclusively* with contention for power and honour over others (which can be perfectly cold).[135] The conflation of meanings – infant rage, self-reproach, social domination – is so marked that it was short-lived. In Greek, *thymos* is

---

133. 'Fukuyama's thesis itself reflects not the disappearance of Marxism but its pervasiveness. His image of the end of history is straight from Marx . . . Marxist ideology is alive and well in Fukuyama's arguments to refute it': Samuel Huntington, 'No Exit – The Errors of Endism', *The National Interest*, Fall 1989, pp. 9–10.

134. *W–19*, p. 120; *LHP–2*, London 1894, p. 105.

135. For these elisions and reversals, compare *Republic*, 439–441 with 581; 'Do we not maintain that the spirited part is wholly bent on winning power and victory and celebrity?' Behind Fukuyama's reading lies Allan Bloom's (moderate) effort to hold these

an affective magma, whose instability of moral definition arises from the absence of any clear conception of the will. But its usage gave no general support for Plato's gloss. The most famous single judgement of *thymos* was made by Euripides: as she surrenders to it, Medea's last words before committing her crime simply speak of *thymos* as 'the cause of the greatest ills to human beings'.[136] Plato himself scarcely persisted with the notion, and when his successor came to *thymos*, its incoherence flew apart – Aristotle simultaneously invoking it as the spring of political rule and freedom, and dismissing it as the rush of a wild beast.[137] The reason why the tripartite soul is both so prominent in the *Republic* and so transient afterwards is, of course, that it is derived from the structure of the Platonic state, whose hierarchy of philosophers, warriors and toilers it is designed to match. 'As the state is held together by three great classes, the producers, the auxiliaries and guardians, *so also* in the soul spiritedness constitutes a third element, the natural ally of reason.'[138] When Plato revised his political doctrine in the more realist key of *The Laws*, where government rests on a class hierarchy of wealth, spirit loses its salience and the soul veers back towards the original Socratic division between reason and the appetites.

What is the effect of Fukuyama's adoption of the tripartite model? In his construction, the role of *thymos* is in one sense antithetical to everything urged by Plato, and yet its profile is no less polymorphous. On the one hand, it is the engine of democracy; on the other, it is the ambition for supremacy. It can represent a pride in personal autonomy or a culture of collective conformity; a sense of equality or a validation of hierarchy. In these variations, a basic antinomy is being repeatedly conjugated, in which the self is both asserted against and assimilated to others. At the limit, Fukuyama offers prefixes to distinguish the two – *megalo: iso* – but the question is whether the compounds share any

---

contradictory usages more or less together: *The Republic of Plato*, New York 1968, pp. 355– 57, 375–77. For a much more extravagant attempt to demonstrate the seamless unity of Plato's whole construction in the *Republic*, see the recent interpretation – decked out with every device of analytic philosophy – of C.D.C. Reeve, *Philosopher–Kings*, Princeton 1988, who renders *thymos*, 'the dark horse of the psychic parts', in more elevated style as 'aspiration', with the naive claim that 'anger essentially involves a belief about the good': pp. 136–37.

136. *Medea*, 1078–80: 'I understand what evils I am about to do, but *thymos* is stronger than my reasonings, the cause of the greatest ills to human beings.'

137. Compare *Politics* at 1327b–1328a, referring directly to Plato, with *Nicomachean Ethics* at 1115a–1117a.

138. *Republic*, 441.

underlying substance. Are the quest for liberty, the talent for industry, the ideal of community, the will to primacy, all manifestations of the same high spirits? The semantic overload appears acute. To sustain it, Fukuyama essentially appeals to Hegel. 'Plato's *thymos* is therefore nothing other than the psychological seat of Hegel's desire for recognition.'[139] The juncture between the two is not without its logic. Hegel, like Plato, developed a theory of the state in parallel to a theory of the mind in the *System der Sittlichkeit* of 1802–3, with a social hierarchy visibly modelled on the moments of the spirit, in the fashion of the *Republic*. The movement of self-consciousness, when it is recapitulated in the *Encyclopaedia*, passes from desire to a struggle for recognition, here indeed associated with 'honour', and then out into the rational reciprocity of universal freedom.[140] The similarities look quite close. But there are two critical differences. The idea of the soul as a repertoire of constant dispositions defining human beings was alien to Hegel, who even refused to credit it of Plato – affecting to believe it was only his vivid imagery that had led to such a misrepresentation.[141] The soul appears in the *Encyclopaedia* as no more than a lowly preamble to consciousness – 'the soul is only the *sleep* of the mind'.[142] Any conception of human nature at all was, of course, rejected yet more categorically by Kojève, who – unlike Hegel – was scathing about Plato's idealism in general, and his doctrine of the psyche in particular.[143] In place of a substantification of the soul, what this tradition generated was a dialectic that developed desire, recognition and free-

---

139. *EHLM*, p. 165.
140. *W–10*, § 432, pp. 221–22; *HPM*, pp. 172–73.
141. *W–19*, pp. 30–31; *LHP–2*, p. 21.
142. *W–10*, § 389, p. 43; *HPM*, p. 29.
143. In his three-volume study of Greek philosophy, Kojève dismissed Plato's psychological doctrine as unworthy of serious consideration: a mixture of edifying or popular opinions, without relation to his theory of Ideas, and self-contradictory claims about the transcendence and autonomy of the soul, which absurdly denied that men had created the world of technology and history. The *Republic* was simply a satire on any State, to mark its distance from an Academy. Aristotle's psychology merited more attention, as a fully-fledged naturalism, which Kojève attacked without remission. Although Aristotle at least granted man's capacity to act in (innate) pursuit of his own satisfaction, rather than being drawn passively towards it as a divine grace, his doctrine was still a crude biologism of human nature. What it yielded was a kind of ancient behaviourism, that reduced the dialectic of master and slave to a division between races, without a glimpse of the struggle for recognition as a contest between one free consciousness and another. Aristotelian virtue – *a fortiori* Platonic *thymos* – was a vitalist value, or as Kojève scornfully put it, a merely veterinary matter. In a remark with more than one echo, he described the *Politics* as a work of apiculture when it spoke of the Greeks, and a manual on termites when it touched on barbarians. *Essai d'une Histoire Raisonnée de la Philosophie Païenne*, Vol. II, Paris 1972, pp. 116–117, 131–132, 184, 329–335, 393.

dom as intelligibly related phases in a single adventure of the spirit. This is why a phenomenology of the mind could generate a philosophy of history. In other words, the movement from the stirring of desire, through the contest for mastery and the work of slavery, to the emergence of modern liberty is a genuine *concatenation*, whose progress explains the structure of world history. It was not just the principle of subjective freedom, singled out by Hegel himself, that lay beyond Plato, but any dynamic conception of this kind at all.

What happens, then, when Fukuyama marries Platonic substance and Hegelian spirit? The original logic of the historical dialectic disintegrates, as human development becomes the field of interplay of three component forces – drives that are persistent and distinct. This is no failing in itself. The unity of the scheme traced by Hegel, or amended by Kojève, was bought at the price of abstraction – it remains a speculative figure, closer to a metaphor than a narrative of the historical record.[144] Fukuyama's account embraces the empirical world in much greater breadth and detail. But its ambition is the same: to explain the logic of universal development. Does the result yield a more grounded equivalent to the Hegelian concatenation? A closer look at the dynamics of Fukuyama's universal history provides the answer. Its starting-point is science, for this alone has given clear-cut directionality to human affairs. Reason, in other words, comes first. Once it takes the form of modern science with the Renaissance, it decisively transforms the world, unfettering material desire in technological development and awakening the need for spiritual recognition in democracy. This sequence, which could be compared to Ernest Gellner's account of modernity, seems unambiguous enough. But it is no sooner advanced than disavowed. Science 'should in no way be regarded as the ultimate

---

144. Its principal weakness, even on its own terms, lies, of course, in its account of the dynamic of labour. Empirically, the suggestion that slaves (however broadly interpreted) progressively transformed the world by their work, so ultimately emancipating themselves for victory over their masters, has no plausibility as a theory of economic development. Kojève seems to have realized this, but the result was only to render his presentation of the master–slave dialectic incoherent at this point. On the one hand, 'the slave who works transforms the natural world in which he lives, by creating within it a specifically human technical world . . . it is *he* who has changed the given world by his labour on it', whereas 'the master evolves because he consumes the products of the slave's work . . . he undergoes history, but does not create it; his "evolution" is passive, like that of nature or an animal species'. On the other hand (a page later), Kojève could write: 'To be sure, the "poor" benefit from technical progress. But it is not they, or their needs or desires, that create it. Progress is realized, started and stimulated by the "rich" or the "powerful" (even in the socialist state)': *ILH*, pp. 497–499. The two claims are plainly incompatible.

cause of change'[145] – for it needs to be explained itself. What has always essentially driven it is desire, for material goods and security. This would seem to yield an economic interpretation of history, not so remote from Marx. If desire is the standing *prius*, however, what explains its sudden ability to galvanize reason into the shape of modern physics? Rather than attempting an answer, Fukuyama shifts his emphasis again, to 'the desire that lay behind the desire of Economic Man'. In this register, 'the primary motor of human history' is 'a totally non-economic drive, the *struggle for recognition*'.[146] Here Hegel is given the palm: the origin of development lies in a battle for prestige that creates the bondage which prompts work that transforms nature. After apparent oscillations, the first mover comes to rest, not in desire or reason, but in *thymos*.

But this is a claim that obtains, so to speak, on the meta-historical plane. It is not cashed into any empirical account of pre-modern origins, before or after the rise of civilization in the Middle or Far East, the Mediterranean or elsewhere. A real macro-history is only sketched from the Industrial Revolution onwards. On this plane, the narrative – nearly always shrewd and lively – does not deliver the order projected above it. Here it is quite clear from Fukuyama's own account that, although economic development to high technological levels is not a *sufficient* condition of political democracy, it is a *necessary* one – and that the reverse does not hold: there can long be remarkably successful industrialization – in the 'market-oriented authoritarianism' of the ROK or Taiwan, the fastest growth of all – without electoral liberalization.[147] In this asymmetry, the priority of *thymos* is overthrown. The affirmation that thymotic passions are what propel history forward is put aside: the stress now falls simply on the defensive claim that the advent of democracy cannot be reduced to the coming of mass consumption, even if economic modernization does prepare the educational ground for it. Silently, the original directionality reasserts itself. Spiritedness becomes in effect a residue – the extra fillip needed to take a society across the threshold from prosperity to parliaments, and the surplus charge that needs to be earthed once they are installed.

The ontological division of the soul, in other words, does not generate a coherent historical sequence. In its general tendency, Fukuyama's narrative veers between a rhetorical priority of spirit and a factual priority of desire. If there is a mediation between the two, it is to

---

145. *EHLM*, p. 80.
146. *EHLM*, p. 136.
147. *EHLM*, pp. 123–25, 134.

be found in the suggestion that the birth of modern science liberated material desires from the thymotic drives which had hitherto dominated history – but how these generated science in the first place is unexplained. The directionality of technique and the strivings of honour remain competing principles of explanation, whose claims of precedence are not to be reconciled. In the design of the account, a true concatenation is missing. It is perhaps significant that the category which is finally most central to Hegel's philosophy of history becomes curiously marginal in Fukuyama's. For there is a sense in which reason is displaced to the side of the construction, as little more than the enabler of desire – as against a spiritedness beyond reason. The contrast with Plato is equally noticeable: where he made *thymos* an ally of reason, Fukuyama makes reason an ally of desire.[148] The result is to tilt the outcome of the enquiry towards the stark dichotomy between a rational hedonism and an elemental agonism with which Fukuyama's reflections conclude.

Their diagnosis of the tensions of 'the old age of mankind' presupposes, of course, that history has indeed reached its appointed term. In its compressed initial statement, Fukuyama's argument could handle most of the objections to it. How does his extended version stand? On the terrain where criticism was originally concentrated, there can be little doubt that his hand is further strengthened. Fukuyama's coolly judicious treatment of nationalism, his critique of the superstitions of great-power 'realism', his relaxed view of advanced capitalism, make an impressive suit. But in laying out his cards more fully, a gap in them can be seen. For the structure of his case has a damaging weakness at the join between its registration of the progress of political democracy and its forecast of the spread of capitalist prosperity. In the real world, there is a visible contrast between the intercontinental sweep of the one and the regional basis of the other. Free elections were extended across a zone numbering some 850 millions in the past two decades; entry into the ranks of advanced capitalism was confined to less than 70 million – essentially, just the two front-line states of the Cold War in East Asia, and a pair of large cities. Fukuyama might have made an argument for the primacy of the struggle for recognition over the mechanism of desire out of this. To have done so, however, would have underlined the empirical imbalance between the two sides of the contention that history has come to an end. South Korea and Taiwan are slender shoulders for the Atlas needed to bear the weight of the Third World. Can their example be so readily broadened? As it happens, Fukuyama

---

148. *EHLM*, p. 372, following Bloom – see *The Republic of Plato*, p. 376.

himself elsewhere displays a significant unease about the East Asian model of capitalism. Is Japan itself, let alone the ROK or Taiwan, really a true liberal democracy? Ruled by a 'benevolent one-party dictatorship', it is nevertheless 'fundamentally democratic, because it is *formally* democratic', since it maintains regular elections and civic rights.[149] But there is an obvious question to ask here. Has Japan ever historically met Fukuyama's own criterion that 'democracy can never enter through the back door; at a certain point, it must arise out of a deliberate political decision to establish democracy'?[150] Decision there was, of course, but taken in Washington. Fukuyama's own misgivings become evident when he speculates that a further weakening of social and family bonds in the US might so discredit liberalism in Japanese eyes that 'a systematic anti-liberal and non-democratic alternative combining technocratic economic rationalism with paternalistic authoritarianism may gain ground in the Far East'[151] – given that the superior performance of East Asian capitalism is already based on much tougher social discipline and less political diversity than in the West. What this line of thought really indicates is an underlying contradiction within the prospectus of universal capitalist democracy. Outside the West, full economic success in building a high-technology capitalism has so far been confined to one region of Asia – whose political cultures conform least to liberal-democratic norms. Where it matters most, the dovetailing of the two great revolutions of our time seems to go awry.

The significance of the misfit is that it points to a larger difficulty in the argument. The enormous change in the world that gives its central force to Fukuyama's case has been the collapse of the USSR and its *glacis* in Eastern Europe. Without this global turning-point, the other parts of his story – restoration of democracy in Latin America, export growth in East Asia, breakdown of apartheid in South Africa – would remain scattered episodes. The conviction that there is no viable economic alternative to the free market owes far more to the failure of Soviet communism than to the success of Korean capitalism. In the same way, the decisive comprobation of liberal democracy was not the retirement of military dictatorships in Latin America or the Pacific which had traditionally paid their respects to it. It was the surrender of bureaucratic regimes in the Warsaw Pact which in the past had always denounced it. If the end of history has arrived, it is essentially because

---

149. *EHLM*, p. 241.
150. *EHLM*, p. 220.
151. *EHLM*, p. 243.

the socialist experience is over. Much of the intuitive appeal of Fukuyama's argument comes, indeed, from the sense that we are witnessing across what was once the Soviet bloc a gigantic historical upheaval that for the first time in history seems to bear no new principle within it, but rather to move as in a vast dream where events are already familiar before they happen. But the dissolution of Stalin's empire still leaves a great question unanswered. It is clear that the primary cause of its downfall was its failure to compete in productivity with the major capitalist powers surrounding it – a fate envisaged by Stalin's opponent over half a century ago.[152] The superior economic performance of the West was the magnet that pulled the system apart, drawing rulers and ruled alike pell-mell into its field of force. The political appeal of liberal democracy counted too, of course, especially among the more educated and privileged. But in broad terms, for the population at large, it was less compelling in its own right than as a concomitant of the consumer wealth perceived abroad. The fall of communism has brought liberal democracy to them, and is bringing capitalism. What kind of levels of consumption can they expect from the change?

To pose this question is to see the real limits of Fukuyama's vision. For his projection of a Taiwanese or Korean future for the rest of the world beyond the OECD not only begs the question of their replicability – which might be answered, with further specification, although this would be a much more demanding task than a simple argument from local example. More deeply, it commits a fallacy of composition. The fact that one or two agents can achieve a goal does not mean that all may do so – the attempt to generalize a target may simply ensure that none can achieve it. The per capita income even of Taiwan is still only half that of the United States. Even on the heroic assumption that its economic growth became normal for all underdeveloped countries, in a common move upwards towards OECD standards of today – is there any material possibility of the Second and Third Worlds reproducing current patterns of First World consumption? Manifestly, there is not. The style of life enjoyed by the majority of citizens of the rich capitalist nations today is what Harrod called oligarchic wealth, and Hirsch subsequently termed a positional good, whose existence – like a site of natural beauty – depends on its restriction to a minority. If all the peoples of the earth possessed the same number of refrigerators and

---

152. 'Socialism could not be justified by the abolition of exploitation alone; it must guarantee to society a higher economy of time than is guaranteed by capitalism. Without the realization of this condition, the mere removal of exploitation would be but a dramatic episode without a future': Leon Trotsky, *The Revolution Betrayed*, New York 1945, p. 78. The chapter is entitled 'The Struggle for the Productivity of Labour'.

automobiles as those of North America and Western Europe, the planet would become uninhabitable. In the global ecology of capital today, the privilege of the few requires the misery of the many, to be sustainable. Less than a quarter of the world's population now appropriates eighty-five per cent of world income, and the gap between the shares of the advanced and backward zones has widened over the past half century.[153] The difference between living standards in Europe and in India and China increased from a ratio of 40:1 to 70:1 between 1965 and 1990 alone. In the eighties, over 800 million people – more than the populations of the EC, USA and Japan combined – became yet more grindingly poor, and one out of three children went hungry.[154] If all human beings simply had an equal share of food, at a diet with less than half American consumption of animal-based calories, without altering any other distribution of goods whatever – scarcely a radical demand – the globe could not support its present population; were US food consumption to be generalized, half the human species would have to become extinct – the earth could support no more than 2.5 billion inhabitants.[155] But even with such staggering inequality, the ozone layer is being rapidly depleted, temperatures are rising sharply, nuclear waste is accumulating, forests are being decimated, myriad species wiped out. This is a scene where Hegel's Spirit, internalizing nature within itself, is lost. Fukuyama has nothing to say about it. It was Cournot who understood what the world market might bring, and criticized the 'economic optimism' of his time for the finite resources it threatened to plunder, the disadvantaged peoples it was likely to condemn, the future generations it could not but despoil.

Today, those generations are multiplying at a rate never seen before in the history of humanity. The population of the globe, which has doubled from two and a half to five billion in the past fifty years, is

---

153. For the detailed figures of this pattern, distinguishing between the 'organic core' of capitalism (North-Western Europe, North America, Japan, Australasia), 'miracle economies' (Italy, Spain, South Korea, Brazil), the Communist countries and the rest of the South, see Giovanni Arrighi's essay, 'World Income Inequalities and the Future of Socialism', New Left Review 189, September–October 1991, pp. 39–65 – a fundamental map of our time. The general problem of positional wealth in an ecological setting with natural entropies is forcefully etched by Elmar Altvater, Die Zukunft des Marktes, Münster 1991.

154. Worldwatch Institute, State of the World 1992, New York 1992, pp. 4, 176.

155. Even with an entirely vegetarian diet, the upper limit for a population receiving an equal distribution for food would be 6 billion, a figure that will be reached in a little over a decade. For these estimates, see the sombre survey by Sir Crispin Tickell, British Ambassador to the UN under Margaret Thatcher, The Quality of Life – Whose Life? What Life? (British Association Lecture, August 1991), an author who must be regarded as above suspicion of exaggeration.

likely to be nearing ten billion by the end of the next half century. Ninety per cent of that increase will occur in the poor countries, where already another 90 million are being added a year. But not all of them will stay there. The ever tighter integration of the world capitalist economy, as it now for the first time comes within sight of encompassing the whole earth, and the increasingly visible polarizations of wealth within it, are generating tremendous pressures for entry into the privileged zones. Already there are some 25 million refugees from political and economic despair in the poor countries. Flows of immigration on a tidal scale are the logical outcome of a bifurcation of the globe that makes residence in the rich countries – of any kind, even as an underclass – of incomparable value, for the positional benefits of their infrastructures and social services alone. Since the First World cannot be reproduced in the Third, without common ecological ruin, increasing numbers from the Third, and the Second, will try to come to the First. The tensions and conflicts that will arise from this crossing of two previously separated universes are easy to predict – their premonitory signals are already evident in Europe. The political economy of the advanced capitalist countries, now paying for the asset-inflation and speculative overdrive that led the boom of the eighties, but failed to restore post-war levels of profit, is likely to suffer new turbulence as it adjusts to the sudden transformation of its parameters with the breakdown of former barriers from the East and South.

That adjustment will not be confined to the financial institutions and corporations of the metropolitan triumvirate. It will involve the states of North America, Japan and the European Community as well. Fukuyama has a view of this, but it is a singularly bleak one. The relations between the post-historical zone of a fortunate liberal capitalism and the zone of misfortune still enmeshed in history will, he suggests, not be close. But they will involve collisions along three axes. Oil supplies must be safeguarded; immigration must be filtered; and advanced technologies – especially, but not exclusively, armaments – must be blocked, where necessary. NATO is a more suitable instrument for enforcing a new world order that would secure these aims than the UN Security Council, whose unity in the campaign against Iraq could prove transient. After effectively criticizing the conceptual basis of Kissinger-style 'realism', Fukuyama admits that such policy recommendations scarcely differ from it. What they amount to, of course, is a set of border patrols. In this prospect, the risks of nuclear proliferation do not gain the relief that might be expected. What many would regard as the major single development capable of blasting any post-history apart is virtually ignored – perhaps as too radically at variance with an

end-state that supposes a well-nigh complete insulation of the more
from the less wealthy states of the world. But even if this were given
greater salience, Fukuyama's prescriptions for dealing with the underdeveloped zone – forcible invigilation and preemption by the dominant
powers – would not alter, but only be executed more urgently. Such is
in any case the consensual wisdom of the hour. But the programme of a
consortium of great powers durably policing the rest of the world, in
the interests of keeping weapons of mass extermination to themselves,
is utopian. The nuclear monopoly of five or six states has neither moral
basis nor practical staying-power. On Fukuyama's own premises, there
is no chance of every lesser or newer power accepting the inequity of
such arrangements indefinitely: how could that be reconciled with the
thymotic striving of the states that feel themselves slaves in the international system? His logic, and current realities, spell out the inevitability
of a struggle for nuclear recognition. The only way that could be
averted is for the nuclear powers themselves to renounce their deadly
ephemeral privilege. So long as there is no sign of that, the lack of right
can only deepen, and the arbitrariness of *de facto* possession become
more exposed, as in the latest attempts, without even pretence of moral
reason, to deny Ukraine or Kazakhstan what accrues without saying to
Russia or Israel. No pacific union can be founded on this myopia.

But if war is unwarrantably minimized as a consequence of nuclear
proliferation in the historical zone, it unexpectedly returns in a strange
after-life in the zone beyond history. In his final chapter Fukuyama,
while avowing that nuclear weapons make traditional wars between
rich states unthinkable, nevertheless seems to endorse Hegel's assumption that wars will continue at the end of history – criticizing Kojève for
the opposite judgement, and dwelling on the redemptive role of war as
a collective bond: even spiritual adventure.[156] The inconsistency of
these musings with the political logic of his portrait of the end of
history is so marked that it invites explanation. The reason why
Fukuyama's argument takes this curious concluding turn, however, lies
in the way he has construed the alternatives for the last men. The
choices before them are effectively two – either the orderly quest for
material pleasures within the framework of an instrumental state, or
the pursuit of thymotic ambitions that explode inordinately beyond it:
Bentham or Nietzsche. What is missing is any conception of the state as
a structure of collective self-expression deeper than the electoral sys-

---

156. *EHLM*, pp. 331–32, 391. The anomaly of these remarks is underlined by the
use that Fukuyama otherwise makes of Kant's theory of perpetual peace, missing from
his essay, but given due importance in his book.

tems of today. Democracy is indeed now more widespread than ever before. But it is also thinner – as if the more universally available it becomes, the less active meaning it retains. The United States itself is the paradigmatic example: a society in which less than half the citizens vote, ninety per cent of Congressmen are re-elected, and the price of office is cash by the million. In Japan money speaks still louder, and there is not even nominal alternation between parties. In France, the Assembly has been reduced to a cipher. Britain lacks so much as a written constitution. In the freshly minted democracies of Poland and Hungary, electoral indifference and cynicism exceed even American levels – less than a quarter of the voters participating in some recent polls. Fukuyama nowhere suggests that any significant improvement is possible in this dismal scene. Reveries of impossible war function as compensation for the absence of any prospect of change in the political quality of peace. Hegel's vision of another kind of state, embodiment of an articulate community rather than mere convenience for rule, has receded, along with the primacy of reason as the realization of freedom – leaving the calculations of desire and the jactations of spirit alone to confront each other. The inadequacy of this as a response to the devitalizing of modern liberty is all too evident. That process is the outcome not just of the power of money and waning of choice within nation-states, but also of their surpassal by international markets and institutions that lack any semblance of democratic control. The European Community, so far the only attempt to transcend national forms for a higher collective sovereignty, still remains yet less accountable to its peoples than the states that compose it. But just as environmental balance cannot be achieved, social equity furthered, nuclear safety assured, so too popular sovereignty cannot acquire new substance, without a different international settlement. The Hegelian problems – poverty, community, war – have not gone away, but their solutions have moved to another plane.

There was one sphere, however, that remained untroubled in Hegel's scheme of things. Beneath the tensions in state and civil society, the family was whole and stable. Today, it is the bed of the fastest currents of change in the rich capitalist world. Fukuyama alludes to the weakening of traditional family patterns, when he speaks of the United States, but it plays little role in his view of the way of the world at large. In fact, this is the arena of the most dynamic struggle for equal recognition in metropolitan societies today. The emancipation of women has achieved more gains in the West over the past twenty years than any other social movement: in law, employment, custom, public doctrine. At the same time, it remains massively far away from real sexual equality, whose ultimate conditions are still scarcely imaginable today. On the other hand, because – unlike the labour movement of the past – it does not directly challenge the central value of this society, private ownership of the means of collective labour, but rather appeals to its formal commitment to individual rights, the established order has found it difficult to muster head-on ideological resistance to it. There is no offically respectable way of rejecting equality between the sexes – only practical expedients for evading it. These, however, have all the inert force of time out of mind – a history longer than that of class divisions themselves. The result is the most glaring single discrepancy between what can be said and what is done in the rich capitalist countries today. It will be difficult to hold that gap constant. It is no accident that where these societies have traditionally contained the most powerful movements of the Left, in Scandinavia, progress has been impressive in gains for equality between the sexes in a period where little has been achieved in advancing it between the classes. There, the beginnings of what is likely to be the real crux of women's liberation, social measures to ensure that maternity is not an economic handicap in relations between the sexes, has already reached the threshold of the political agenda. The structural upheaval that would be involved, in transfer payments and work patterns alike, if equalization of this kind were ever to occur, is the guarantee that it is an unforeseeable distance away. It is far from clear to what extent the capitalism we know today could accommodate it. But just for that reason, any sounding of the end of the century that misses this current is deficient. Rather than looking at the issue of equal rights where it is actually causing most change, Fukuyama diverts it to the fate of viruses – as if it could be deflated by a mere *reductio ad absurdum*. Here too the resort, unusual in this work, to a persiflage suggests an uncomfortable awareness of possibilities not allowed for. The end of history may see the last men, as they now are. Women willing to see themselves as the ultimate exemplars of their sex are likely to be fewer.

6. Socialism?

These are all evident limitations of Fukuyama's construction. But if the extended version of it is more vulnerable than the initial sketch, just because it is richer and therefore more specified, it still puts the same onus on any critique. For Fukuyama's case to fail, it is not enough to show that it understates or overlooks the defects in the world order dominated by liberal capitalism. It must be possible to indicate a credible alternative to it, without resort to mere gestures at the unpredictable or changes that are no more than terminological. Fukuyama's original claim was that capitalist democracy is the final form of freedom discovered, which brings history to an end – not because there are no problems left, but because the solutions to them are now known in advance. These can be found in the pattern of society that already exists in North America, Western Europe and Japan, to which it is only a matter of time before the Second and Third Worlds approximate. The solutions prove on inspection to be less available or secure than advertised. But it could still be that nothing else is feasible. Fukuyama's vision is not artificial or implausible, because it appeals to the widespread conviction that the collapse of the Soviet bloc has shown just this to be the case. What the end of history means, above all, is the end of socialism.

The fate of the communist world does not, of course, stand alone. The cascade of bureaucratic regimes falling within a space of two years, from the Gobi to the Adriatic, burying the USSR with it, has been far the most spectacular episode. The tradition of the Third International has ended in ruin, while its rival in the West has survived. But the heirs of the Second International have become increasingly sterile. The historical achievements of European social democracy after the war were welfare services and full employment – at the outer limit, some nationalizations. All of these have been diluted or abandoned today, without substitutes, and loss of direction has led to decline in power. Today, the classic Nordic bastions of social democracy are for the first time since the twenties under predominantly conservative rule. Meanwhile, in the Third World the dynamic of national liberation is largely exhausted, and the movements that wore socialist colours in the struggle for it have shed them, from Yemen to Angola. The symbol of the hour is an American viceroy in London brokering victory in the Horn between one guerrilla force repenting sympathy for China and another for Albania, at their mutual request. None of the political currents that set out to challenge capitalism in this century has morale or compass today.

The reasons for this common disarray lie deeper than the current captions – the evils of totalitarianism, the corruptions of welfare or security, the delusions of autarky. The foundations of the classical conception of socialism were fourfold. They comprised a historical projection, a social movement, a political objective and an ethical ideal. The objective basis for the hope of transcending capitalism lay in the increasingly social nature of the forces of industrial production, rendering private ownership of them – already generating periodic crises – in the long run incompatible with the logic of economic development itself. The subjective agency capable of assuring a transition to social relations of production was the collective labourer produced by modern industry itself, the working class whose self-organization prefigured the principles of the society to come. The leading institution of that society would be the deliberate planning of the social product by its citizens, as freely associated producers sharing their basic means of livelihood in common. The central value of such an order would be equality – not regimentation, but a distribution of goods appropriate to the needs of each and an expectation of tasks in keeping with the talents of each, in a society without classes.

Today, all of these elements of the socialist vision have fallen into radical doubt. The secular trend towards increasingly social forces of production, as it was understood by Marx or Luxemburg – that is, the growth of ever larger and more interconnected complexes of fixed capital, requiring centralized management of them – continued from the industrial revolution to the long boom after the Second World War, but in the past twenty years it has been reversed. Technological advances in transport and communications have since broken up manufacturing processes and decentralized plants, at an accelerating rhythm. Meanwhile the industrial working class, whose ranks multiplied in the metropolitan countries up to mid-century, has since gradually declined in size and social cohesion. On a world scale, its absolute numbers have grown in the same period, as industrialization has spread to the Third World. But since global population has risen much faster, its relative size as a proportion of humanity is steadily shrinking. Centralized planning achieved remarkable feats in conditions of siege or war, in communist and capitalist societies alike. But in peacetime conditions, the command-administrative system in the communist countries proved quite unable to master the problem of coordination in increasingly complex economies, leading to waste and irrationality far exceeding those of market systems in the same period, and eventual symptoms of potential breakdown. Equality itself, always at least a rhetorical value of public life after the Second World War, however radically denied in reality, is now widely discounted as either possible or desirable. Indeed, for the common sense of the time, all the ideas that once made up a belief in socialism are so many dead dogs. Mass production has been overtaken by post-Fordism. The working class is a fading memory of the past. Collective ownership is a guarantee of tyranny and inefficiency. Substantial equality is incompatible with liberty or productivity.

How conclusive is this popular verdict? In point of fact, none of the objective changes that have transformed the credit of socialism is without its ambiguity. Socialization of the forces of production understood as their physical concentration – massing of plant-size and geographical location – has certainly declined. But understood as technical interconnexion – the linkage of multiple productive units in an ultimately integrated process – it has enormously increased. Self-sufficient manufacturing systems have become far fewer as multinational enterprise has spread, creating a network of global interdependencies unimaginable in the time of Saint-Simon or Marx. The industrial proletariat of manual workers in manufacturing and mining has significantly decreased in the rich capitalist countries, and on present trends of productivity and population will never recapture numerical predominance on a world scale. But the number of wage-earners, still a minority of the earth's population at mid-century, has been increasing at a pace without precedent, as the peasantry moves off the land in the Third World. Command planning has been discredited and dismantled in the former Soviet bloc. In the capitalist world, however, corporate planning has never been so complex and ambitious, in the scale and range of its calculations – girdling the earth and stretching time. Even equality, everywhere decried as a fetter on economic progress, has been in the same period steadily extended as a legal claim and customary norm. The sources of socialism, as it was traditionally conceived, have not so simply dried up.

To register this, however, involves no assurance that they will prove more effective in the future than in the past. The test for the validity of socialism as an alternative to capitalism lies in whether it retains a potential for solutions to the problems confronting the latter in its hour of historical triumph. In the epoch of *The Communist Manifesto,* Mill remarked that 'if the choice were to be made between Communism with all its chances, and the present state of society with all its sufferings and injustices; if the institution of private property necessarily carried with it as a consequence, that the produce of labour should be apportioned as we now see it, almost in an inverse ratio to the labour – the largest portions to those who have never worked at all, the next largest to those whose work is merely nominal, and so in a descending scale, the remuneration dwindling as the work grows harder and more disagreeable, until the most fatiguing and exhausting bodily labour cannot count with certainty upon being able to earn even the necessities of life; if this or Communism were the alternative, all the difficulties, great or small, of Communism would be but as dust in the balance.' But that was not the case, he pointed out. For 'to make the comparison applicable, we must compare Communism at its best, with the regime of private property, not as it is, but as it might be made. The principle of private property has never yet had a fair trial in any country.' Only the future could decide between the comparative advantages of the two systems, in which the final criterion would probably be which was 'consistent with the greatest amount of human liberty and sponta-neity'.[157] The system of private property did transform itself, even if not quite in the way Mill envisaged, and the comparison has turned to its advantage. But the question as Mill posed it is still unsettled. For the boot is now on the other foot. Has socialism been given a fair trial – have we seen it, not as it actually existed, but as it might exist, 'at its best'? The changes involved might be as far from the expectations of Marx as were those that altered capitalism from the ideas of Mill. But for such a possibility to have meaning, it is not utopian circumstances that should be looked to, but the real conditions of the world in the next century. What are the prospects that socialism could cope with these more successfully than capitalism?

Intellectually, the culture of the Left is far from having been demobi-lized by the collapse of Soviet communism, or the impasse of Western social democracy, as a glance at the distinguished recent symposium *After the Fall* shows.[158] In this sense, the vitality of the socialist tradition continues to be displayed on many sides. Amidst a range of proposals for renewal, two themes stand out as most consensual. A socialism beyond the experience of Stalinist tyranny and social-demo-cratic *suivisme* would represent neither an impossible abolition of the market, nor an uncritical adaptation to it. Differing forms of collective ownership – cooperative, municipal, regional, national – of the major means of production would be combined with market exchanges

---

157. *Collected Works*, Vol. II, Toronto 1965, pp. 207–208.

158. Robin Blackburn, ed., *After the Fall – the Failure of Communism and the Future of Socialism*, London 1991. Among the many significant contributions to this volume, Habermas's essay 'What does Socialism Mean Today?' is of particular interest here. Written with rare passion, it reveals once again the depth of his personal commitment to the Left, while also reproducing in more political key some of the paradoxes of his writing on modernity. Here he asks whether, after the collapse of communism and the deadlock of social democracy, the Left 'must now retreat to a purely moral standpoint, keeping socialism as nothing more than an ideal', without an objective anchorage in existing society – and replies that to do so would be to 'defuse socialism and reduce it to a regulative notion, of purely private relevance'. Yet he also argues that 'a dynamic of self-correction cannot be set in motion without introducing morality into the debate, without universalizing interests from a normative point of view', and 'rethinking topics morally'. Less categorical than before in scouting popular sovereignty, Haber-mas's agenda for the Left still remains essentially remedial, 'to prevent the institutional framework of a constitutional democracy from becoming desiccated': pp. 37–38, 43–45. But as the wider problems of world poverty and insecurity have gained more relief in his thinking, the accent has changed.

between them, under the guidance of broad public planning of macro-economic balances. The most impressive of such conceptions, developed by Diane Elson, turns the tables on the familiar notion that it is the advent of an economy increasingly based on information that has rendered any alternative to capitalism obsolete, by calling for abolition of the anachronisms of commercial secrecy. Here the objective is a socialization of the market that transfers powers to producers in competing enterprises with knowledge of each other's techniques and costs, and secures the freedom of households with guarantees of basic income.[159] The mechanisms of planning in a socialized market of this kind could be of various kinds, but all involve some central controls over the credit system. Such controls, in turn – this is the second principal theme of current literature – would have to be accountable to a democracy far more articulated in its forms than anything the capitalist version has to offer: encouraging electoral participation rather than indifference, minimizing barriers between deputies and constituents, opening and regulating executive processes, diversifying arenas in which decisions are taken, securing representation of gender as well as of number. Among schemes along these lines, David Held's model of a developed democracy is one of the most detailed so far.[160] Finally, of course, there is general agreement that the social forces needed to work towards a socialism of this kind would have to embrace a much broader coalition of wage-earners than was envisaged in earlier conceptions relying on the industrial labour-force alone.

No refoundation of the socialist project, whatever its particular direction, could hope to be credible that failed to come to terms with the historical experience of the Second and Third Internationals. Mere repudiations are no more use today than were simple pieties yesterday. Any culture of the Left that tries to start again *ex nihilo*, or take shelter in the principles of 1789 (or 1776), will be stillborn. Serious reflection on the political and intellectual legacy of the modern socialist movement, in its various forms, reveals many riches that were forgotten as well as roads that were mistaken – also many more interconnexions with the critics of socialism than have been customarily remembered. It is not an accident that the most fundamental survey of the problems confronting any socialism of the future should also be the richest stock-taking, with many surprises, of the main tradition of the past: Robin Blackburn's balance-sheet of the economic and political heritage

---

159. 'Market Socialism or Socialization of the Market?', *New Left Review* 172, November–December 1988, pp. 3–44.
160. See *Models of Democracy*, Cambridge 1987, pp. 267–299.

of Marxism.[161] Its theme is complexity – of the circumstances in which the October Revolution was made and unmade; of the differing strands within Bolshevik and social-democratic thought confronting the Soviet experience; of the structure of any possible society beyond capitalism, which nearly all of them underestimated. In this reconstruction, Kautsky and Mises, or Hayek and Trotsky, turn out to have had more in common than might be imagined, in their critique of the idea of a universal intelligence capable of rationally directing the countless transactions of a modern economy; but the very dispersal of knowledge on which social and technological progress depends also tells against the presumptions of unaccountable private management. Here the idea of a socialism after communism is posed on the appropriate contemporary scale. The effect is to bring into relief the real exigencies, but also some of the difficulties of an alternative to the present world order.

For the central case against capitalism today is the combination of ecological crisis and social polarization it is breeding. Market forces contain no solution to these. Driven by the imperatives of private profit, their logic is to disregard environmental damage and to entrench positional hierarchy. The global consequences of their spontaneous development are the visible refutation of Austrian conceptions of it as a beneficent catallaxy. Here, if anywhere, the case for deliberate collective intervention – the constructivist *taxis* rejected by Austrian theory – would seem unanswerable. At this higher level, where the fate of the earth itself will be decided, do not the classical arguments of socialism for intentional democratic control of the material conditions of life stage their comeback? If there is to be, as the most prescient analysts insist, an Environmental Revolution comparable in significance only to the Industrial and Agricultural Revolutions before it,[162] how could it be other than consciously realized – that is, planned? What else are the targets already feebly set by various national governments and international agencies? The reply to these questions is in one sense obvious. But in another sense, it remains politically ambiguous. For the paradox

---

161. 'Fin-de-Siècle: Socialism after the Crash', in *After the Fall* – an essay which makes good its dictum that 'a doctrine's capacity for integral self-criticism and self-correction is as important as the starting-point since the latter is bound to be mistaken or inadequate in various ways': p. 180.

162. 'The pace of the Environmental Revolution will be far faster than that of its predecessors. The agricultural revolution began some 10,000 years ago and the Industrial revolution has been under way for two centuries. But if the environmental revolution is to succeed, it must be compressed into a few decades . . . Muddling through will not work': Lester Brown, 'Launching the Environmental Revolution', *State of the World 1992*, pp. 174–75.

is that the terrain on which the socialist economic critique of capitalism has most contemporary power also poses it with even more difficult tasks than those it failed to acquit in the past. The central stumbling-block to a planned economy is the coordination problem – its incapacity, as the Austrians saw it, to match market pricing as an information system, in conditions of dispersed knowledge. (The incentive problem, or lack of an entrepreneurial function, occurs at a lower analytic level, and could be regarded as more remediable.) There are simply too many decisions to process, a complexity defying any conceivable computation. If socialist planning was defeated by this problem at the level of single national economies, how could it handle the immeasurably greater complexities of a global economy? Is it not more likely that ecological balance will be reached by selective regulation, that deters or proscribes certain forms of production within the world market, rather than stipulating any – as energy taxation or pharmaceutical legislation does (more or less badly) today?

A solution of this kind, within the familiar framework of capitalism, is nevertheless quite unworkable. For the central problem is not simply the (rising) absolute levels of damage to the biosphere, but the relative contributions to it of rival national economies. This, however, could only be resolved by a mixture of deterrents and quotas: in other words, not just prevention, but allocation – or planning proper. Allocation, however, inevitably poses the issue of equity. On what principles should the consumption of fossil fuels, the production of nuclear waste, the emission of carbon, the substitution of CFCs, the employment of pesticides, the logging of forests, be distributed among the peoples of the world? Here the market, however curbed, has nothing to offer. The malignant appropriation of the world's riches by a privileged minority, with which the destruction of its resources is now fatally interwoven, threatens any common solutions to the massive dangers now gathering momentum. Socialism meant planning, not for its own sake, but in the service of justice. It is quite logical that Austrian economic theory, as the most cogent rationale of capitalism, should exclude the idea of justice even more rigorously than that of planning. But it is precisely an alliance of the two that is required for any genuine global settlement. The environmental revolution will not occur without a new sense of egalitarian responsibility.

Much the same paradox recurs on the ground of representative institutions proper. The attenuation of democratic forms in the major capitalist societies is increasingly evident. The executive branches of the state have gained steadily greater power at the expense of legislative assemblies. Policy choices have narrowed and popular interest in them declined. Above all, the most important changes affecting the well-being of citizens have been transferred sideways to international markets. In these conditions, the construction of effective supranational sovereignties is the obvious remedy to the loss by national states of so much of their substance and authority. Western Europe contains the one significant start towards such a federation. The European Community was created principally by Christian Democrats, and the Treaty of Rome was expressly designed as the framework for a robust continental capitalism. It took a considerable time for many socialists to see it as an opportunity for long-term advance in another direction. Today that awareness is much more widespread. On any realistic reckoning, it is clear that a major task of the Left will be to press towards the completion of a genuine federal state in the Community, with a sovereign authority over its constituent parts. That, of course, will require a democratically empowered European legislature, rather than the shadow parliament of the present – just the prospect that is anathema to the Right across the region. Such a Union is the only kind of general will that can contest the new power of the invisible hand as the arbiter of collective destinies.

But realism also dictates an awareness that, just as the larger an economy the more difficult it is to plan, so the greater the territory and population of a state, the less subject it tends to become to democratic control. The United States, with its lawless executive and paralytic legislature, is the most vivid example of this today, as Russia might become tomorrow. Scale tends to afford economies in civic participation too. The reason is partly that it renders central government spatially and structurally more distant from its electorate, increasing its bureaucratic autonomy. But it is also because it sharply raises the costs of political organization, giving disproportionate advantages to groups that are concentrated in numbers and well-endowed with resources – hence with good internal lines of communication and ample means of opinion formation – as against widely scattered masses lacking the expensive requirements for their own voluntary association. The path to a more relevant democracy today points beyond the nation-state; but the price of it is likely to be a more remote one too. The socialist critique of capitalist democracy will thus confront many of the same problems it now diagnoses, in a yet more acute form at the very level towards which its own programme should move. Here too the dialectical figure seems to shift into reverse: the contradictions of capitalism do not resolve but augment the difficulties of socialism.

If this is true of economic principles and political institutions, what of social agency? The classical proletariat of industrial workers has declined in absolute numbers in the advanced countries, and in relative size as a proportion of the world's population. At the same time, the number of all those who depend on wages for their livelihood has vastly increased, although it still probably falls short of a majority of humanity. The greatest single change in global society since the Second World War, after the contraction of the peasantry, has been the entry of women into the paid labour-force of rich and poor countries alike. With this change, the human potential of opposition to the dictates of capital has become more truly universal than it was at the height of the traditional labour movement, confined to only one sex. Migration is also mixing populations once again, on a scale not seen since the previous century. How far do these transformations offer a realistic basis for resuming a socialist project? The answer is at best deeply ambiguous. For if their net effect is to broaden the social forces open to the appeal of a different kind of world order, it is also to divide them. Even within the metropolitan industrial working class itself, there is less occupational similarity and cultural likeness than in the past. Outside it, heterogeneity of every kind – income, employment, gender, nationality, faith – proliferates. Many of these divisions, of course, operated in the past too. But the core support of the classic labour movement was nevertheless relatively homogeneous: it was essentially manual, overwhelmingly male and predominantly European. No equivalent to such coordinates obtains today. The distances between a Korean seamstress, Zambian field-hand, Lebanese bank-clerk, Filipino sailor, Italian secretary, Russian miner, Japanese auto-worker, are vastly greater than those that were once bridged in the ranks of a unitary Second International, even though not a few might even be employees of the same conglomerate. The new reality is a massive asymmetry between the international mobility and organization of capital, and the dispersal and segmentation of labour, that has no historical precedent. The globalization of capitalism has not drawn the resistances to it together, but scattered and outflanked them. In due course, perhaps, an 'interstitial surprise' of the kind tracked by Michael Mann – the emergence of a new social agent catching all others unawares – may appear. But for the moment no change in this unequal balance of forces is in sight. The potential extension of social interests in an alternative to capitalism has been accompanied by a reduction in social capacities to fight for one.

All these difficulties have a common origin. The case against capitalism is strongest on the very plane where the reach of socialism is weakest – at the level of the world system as a whole. That weakness has always been there, from the earliest hopes of revolution in one country, or even continent, expressed by Marx and his contemporaries. But increasingly, as the twentieth century advanced, the movement that prided itself on having overcome national boundaries fell ever further behind the system it set out to replace, as the civilization of capital became steadily more international, not just in its economic mechanisms – with the arrival of the multinational corporation – but also in its political arrangements, with the machinery of NATO and the G–7. The contrast with the record of what was once the 'socialist camp' says everything. The age continues to see nationalisms exploding like firecrackers across much of the world, not least where communism once stood. But the future belongs to the set of forces that are overtaking the nation-state. So far, they have been captured or driven by capital – as in the past fifty years, internationalism has changed sides. So long as the Left fails to win back the initiative here, the current system will be secure.

Where, then, does this leave socialism? History suggests a range of ideal-typical outcomes, which more or less set the spectrum of possibilities. In stylized fashion, these can be taken as paradigms for different versions of the future. The first possibility is that the experience of socialism in this century will simply be regarded by historians of the future as something like the Jesuit experiment in Paraguay. This was an episode that fascinated the Enlightenment – Montesquieu and Voltaire, Robertson and Raynal all reflected on its significance. For over a century, between the 1610s and the 1760s, the Jesuit fathers organized Guaraní tribes into egalitarian communities under their authority in the territories upstream from the River Plate. In these settlements, each Indian family had the right to a personal field, tilled privately, but the bulk of the land was cultivated collectively as God's property by the obligatory labour of the whole community, to the sound of religious song and music. Its produce was distributed for the benefit of all those who worked the fields, with a reserve for the ill, the old and the orphans. There were storehouses, workshops, small factories and well-built towns. But there was no money. Simply, a tradable surplus of *yerba* was exported to Buenos Aires, to pay for manufactures which the reductions did not produce. The Jesuits devoted great care to the education of their charges, ingeniously adapting their doctrinal duties to local beliefs. There was conscription, and the Guaraní cavalry did outstanding service for the Spanish monarchy outside the borders of the Jesuit domain. But no Spanish official was permitted to reside within it, no traders (with a few designated exceptions) could visit it, and no Spanish was taught to the Indians, who were given instruction and literacy in their own language, under the autocracy of the Order.

In its complete reversal of the treatment meted out to the native populations everywhere else in the Americas, in its careful isolation from the surrounding Viceroyalty, in its relative prosperity (exaggerated by legend), the Jesuit state in Paraguay came to attract the hatred and greed of the local landowners, the suspicion and jealousy of the court in Spain. Ultimately, in a sudden decree, Madrid ordered the expulsion of the Order from Paraguay. The operation, ruthlessly conducted by the Viceroy, met no resistance. The fathers obeyed their instructions from Rome. The Indians were disarmed with promises of the preservation of their communities and the provision of a university that they had missed. But once the Society was gone, their lands were soon seized, their townships destroyed, their populations dispersed. Today, all that is left of an experience that had won the ambivalent admiration of the *philosophes* are a handful of handsome church ruins, and perhaps the survival of the local idiom.[163] In Europe, the Jesuits adjusted their ambitions and eventually became an inoffensive part of the overall scene, their name respected and their cause absorbed in a civilization moving in another direction. In the nineteenth century, their singular experiment in Paraguay was occasionally mourned by romantic socialists like Cunningham Grahame, a friend of William Morris, or deprecated by rational conservatives like Cournot.[164] But in the consensus of later generations, when it was remembered at all, it was seen as a weird historical sport – an artificial social construction, contradicting every known law of human nature, doomed to rapid extinction. In the same way, future – even present – historians might look back on the cycle of attempts to build socialism in the twentieth century as a set of exotic aberrations in backward lands, fated to vanish after briefly disturbing the main course of history as it proceeded to its appointed conclusion, leaving only the innocuous traces of absorption in more advanced regions. Already in the seventies François Furet spoke of the 'closing of the socialist parenthesis', as civilization resumed its

---

163. Raynal's verdict has a contemporary ring. In the benevolent security of the Paraguayan missions 'perhaps never was so much good done to men, with so little ill', yet the Guaranís did not resist the expulsion of the Jesuits because, he thought, they had fallen into a kind of melancholy under too uniform a mode of life, that deprived them of licence or tumult, emulation or passion, as well as the freedoms of the forest: *Histoire Philosophique et Politique des Etablissements et du Commerce dans les Deux Indes*, Vol. 4, Geneva 1780, pp. 303–304, 320–23.

164. R.C. Cunninghame Graham, *A Vanished Arcadia*, London 1900; Cournot, *Revue Sommaire*, p. 311. The most interesting modern reflection is Bartolemeu Melía, 'Las Reducciones Jesuíticas del Paraguay: un Espacio para una Utopía Colonial', *Estudios Paraguayos*, September 1978, pp. 157–168.

long-term development towards liberal capitalism. In the perspective of that progress, the eventual fate of socialism would be oblivion.

The second possibility is that the outcome of modern socialism would be closer to the legacy of the first revolution against divine right monarchy. In England in the 1640s, the dynasty and episcopacy were overthrown, a revolutionary army emerged, a republican state was founded, and an extraordinary ferment of radical ideas bubbled up. The most remarkable of these, as a collective achievement, was the first theory of modern democracy that emerged in the ranks of the Levellers. Their political demands included widespread male suffrage, a written constitution, entrenched clauses to protect civil liberties, annual parliaments, popular election not only of MPs, but of military officers and civil servants as well. This was a programme so far ahead of its time that most of its concerns have even today still not been realized in Britain, which has neither republic, nor written constitution, nor a bill of rights, let alone annual parliaments or an elected officer corps. The Leveller vision of democracy, the product of popular mobilization during the Civil War and the experience of rank-and-file representation in the General Council of the Army, did not outlast the military struggle against the monarchy, as an effective movement. But the Leveller moment in the Civil War remains the most deeply impressive political spectacle of its time. It is not surprising that its ideals should have won such frequent admiration from contemporary historians.

Yet what was their actual historical legacy? The English monarchy was restored in 1660, and within another fifty years a stable aristocratic oligarchy was in place, that lasted down to the epoch of the industrial revolution. In this development, the memory of the radical ferment of the English Republic was completely effaced. Neither the Commonwealth itself, nor the Levellers who had fought to democratize the revolutionary state, left any durable traces in British political life. The Putney Debates were only rediscovered in the late nineteenth century, and the Leveller programmes seriously examined in this century. Just as the English Revolution left no major institutions behind, so it bequeathed no continuous heritage of ideas, living on as an active influence in subsequent generations. The reason lay not so much in its political defeat as in the intellectual change that occurred after it was over. For the great revolutionary excitement at mid-century was still cast in essentially religious terms. The Civil War issued into a Puritan Revolution, whose principal leaders and militants were committed to the creation of a Commonwealth of the Godly, in a mental universe still saturated with Biblical myths and Protestant doctrines. It was this theological casing which cut it off so abruptly. Providence, sign of the Lord's blessing when Cromwell's armies were victorious, became proof of divine anger when the Republic fell, leading to a characteristic collapse of morale. More profoundly, however, the religious stamp of the Revolution came to seem anachronistic, as polite culture and popular beliefs became increasingly secularized over the next century.

The result was a gap of some hundred and forty years between this the English Revolution and its historical successor in France. The Declaration of the Rights of Man, the slogans of Liberty, Equality and Fraternity, were objectively sequels to the Leveller Agreements of the People. But subjectively, there was little or no connexion between them, because the whole language of political insurgency had changed. Now, whatever other energies it drew upon, the vocabulary of revolution was radically secular, indeed for the most part intransigently anticlerical. So it might be said that Leveller democracy did not quite suffer the fate of Jesuit equality, since after the elapse of another century, its equivalent did reappear – much more strongly, explosively and durably, but in the form of a transvaluation. In this process, ideas at work in the Good Old Cause found expression in a very different idiom, with other connotations and justifications. If something like this were to unfold at the end of the twentieth century, socialism would indeed disappear – but at some later date we could expect to find its characteristic goals and values recoded into some new compelling vision of the world, objectively related but subjectively disconnected from its predecessor. Some might imagine that a certain ecologism could fit this role – discarding what it would see as the religious dimensions of socialism, faith in the proletariat and disdain for nature, but rearticulating other of its key themes: above all, conscious collective control of economic practices, in the interests of equal life-chances for all humanity.

A third possibility is that the trajectory of socialism might rather come to resemble that of the Jacobinism unleashed by the French Revolution itself. Unlike the Levellers, the Jacobins – less committed to personal liberty, more effective in state construction – succeeded in winning power, although they did not hold it for long. Their rule was the radical crest of a revolutionary process which lasted a decade, convulsing the European scene. Like the English before it, the French Revolution created no lasting political order, it too issuing into a military dictatorship followed by a restoration. But this time the old order had to be reimposed from without, for the Revolution itself had gone much further: setting in train deeper popular mobilization, broader ideological development, vaster strategic consequences for Europe at large. In so doing, it had become not just a national but a universal event, whose memory could not be forgotten. Within France itself, just because the restoration had been external, the revolutionary legacy could not long be suppressed. Fifteen years later, Paris was covered in barricades and the government in flight. The July Monarchy lasted little longer, before being consumed in the flames of 1848. The French Revolution, in other words, founded a cumulative political tradition, inspiring successive later attempts to realize the principles of 1789 or 1794 – not only in France, but in Europe as well, and ultimately even beyond it.

On the other hand, this tradition also quite soon underwent a decisive mutation. For out of the bourgeois-democratic matrix of the French Revolution, there issued the distinct and eventually antagonistic conceptions of modern socialism. In this process, there was no break in temporal continuity, of the kind that lay between the age of the Levellers and that of the Jacobins. The birth of socialist ideas effectively overlapped with the emergence of the secular notions of popular sovereignty and equality before the law that would become the normal foundations of capitalist democracy. Babeuf, the first thinker of the socialist tradition proper, was an actor in the Revolution itself. Saint-Simon, its first systematic theorist, was a volunteer in the American War of Independence, and a witness of the Revolution, who developed his doctrines in reaction to it under the Restoration. Fourier published his first scheme for phalansteries under Napoleon. Marx himself was profoundly steeped in the heritage of what he often called simply the 'Great Revolution', and modelled the proletarian upheaval to come by backward projection from it. So when the 1848 Revolution broke out, it was natural that the Second Republic should see a brief united front between old Jacobins and new Socialists, Ledru-Rollin and Louis Blanc. As late as the Commune, a coalition between the two still held in Paris. But as Cournot noted, watching the red flags with foreboding, the proximity was now deceptive. Socialism did present itself as the heir of the Revolution, the only programme capable of giving effective reality to liberty, equality and fraternity. But it was also a genuine mutation. This was a different species of movement from the Jacobin, aiming at another kind of society than Robespierre's Republic of Virtue, which involved a break with its respect for private property, a critique of its understanding of the past, a reordering of the trinity of 1789, and a wager on a new social agent that only emerged with the spread of modern industry, after the French Revolution was over.

Were the Jacobin paradigm to be pertinent, socialism too would undergo a similar mutation in its turn – with the overlapping emergence of a new kind of movement for the radical transformation of society, in some respect acknowledging its debt to socialism, but in others criticizing and repudiating it quite sharply. This, of course, is something like the role that feminists often attribute to the struggle for sexual equality. The modern origins of campaigns for women's emancipation go back to the time of the Second International, when the central texts of the labour movement themselves spoke of abolishing inequality between sexes as well as classes, and Bebel's work on *Woman in the Past, Present and Future* was the most popular single book in the literature of German social democracy – just as the central text of modern feminism, de Beauvoir's *Second Sex,* was to be written from a declared socialist standpoint. But suffragism and its successors nevertheless always represented a distinct historical tradition, and as socialism came to accord steadily less place to sexual equality in the twentieth century, the distance between the two widened. The contemporary forms of second-wave feminism have generally been marked by clear differentiation from socialist traditions. If the social changes it has achieved still remain quite modest, the structural consequences of real sexual equality for a capitalist economy and society look imponderably large. Whether it will come to this, no one can now say. But feminists might well argue that, by contrast with the uncertain future of the labour movement, the cause of women's emancipation can be reasonably confident that it has the better part of its life in front of it.

There is another possibility, which is that the destiny of socialism might after all prove closer to that of its historical rival, liberalism. If the economic origins of modern liberalism lay in classical political economy, as formulated by Smith and Ricardo, and it became a political doctrine in the time of the Restoration, given classical expression by Constant, the two streams did not fully merge until the mid nineteenth century, in the epoch of Gladstone and Cavour. Then, as a general theory of free trade and the rule of law, a market society and a limited state, whose influence was much broader than the parties which bore its name, it became the ruling conception of progress in the Old and New Worlds alike. By the turn of the century, having presided over substantial economic growth and international peace, liberalism seemed set to guide the civilization of the Belle Epoque into a world of wider prosperity and less restricted democracy.

From this zenith, the descent was abrupt. With the outbreak of the First World War, liberal civilization suddenly collapsed into industrial barbarism. As millions fell in the inter-imperialist killing, under the leadership of its most respectable politicians and ideologues, its value-order seemed bent on committing moral suicide. The profound discredit that ensued from this debacle was then followed by the devastating blow of the deepest slump in world history, between the wars. If the Great War seemed to spell the unhingeing of the constitutional state, the Depression appeared to demonstrate the bankruptcy of the free market. Still worse was to come, when the combined legacy of Versailles and Black Friday brought Nazism to power within the framework of parliamentary democracy, while the world market broke up into autarkic blocs. By the end of the first third of the century, it looked to many observers as if liberalism might be destroying itself from within as a major historical force.

Events proved otherwise. In and through the ordeal of the Second World War, liberalism staged a remarkable recovery. In the struggle against fascism, the American economy recovered its dynamism, and the Anglo-Saxon states their reputation. With the return of peace, liberal democracy based on universal suffrage was for the first time generalized across the whole advanced capitalist zone, and consolidated with the economic assistance and political supervision of the United States. At the same time the world capitalist economy was durably re-liberalized, and as international free trade revived on a gold–dollar standard, a long boom brought rapid growth and mass prosperity without precedent across the OECD. By any historical measure, this was a formidable dual transformation. Liberalism now looks forward to a third achievement, of comparable order – the gradual spread of its economic and political model throughout the less developed world. Scarcely any country in the Third World launched industrialization on free market lines, or started out as a true constitutional state. But once accumulation has reached a certain threshold, political democracy and economic deregulation have begun to exhibit a certain trend-line in selected regions of the South too. This, of course, is the story told by Fukuyama.

Socialism, for its part, emerged onto the world stage at just the moment when liberalism entered into its modern crisis. At a time when most liberal thinkers was still bathed in the euphoria of Herbert Spencer, convinced that industry would spread peace between states, Luxemburg and Lenin, Hilferding and Trotsky were predicting the outbreak of the imperialist war that would bring the *fin-de-siècle* settlement to an end. It was the Marxist tradition which likewise foresaw the possibility of the Great Depression, and Marxists who first perceived the full consequences of the fascism that emerged from it. At the same time, as Marx himself – and following him Russian Marxists – had also thought possible, a socialist revolution did indeed break out in Russia, and lead to the creation of a communist state in what European observers had long thought would probably be the second major power in the world in the twentieth century. That state was in turn the prime force in the defeat of European fascism in the Second World War – a defeat which laid the foundations for the historical recovery of liberalism in the West, while a second great revolution broke out in Asia.

No political movement ever realizes exactly what it sets out to achieve, and no social theory ever foresees just what goes on to occur. There is no difficulty in enumerating all the mistaken claims and predictions made by Marx, Luxemburg or Lenin. But no other body of theory in this period – the first third of the century – came near to the twofold successes, of anticipation and accomplishment, of the socialist tradition. On the other hand, these proved in practice to be as vulnerable to time – and their own crimes – as those of liberalism before them. Already before the defeat of Nazism, Stalin's regime had made war on its peasantry and unleashed the purges, in two great waves of mass terror that can only be compared in toll of lives to the First World War, and may have exceeded it. If the moral–political balance with liberalism was thereby lost, the economic balance soon gave the East no advantage over the West either. The stormy Soviet industralization of the thirties, which secured victory over Hitler, unfolded against a background of depression and stagnation in the West. But after 1950 capitalism entered on the most dynamic boom in its history, and when recession set in again twenty years later, its growth rate proved to be well above that of the Soviet bloc, by now sunk in acute economic stagnation and social paralysis under unreconstructed bureaucratic rule. The social-democratic branch of the socialist tradition, on the other hand, which had not challenged the murderous plunge into the First World War, and furnished little remedy against the Depression, flourished within West European capitalism after the Second World War, pioneering welfare systems that were to render it significantly more humane than its American or Japanese counterparts. But with the altered economic conditions of the eighties, these too entered into crisis as social-democratic parties steadily lost office or abandoned commitments to their traditional goals. By the end of the decade, communism was everywhere in crisis or collapse, and social democracy was rudderless. The historical potential of socialism at large, even allowing for the lesser discredit (but also lesser weight) of social democracy, seems to many as thoroughly exhausted as did that of liberalism fifty years ago.

If the liberal paradigm were pertinent, however, an ulterior redemption of socialism as a movement could not be excluded. Liberalism recovered, despite every dire prediction, by adopting diluted elements of its antagonist's programme – state monitoring of macroeconomic balances, securing of social peace through welfare schemes, broadening of democracy to all adults. Communism tried to modernize itself in similar fashion, by introducing elements of the rule of law and of competitive markets. The result was a complete failure, at any rate in the Soviet bloc. There capitalism is now politically and intellectually triumphant. On the other hand, full privatization of large-scale property – that is, a complete economic reproduction of capitalism and its concomitant social structure – is still some way off. Its achievement will require a feat of long-run social engineering without precedent in the liberal tradition, in harsh conditions. The resources needed to finance it are already overstretched in the superintending powers. For the underlying structural malaise of advanced capitalism, revealed in the seventies, has not been overcome. Rates of profit are still no more than half those of the long post-war boom – and have been sustained at this level only by massive credit expansion, postponing the day of reckoning. The advent of any severe new crisis in the OECD would change all political calculations, West and East, unpredictably. The tightening of the linkages in the global capitalist order is anyway bound to force the tremendous pressures of poverty and exploitation in the South into the arena of the North for the first time. All these tensions could create a new international agenda for social reconstruction. Were it able to respond effectively to them, socialism would not so much be succeeded by another movement, as redeemed in its own right as a programme for a more equal and livable world.

Historical analogies are never more than suggestive. But there are occasions where they may be more fruitful than predictions. It would be surprising if the fate of socialism reproduced any one of these paradigms in all fidelity. But the set of possible futures now before it falls within a range such as this. Oblivion, transvaluation, mutation, redemption: each, according to their intuition, will make their own guess as to which is more probable. Jesuit, Leveller, Jacobin, Liberal – these are the figures in the mirror.

1992

Index